# A la Carte

*Selected Papers on Maps and Atlases*

# A la Carte

*Selected Papers on Maps and Atlases*

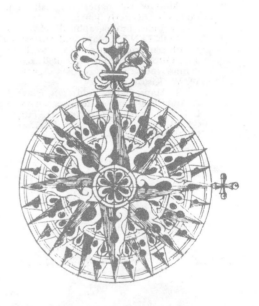

*Compiled by* Walter W. Ristow
*Geography and Map Division*

Library of Congress · Washington · 1972

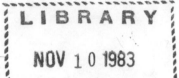

**LIBRARY**

**NOV 1 0 1983**

**UNIVERSITY OF THE PACIFIC**

412131

Western
Americana

GA
231
R5

**Library of Congress Cataloging in Publication Data**

Ristow, Walter William, 1908–      comp.
  A la carte.
  Most of the papers originally appeared in the Library of
Congress Quarterly journal.
  Includes bibliographical references.
  CONTENTS: Maps and atlases of the sixteenth and seven-
teenth centuries: Peter Apian's world map of 1530, by F. R. Goff.
The Oztoticpac lands map of Texcoco, 1540, by H. F. Cline. A
manuscript atlas by Battista Agnese, by L. Martin, edited by
W. W. Ristow. [etc.]
  1. Maps, Early—Addresses, essays, lectures.
2. America—Maps—Addresses, essays, lectures.
I. U. S. Library of Congress. II. Title.
GA231.R5              912.73              75–173026
ISBN 0–8444–0004–1

*Cover: Compass rose, from the Gabriel Tatton map of the
Pacific Ocean, 1600. (See page 42.)*

*End papers: World map by Ortelius. (See pages 52–53.)*

For sale by the Superintendent of Documents, U.S. Government Printing Office
Washington, D.C. 20402 - Price $6.85
Stock Number 030–004–00010–8
Catalog Number LC 5.2:M32/3

# Preface

The study of early maps and atlases has in recent years engaged the interest of an increasing number of American scholars from a variety of disciplines. A small but dedicated group of professional geographers has been concerned with the origins and development of geographical thought and knowledge, including the representation of geographical data on maps and charts. Professional historians have devoted their attention to the period of discoveries and the cartographic revolution it induced. Others with this specialization have chronicled the unrolling of the map of the United States as the trans-Mississippi country was explored and surveyed in the nineteenth century.

Frontiers of cartographic history have, happily, also been advanced by a number of individual researchers whose interest in the study is primarily avocational or recreational. Lawyers, doctors, brokers, bankers, merchants, journalists, and industrialists are represented in the rapidly growing fraternity of map collectors and cartophiles.

Whether his interest is scholarly and professional, or casual and avocational, the student of old maps and atlases looks to the Library of Congress as one of the principal research and reference centers on the history of cartography. In the custody of the Library's Geography and Map Division are more than three and a quarter million maps and some 32,000 atlases, by far the largest cartographic collection in the Western Hemisphere. Included are rare manuscript and printed maps dating from as early as the fifteenth century and a good representation of maps from subsequent periods and schools of cartographical history and evolution.

Invaluable to the researcher is the Geography and Map Division's bibliography of cartography. This analytical card catalog, accumulated over a period of more than seven decades, includes references to cartobibliographies, biographies of mapmakers, engravers, and publishers, cartographic techniques and procedures, descriptions and analyses of distinctive maps, atlases, and globes, and general and specialized books on the history of the cartographic art.

In addition to providing informed assistance to researchers, Library specialists have, through the years, compiled comprehensive cartobibliographies and prepared scholarly studies relating to the history of cartography. During the past three decades a number of such papers, describing unique or interesting early maps and atlases, have been published in the *Quarterly Journal of the Library of Congress*.

Because of their permanent reference value and to make them available in a convenient format to a wider audience, the papers are reprinted in this volume. They include contributions by nine present and past staff members of the Library of Congress, among them specialists from the Exhibits Office, the Map Division (known since 1965 as the Geography and Map Division), the Hispanic Foundation, the Manuscript Division, the Rare Book Division, and the Subject Cataloging Division. All the papers, with the exception of those by the late Lawrence Martin, have been reviewed, edited, and brought up to date by the original authors. Martin's contributions have been edited and, in several instances, extensively revised and expanded by the compiler.

Two papers not originally published in the *Quarterly Journal* have been included because of their close relationship to one or more of the *Journal* articles. They describe, respectively, "John Smith's Map of Virginia" and "John Disturnell's Map of the United Mexican States, 1847." The former was initially issued in a descriptive leaflet to accompany a facsimile edition of Smith's Map of Virginia, published by the Library in 1957. Lawrence Martin's study on Disturnell and his map of Mexico was included in volume 5 of Hunter Miller's *Treaties and Other International Acts of the United States of America* (Washington, 1937), which has been out of print for a number of years.

The 20 papers are arranged in two groups. In the first are seven articles that describe unique and distinctive sixteenth- and seventeenth-century maps and atlases in the Library's collections. American maps are featured in the 13 papers of the second group. Maps and mapmakers of colonial America and eighteenth- and nineteenth-century cartographic works of United States publishers are included. "The Hotchkiss Map Collection," described by Mrs. LeGear, contains manuscript as well as printed Civil War maps. Latin America is represented by the Disturnell paper, already mentioned, and by the interesting group of manuscript boundary maps of South America prepared according to provisions of the Treaty of San Ildefonso.

This is the rich and varied offering presented between the covers of *A la Carte*. Individually the selections provide detailed information about a number of unique or distinctive early maps and atlases. Collectively the papers illuminate many fascinating milestones and landmarks along the evolutionary trail of cartographic history.

Walter W. Ristow, Chief
Geography and Map Division
Reference Department

*June 30, 1970*

# Contents

v   Preface

ix  About the Authors

## MAPS AND ATLASES OF THE SIXTEENTII AND SEVENTEENTH CENTURIES

2   Peter Apian's World Map of 1530
    *by Frederick R. Goff*

5   The Oztoticpac Lands Map of Texcoco, 1540
    *by Howard F. Cline*

34  A Manuscript Atlas by Battista Agnese
    *by Lawrence Martin, edited by Walter W. Ristow*

39  Rosenwald Gift of 16th-Century Maps
    *by Clara E. LeGear*

45  Gerardus Mercator's Atlas of 1595
    *by Clara E. LeGear*

51  Sixteenth-Century Atlases Presented by Melville Eastham
    *by Clara E. LeGear and Walter W. Ristow*

62  America and Africa: Two Seventeenth-Century Wall Maps
    *by Walter W. Ristow*

## AMERICAN MAPS OF THE SEVENTEENTH TO NINETEENTH CENTURIES

78  Maps of Early America
    *by Clara E. LeGear*

91  Captain John Smith's Map of Virginia
    *by Walter W. Ristow*

96  Augustine Herrman's Map of Virginia and Maryland
    *by Walter W. Ristow*

102 John Mitchell's Map of the British and French Dominions in North America
    *compiled and edited by Walter W. Ristow from various published works of Lawrence Martin*

114 The Walker-Washington Map
    *by Paul G. Sifton*

121    John Ballendine's Eighteenth-Century Map of Virginia
       *by Arthur G. Burton and Richard W. Stephenson*

126    The Federal City Depicted, 1612–1801
       *By Nelson R. Burr*

144    The Federal City in 1793
       *by Frederick R. Goff*

153    *From an Actual Survey,* Early Maps of Pennsylvania and Virginia
       *by Walter W. Ristow*

162    John Melish and His Map of the United States
       *by Walter W. Ristow*

183    The Hotchkiss Collection of Confederate Maps
       *by Clara E. LeGear*

189    South American Historical Maps
       *by Lawrence Martin, revised and expanded by Walter W. Ristow*

204    John Disturnell's Map of the United Mexican States
       *by Lawrence Martin, edited and abridged by Walter W. Ristow*

222    How to Order Photoreproductions

223    Index

# About the Authors

**Nelson R. Burr,** a native of Hartford, Conn., received his undergraduate and graduate training at Princeton University. He held various positions with the Historical Records Survey from 1936 to 1941, including that of Assistant State Director for Connecticut. In that post he directed the inventory of church records, which led to his lasting interest in the history of religion in America. Dr. Burr began his service with the Library of Congress in 1942, serving from 1945 to 1957 in the Exhibits Office, where he compiled catalogs for exhibits celebrating the centennials of a number of the States. On leave from 1957 to 1959, he compiled a *Critical Bibliography of Religion in America,* which was published in two volumes in 1961. Among his other publications are *The Anglican Church in New Jersey, The Story of the Diocese of Connecticut,* and *Narrative and Descriptive Bibliography of New Jersey.* From 1959 until his retirement in July 1967 Dr. Burr was a cataloger in the Subject Cataloging Division.

**Arthur G. Burton,** Assistant Exhibits Officer, came to the Library of Congress with the 1953 class of special recruits, after receiving a master's degree in library science from Columbia University. Before joining the staff of the Exhibits Office in 1957, Mr. Burton was in the General Reference and Bibliography Division and served as editor-bibliographer of the Library's Alfred Whital Stern Collection of Lincolniana. He is the author or co-author of a number of catalogs and articles relating to Library of Congress exhibits.

**Howard F. Cline** (1915--1971) was Director of the Library's Hispanic Foundation from 1952 until his death. He completed both his undergraduate and graduate work at Harvard, receiving a doctor's degree in 1947, and taught at Harvard, Yale, and Northwestern Universities. A recognized authority on Latin America, he was the author of several books and papers on the anthropolgy, geography, and history of Mexico and Middle America.

**Frederick R. Goff,** a graduate of Brown University, has been Chief of the Library of Congress Rare Book Division since 1945. He has a well-deserved reputation in the rare book field as a bibliographer and author of scholarly papers. An especially noteworthy contribution is the *Third Census of Fifteenth Century Books Recorded in North American Collections* (Bibliographical Society of America, 1964), which Dr. Goff compiled and edited. Americana is a major interest of Dr. Goff, but he is not insensitive to the interest and romance of the early cartographical history of America.

**Clara Egli LeGear,** when she retired in December 1961, had completed 47 years of service in the Library of Congress, all but one of which was in the Map Division, predecessor of the Geography and Map Division. Since her retirement she has continued her professional studies under an appointment, by the Librarian of Congress, as Honorary Consultant in Historical Cartography. Perhaps best known among her many scholarly contributions are volumes 5 and 6 of the *List of Geographical Atlases in the Library of Congress*. Volume 7 of this invaluable cartobibliographical reference work, also compiled by her, is in press. Mrs. LeGear is an authority on the history of cartography and has published a number of papers in the field.

**Lawrence Martin** (1880–1955) was Chief of the Library of Congress Map Division from 1924 to 1946. A native of Massachusetts, he received bachelor's and doctor's degrees from Cornell and a master's degree from Harvard. His early professional specialization was in physical geography, and from 1906 to 1917 he taught physiography at the University of Wisconsin. In World War I he taught map-reading and served in Military Intelligence, attaining the rank of lieutenant colonel. His experience as one of a group of specialists who worked in Paris with the Peace Commission fostered an interest in boundary studies and in political and historical geography and cartography. After returning to civilian life Martin was Geographer in the Department of State for several years before his appointment to the staff of the Library of Congress. The cartographical research he carried on while he was Chief of the Map Division was largely focused on several maps, and their makers, important in the history of the United States.

**Paul G. Sifton,** specialist in American cultural history in the Manuscript Division, has been with the Library since October 1965. From 1958 to 1965 he served as historian at Independence National Historical Park, Philadelphia. He graduated from George Washington University in 1951 and held a Fulbright grant to the University of Grenoble and the Sorbonne in 1951–52. After receiving his master's degree from the University of Pennsylvania in 1953, he taught at Wayne State University and at the University of Kiel, West Germany. He was awarded a doctor's degree from the University of Pennsylvania in 1960. His dissertation was entitled "Pierre Eugène Du Simitière (1737–1784): Collector in Revolutionary America."

**Richard W. Stephenson** received his training in geography at Wilson Teachers College and George Washington University. Since joining the staff of the Library of Congress in 1951, he has held various positions in the Geography and Map Division, serving at present as Head of the Reference and Bibliography Section. Three cartobibliographies, *Selected Maps and Charts of Antarctica, Civil War Maps,* and *Land Ownership Maps: A Checklist of Nineteenth Century United States County Maps in the Library of Congress,* all compiled by Mr. Stephenson, have been published by the Library.

**Walter W. Ristow,** on the staff of the Library's Geography and Map Division since 1946, is now Chief. A graduate of the University of Wisconsin, he has a master's degree from Oberlin College and a doctor's degree from Clark University, with a major in geography. From 1937 to 1946 Dr. Ristow was, successively, Head of the Map Room and Chief of the Map Division, New York Public Library. He has published several monographs and professional papers, largely dealing with the history of American cartography. He edited and prepared descriptive text for a facsimile edition of Christopher Colles' *Survey of the Roads of the United States of America* (Harvard University Press, 1961).

# Maps and Atlases of the Sixteenth and Seventeenth Centuries

# Peter Apian's World Map of 1530

## BY FREDERICK R. GOFF

I N 1958 the Library of Congress acquired a copy of Pomponius Mela's *De orbis situ libri tres,* printed at Basel by Andreas Cratander during the month of January 1522. This is a handsome Renaissance volume which possesses interest for several reasons. Not only is the classical text the work of the earliest Roman geographer, but this is the second edition to contain the commentaries of Joachim Vadianus (1484–1551), a distinguished Swiss geographer. The first edition, of which the Library has three copies, was published in Vienna in 1518. Both editions are described by Henry Harrisse in his *Bibliotheca Americana Vetustissima* (see numbers 92 and 112), since in Vadianus' letter to Rudolphus Agricola appended at the end there is found a brief passage relating to America. The 1522 edition is also described under number 63957 in volume 15 of Joseph Sabin's *A Dictionary of Books Relating to America,* where one copy is located in the John Carter Brown Library, in Providence, R. I. Sabin states that the elaborate woodcut border surrounding the title, signed "1519 HF," is the work of Hans Holbein. Others have suggested, probably with greater validity, that this is not the work of Holbein but of Hans Furtenbach.

The Library's copy of the 1522 edition, bound in contemporary brown blindstamped calf, has been rebacked, but it is a large copy in good condition. This edition appears to be relatively common since the National Union Catalog locates 11 copies altogether, not including the present one. The Library's copy, however, contains a map, inserted between signatures a and b, which does not appear to be present in any other copies; and indeed it should not be, for the map, which is dated 1530, obviously could not have been added at the earliest until eight years after the volume was published. It is evident, in fact, through the presence of wormholes in signatures a and b, but not affecting the map, that the map was inserted much, much later. A further indication is the presence on the verso of the map of apparent traces of an adhesive, suggesting that before its insertion in the volume it had probably been mounted in some fashion.

The map itself is of the highest significance in the cartographic history of the New World, for it is one of the earliest engraved maps to carry the name "America."

Reprinted from the May 1958 issue of the *Library of Congress Quarterly Journal of Current Acquisitions.*

*From the Rare Book Division.*

The earliest map on which the name appeared is the unique map of heroic size executed by Martin Waldseemüller in 1507; the sole surviving copy is now located in Wolfegg Castle in Württemberg. Until the relatively recent discovery of that map, the earliest engraved map on which the name "America" appeared was thought to be the woodcut map engraved by Peter Apian in 1520. Although much smaller in scale than Waldseemüller's 1507 map, Apian's woodcut engraving derived from it. Apian's map was prepared for inclusion in the edition of Caius Julius Solinus' *Polyhistor* that was printed in Vienna in 1520; it was probably engraved at the expense of Luc Alantse of Vienna, whose monogram appears in the lower left-hand corner. The fact that it was prepared for inclusion in a bound volume undoubtedly accounts for the relatively large number of copies that have survived. The Library of Congress alone has no fewer than four copies, including one in the Rosenwald Collection. Copies that have not suffered from the binder's knife are relatively scarce, however. An untrimmed copy with all four points of the compass designated outside of the border must measure at least 30 x 43 cm. The title of this map reads as follows:

Tipvs Orbis Vniversalis Ivxta Ptolomei Cosmographi Traditionem Et Ame/Rici Vespvcii Alior[um]qve Lvstrationes A Petro Apiano Leysnico Elvcbrat[us]/An Do. M.DXX.

The world map found in the Library's copy of the Pomponius Mela of 1522 is a re-engraving of the Peter Apian map of 1520. Its title is identical with that of the earlier map except for the year M.DXXX. With its upper, lower, and right margins trimmed, it measures 29 x 41 cm. A perfect copy would probably be a little less wide than the earlier map of 1520. The cartographic features are virtually the same. Other than the date, the significant differences appear to be the heavier neat line, the disappearance of the monograms, the differing armorial shields in the lower left- and right-hand corners, and the colophon to the right of the left shield, which reads: "ghedruct tāt/werpen by mij/Peter de Wale i/de guldē/hant." The shield in the lower right corner carries the arms of Antwerp with those of the Empire; that in the left-hand corner carries only the arms of the Empire.

The map is described briefly under number 190 in Henry Harrisse's *The Discovery of North America* (London, Paris, 1892). Harrisse states that he "once saw that map inserted in a copy of Peter Martyr's *Decades* published at Alcalá in 1530," and refers to the Heber and Murphy copies of that book as containing this 1530 map. The next reference that has been located is found in Fernand G. van Ortroy's *Bibliographie de l'oeuvre de Pierre Apian* (Besançon, 1902), entry 2. His description derives from the copy in the John Carter Brown Library, which had been inserted in that library's copy of Peter Martyr's *De Orbe Novo* (Alcalá, 1530), formerly owned by Ternaux-Compans. Ortroy refers to the existence of two other copies also inserted in the 1530 Peter Martyr, one owned formerly by Richard Heber and the other by Henry C. Murphy. The Heber copy was sold at auction in 1835; it was this that John Carter Brown acquired in 1846. The 1884 sale catalog of the library of Henry C. Murphy, sold by George A. Leavitt & Co., describes under number 1607 the 1530 Peter Martyr; and the note beneath that entry says: "The map engraved on wood in this volume is very rare and wanting in many copies. It is the first edition of the eight decades, and contains the same map as that in the Solinus Camers of 1520." This seems to say quite clearly that the map in the Murphy copy was the fairly common Apian map of 1520 that is usually to be encountered in the 1520 Solinus. Thus the two "additional" copies of the Peter de Wale engraved map of 1530 mentioned by Ortroy do not exist.

Correspondence with eight present-day owners of the 1530 Peter Martyr, other than the John Carter Brown Library, does not reveal the presence of any maps in their copies of the book. In fact, the only other copy of the 1530 map that has possibly been recorded is a mutilated copy reported by A. L. van Gendt of Blaricum, the Netherlands, to be in the municipal library of Antwerp. In response to a request for a reproduction, we received a photograph not of the 1530 world map, but rather the one that Peter Apian prepared to accompany his *Cosmographia* of 1545. Dr. Schmook, Director of the Stedelijke Bibliotheek, later informed us that the 1530 world map "doesn't exist in Antwerp." Mr. Van Gendt believed that the purported Antwerp copy was reproduced on plate I of Jean Denucé's *De Geschiedenis van de Vlaamsche*

*Kaartsnijkunst* (Antwerp, 1941). Actually this plate reproduces the John Carter Brown Library copy. The scant textual description of the map, found on page 15, is of little help.

The Société Royale de Géographie d'Anvers in its 1926 catalog of the exposition held during that year reproduced the 1530 map after a copy at that time in the possession of M. Van Ortroy in Antwerp. This, we have ascertained, is also a reproduction of the copy in the John Carter Brown Library; Ortroy in his bibliography of Apian indicated that he had secured a photograph of the Brown copy. This undoubtedly served as the source of the 1926 Antwerp reproduction. Leo Bagrow's *Geschichte der Kartographie* (Berlin, [1951]) briefly mentions the 1530 map under the name of "Wale" but does not locate a copy. De Wale's name is omitted, however, from the list of cartographers in the 1964 English edition of Bagrow's *History of Cartography*, revised and enlarged by R. A. Skelton. Thieme-Becker lists Peter de Wale as a painter and designer, indicating further that he was a member of St. Luke's Guild in Antwerp. That catalog refers to a woodcut by Wale of two skeletons that is dated 1530, the year of the map, but no mention is made of it; since he died during April 1570, one would assume that the engraver was a relatively young man at the time he re-engraved the Apian world map.

In summary, it would appear that the 1530 map engraved at Antwerp by Peter de Wale is a cartographic wood-engraving of excessive rarity. In our exhaustive survey there have been identified with certainty only two original copies, one purchased by John Carter Brown in 1846 and now reposing within the library which bears his name, and the other acquired by the Library of Congress in 1958 from an antiquarian bookseller in the Netherlands. Of these surviving copies, the one owned by the Library of Congress appears to be in better condition. Three points of the compass, "SEPTENTRIO," "ORIENS," and "MERIDIES," found outside the margin, have been cut away, and a small tear at the top affects three letters of the name "Ptolomei" in the title. In the Providence copy all four compass points have been cut away and a large tear one inch deep in the upper right-hand margin seriously affects the representation of the Pacific area south of Japan.

# The Oztoticpac Lands Map of Texcoco, 1540

## BY HOWARD F. CLINE

Reprinted from the April 1966 issue of the *Quarterly Journal of the Library of Congress*.

Tʜᴇ ᴅɪʟɪɢᴇɴᴄᴇ and sophistication of present-day collectors have made documentary discoveries of any importance extremely rare. When scholars do establish the history and the authenticity of a hitherto unidentified piece, it is a cause for some excitement. In April 1965 mapmounters in the Government Printing Office delivered to the Geography and Map Division of the Library of Congress a remarkable pictorial document which they had mounted on rag paper and backed with cotton muslin. Although it was clearly the property of the Library, there was no indication of its provenance. Tentatively identifying it as a Mexican Indian document, Walter W. Ristow, then Associate Chief of the division, asked the writer as Director of the Hispanic Foundation in the Library to study the map in more detail.

His preliminary studies of the Oztoticpac Lands Map revealed it to be a complicated mystery, here unfolded as far as present facts permit. Its closing scenes remain to be written when data now lying in unplumbed archives become available. Information from a wide variety of printed and manuscript sources does permit us to piece together the broad outlines of events and to relate this Library of Congress item to other important contemporary materials for Mexican ethnohistory. The present version carries investigations through November 1966 and revises earlier conclusions.[1]

Library of Congress records do not reveal any reliable information about the previous history of the Oztoticpac Lands Map. Possibly transferred to the Library as early as 1905, the item remained until April 1965 as a curiosity and a "problem piece" in a backlog. Search of official records and inquiry among even the oldest employees have failed to furnish any clues about its previous background. Intensive search in the published literature on pictorial documents and review of unpublished data being collected in the Hispanic Foundation on these documents for the *Handbook of Middle American Indians* similarly have produced no known mention of this document. Hence our inquiries have no previous background and must begin with the document itself.

The Library of Congress' Oztoticpac Lands Map is reproduced as figure 1. It is on native paper, which probably had a figbase. It measures about 76 x 84 cm. (30 x 33

5

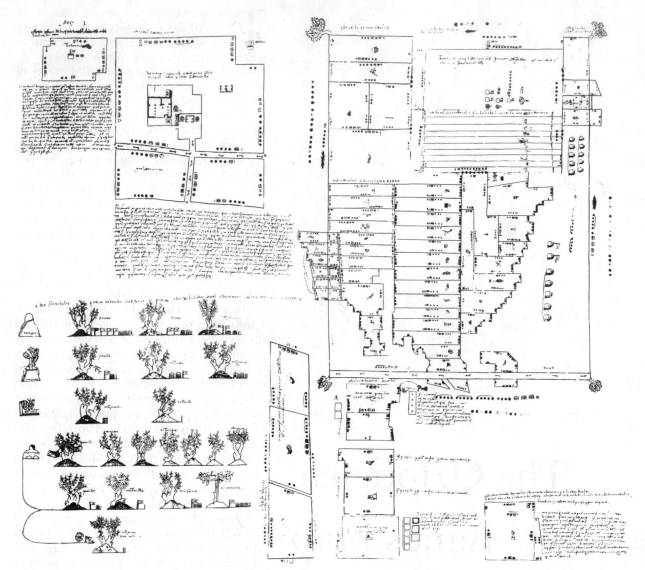

*Figure 1. Oztoticpac Lands Map of Texcoco. From the collections of the Geography and Map Division.*

inches). It is remarkably well preserved, with only minor worm damage. Originally the map was folded, apparently into four parts, and some of the writing along the folds has become illegible. Although the document has been drawn primarily in black ink, red, seen in faded lines around certain areas, apparently denotes that they were owned by native nobility. Red is also used for some of the native numerals.

Seemingly there are four kinds of black ink, reflecting as many hands. The basic document is by one or more skilled Indians and is drawn in firm black. An interpreter has added a number of glosses in Nahuatl, the language spoken then as it is now by Aztecs; another hand, the same that might well have added the native numerals in red, supplied the shorter Spanish glosses in black. Across the top of the map is yet another Spanish legend, by a fourth hand, in badly faded European ink. The Photoduplication Service of the Library rephotographed the legend under both ultraviolet and infrared light, but so badly worn has been this part of the manuscript that such attempts did not improve its legibility.

To permit systematic description of this Aztec pictorial document, the writer has divided it into seven main parts, to each of which he has arbitrarily assigned a Roman numeral. Within each of the parts, separate elements have been given letters and Arabic numbers. Main divisions are shown on the diagram (figure 2). The legend at the top

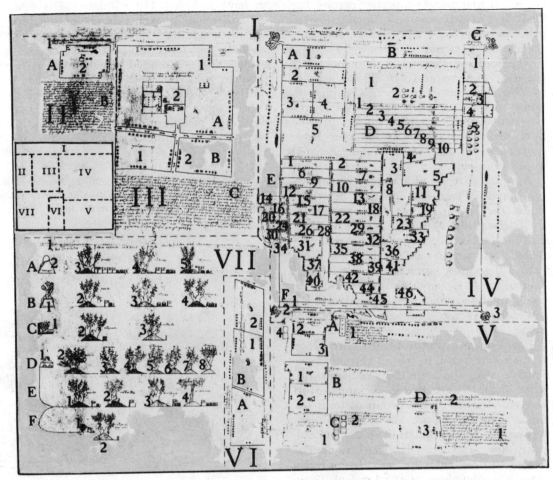

has been designated part I. Fortunately, even though this descriptive Spanish title is virtually obliterated, other features of the map and related documents provide infor-

*Figure 2, above. Map with divisions and reference points added to facilitate discussion of details.*

*Figure 3. Plan of the estate of Tollancinco, from part II of the map, with a transcription of the Spanish gloss.*

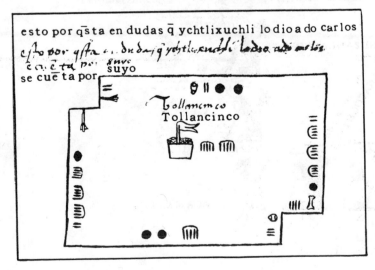

esto por q̄sta en dudas q̄ ychtlixuchli lo dio a do carlos

se cue̅ ta por suyo

mation about its time, place, and purposes.

The first clues come from part II, in the upper left quadrant. Above a plan labeled "Tollancinco" (figure 3) is a Spanish gloss, and below it a long Nahuatl text. The Spanish gloss states, "this, because there is doubt that Ixtlilxochitl gave it to Don Carlos, is counted as his." From the gloss we almost immediately have a locale, a tentative date, even a purpose for the Oztoticpac Lands Map. It concerns properties of the native nobility of Texcoco, among whom were Don Carlos Chichimecatecotl and his half brother Ixtlilxochitl. Since Don Carlos died in 1539, the document probably hovers chronologically around that year, although its date of composition will be discussed further in this article. The fact that the map begins with an inventory of properties, with others coming later in the document, tells us we are dealing with land litigation matters. For the moment, the main consid-

7

eration is that these properties involve the lords of Texcoco, a well-documented Aztec place of great importance before and after the Spanish Conquest.

The lords of Texcoco, Indian nobles at the time of Fernando Cortés' conquest of Mexico, figure prominently in the interpretation of the Oztoticpac Lands Map. Various native and European sources provide data on them, but contradictions leave numerous inconsistencies and debated points unresolved.[2]

An interesting graphic treatment appears on Mappe Tlotzin, a portion of which shows the various rulers of Texcoco and their wives from about A.D. 1263 to about 1539; it has been excerpted here as figure 4.[3] Table 1, providing data on these and other rulers, draws on numerous pictorial and textual sources, notably Bernardino de Sahagún and Fernando Alva Ixtlilxochitl, a descendant of the Texcocan noble of that name.[4]

Based on oral traditions, the chronology of the rulers shown in table 1 becomes more reliable after the time of Nezahualcoyotl, when records were better. Nezahualcoyotl was grandfather to the group of lords (señores) with whom we are primarily concerned. Famed as warrior, poet, philosopher, and legislator, he sired numerous descendants, two of whom were by his legitimate wife, daughter of the Lord of Tenochitlan (Mexico City). One of these sons he executed for treason. The other, Nezahualpilli, inherited the kingdoms.[5]

By some 40 women, Nezahualpilli is said to have fathered 145 children.[6] His first child-wife bore him no heir; she engaged in organized adultery, having a long series of noble lovers killed and a statue of each made. These crammed her bedroom, explained away as "gods of Tenochitlan," until she made the mistake of allowing three paramours to live, one of whom flashed a medallion which Nezahualpilli recognized as a gift he had presented to his

*Figure 4. Rulers of Texcoco, ca. 1263-1539, adapted from Mappe Tlotzin, as published in the 1885 edition of J.M.A. Aubin's* Mémoires sur la peinture didactique et l'écriture des anciens mexicains . . . . *Original in the Bibliothèque Nationale, Paris.*

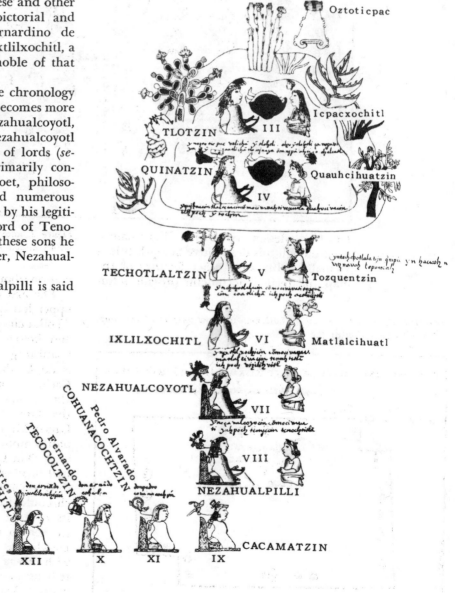

TABLE 1. *Chichimec and Acolhua Rulers of Texcoco, 1115–1582*

| Order | Ruler | Rule Began | Died | Reign (Years) | No. in figure 5 |
|-------|-------|-----------|------|---------------|-----------------|
| I | XOLOTL | 1115 | 1232 | 117 | |
| II | NOPALTZIN | 1232 | 1263 | 31 | |
| III | TLOTZIN POCHOTL | 1263 | 1298 | 35 | |
| IV | QUINATZIN TLALTECATZIN | 1298 | 1357 | 59 | |
| V | TECHOTLALTZIN | 1357 | 1409 | 52 | |
| VI | IXTLILXOCHITL OMETOCHTLI | 1409 | 1419 | 10 | |
| | **Tepanec Interregnum** | | | | |
| VII | NEZAHUALCOYOTL | 1431 | 1472 | 41 | |
| VIII | NEZAHUALPILLI | 1472 | 1516 | 43 | 1 |
| IX | CACAMATZIN | 1517 | 1519 | 2 | 5 |
| | **Spanish Conquest** | | | | |
| X | Fernando TECOCOLTZIN | 1520 | 1521 | 1 | 17 |
| XI | Pedro Alvarado COHUANACOCHTZIN | 1521 | 1525 | 4 | 9 |
| XII | Fernando Cortés IXTLILXOCHITL | 1525 | 1531 | 6 | 10 |
| XIII | Jorge Alvarado YOYOTZIN | 1532 | 1533 | 1 | 12 |
| XIV | Pedro TETLAHUEHUETZQUITZIN | 1534 | 1539 | 5 | 8 |
| XV | Antonio Pimentel TLAHUILOTZIN | 1539 | 1546 | 7 | 21 |
| XVI | Hernando Pimentel IHUAN | 1546 | 1565 | 19 | 34 |
| XVII | Diego TEUTZQUITZIN | 1565 | 1577 | 12 | 35 |
| | **Vacancy** | | | | |
| XVIII | Don Cristóbal | 1579 | ? | 3 plus | |

wife. He had her, the surviving lovers, and their accomplices publicly executed.[7]

Nezahualpilli took a second wife, whose offspring were considered legitimate by some. The vast majority of Nezahualpilli's issue was natural. He designated no legal heir to the realms which, in alliance with related Aztec dynasties of Tenochitlan (modern Mexico City) and Tlacopan (Tacuba), had created a rich Texcocan empire. This Triple Alliance in the fifteenth century had conquered nearly all the area of modern Mexico, levying tribute payments and services due on a vast number of provinces and communities, incomes of which were divided among the realms of Texcoco (two shares), Tenochitlan (two shares), and Tacuba (one share).[8]

Succession to the throne of Texcoco was thus a major economic and political prize on the eve of the Conquest and for some years thereafter. These tangled matters are partially reflected on the Oztoticpac Lands Map, which involves ownership of properties claimed by various sons of Nezahual-pilli, the lords of Texcoco. A schematized chart of the principal figures, all brothers or half brothers because of their common father Nezahualpilli, appears as figure 5 on the following page.

Let us now identify our major protagonist, Don Carlos. He is No. 20 on figure 5; he has often been confused in the secondary literature with No. 18, Carlos Ahuaxpizin, another natural son.[9] Our Carlos had a colorful career, which ended spectacularly when Spanish officials executed him on November 30, 1539, in the public square of Mexico City, upon his conviction by the Inquisition for heretical dogmatizing, with additional charges of idolatry and immorality.[10] Execution by the Spanish of one of the powerful lords of Texcoco, for whatever reasons, was a critical event. It damaged the prestige of the Inquisitor, Bishop Juan Zumárraga, who was officially reprimanded for his action.[11] Modern students still disagree about the necessity or justice of Don Carlos' severe sentence.[12] His execution left in its wake litigation related to

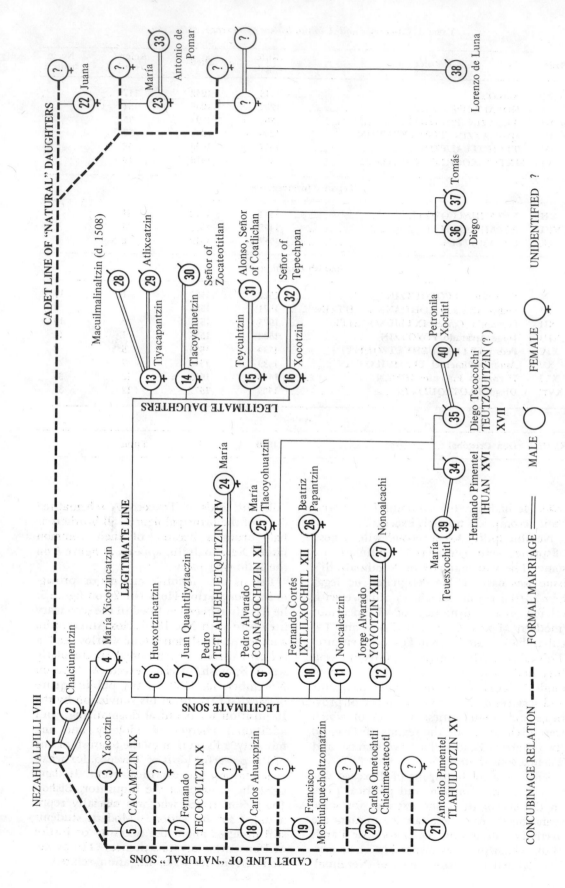

Figure 5. Heirs of Nezahualpilli. The roman numerals indicate the order of succession after Nezahualpilli, who was eighth hereditary Lord of Texcoco.

lands of the lords of Texcoco, with which the Oztoticpac Lands Map is primarily concerned.

The Texcocan lords drew revenues of various kinds from their own private estates as well as from tribute-paying communities. If, as is most probable, Tollancinco was such a private property, its returns are shown in the middle of the estate (figure 3). There appears a container of items, which may be cacao beans, money, or beans, with a flag in them; the flag is a symbol for 20, hence 20 such containers are signified. Beside the container are native numerals for 10, probably to indicate that at 10-day intervals the rental goods were to be given the landlord. Equally possible is the interpretation that 10 such containers were to be delivered every 20 days.

The long Nahuatl gloss relates to the history of the land parcel. Couched as is much Indian prose in highly figurative language, its meaning is not wholly clear.[13] It is the testimony of a Texcocan Indian named Benito Ciuaiunti concerning an episode he had witnessed 10 years earlier. Don Carlos had gone to the palace and had asked Benito to intercede for him. Benito had told the ruler, Don Hernando (also called Fernando) that Don Carlos was sent by a priest who was inquiring about a house. When he was told that the one he asked about belonged to Yoyocin (Yoyotzin), he ordered Don Carlos to ask Don Hernando for another that was vacant. Hernando smiled at his younger brother Carlos and told him their father had already shown him favors, at which Don Carlos left. Hernando told Benito that his younger brother Carlos had said that the government was taking all the properties. Hernando explained that Cacamacin (Cacamatzin) had given him the Ocotepec property and that some time ago he had given it to Yoyocin.

Benito's testimony confirms the fact that we are dealing with Texcocan property belonging to the sons of Nezahualpilli. It also sets upper chronological limits. Don Fernando Cortés Ixtlilxochitl died in 1531, hence this document cannot postdate 1541 if Benito's statements concerning happenings 10 years before are correct.

The mention in the gloss of persons shown on figure 5—Cacamatzin (5), Yoyotzin (12), Ixtlilxochitl (10)—not only assures us that we are dealing with the lords of Texcoco but raises certain questions of relationships among them. Fortunately they can be answered provisionally. It is clear from this account that Don Carlos was considered one of the half brothers; however he was never a ruler. After ousting two natural sons who ruled from 1517 to 1521, one after another of the legitimate brothers successively grasped the reins of rule, drawing their power from their legitimate lineage, but even more, from their newly developed relationships with the conquering Spaniards.[14]

On the death of Pedro Tetlahuehuetzquitzin (8), the last legitimate brother, in 1539, and the execution that same year of Don Carlos, who had unsuccessfully tried to become lord, one of the last of the natural half brothers, Antonio Pimentel Tlahuilotzin, was recognized both by Spaniards and Indians as "lord of Texcoco."[15] When he died in 1546 various sons of the legitimate brothers succeeded to what had become primarily an honorific post, its influence shrunk. These genealogical details become important in dating our document and relating it to others.

At the coming of the Spaniards in 1519, the throne of Texcoco, then a vast and rich realm, was in violent dispute between the half brothers Cacamatzin and Ixtlilxochitl. Montezuma, lord of Mexico, aided his nephew Cacamatzin (a natural son) against the younger legitimate brothers. These Texcocan Aztec fratricidal struggles facilitated European conquest of Mexico. They arrayed nearly half the Aztec Empire against the other half, permitting Cortés to secure native allies from the discontented communities hoping to escape the imperial yoke.[16]

To further his own ambitions, Ixtlilxochitl became one of the staunchest native allies of Fernando Cortés and Pedro Alvarado and aided them greatly in capturing Mexico. Upon final Spanish victory over Mexico City, Cortés in 1521 gave Ixtlilxochitl and the brothers who had sided with him the ruling positions they had sought earlier in Texcoco and its dependencies. Actually Ixtlilxochitl and his brother Cohuanacochtzin more or less divided the kingdom of Texcoco between themselves. The former ruled the northern areas from Otumba; the latter from the city of Texcoco governed its southern provinces.[17] On the death of Cohuanacochtzin while with

Cortés in Central America in 1525, Ixtlilxochitl inherited the whole kingdom. He then moved from Otumba to Texcoco and occupied the ancestral palace (shown on figure 9) until his death in 1531.[18]

In 1524, when the Texcocan Aztecs were baptized officially, Ixtlilxochitl took the Christian name of Fernando Cortés, his godfather. His ranking brother became Pedro Alvarado Cohuanacochtzin to honor his patron. Other brothers and their wives selected Christian names (figure 5).[19] About this time the conquistador Fernando Cortés took young Don Carlos Chichimecatecotl into his household and reared him as a nominal Christian. This upbringing was nearly the sole defense Carlos could advance in 1539 when the Inquisition charged him with idolatry.[20] Part IV of the Oztoticpac Lands Map shows plots of ground which Cortés gave to Don Carlos.

Any lingering doubts about the place of the map and the personages are quickly dispelled when its part III is examined (figure 6). It consists of a plan, plus a short Spanish and a much longer Nahuatl gloss. Information from part III confirms what part II had suggested, that lands belonging to the descendants of Nezahualpilli were in litigation, with this document being used to determine which properties belonged to whom.

At the top of part III of the Library of Congress Map is a statement (in Spanish): "This certainly belongs to the seigniory," reinforced by a Nahuatl gloss inside the boundaries, stating "The palace of Oztoticpac belongs to the government. It is not the property of Don Carlos." A minor gloss identifies a plot owned by Don Antonio Pimentel Tlahuilotzin.

Under the drawing of part III is a long passage in Nahuatl. Like that in part II it is testimony by an Indian, Zacarías Tlacocoua, and relates to the history of the Oztoticpac area.[21] Zacarías reported that five years earlier Don Carlos asked him to talk to the ruler and tell him that in the Oztoticpac lands were two houses, apparently vacant, which Don Carlos sought. As instructed, Zacarías consulted the ruler, who said that the younger brothers among the señores should be sounded out. So Zacarías talked with Don Francisco Mochiuhquecholtzomatzin, who raised some objections, saying that Oztoticpac was already the home of the younger brothers. Zacarías said he re-

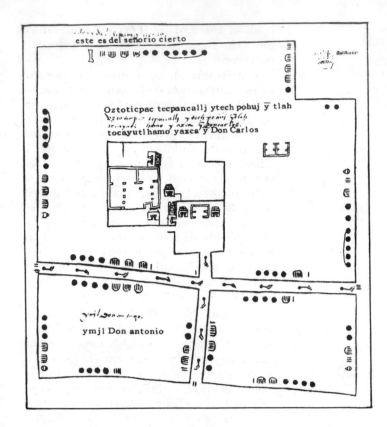

*Figure 6. Detail from part III of the Oztoticpac Lands Map, with transcription of the Spanish gloss provided.*

ported this to Don Pedro, the ruler (now deceased), who seemingly disregarded the counsel of Francisco by stating that Don Carlos could settle in the area while he looked for another dwelling and lands which could be purchased; Pedro agreed to purchase them for his younger brother Carlos. So Don Carlos settled at Oztoticpac. Zacarías adds, "And it was reckoned with the land of Texcoco; it was not ascribed to him. He told me it was not the property of those belonging to the palace."

The testimony of Zacarías in the Nahuatl gloss substantiates the previous chronological note. The map could not have been made later than 1544, since the witness talked to Don Carlos, who died in 1539, while he was still alive. Yet another Nahuatl gloss (V–D–1) tells us that Don Carlos died on the day dedicated to Maria Magdalena; hence the document postdates 1539. We have now narrowed its composition to the years 1539–41 on the basis of direct native testimony. A reasonable date which we shall use for it is 1540, plus or minus a year.

The statements of Zacarías also reveal that Oztoticpac was a place within Texcoco, not the Aztec village of the same name northeast of that city. From published records of the Inquisition procedure against Don Carlos we further learn that Oztoticpac was one of two estates within the city of Texcoco assigned to Don Carlos; he first occupied it in 1532, when he took a niece as his concubine.[22] The idols on which the Inquisition's charges of idolatry were based were not kept here. They were found in his other house, although its name is not given, but which may well be the Ocotepec mentioned above.

Zacarías' long statement is an integral part of the map, as was that of Benito in part II. Both strongly buttress the view that the seignorial lands occupied by Don Carlos were not his property but rather belonged to the family as a whole. From this we can reasonably infer that the Oztoticpac Lands Map was prepared by and for the Texcocan señores, probably at the order of Antonio Pimentel Tlahuilotzin, who succeeded Don Pedro as governor in 1540 and ruled until 1546.

Perhaps the most striking and unusual feature of part III is that it corresponds in major details to a well-known cognate Mexi-

*Figure 7. Humboldt Fragment VI. In the Deutsche Staatsbibliothek, Berlin. Photo by Deutsche Fotothek Dresden (Kramer).*

can pictorial document which was acquired in Mexico by Baron Alexander von Humboldt in 1803. He published a lithographic version of it in his famous *Vues* (1813), entitled "Pièce de procès en écriture hiéroglyphique." [23] In 1806 Humboldt donated this and other original manuscripts to the Royal Library and Museum in Berlin.[24] The Humboldt document, usually known as Humboldt Fragment VI, was republished (1893), with a commentary by the great German scholar of ancient Mexico, Eduard Seler.[25] Although because of World War II most of the American Indian Manuscripts collection in the former Royal Berlin Library was lost or dispersed, Humboldt Manuscript 1, containing Fragment VI, survived intact in that repository, which has now been renamed Deutsche Staatsbibliothek. The photograph, reproduced here as figure 7, was kindly furnished by the Chief of its Manuscripts Division.[26]

Comparison between Humboldt Fragment VI and our part III, each by a distinct native artist, indicates that the German manuscript has some features not found on the Oztoticpac Lands Map. It carries a gloss in Spanish: "Ciudad de Tetzcuco" (City of Texcoco). Further, the Humboldt manuscript contains personages around the borders which do not appear on the Library of Congress document. The latter has, however, native glosses not seen on the Berlin item; these identify plots of land within Texcoco, notably the palace of Oztoticpac and the lands owned by Don Antonio

Pimentel Tlahuilotzin. The two documents are intimately related, linked by the exact correspondence of main iconographic and numerical elements.

Common to both is an identical, complicated palace complex, with an adjacent single house plan to its right. Slightly variant in depiction but identical in meaning are native signs and numerals along the inside of boundary lines of the main plot and of the smaller, related areas. These are separated from the larger parcel by a road, indicated by footprints, just as a similar pathway divides them from each other.

It is thus obvious that Humboldt Fragment VI and part III of Oztoticpac Lands Map are related, but the nature of the relationship is less evident. Fortunately, historical records provide sufficient clues on which to base reasonable hypotheses. Before summarizing these, however, it seems important to correct some misconceptions introduced by Seler in his pioneering commentary on Humboldt Fragment VI, as what he stated would apply with equal force to the same matters shown on the Oztoticpac Lands Map.

A basic misapprehension was Seler's belief, based on the Spanish gloss, that the land plan referred to the whole city of Texcoco, rather than to one important part of it, the lands and palace of Oztoticpac. Seler even chided his master, Humboldt, for considering the depiction as an estate rather

*Figure 8. Oztoticpac place glyphs, from Texcocan pictorial documents.*

Humboldt Fragment VI                    Codex Xolotl

Mappe Reinisch        Mappe Tlotzin        Oztoticpac Lands Map        Mapa de Sigüenza        Codex Mendoza

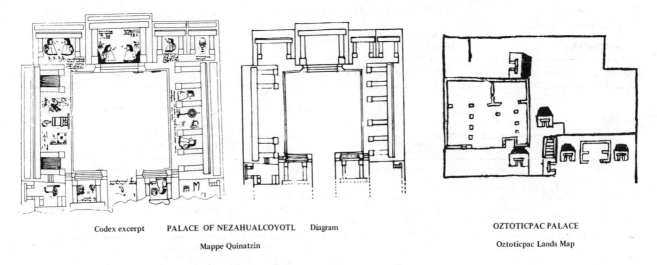

Codex excerpt     PALACE OF NEZAHUALCOYOTL     Diagram                    OZTOTICPAC PALACE

Mappe Quinatzin                                                          Oztoticpac Lands Map

*Figure 9. Texcocan palaces, from two contemporaneous maps. Mappe Quinatzin is in the Bibliothèque Nationale, Paris, and was first published in Aubin's* Mémoires.

than the whole community. Possibly because of his mistaken premise, Seler failed to unravel the meaning of the place-sign at the top of Humboldt Fragment VI, a flag over a cave. Comparative study of other Texcocan pictorial documents shows it to be Oztoticpac (figure 8), indicating that our two cognates are concerned with the same place.[27]

A second, less important misinterpretation was Seler's statement that the palace-complex on Humboldt Fragment VI (and also on the Oztoticpac Lands Map) was one described at length in 1582 by Juan Bautista Pomar as that of Nczahualcoyotl. Other sources provide data on the latter, and it is pictured on Mappe Quinatzin, another Texcocan pictorial document approximately contemporaneous with the two we are discussing.[28] Figure 9 makes possible a comparison between the plans of the Palace of Nezahualcoyotl and the Palace of Oztoticpac.

Built in the fourteenth century by Quinatzin, the Palace of Oztoticpac was for many years the principal feature of Texcoco, housing the ruler and his court.[29] Although overshadowed by the buildings erected by Nezahualcoyotl and Nezahualpilli, it served as council hall for the lords of Texcoco up to the time of the Spanish Conquest.

In his commentary on Humboldt Fragment VI, Seler correctly outlined the Aztec numerical system, shown on that and other Texcocan documents.[30] Numerals 1 through 19 appear as vertical lines, grouped into fives. In the Mexico City area such units may be open circles. A basic unit, 20, is shown two ways: for objects and people, a flag (*pantli*) is used; in land measures of Texcoco, 20 is a solid circular dot, five of which equal 100. A sign for many hairs (*zontli*) depicts 400.

Both Humboldt Fragment VI and Oztoticpac Lands Map, as well as other Aztec pictorial documents, carry conventional signs for native land measures. Surprisingly little information about such symbols is found in the published literature.[31] A summary of our present knowledge, based on published and unpublished materials, appears as figure 10. It should be clearly understood, of course, that the modern equivalents are only approximations. Within short distances in the Valley of Mexico the same unit varied in length. (See following page.)

If we apply these equivalencies in figure 10 to the Oztoticpac Palace areas shown on the two maps, we find that the main lot was roughly 678 feet by 633 feet. The plot labeled "Lands of Don Antonio" would be approximately 370 by 254 feet, and the adjoining area about 378 by 208 feet.

Turning from the common visual elements of thcsc two related Texcocan pictorial documents, we can now note their probable chronological relationships and diverse purposes. This will throw wholly new light on Humboldt Fragment VI, as Seler's commentary made no attempt to go beyond the erroneous suggestion that the document was a sort of census of the

Figure 10. Aztec land measures.

| SYMBOLS | | NAHUATL | | SPANISH | NOTES | EQUIVALENTS | |
|---|---|---|---|---|---|---|---|
| Texcoco | Mexico | Term | Molina definition | | | Inches | Meters |
| | | | | linea (line) | smallest Spanish measure | 0.076 | 0.0019 |
| | | | | dedo (finger) | 9 lineas | 0.690 | 0.0175 |
| | | cemmapilli (one thumb) ynicatoueymapil | pulgada medida | pulgada (thumb; inch) | 12 lineas | 0.916 | 0.233 |
| | | cemmatl (one hand) [possibly palmo, q.v.] | | mano (hand) | handbreadth | 4.00? | 0.1016 |
| | | cemizte(i)l | xeme | jeme | distance from end of thumb to end of forefinger, extended | 5.00? | 0.127 |
|  | 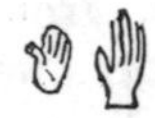 | [cemmatl]? [(one hand)]? | | palmo (palm) | 9 pulgadas; fingertips to wrist | 8.23 | 0.209 |
| | | | | palmo mayor (great palm) | 12 dedos | 8.73 | 0.222 |
| | | tlacxitamachiualoni xocpalli[PC] | pie medida comun | pie (foot) | 12 pulgadas; 16 dedos | 10.97 | 0.279 |
| | | cemmolicpitl | codo medida hasta la punta del dedo mas largo de la mano | codo (elbow) | .5 vara | 16.50 / 17.5? | 0.418 / 0.445 |
| | | cemmatzotzopaztli | codo medida hasta la punta del dedo menor | | | 14.0? | 0.356 |
| 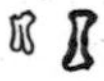 |  | omitl[PC] (bone) | | | | 16.5? | 0.418 |
| |  | octacatl | vara de medir | vara (rod; staff) | 2 codos; 3 pies; 4 palmos | 32.99 | 0.838 |
| | | tlalquauitl[PC] (land stick) | | | | | |
| | | | | brazo (arm) | | | |
| |  | cenciyacatl | brazo medida del sobaco [armpit] a la mano | | | 36.0? | 0.914 |
| | | cemacolli | brazo medida del un ombro a la mano | | | 38.0? | 0.965 |
| | | ciacatl[PC] | [possibly "codo"?] | | | | |
| | | | | braza (fathom) | 2 varas | 65.88 | 1.57 |
| | | cemmatzotzopaztli [see above, "codo"] | braza desde el hombre hasta la punta de los dedos | | | 42.0? | 1.067 |
|  |  | cenyollotli (one heart) | braza medida del peche a la mano | | | 50.0? | 1.27 |
|  | 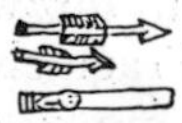 | cenmitl (one arrow) | braza medida desde el codo hasta la otra mano | | | 65.0? | 165 |

NOTE: PC indicates data from Pedro Carrasco. Arbitrary equivalents assigned by Cline indicated by "?".

Indian city of Texcòco. Both the dating and the purpose of Humboldt Fragment VI rest on identification of the seated figures shown at its top and sides (figure 11).

Seler stated that the Spaniard in the middle of a row of three figures at the top was Viceroy Antonio de Mendoza. Mendoza served in that post from October 1535 until 1551.[32] On Humboldt Fragment VI his name glyph is missing, but it appears on other Mexican pictorial documents, notably Telleriano-Remensis (f. 46) and Vaticanus B (f. 93).[33]

The Viceroy is flanked on Humboldt Fragment VI by two figures, undoubtedly *oidores* (judges) of the Royal Audiencia. One has a native name glyph. For the moment we can assume that these oidores served during the time that the Indian litigant, Antonio Pimentel Tlahuilotzin, was governor of Texcoco, 1540–46. Table 2 lists such oidores.

The only one of these identified in the published literature seems to be Francisco Ceynos. His glyph was identified and published from Codex Osuna by Seler. Without elaborating further, Seler said it apparently "represents the prickly point of a leaf." [34] It does not correspond to the one glyph we have for an oidor.

TABLE 2. *Oidores of the Audiencia of Mexico, 1539–46*

| Name | Served | |
| --- | --- | --- |
| | From | To |
| Francisco Ceynos | 1531 | 1546 |
| Francisco de Loaysa | 1535 | 1542? |
| Alonso de Tejada | 1535 | 1548 plus |
| Gómez de Santillan | 1536 | 1550 plus |
| Antonio Rodriguez Quesada | 1546 | ? |

Joaquín Galarza has identified that glyph.[35] Analyzing its elements as "pelota de hule" (*olli, ulli*), "plan del juego de pelota" (*tlachtli*), and the symbol for Quetzalcoatl (ojo del dios con máscara de Ehecatl), he arrives at "tlach-olli" for Antonio Rodriguez, and "Quetzaltla" for Quesada. Hence the oidor to the Viceroy's left is probably Antonio Rodríguez Quesada. We know little about him except that he was appointed about 1546, and as oidor supervised the Indian boys' curriculum at the famous native school of Santa Cruz Tlatelalco. It is also reported that he had a large house constructed by Indian labor.[36]

Thus the unidentified oidor may be one of three persons serving on the bench during these years. Francisco Loaysa seems

Figure 11. Details from Humboldt Fragment VI showing Texcocan court and four land litigants with their native name glyphs.

VICEROY       OIDOR       OIDOR

Antonio de Mendoza

Francisco Ceynos ?
Gomez de Santillan ?
Alonso de Tejada ?

Antonio Rodriguez Quesada

Antonio Pimentel Tlahuilotzin

Pedro de Vergara

Vicencio de Riverol

Alonso de Contreras

ruled out; his term did not overlap Rodriguez Quesada's, narrowing the choice to Francisco Ceynos, Alonso de Tejada, or Gómez de Santillan.

The other figures, with one exception, can be directly identified from glyphs. On the left margin are two Spaniards, one with a name glyph above an Indian, the other below. Opposite them is another Spaniard with a name glyph, partially missing. These are obviously litigants.

Seler identified the Indian as Antonio Pimentel Tlahuilotzin, signified by his bow, *tlahuitolli*.[37] Don Antonio seemingly took office in 1540 as twelfth in the hereditary line of señores of Texcoco listed by Sahagún's informants for Primeros Memoriales and included by him as such in his *History*. Don Antonio ruled about six years, apparently dying in 1546.[38]

Above him the Spaniard has a name glyph, which Baron Humboldt thought might be "Aquaverde" because of the green water sign.[39] However, Joaquín Galarza much more correctly reads the elements as "mat" (*petatl*), "rushes" (*otlatl*), and "water" (*atl*). Phonetically this yields PETLO —TLA, for Pedro (de) Vergara.

Opposite him on the other side of the plot sits the Spaniard whose glyph Galarza has also deciphered. Its elements are "jar" (*comitl*), "teeth" (*tlantli*), "bean" (*etl*), and "face" (*xayacatl*). Phonetically these provide COM-E-X[sh]AY. The result, "Comtlesha" is probably the native pronunciation of "Contreras."

The fact that Don Antonio, Pedro de Vergara, and Alonso de Contreras were actually engaged in litigation before the Audiencia provides us with the probable name of the Spaniard below Don Antonio on Humboldt Fragment VI. He would be Vicencio de Riverol, lawyer for Pedro de Vergara (and probably Don Antonio). The appearance of these figures indicates also that Humboldt Fragment VI is probably connected with that suit, which we shall briefly review.

On December 31, 1540, Pedro de Vergara petitioned Oidor Francisco de Loaysa to order the Inquisition to return to him certain fruit trees which its officials had sequestered from the property taken from Don Carlos.[40] He averred that about three years before (i.e., 1537) he and Don Carlos had verbally arranged for Vergara to provide Castilian trees from which Don Carlos

was to obtain seedlings and scions to graft on native trees which he owned; Vergara and Don Carlos were to share half and half the products of the seedlings and grafted trees. Vergara claimed that the day before his execution, don Carlos called him to the Inquisition jail and affirmed the earlier contract in presence of witnesses. Vergara wanted his own trees back, plus half of the grafted ones. Oidor Loaysa endorsed his petition and on January 10, 1541, remanded it to the Fiscal of the Inquisition for reply.

After delays, Vergara seemingly established the fact of the contract through testimony and was about to regain his property when complications arose. His lawyer Vicencio de Riverol (who had defended Don Carlos in 1539) requested the Audiencia to issue a restraining order against one Alonso de Contreras, who, he said, had been moving and uprooting the trees on the Oztoticpac estate, to the detriment of Vergara's interest in them. Such an injunction was issued January 10, 1542. Three days later, however, Alonso de Contreras challenged the Audiencia's action. His lawyer stated that Contreras had purchased the Oztoticpac property with his own money from the Inquisition, and this included the grafted trees on it; further, it was charged, until Vergara could produce a written contract, his claims were invalid. Oidor Loaysa on January 16, 1542, ruled that the injunction would remain in force, but that the claims by Contreras should be heard in the Audiencia court. That terminates the fragment of the suit now available.

It would seem clear, however, that Humboldt Fragment VI probably is related to the ensuing legal actions after January 16, 1542. Vergara and Don Antonio would have common cause in having Oztoticpac ruled the property of the señores of Texcoco, with Don Carlos as life-tenant; the trees apparently were clearly his. If these facts could be established, the Inquisition had exceeded its authority by selling Oztoticpac to Contreras, hence his claims would be dismissed. This, then, seems to be the story behind Humboldt VI.

Despite diligent search by scholars, certain reports that might clear up the fate of Don Carlos' estate, including these trees, have not come to light. We know that inquiries were ordered. To official ears in Spain had come echoes of the scandal over the severe treatment of Don Carlos. Hence the Royal Visitor, Francisco Tello de Sandoval, when ordered overseas to inspect the realms of New Spain and to correct abuses (1544–47), was specifically instructed by Spanish Church authorities to determine what had become of Don Carlos' estate and heirs. If Tello ever prepared a report on these matters, it has not yet been found, although other of his records survive.[41]

The facts that have been uncovered require a revision of the date previously assigned to Humboldt Fragment VI and its relationship to the Oztoticpac Lands Map. The former can be dated with relative precision at 1546. That is the only year when Don Antonio was still living and when Antonio Rodríguez Quesada, both identified on the document, was serving on the bench. Earlier I had suggested that these two Texcocan pictorials "probably are related documents for the same litigation. The former [Humboldt Fragment VI] could well be an earlier and simpler land claims document which was greatly expanded in detail and coverage at a later stage . . . to form the later, more complex Oztoticpac Lands Map."[42] This hypothesis now should be restated to the effect that an earlier, complex litigation that produced the Oztoticpac Lands Map was not directly related to that shown on Humboldt Fragment VI, and that the latter pictorial is based upon the former. The main common link between the documents rests primarily on the fact that the disputed fruit trees were part of the Oztoticpac Palace complex assigned by the Lords of Texcoco to Don Carlos. We shall return to the fruit trees when we discuss part VI of the Oztoticpac Lands Map.

The nature of the litigation reflected on the Oztoticpac Lands Map is suggested by relating the pictorial document to printed materials. If the information it provides is properly interpreted, parties to the suit would include the traditional señores of Texcoco, seeking to validate and maintain their claims to traditional family lands; possibly the heirs of Don Carlos, seeking to segregate his estate owned personally from that of the other señores; and, opposing them, a "new community" created by Spanish administrators in 1540, who partitioned certain lands of Texcoco and gave them to the commoners of a small area known as Tetzcocinco. Unfortunately, the related materials are not wholly satisfactory and require explanation.

TABLE 3. *Selected Days and Dates, 1537–40*

| Year | Date | Weekday |
|------|------|---------|
| 1537 | January 4 | Wednesday |
| 1538 | January 4 | Thursday |
| 1539 | January 4 | Tuesday |
| 1540 | January 4 | Monday |

The documentary material in question was published by McAfee and Barlow in 1946. From various corrupt Nahuatl copies they reconstructed and translated what they called "The Titles of Tetzcotzinco," among them a short piece labeled "The Land Grants of Don Antonio Pimentel."[43] The recital begins by saying that on August 15, 1537, when Don Antonio governed, a repartition of Texcocan lands was made. On Monday, January 4, in presence of the Guardian, Fray Juan de Alameda, and by his order, lands were given in perpetuity to Tetzcocinco, and "a new *communidad* was established in the city of Texcoco." The document incorrectly further states "Don Antonio became governor in the year of 1537." The remainder of the document summarizes the conditions under which Don Antonio gave the lands and the recipients who were to hold them.

This document is misdated. Its correct date is 1540, not 1537. From several other sources we know that from 1534 through 1539 Pedro Tetlahuehuetzin was señor and governor of Texcoco, succeeded after a short interregnum by Don Antonio in 1540. More convincing, however, is the fact that Monday, January 4, could occur only in 1540, as table 3 shows. Calendars for these years were reconstructed by the detailed records of dates and days provided by the Inquisition records of Don Carlos' trial.

This revised date is consistent with our earlier dating of the Oztoticpac Lands Map, from internal evidence, at about 1540. The material itself implies that the dispute for which the latter document is evidence concerns the claims of the "new community" to Texcocan lands. This view is strengthened by data from other parts of the Oztoticpac Lands Map, to which we shall shortly turn.

Let us summarize this lengthy discussion of part III of the Oztoticpac Lands Map. It deals with a property in litigation, lands of Oztoticpac, stated in Spanish and Nahuatl to belong to the seignorial lands of the rulers of Texcoco. The long Nahuatl gloss tells how it was given as life tenancy to Don Carlos. We have also now seen that part III, prepared about 1540, precedes its cognate, Humboldt Fragment VI, by at least five years. It now seems quite probable that the latter is derivative from the Oztoticpac Lands Map and was submitted in connection with a 1546 suit by Alonso de Contreras against codefendants Pedro de Vergara and Antonio Pimentel Tlahuilotzin over grafted fruit trees planted around the Oztoticpac palace, trees that had been part of Don Carlos' estate at his death in November 1539.

All of the upper right quadrant of the Oztoticpac Lands Map, which has been designated as part IV (figure 12), refers to a complicated area, including an estate which the Nahuatl gloss identifies as Octicpac. The Spanish note states that Don Pedro Tetlahuehuetzquitzin gave this land to Don Carlos. The Nahuatl note repeats this and adds that the red or colored lines outline the land of Don Carlos. It will be recalled from the testimony of Zacarías Tlacocoua in part III that Don Pedro had earlier promised his younger half brother Don Carlos to buy him a house and land, possibly this property.

The total area is denoted by four large stylized trees as boundary markers at the corners. Again using the published equivalencies, we find this to be a fairly sizable tract, approximately 2,167 feet by 1,667 feet. Within the larger area, the holdings of Don Carlos are delimited by the red lines, running between smaller boundary signs, maguey plants topped by flags. His lands in fact are divided into two parts: a fairly sizable single plot occupying about half the circumscribed area, with the other (lower half) divided into ten smaller tracts, each with its toponymic glyph and individual dimensions. The larger single tract is about 770 feet across by 410 feet deep. The subdivided area is the same distance across, but only about 354 feet deep, giving an average depth of each plot of about 12 yards. According to a Spanish gloss, these lands belong to renters, whose ten portraits are shown to the right. To the left, across a right of way, red lines bifurcate two other plots, presumably also belonging to Don Carlos.

The remainder of part IV shows numerous small landplots, each with a toponymic glyph and dimensions. Three different Spanish glosses designate these as property of the commoners (*maceguales*) rather than a part of Don Carlos' property. The glosses also reaffirm that the total litigation shown on the Oztoticpac Lands Map pitted the commoners against the claims of the señores to lands held during his lifetime by Don Carlos. This, as suggested above, may well be directly connected with the "new community" of Texcoco, established by Antonio Pimentel Tlahuilotzin and recorded in the January 4, 1540, land grants document.

In that action, Don Antonio gave the communities of Tetzcocinco and Santa Maria Nativitas a specified tract, to hold perpetually as a group. The boundaries were to run from the large ancient trees in Acoliuhyan (variant: Aculco), across to one at Tochatlauhtli, a dry barranca below Tezcotzinco, thence to another tree on the hilltop at Xocotlan, and from there down the San Juan road to the Rio Grande. These landmarks seem to fit quite accurately those shown on our map. The Octicpac tract owned by Don Carlos was only a small part of the larger Tetzcocinco 1540 donation and was obviously excluded from it. For these reasons the area we previously labeled "Octicpac" has now been renamed "Tetzcocinco." [44]

The general significance of part IV is to provide further details on the litigation with which the whole document is concerned and, at the same time, data on land tenure systems. While not an exact parallel, this portion of the Oztoticpac Lands Map corresponds in general to yet another of the Humboldt Manuscripts (Fragment VIII), and to various other Aztec pictorial cadastral documents of the sixteenth century. [45] Part IV thus provides comparative material of consequence, especially in view of the fact that it is imbedded in a known historical context.

Parts V and VI are much the same, in that each treats small individual land plots and properties clearly owned by Don Carlos. The plots have toponymic glyphs and related Spanish and native glosses which give additional miscellaneous information about the history of the plots and related matters (figure 13 on following page).

The area called "Totocinco," for instance, was a piece of land originally owned by a Don Carlos Coatlecouztin, who sold it

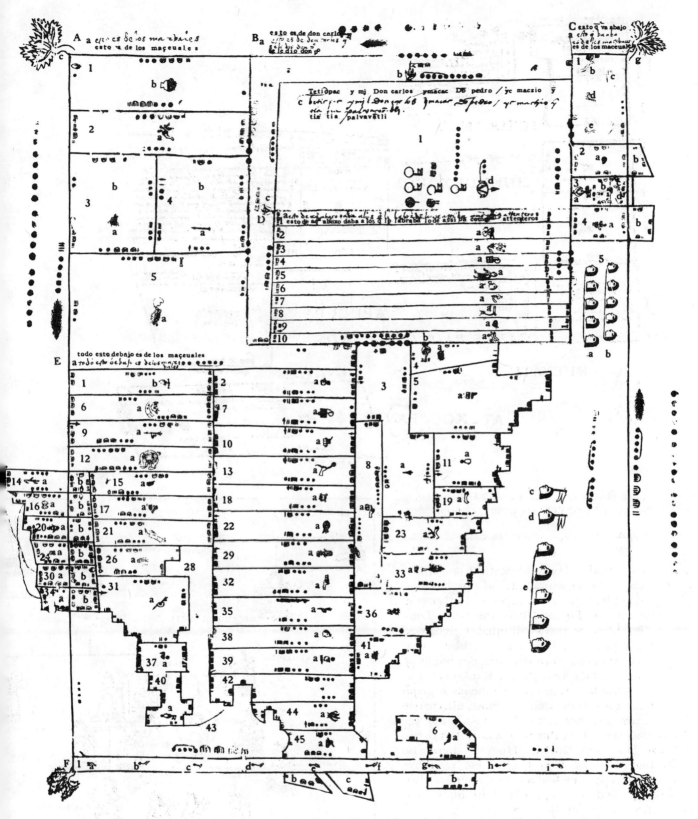

*Figure 12. Detail of part IV of the Oztoticpac Lands Map, with transcription of Spanish gloss supplied. The heads at the right indicate the Indian families who farmed the plots.*

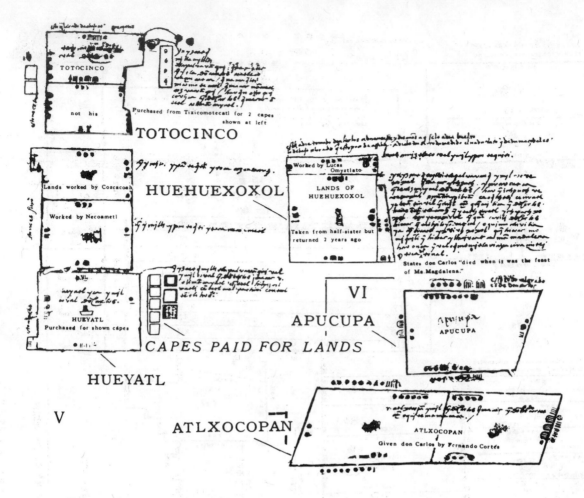

Figure 13. Lands of Don Carlos Chichimecatecotl, from parts V and VI of the Oztoticpac map.

Figure 14. Relatives of Don Carlos Chichimecatecotl.

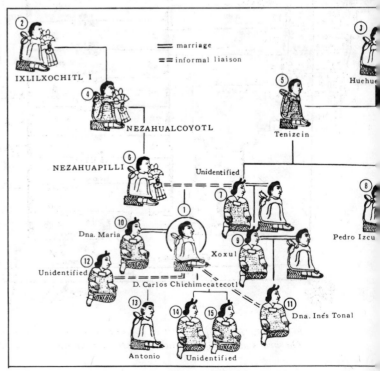

to a certain Tixicomotecatl, from whom Don Carlos Chichimecatecotl purchased it, paying him two plain capes and other considerations. To the left of the main Totocinco plots are two small squares, signifying the capes, above which is a rabbit's head with two dots. Normally this sign might be considered an Aztec date, 2 Rabbit (1494 or 1546) but here it seems to be the name glyph for Don Carlos, one of whose alternative names was Ometochtli ("Two Rabbit"); the gloss states that this plot was certainly his.

The lands labeled "Hueyatl" were also purchased by Don Carlos. He paid five plain capes, one feathered cape, one seamed cape, and one cape edged in black, also shown on figure 13.

The plot designated "Lands of Huehuexoxotl" has special interest, partly because of its important historical and genealogical data. The gloss indicates that Don Carlos died on the feast of Mary Magdalene and at that time provided well for his concubine. It supplies further notes on the disordered love life of Don Carlos, which helped the Inquisition prove charges of immorality against him.

The Nahuatl gloss indicates that Don Carlos took the plot of land, then returned it to his half sister Xoxul, who had inherited the property from their common great-grandfather (Huehuexoxol). Her daughter was Inés Tonal, the niece Don Carlos kept as a concubine, siring two daughters by her, one of whom died. The fact that he not only lived in sin with Inés, but also that he preached concubinage as an admirable doctrine weighed heavily against him in his 1539 Inquisition trial. Added

to this was strong evidence that Carlos had furtively hidden himself in the sleeping apartment of Maria, the recently widowed wife of his half brother Pedro Tetlahuehuetzquitzin. Discovered in the night, he was forcibly ejected by her servants, causing a notable scandal. By an unknown female, Don Carlos also had a son, Antonio, who as a lad of about 10 years appeared in 1539 as a witness against his father.[46]

In addition to his extramarital exploits, Don Carlos had been married to a Doña María by the Catholic Church in 1535. There is no record of children by that union. His formal and informal family relations are shown on figure 14, and data about them are summarized in table 4.

Support for our thesis that the litigation shown on the Oztoticpac Lands Map arose

TABLE 4. *Family of Don Carlos Chichimecatecotl*

| No. | Name | Relationship | Notes |
|---|---|---|---|
| 1 | Carlos Chichimecatecotl | Self | Also known as Carlos Brabo; Ometochtzin. |
| 2 | IXTLILXOCHITL I | Paternal great-grandfather | Ruled to 1419, when died. |
| 3 | Huehuexoxol | Maternal great-grandfather. | Lands he gave to Carlos' grandmother shown on Map, V–D–3. |
| 4 | NEZAHUALCOYOTL | Paternal grandfather | |
| 5 | Tenizcin | Maternal grandfather | Map states (V–D–1, Nahuatl) "grandfather of Don Carlos." |
| 6 | NEZAHUALPILLI | Father | |
| 7 | Unidentified | Mother | Granddaughter of Huehuexoxol. |
| 8 | Pedro Izcutecatl | Uncle | Brother of D. Carlos' mother. Custodian of Oztoticpac, 1537–39. |
| 9 | Xoxul | Half-sister | Daughter of D. Carlos' mother; brother is Carlos. |
| 10 | Dna. María | Wife | Married, 1535, at which time Carlos gave up concubine Inés. |
| 11 | Dna. Inés Tonal | Half-niece; concubine | Daughter of Xoxul. Baptized, 1524; met Carlos, 1532, lived with him until 1535. Bore him 2 daughters, 1 living in 1539. |
| 12 | Unidentified | Concubine | Mother of son Antonio, no. 13. |
| 13 | Antonio | Son | b. about 1528. |
| 14 | Unidentified | Daughter | b. about 1533? Deceased before 1539. |
| 15 | Unidentified | Daughter | b. about 1534; living with mother Inés in Ixtapalapa, 1539. Carlos furnished them with maize. |

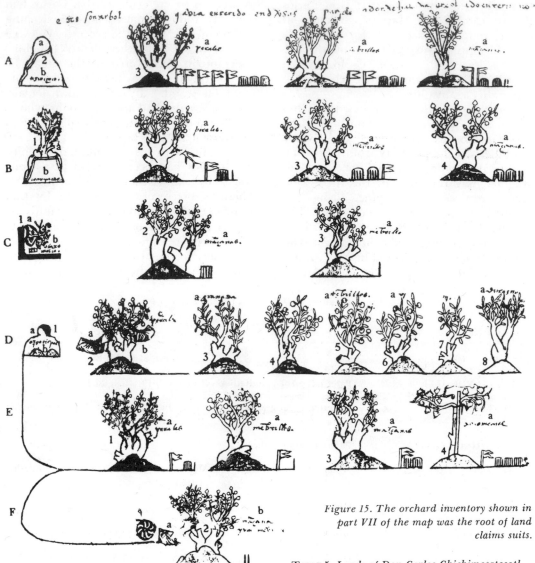

Figure 15. The orchard inventory shown in part VII of the map was the root of land claims suits.

TABLE 5. *Lands of Don Carlos Chichimecatecotl*

| Plot name or description | Mode of acquisition or ownership |
|---|---|
| Totocinco | Part purchased; part "Not his" |
| Lands worked by Cozcacoah | Purchased |
| Lands worked by Necoametl | Purchased |
| Hueyatl | Purchased |
| Huehuexoxol | Part a legacy; part "worked by Lucas Omyzlato" |
| Apucupa | "Belongs to Don Carlos" |
| Atlxocopan | Given Don Carlos by Fernando Cortés |

between the village commoners and the hereditary ruling family seems also to come from the Spanish gloss to Lands of Huehuexoxol. It summarizes data also contained in the Nahuatl gloss, concerning the fact that Don Carlos had taken it as a common inheritance from his sister but had returned it to her two years previously. But for our purposes the statement in Spanish that the "interpreter for the commoners has measured all this" is important.

It confirms that such a group was party to the suit and clarifies the fact that a second set of measurements on nearly all parts of the map were presumably placed there when representatives of the Indian commoners verified the pictorial document independently against claims on it made by the Texcocan señores. In nearly every case in parts V and VI there are statements in Nahuatl or Spanish mentioning that the properties were owned by Don Carlos, with explanations of how acquired, or notes indicating they did not belong to him, hence presumably could be claimed by the commoners. These several parcels are listed in table 5.

The information thus provided by parts V and VI tends to be genealogical, minor, and local, although it does have certain eco-nomic and social interest. Its value is far outweighed by the exciting and significant depictions in VII, the lower left quadrant (figure 15).

Part VII consists of a partly illegible and obscure Spanish gloss, plus six rows of grafted fruit trees, the first four rows of which have glossed toponymic glyphs pre-ceding them. Following each of the grafted trees, a Spanish notation gives its species, and native numbers, presumably specifying the quantity of such varieties within the

Figure 16. Modern map showing areas to which the toponymic glyphs in part VII of the Oztoticpac Lands Map refer. The village of Oztoticpac is indicated to the north of the Texcocan estates of Oztoticpac.

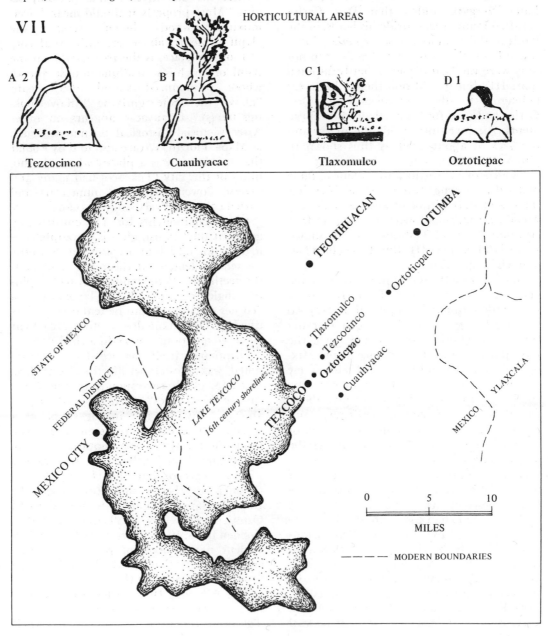

place indicated by the toponymic glyph. Figure 16 reproduces the major glyphs, with a map providing locations to which they refer.

We have already noted in connection with Humboldt Fragment VI that fruit trees planted by Don Carlos in partnership lay at the root of the suit which that document depicts. Those were located on the Oztoticpac lands, in two of the five orchards shown on part VII of the Oztoticpac Lands Map.

From Vergara's original petition we learn that "Don Carlos grafted many of the said trees on his own lands and outside them." Later Vergara added that Don Carlos "grafted many trees outside his lands, in the lands of the commoners (maceguales)." Presumably on the Oztoticpac Lands Map not only were the Oztoticpac orchards disputed (part III), but in addition these other areas belonging to the commoners which Don Carlos had used for his horticultural experiments. An inventory of all the places and trees, as of about 1540, is thus shown in part VII.

"Tezcocinco," the location of one of these orchards, became Santa María Nativitas Tetzcocinco. It will be recalled that Viceroy Mendoza confirmed ownership of it to Don Antonio Pimentel Tlahuilotzin. It is shown as his land on part III. But Tezcocinco had a much longer history.

One source tells us that in the year 4 Cane (1170 or 1248) some 2,000 Toltec Indians of the Tlailotlaque tribe appeared in Texcoco under a leader named Tempatzin, carrying their idol Tezcatlipuca, having made the long journey from their homes in the Mixteca of southern and western Mexico. They petitioned for land, which the ruler of Texcoco, Tlotzin, was delighted to give them, for they were famed as craftsmen and artists. Tlotzin selected 400 of the most skilled and gave them and their leader the area of Tezcocinco.[47]

Another published source is a grant of water rights from Nezahualcoyotl to the Indian descendants of the original settlers and others who had come into the area. The grant conveyed exclusive rights to various waters brought by the aqueduct shown on the place glyph. Nezahualcoyotl indicated one of the boundaries of Tezcocinco to be the adjoining Cuauyacac area, discussed below. To commemorate the grant and importance of Tezcocinco, Nezahualcoyotl had his portrait cut in stone on the hillside.[48] Utilizing the water supply and pleasant site, his son Nezahualpilli built royal gardens and baths there on the hill, which Pomar described as small and slightly to the east of Texcoco. He said that the etymology of the place-name was unknown, having persisted from earlier Chichimec times before the Aztecs of Texcoco settled in the area.[49]

Pomar also identifies Cuauyacac, location of other orchards, as a place about a mile east of Texcoco, on a hill within which was a notable cave. He gives its meaning as "where the uncultivated area (monte) begins." More properly it should mean "overlooking the woods," shown in rebus by the glyph elements: above the hill, usual convention for place, is the tree (cuah), in the trunk of which is seen a human nose, yacatl, whose pronounced sound also means "above" the whole signifying "hill overlooking tree(s)." Cuauyacac appears on other Aztec pictorial historical documents, such as Mapa Tlotzin. We are also told by Pomar that in 1582 it was a place "where the nobility of this city [Texcoco] had many and diverse flower gardens of numerous and varied colors and very singular odors. . . ."[50]

Glyph components for Tlaxomulco suggest that the Spanish gloss is incomplete, as it does not take into account the butterfly (papalotl) element in the rebus. However, the teeth (tla, tlalli, land; tlan, teeth) plus the angle, xomul, yields "Tlaxomulco," a "corner of land." It can be tentatively identified as Quauhximalco, a hilly area near Texcoco mentioned by Ixtlilxochitl.[51]

Oztoticpac itself, as we have already noted, was an estate within the city of Texcoco. Its glyph corresponds to the name "above the caves" (oztotl, cave; icpac, above), a stylized hill in the shape of a woman whose breasts represent the caves. From the records of the Inquisition it appears that Don Carlos had two houses within Texcoco, but that he resided in Oztoticpac. When Bishop Zumárraga, the Inquisitor and his cloud of witnesses visited Oztoticpac in July 1539, they found 4 wooden bows, 10 or 12 arrows, a bed, and an ancient native book of paintings, apparently a ritual calendar which set forth the "count of the fiestas of the Demon."[52]

The fact that Don Carlos was executed for having these ancient things caused other Texcocan Indian nobles to destroy their own native documents, according to Pomar, who avidly sought them in 1582 to write his lengthy report to the King. For our immediate purposes, however, it is important to note that there was growing on the Oztoticpac estate in 1539 a field of wheat, plus "trees of various kinds, grouped together around the house."[53] These trees are the ones with which the Vergara suit and Humboldt Fragment VI are concerned.

The main Oztoticpac glyph is connected by a line to a smaller and final group of fruit trees, preceded by an unglossed glyph. The latter has not been identified. It possibly represents the other house or estate of Don Carlos, which the Bishop visited the same day in 1539. It was in the second house that the damning idols were uncovered.

Unique among all known Mexican Indian pictorial documents is the depiction of grafted fruit trees shown on the Oztoticpac Lands Map of the Library of Congress. Other well-known documents provide important information on indigenous plants, but no others show the blending of native fruit trees with European varieties, a major contribution of this particular document.[54]

By 1540 the Texcocan Aztec orchardist activities in the four or five indicated places were considerable, both in quantity and variety. The general gloss for part VII, although obscure in part and not wholly legible, suggests that the introduction of grafted trees had created valuable properties from those previously abandoned or of small worth.[55] Table 6 summarizes the stands of fruits, tabulated from the native numerals following each variety. In the case of Oztoticpac, where peaches and pomegranates are shown, the number of such trees is omitted on the map. The tabulation

therefore provides a minimum total. It will be noted that quince and apples are the most numerous. Oztoticpac and Texcocinco are most concerned with this form of horticulture.

The data from the pictorial document accord with the descriptions of later activities reported in 1582 by Pomar. After discussing pines, oaks, and other industrial woods, he noted that sabine pines had been planted in Texcocinco, brought from other parts of the Valley of Mexico. He continues:

The natural fruit trees of this land, and which yield well, are cherries, which in tilled and cultivated soil give numerous and good fruits, very tasteful and reasonably nutritious. There are apple trees which yield a yellow and slightly red fruit, about the same size and taste of those in Castile, which we call "apples of San Juan." Some of these are better than others, depending on the care which is given the trees, or the good or bad qualities of the soil in which they grow. These and the cherries pass to the Indians, who store them to eat as a gift in winter. . . . They also have trees which yield black mulberries.

In another passage the same author stated that the Spanish fruits imported and grown in Texcoco included peaches of all varieties —common (*melocotones*), apricots, *priscos*, and a variety called "Damascus." There were also large pears, muscadines, and winter apples, and quince better than in Spain itself. Pomegranates and plums grew poorly; the little fruit they yielded was costly and bad. The same applied to figs, olives, and staked grapevines. If carefully cultivated, however, grapes—especially muscatel—would yield. Of only limited success were oranges, limes, citrons, and similar species, except in sheltered patches in the north of the realm.[56]

Pomar's general descriptions of the fruits offer some difficulties for precise botanical identifications. Table 7 provides a provisional key to them, with English, Spanish, Nahuatl, and botanical names. It is notable that in 1571, when Molina wrote his *Vocabulary*, only apples, cherries, and perhaps plums had authentic Aztec names; other fruits were called by loanwords from Spanish, suggesting that they were recently introduced.

Of major importance to cultural and horticultural history in Mexico are the tree grafts on part VII of the Oztoticpac Lands Map. Tree grafting in the Old World has an ancient origin, as evidenced in Greek

TABLE 6. *Fruit Orchards, Oztoticpac Lands Map*

| Variety | Texcocinco | Cuauyacac | Tlaxomulco | Oztoticpac | Total |
|---|---|---|---|---|---|
| Pears | 15 | 26 | -- | 26 | 67 |
| Quince | 52 | 30 | 1 | 42 | 125 |
| Apples | 52 | 17 | 5 | 29 | 103 |
| Pomegranates | -- | -- | -- | ? | ? |
| Peaches | -- | -- | -- | ? | ? |
| Grapevines | -- | -- | -- | 27 | 27 |
| Total | 119 | 73 | 6 | 124 | 322 |

TABLE 7. *Fruits Grown in Texcoco, 1582*

| English | Spanish | Nahuatl | Botanical |
|---|---|---|---|
| APPLE | manzana | texocotl | *Pyrus malus*, Linn. |
| winter apple | manzana de invierno; manzana de por San Juan. | | |
| APRICOT | albaricoque | | *Prunus armeniaca*. |
| CHERRY | cerezo; cereza | capulin | *Prunus cerasus*, or *Prunus avium*, Linn. |
| CITRON | cidra | cidraquauitl | *Citrus medica genuina*. |
| FIG | higuera | hicoxquauitl | *Ficus carica*. |
| GRAPE | uva; parra | xocomecatl; xocomecaquauitl. | *Vitis vinifera*. |
| muscatel | moscatel | ytac xocomecatl | *Vitis rotundifolia*. |
| LIME | lima | limaquauitl; xocoquauitl. | *Citrus medica acida*. |
| MULBERRY | mora | amaxocotl; amacapulin | *Morus nigra*, Linn. |
| OLIVE | azeituna; oliva | azeitequauitl | *Olea europea*. |
| ORANGE | naranja | naranjaxocotl | *Citrus aurantium bergamia*. |
| PEACH | durazno | duraznoquauitl | *Prunus persica*, Stokes |
| common peach | melocoton; durazno de Damasco; prisco. | xocotlmelecoton; xuchipaldurazno; cuzticdurazno. | *Amygdalus*. |
| PEAR | pera; pera mayor | peral ytla aquillo | *Pyrus comunis*, Linn. |
| muscadine | cermeña | | |
| PLUM | ciruela | ciruelaquauitl; macaxocotl. | *Prunus domestica*, Linn. |
| POMEGRANATE | granada | granandaquauitl | *Punica granatum*. |
| QUINCE | membrillo | xocotl mébrillo | *Cydonia oblanga*, Mill. |

texts and the Bible (Romans, xi: 16–24).[57] The history of tree grafting in sixteenth-century Spain and in colonial New Spain, however, seems never to have been systematically examined. But the pictorial data on the Oztoticpac Lands Map, coupled with information from manuscript sources about the very trees shown, give new and unusual information.

We know from another passage by Pomar that in 1582 the grafting of fruit trees was common in Texcoco, and easy. However, the depictions on the Oztoticpac Lands Map provide specific new information. They were reviewed by a modern specialist, Dr. Freeman S. Howlett, who reported that an ancient and simple technique known as "cleft grafting" was apparently used by Don Carlos and Vergara for the quince and apple trees. Seemingly the Aztec artists have shown a "whip and tongue" type of grafting for the grapes (figure 17). He suggests that yet a third technique, "budding," was employed for peaches, a more usual and successful approach with stone fruits (figure 17). Two or three years after the budding, the point of original union is nearly indistinguishable, hence its apparent absence at the hands of the observant Texcocan draftsmen. In passing, Dr. Howlett noted, "As far as I know this is the earliest known lawsuit or conflict described in horticultural literature anywhere in the world." [58]

In summary, part VII alone makes the Oztoticpac Lands Map highly significant. The depiction of horticultural practices ranks it among the important Indian pictorial documents which provide noteworthy economic and cultural data for the immediate post-Contact period. The very lack of such reliable information on the pre-Conquest and Spanish colonial practices suggests that systematic investigation of textual and related Indian pictorial materials would reveal important new insights into acculturation.

1 Original preliminary description and hypotheses appeared as an article by Howard F. Cline, "The Oztoticpac Lands Map of Texcoco, 1540," in the *Quarterly Journal of the Library of Congress*, 23: 76–115 (April 1966); additional material was included in his "The Oztoticpac Lands Map of Texcoco, 1540; Further Notes," presented at the 37th International Congress of Americanists, Mar del Plata, Argentina, September 1966, and scheduled for inclusion in its published *Proceedings*.

The author wishes to acknowledge professional and technical help given him by various colleagues. These include Charles Gibson, Henry B. Nicholson, Donald Robertson, Ignacio Bernal, Pedro Carrasco, Joaquín Galarza, Richard N. Greenleaf, Freeman S. Howlett, Arch C. Gerlach, and Jorge I. Rubio Mañe, with special appreciation to John B. Glass, who furnished much useful data, and to Charles Dibble, who translated the Nahuatl portions of the document.

2 Texcocan sources are cited and analyzed in detail by Charles Gibson, "Llamamiento general, repartimiento, and the Empire of Acolhuacan," *Hispanic American Historical Review*, 36:1–27 (February 1956). For most purposes, Fernando Alva Ixtlilxochitl, *Obras históricas* (2 vols. Mexico City, 1891–92), is the major source, although Diego Durán, *Historia de las Indias de la Nueva España y islas de tierra firme* (2 vols., atlas, Mexico City, 1867, 1880), is important because Durán was raised in Texcoco. Through the courtesy of the Spanish Ambassador, the Hispanic Foundation in December 1965 was permitted to microfilm the text and photo-reproduce in color the pictorial sections of the Durán *Historia* manuscript, deposited in the Biblioteca Nacional (Madrid) and displayed at the New York World's Fair in 1964–65; the 1867–80 printed version has serious defects. As a major element of the Aztec nation, Texcoco and its history are covered in numerous general sources and treatments, among them H. H. Bancroft, *Native Races* (5 vols., San Francisco, 1882–83), especially vol. 2, "Civilized Nations," and vol. 5, "Primitive History." The standard modern summary, now somewhat outdated, with useful bibliography, remains George C. Vail-

*Figure 17. Grafted trees and vines from part VII of the Oztoticpac Lands Map. Transcription of the Spanish gloss provided.*

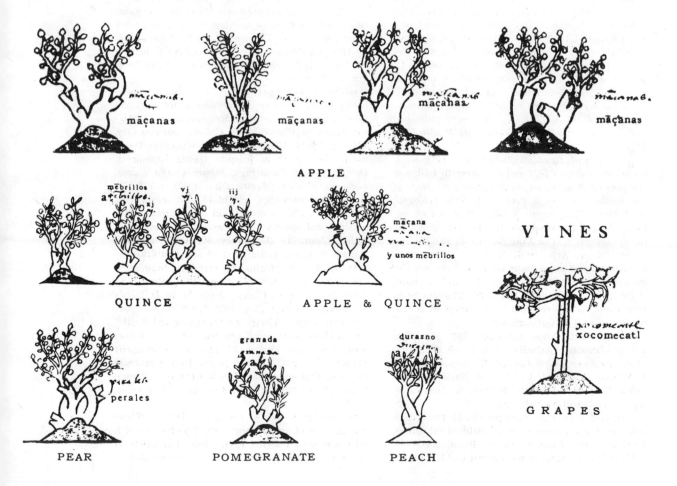

lant, *Aztecs of Mexico; Origin, Rise and Fall of the Aztec Empire* (New York, 1941).

3 Also known as "Histoire du royaume d'Acolhuacan ou de Tezcuco," it is in the Bibliothèque Nationale (Paris), Fonds Mexicains, 373. It was first published in 1849 by J. M. A. Aubin, later in color, in his *Mémoires sur la peinture didactique et l'écriture des anciens mexicains . . . précédés d'une introduction par E. T. Hamy* (Paris, 1885. Recherches historiques et archéologiques, Mission Scientifique au Mexique et dans l'Amérique Centrale). Paul Radin, *The Sources and Authenticity of the History of the Ancient Mexicans* (Berkeley, 1920), reprints the Aubin lithographs in black and white, with commentary, p. 18–19, 35–38. Donald Robertson, *Mexican Manuscript Painting of the Early Colonial Periods: The Metropolitan Schools* (New Haven, 1959), p. 140–141, discusses the artistic composition of the Mappe Tlotzin and its relation to other Texcocan manuscripts.

4 Bernardino de Sahagún, O.F.M. (1499–1590), wrote numerous works, the most important of which was his *Historia general de las cosas de Nueva España,* which underwent numerous revisions at his hands for 50 years. His Texcocan lineages, with separate drawings, taken from an early version, are conveniently found in Bernardino de Sahagún, *Florentine Codex, General History of the Things of New Spain, in Thirteen Parts. Book 8, Kings and Lords.* Translated from the Aztec into English, with notes and illustrations, by Arthur J. O. Anderson and Charles E. Dibble. Part IX (Santa Fe, N. Mex., 1954. Monographs of the School of American Research, No. 14, Part IX), p. 9–11, illustrations 28–41. Fernando de Alva Ixtlilxochitl apparently prepared in 1602–9 his "Relaciones" and "Historia Chichimeca" as documentation for his claims as legitimate heir. Edited by A. Chavero, they were published under the title *Obras históricas* (2 vols. Mexico City, 1891–92).

5 Ixtlilxochitl, *Obras,* 1:309–323. Born 1402, Nezahualcoyotl ruled to 1472 and is universally hailed as the greatest Aztec figure. Frances Gillmor's *Flute of the Smoking Mirror: a Portrait of Nezahualcoyotl, Poet-King* (Albuquerque, N. Mex., 1949) is a sympathetic biography, supplemented by her biography of Montezuma I, *The King Danced in the Marketplace* (Tucson, Ariz., 1964). Both cite a large body of pictorial and prose documentary sources. See also Bancroft, *Native Races,* 5:382–429 and Vaillant, *Aztecs,* p. 97–102. Ixtlilxochitl, 2:222, 241, says Nezahualcoyotl had 60 sons and 57 daughters by concubines, but only 2 legitimate sons.

6 Ixtlilxochitl, *Obras,* 2:248–249, 267; and Juan Bautista Pomar, "Relación, Tezcoco, 9 de marzo, 1582," in Ángel María Garibay K., *Poesía Nahuatl,* I (Mexico City, 1964. Universidad Nacional Autónoma de México, Instituto de Historia, Fuentes indígenas de la cultura Nahuatl), p. 176.

7 All told, more than 2,000 persons died as accomplices in this bizarre episode; see Ixtlilxochitl, *Obras,* 1:285–286; and Bancroft, *Native Races,* 5:448–449.

8 The Triple Alliance was formed in 1431; for in-

formation on it see Bancroft, *Native Races,* 5:395–399; and Robert H. Barlow, "La fundación de la Triple Alianza," in Instituto Nacional de Antropología e Historia (México), *Anales,* 3:147–155, and his detailed *The Extent of the Empire of the Culhua Mexica* (Berkeley and Los Angeles, 1949). Important new data are in Charles Gibson, *The Aztecs Under Spanish Rule: A History of the Indians of the Valley of Mexico* (Stanford, 1964).

9 Most of the information appearing under "Ahuaxpitctzatin" in Rafael García Granados' useful but uncritical *Diccionario biográfico de historia antigua de Méjico* (Mexico City, 1952–53. Universidad Autónoma de México, Instituto de Historia, *Publicaciones,* primera serie, 23), 1:34–37, relates to Carlos Chichimecatecotl. Richard E. Greenleaf, *Zumárraga and the Mexican Inquisition, 1536–1543* (Washington, 1961. Academy of American Franciscan History, Monograph series, 4), p. 68–74, provides data on Don Carlos Chichimecatecotl but makes incorrect statements, based on data relating to Carlos Ahuaxpizin; he lumps various brothers together by naming his subject "Don Carlos Ahuaxpitzatzin Ometochtzin Yoyotzin Ixtlilxochitl Mendoza," characterized as "an obscure person in Texcocan history until the Zumárraga trial of 1539" (p. 68, n. 4). Gibson, *Aztecs,* p. 170–171, more correctly indicates the succession in Texcoco following the death of Nezahualpilli (1516), although omitting some figures.

10 *Proceso criminal del Santo Oficio de la Inquisición y del Fiscal en su nombre contra Don Carlos, indio principal de Tezcoco,* edited by Luis González Obregón (Mexico City, 1910. Archivo General y Público de la Nación, *Publicaciones,* 1). Cited hereafter as *Proceso.*

11 Two strong reprimands dated 1540 are published in *Un desconocido cedulario del siglo xvi perteneciente a la Catedral Metropolitana de México,* edited by Alberto María Carreño (Mexico City, 1944), p. 13–14, 160–161, and reproduced as Documentos 18 and 19 in Joaquín García Icazbalceta, *Don Fray Juan Zumárraga, primer obispo y arzobispo de México* (Mexico City, 1947), 4:170–173. Greenleaf (*Zumárraga,* p. 14–15, 74) notes that Zumárraga's actions resulted in his removal as Inquisitor and speeded the "exemption movement" which ultimately (December 30, 1571) removed Indians from the jurisdiction of all inquisitions.

12 José Toribio Medina, *La primitiva Inquisición americana, 1493–1569* (Santiago de Chile, 1914), 1:141–175; Mariano Cuevas, *Historia de la Iglesia en México* (Mexico City, 1921 [1946 ed.]), 1:369–379, 431; Robert Ricard, *La "conquête spirituelle" du Mexique; essai sur l' apostolat et les methodes missionaires des Ordres Mendiants en Nouvelle Espagne de 1523–24 à 1572* (Paris, 1933. Université de Paris. Travaux et mémoires de l'Institut d'Ethnologie, 20), p. 320–322; and Greenleaf, *Zumárraga,* p. 75.

13 Translation by Dr. Charles E. Dibble. There remain some obscurities and textual problems which have not been resolved to his full satisfaction. A literal translation appears in Cline, "Further Notes."

A parallel line of native lords for the Tulancingo village area is treated in Pedro Carrasco, "Los caciques chichimecas de Tulancingo," *Estudios de cultura Nahuatl,* 4:85–91 (1963).

14 Many of the materials cited in note 2 continue their coverage into the Spanish period. The Texcocan views are stated in Ixtlilxochitl, *Obras;* with the coming of the Spaniards, Texcocan history merges with the vast literature on the Conquest, and especially the role of Fernando Cortés.

15 Gibson, *Aztecs,* p. 170–171, notes the evolution of differences between "lord" (*tlatoani*) and "governor" (*gobernador*) as Spaniards cut down the size of the Texcocan realm and reduced the powers of the tlatoani-governor. Surviving letters from the latter lament the situation and cast light on the gradual diminution: Hernando Pimentel Ihuan (Nezahualcoyotl), "Memorial dirigido al rey por . . . cacique y governador de la provincia de Tezcuco," undated but ca. 1545, in Manuel Orozco y Berra, *Historia antigua y de la conquista de México* (Mexico City, 1880), 2:201–203, indicating reductions since the Conquest; reprinted, with omissions, in *Divulgación historica,* 4:508–509 (1942–43). "Carta de don Hernando Pimentel, cacique principal de Texcuco, al rey don Felipe II . . . Texcuco a 6 de abril de 1562," in Francisco del Paso y Troncoso, comp., *Epistolario de Nueva España, 1505–1818* (Mexico City, 1939–42. Biblioteca Histórica Mexicana, segunda serie), 16:74–75, complaining of reduced area, asking redress, especially for four towns; "Tasaciones de tributos de la ciudad de Tescuco y su provincia . . . 26 de septiembre de 1544," *ibid.,* 4:128–130, indicating that on petition of Hernando (Pimentel), governor, and Diego, a principal Indian, tributes for 1547 and the following 3 years would be the same as from the 1544 assessment if they were allowed to keep their posts; in 1556 annual Texcocan money payments were commuted to annual payment to the Crown of 8,000 *fanegas* of maize, reconfirmed in 1562.

16 Gibson, *Aztecs,* p. 20–25, stresses the disruptive effects of rivalries within the Triple Alliance, climaxed by the Cacama-Montezuma struggles against Ixtlilxochitl. A narrative of the period is found in Bancroft, *Mexico,* 1:118 ff. Much of the enormous literature on Cortés is cited in Henry R. Wagner, *The Rise of Fernando Cortés* (Los Angeles, 1944).

17 Ixtlilxochitl, *Obras,* 1:335–346, the "Thirteenth Relation," covers the period from 1519, and 1:387–388, the division of the kingdom.

18 Ixtlilxochitl, *Obras,* 1:417. Cortés had taken with him to Guatemala, as hostages, the main nobles among the Aztecs; for various reasons he executed nearly all of them except Ixtlilxochitl, who unsuccessfully tried to save his brother Cohuanacochtzin from hanging; the episode is recorded in Bancroft, *Mexico,* 2:205–206, and at greater length in his *History of Central America* (San Francisco, 1883), 1:551–557. According to Ixtlilxochitl, *Obras,* 2: 301–304, the earlier Ixtlilxochitl, who was born in 1500, had a short but eventful life; by the age of 3 he had killed his wet nurse for adultery; at the age of 6 he was sentenced to death by his father's councilors, and, on reversal of their sentence by the king, killed them; at age 14 he first went to war and at 16 became a major leader.

19 Ixtlilxochitl, *Obras,* 1:398–400, who incorrectly includes Lorenzo de Luna; Ixtlilxochitl's mother, Tlacoxhuactzin, refused at first to be baptized, until he threatened to burn her alive. Previous native marriages were resanctified by the Church on October 14, 1526, at which time Fernando Cortés was best man for Ixtlilxochitl.

20 *Proceso,* p. 66–67; and Greenleaf, *Zumárraga,* p. 73.

21 Provisionally translated by Dr. Charles E. Dibble, the full text appears in Cline, "Further Notes."

22 *Proceso,* p. 7–8, 9, 12 (stating that the house in which idols were found had belonged to Don Carlos' maternal grandfather Tlalchachi), 21, 27, 56–57.

23 Alexander von Humboldt, *Vues des Cordillères et monumens des peuples indigènes de l'Amérique* (Paris, 1810 [i.e., 1813]), p. 56, planche 12 bis. For Humboldt's Mexican travels, see Helmut de Terra, *Humboldt; the Life and Times of Alexander von Humboldt, 1769–1859* (New York, 1955), p. 149–171.

24 Friedrich Wilken, *Geschicte der Königlichen Bibliothek zu Berlin* (Berlin, 1828), p. 29, 155–56, 234; *Index librorum manuscriptorum et impressorum quibus Bibliotheca Berolinensis aucta est. Annis 1837 et 1838. Praemissa est historia Bibliothecae Regiae A. 1828–1839 vernaculo sermone scripta* (Berlin, 1840), p. xvi; *Katalog der Schausammlung der Preuszichen Staatsbibliothek* (Berlin, 1925), p. 54; Howard F. Cline, "The former Manuscriptae Americanae of the K. Bibliothek, Berlin (presently Deutsche Staatsbibliothek)" in Hispanic Foundation, *HMAI Notes,* No. 24, p. 3–6. Ulf Bankmann and others in Germany kindly provided unpublished data on the Humboldt and other manuscripts in this collection. See note 26.

25 *Historische Hieroglyphen der Azteken im Jahr 1803, im Konigreich Neu-Spanien gesamlet von Alexander von Humboldt . . .* (Berlin, 1893) handsomely publishes at nearly full size (including the 14-foot No. I) the 16 Humboldt Fragments; for this separate album by the Royal Library (Berlin) a commentary was specially prepared by Eduard Seler, *Die mexikanischen Bilderhandschriften Alexander von Humboldts in der königlichen Bibliothek zu Berlin* (Berlin, 1893). With some omissions and revisions, Seler included the same work in his *Gesammelte Abhandlungen* (Berlin, 1902–23), 1:162–300 (1902), with reduced plates. The 1893 version of his essay was translated as "The Mexican Picture Writings of Alexander von Humboldt in the Royal Library at Berlin" and published in *Mexican and Central American Antiquities, Calendar Systems and History, Translated From the German Under the Supervision of Charles P. Bowditch* (Washington, 1904. Smithsonian Institution, Bureau of American Ethnology, Bulletin 28), p. 123–229; Karl von den Steinen prepared colored plates of the Humboldt Fragments for that publication, but they appeared in reduced size, in black and white, in-

ferior to the 1893 *Historische Hieroglyphen*. For convenience we cite the 1904 translation; Fragment VI, ibid., p. 190–196, plate XI. An older description, based primarily on Seler, is P. J. J. Valentini, "Humboldt's Aztec Paintings," *The Cosmopolitan*, 18:331–339 (Jan. 1895).

[26] Dr. Hans Lülfing, Chief, Manuscripts Division, Deutsche Staatsbibliothek (DSB), in December 1962 furnished much information on the present whereabouts of former Manuscriptae Americanae; manuscript 1, containing Fragments II–XVI, is the only one remaining in DSB; manuscript 2, Humboldt Fragment I, is now in West Berlin; the other 13 manuscripts were acquired after Humboldt's 1806 gift. Dr. Lülfing kindly furnished a color transparency and a black and white photograph of Humboldt Fragment VI for this article.

[27] Seler, "Picture Writings," p. 190–193. On p. 196, after describing the glyph, Seler wrote, "Although various suggestions occur to me, I do not venture to express a definite opinion in regard to the meaning of this object." The writer is indebted to John B. Glass for identifying the glyph and furnishing comparative materials. Robertson, in his *Mexican Manuscript Painting*, p. 175, briefly discusses the Humboldt Fragment VI, which he reproduces from the original as plate 68.

[28] Seler, "Picture Writings," p. 190–191. Juan de Torquemada bases his account of Nezahualcoyotl's palace in *Monarchia indiana* (2 ed., Madrid, 1723), 1:167–168, on "cuenta cierta . . . escrita en los libros de su gasto, y autorizada por un nieto suio, que despues de ser Cristiano, se llamó Don Antonio Pimentel." See also Pomar, "Relación, 1582," p. 218–219. Ixtlilxochitl (*Obras*, 1:398–399, 402) claims that the first organized church services were held in it on June 12, 1524. Mappe Quinatzin is also known as "Cour chichimèque et historie de Tezcuco," Bibliothèque Nationale (Paris, cited as BNP) manuscripts 11–12, published first by Aubin in 1849 and republished in color in his "Peinture didactique," with commentary; Radin, *Sources*, p. 19, 38–41, plates 16–17, abstracts Aubin and reproduces his plates; Robertson, *Mexican Manuscript Paintings*, p. 135–140, plates 13, 46–47, analyzes artistic features. Ixtlilxochitl, *Obras*, 2:173–181, describes a source, probably this or a parallel. One Spanish gloss reads "78 years ago Nezahualpilli was born [1464]," giving a 1542 date to Mappe Quinatzin; another says Nezahualcoyotl came to Tezcoco in the year 4 Xochitl, 115 years ago [1431], giving a 1546 date. See also Robert H. Barlow, "Una nueva lámina del Mapa Quinatzin," *Journal de Société des Americanistes*, n.s., 39:111–124 (1950); this is BNP manuscript 396, showing various crimes and punishments.

[29] Ixtlilxochitl, *Obras*, 2:51, 79, 385; various buildings by Nezahualcoyotl are described, ibid., 2:209–212.

[30] Seler, "Picture Writings," p. 191–192.

[31] Gibson, in *Aztecs*, p. 257–258, note 4 (p. 538–539), summarizes, saying that "the subject needs systematic restudy based on records of colonial lands."

Daniel G. Brinton's *The Lineal Measures of the Semi-Civilized Nations of Mexico and Central America* (Philadelphia, 1885) is short and unsatisfactory. For Spanish colonial measures shown in figure 10, materials in Manuel Carrera Stampa, "The Evolution of Weights and Measures in New Spain," *Hispanic American Historical Review*, 29:2–24 (February 1949) have been utilized. The Aztec terms in figure 10 come from Fray Alonso de Molina, *Arte de la lengua mexicana y castellana* (Mexico City, 1571); the Library of Congress copy seems to have been that of Molina and contains numerous additions and corrections to the published text. The writer is grateful for aid given by Dr. Pedro Carrasco in working out Texcocan measures, many on documents collected by him.

[32] Seler, "Picture Writings," p. 195; and Arthur S. Aiton, *Antonio de Mendoza, First Viceroy of New Spain* (Durham, 1927), p. 41, 191.

[33] José María Arreola, "Jeroglíficos mexicanos de apellidos españoles," *Ethnos* (Mexico), Ep. I/1:17–21 (1920), fig. 8.

[34] Seler, "Picture Writings," p. 187, fig. 43–s; 195.

[35] Personal communications.

[36] Arthur Scott Aiton, *Antonio de Mendoza* (Durham, 1927), p. 59, 106; and Gibson, *Aztecs*, p. 222.

[37] Seler, "Picture Writings," p. 194–195.

[38] Dibble and Anderson, *Florentine Codex . . . Book 8*, p. 10.

[39] Humboldt, *Vues des Cordillères*, p. 56.

[40] "Proceso de Pedro de Vergara, soltero, contra el Fiscal del Santo Oficio, sobre los árboles de Don Carlos," manuscript in the Archivo General de la Nación (México), Inquisición, vol. 139, exp. 11, fols. 60–72v. The writer is grateful to Dr. Richard Greenleaf for calling this important item to his attention and to Dr. Jorge Ignacio Rubio Mañe, Director of the Archivo, for preparing a transcript of it.

[41] Tello's general instructions from the Crown appear in Vasco de Puga, *Provisiones, cédulas, instrucciones de su Magestad, ordenanzas . . . dende el año 1525 hasta este presente de 63* (Mexico City, 1563; reissued, 2 vols., 1878, and facsimile, 1945), fol. 94–95v (1878, omits 94–94v), 97–98, 446–454. "Instrucción de lo que el muy reverendo licenciado Francisco de Sandoval . . . [no date]," Medina, *Primitiva Inquisición*, 2:6–8, contains the text of a special instruction re Don Carlos.

[42] Cline, "Oztoticpac Lands Map," p. 91.

[43] "The Land Grants of Don Antonio Pimentel," in "The Titles of Tetzcotzinco (Santa María Nativitas)," translated and annotated by Byron McAfee and R. H. Barlow, *Tlalocan*, 2:110–127 (1946); the Antonio Pimentel grant is discussed on p. 119–122. Antonio signed the document as governor, Pedro Tlahuehuetzquitzin as alcalde, and Jorge Yoyotzin as scribe. According to information supplied by Charles Gibson, these land titles may be found in "Colección antigua," t. 254, fols. 261–265, Museo Nacional de Antropología (Mexico City), nineteenth-century copies from an unknown source, and in BNP manuscript 288, Pichardo copy from an unknown source; related, unpublished materials are in

the British Musuem, MS 42567, cuad. 9; and a deviant copy was published by Guillermo Echaniz, *Datos relativos a Tetzcuzinco* (Mexico City, 1944), from an unknown copy.

44 Cline, "Oztoticpac Lands Map," p. 95–96.

45 Humboldt Fragment VIII is discussed and illustrated in Seler, "Picture Writings," p. 200–209; on this document and Codex Vergara (BNP), in addition to glyphs giving the name of the landplot, another glyph indicates the nature of the soil (hilly, sandy, etc.); this is missing from the Oztoticpac Lands Map.

46 *Proceso*, p. 11 (Pedro Izcutecatl re Inés); 14–15 (Inés re relations with D. Carlos); 32–33 (María, wife of Antonio de Pomar, sister of D. Carlos, noting later "andaba como loco . . . siempre ha procurado de señoriar y mandar a todos por fuerza, y ser señor de Tezcoco"); 33–37 (María, widow of Pedro, and her servants); 38 (María, wife of D. Carlos); 37 (Antonio, son of D. Carlos); 54 (Doña María, sister of D. Carlos, re his instructions about concubinage); 55–61 (D. Carlos, admitting concubinage, rejecting other charges). See also Greenleaf, *Zumárraga*, p. 69–72. I find no corroboratory evidence for Greenleaf's statements that Don Carlos had been a star student at the Franciscan school for Indians, Colegio de Santa Cruz de Tlatelolco (ibid., p. 36, 68); the school was founded in 1534 when Carlos was living in Oztoticpac with Inés, and where he continued to reside after his marriage in 1535. Standard sources on Tlaltelolco do not mention him: Fernando Ocaranza, *El imperial Colegio de Indios de la Santa Cruz de Santiago Tlaltelolco* (Mexico City, 1934); Francis Borgia Steck, *El primer colegio de América: Santa Cruz de Tlaltelolco, con un estudio del códice de Tlaltlolco por R. H. Barlow* (Mexico City, 1944. Centro de Estudio Franciscanos).

47 Ixtlilxochitl, *Obras*, 1:289–290, 295, 2:70, 74–75. The barrio Tlailotlapan of Texcoco survived, named for these Toltec (ibid., 1:289). The scene is shown on Mappe Quinatzin, with a gloss in Nahuatl stating "In the time of Quinatzin the Tlailotlaques and the Chimalpanecas arrived, 172 years ago." Their arrival is also recorded by Codex Xolotl. The introduction of written and painted documents in Texcoco is said to date from this immigrant group.

48 McAfee and Barlow, "The Water Grants of Nezahualcoyotl," in "The Titles of Tetzcotzinco," *Tlalocan*, 2:111–119. A discussion of the grant and related matters appear in Ángel Palerm and Eric R. Wolf, "El desarrollo del área clave del imperio texcocano," *Revista mexicana de estudios antropológicos*, 14/1:337–349 (1954–55). See also Bancroft, *Native Races*, 5:404, 427–428.

49 Pomar, "Relación, 1582," p. 155, 208–209; Ixtlilxochitl, *Obras*, 2:210–212 (gives a long description), 221, 237; and Orozco y Berra, *Historia antigua*, 3:316–317.

50 Pomar, "Relación, 1582," p. 208, 210; and Ixtlilxochitl, *Obras*, 2:100. Garibay, in *Poesía Nahuatl*, I (see note 6), p. 224, notes that this "bosquecillo" retains its name and is used for cereal cultivation.

51 Ixtlilxochitl, *Obras*, 2:66.

52 *Proceso*, p. 7. The bed and its covering, being of little value, were given to Carlos' wife, María.

53 "Arboles de diversas maneras, cercada junto a la dicha casa," *Proceso*, p. 7. See also Pomar, "Relación, 1582," p. 153.

54 Most important of these is *Libellus de medicinalibus indorum herbis . . . 1552*, a Latin treatise usually known as Codex Badianus or Codex Barberini; it has been published in translation and with extensive annotations by Emily W. Emmart, *The Badianus Manuscript (Codex Barberini, Latin 241), Vatican Library; an Aztec Herbal of 1552* (Baltimore, 1940). Zelia Nuttall, in her "El cultivo de árboles frutales en Coyoacán a fines del siglo xviii," *Mexico Forestal*, 3/6–7:90–92 (junio-julio 1925), refers to the brief mention of grafted trees in eighteenth-century titles to her land in Coyoacán.

55 "These are trees which were grafted in unused [dexadas] places where trees were found; before these grafts there were no fruits at all" [writer's transcription and translation].

56 Pomar, "Relación, 1582," p. 211, 212.

57 Robert J. Garner, *The Grafter's Handbook* (New York, 1958), p. 34–35. Woodrow Borah, in his *Silk Raising in Colonial Mexico* (Berkeley and Los Angeles, 1943), p. 5, 6, says that in 1522 Cortés asked the Spanish Government for livestock, cuttings, seeds, mulberry trees, and silkworm eggs, which apparently came in 1523. Antonio Pimentel Tlahuilotzin (litigant of Humboldt Fragment VI) had planted mulberries and gathered silk on his lands, according to Pomar, "Relación, 1582," p. 214, but in 1582 no silk was raised. Borah traces the history of silk raising to 1580 (p. 1–31), noting Don Antonio's participation in the silk boom (p. 18).

58 Private communication. Dr. Howlett is chairman of the department of horticulture at the Ohio Agricultural Research Center, Wooster, Ohio.

# A Manuscript Atlas by Battista Agnese

# BY LAWRENCE MARTIN·EDITED BY WALTER W. RISTOW

Reprinted from volume 1, number 2 (1944), of the *Library of Congress Quarterly Journal of Current Acquisitions.*

A RARE manuscript atlas by Battista Agnese, probably made in 1544, was acquired by the Library of Congress in 1943. The handsome volume, bound in contemporary brown tooled leather and stamped in gold, has 15 vellum leaves, with 10 colorfully illuminated hand-drawn maps. Purchased from Lathrop Harper of New York, the atlas is known to have been earlier in the famous Fürstliche Stollberg-Wernigerodische Bibliothek, Wernigerode, Saxony. It was still in that library when Walter Ruge included a description of it in 1916 in his "Älteres kartographisches Material in deutschen Bibliotheken." [1] The original owner of the volume was Heronimous Ruffault, the Abbot of St. Vaast (Vedasti), in France. On the verso of the first leaf there is a decorative inscription that reads "REVERENDISSIMVS Ī CHRISTO PATER DŃS HIERONIMVS RVFFAVLT ABBAS SĀCTI VEDASTI ET SANCTI ADRIANI."

The late Henry R. Wagner, distinguished authority on the history of cartography, published a detailed study on Agnese and his atlases in 1931.[2] After examining some 60 separate Agnese atlases, Wagner classified them into three types as follows:

Type I. Pre-Californian, from about 1535 to the end of 1541.

Characteristic features are the absence of California, delineation of Yucatan as an island, separation of England and Scotland, and the misplacing of Taprobana (as Ceylon) on the oval world map.

Type II. Post-Californian, from about 1542 to about 1552.

Atlases in this group show the peninsula of California. With one exception, only the routes of Magellan and that to Peru are shown on the oval world map. Also, with some few exceptions, North America is of the Verrazano type, and Yucatan is drawn as an island. On the map of Northwest Europe, Scotland has a square shape. In most atlases of this type Scotland and England are separated by a narrow strait.

*Plate 6.*

Type III. Post-Californian with a new map of Scotland, from about 1552 to 1564.

In addition to containing a new map of Scotland, these atlases show Yucatan as a peninsula. Also, on the oval world map the Verrazano shape of North America has been dropped. Taprobana appears in its proper place as Sumatra and the island of Ceylon has been reduced to its proportionate size.

Number 33 in Wagner's list of Agnese atlases is the copy now in the Library of Congress. From photographs and from information furnished by Otto Lange of Florence, who at one time had offered the atlas for sale, and by Lathrop C. Harper of New York City, who owned it in 1931, Wagner classified it in his type 2 group and described it as follows:

The atlas comprises a declination table and an armillary sphere on single pages, an uncompleted double-page zodiac with a small Atlantic hemisphere in the center, and 10 maps 29.5 x 19.5 [cm.]: Nos. 1, Pacific Ocean, Vermeio type; 2, Atlantic Ocean; 3, Indian Ocean; 4, Northwest Europe; 5, Spain and Northwest Africa; 6, West Mediterranean; 7, Central Mediterranean; 8, East Mediterranean; 9, Black Sea; 10, Oval world-map. In the back cover there is a compass (with the needle missing) surrounded by a windrose, and according to Ruge's description, the binding may be a characteristic Agnese binding. The verso of the first leaf contains an inscription that it belonged to Heronimous Ruffault, the abbot of St. Vedasti and St. Adrian, and in the front is a notation in a later hand that this man was abbot from 1537 to 1563 of S. Vaast, a Benedictine convent in Arras.[3]

Of more than 60 Agnese atlases that have been identified and described, at least 16 are known to be in collections in the United States. The Huntington Library has five, the Newberry Library three, the John Carter Brown Library and the Morgan Library two each, and there are single copies in the New York Public Library, in the Library of the Hispanic Society of America, in the hands of an American dealer [in 1943], and in the Library of Congress. The only other known copy in the Americas is in the Sociedad de Geografía of Mexico.

"All we know about Battista Agnese," wrote Wagner in 1931, "is found on his own maps. He described himself as a Genoese and dates his maps from Venice. The Italian geographers who have manifested some interest in his work have so far failed to unearth a single other fact about his life, and the investigators in the Vene-

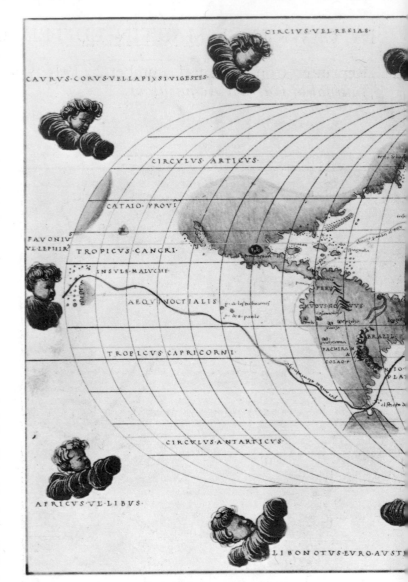

tian archives seem never to have found his name mentioned. This is the more remarkable because he was one of the most prolific map-makers of the sixteenth century." [4]

Similarly, Winsor wrote, in 1897, that "what we know of Agnese's career is almost wholly derived from his works; and at least half of these, as we recognize them, are anonymous and undated. There has been some difference of opinion as to the length of his cartographical service. Wieser and Kretschmer assign to him atlases in the British Museum of as early dates as 1527 and 1529. Kohl puts his earliest work in 1530. Harrisse starts his career with a group of portolanos known to have been made in 1539. Kohl does not trace him beyond 1545. Harrisse and Kretschmer date his latest

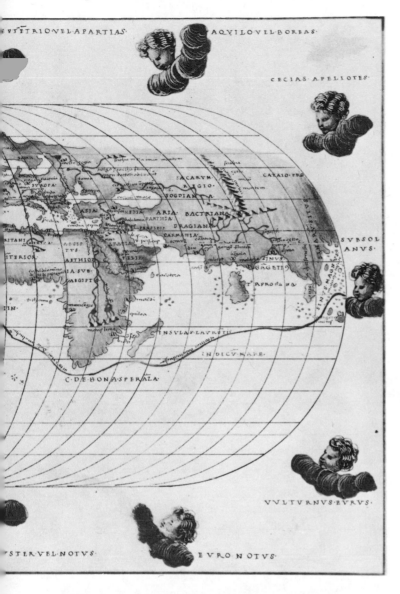

Labels visible on the map image:
VTERIOVELAPARTIAS· · AQVILOVELBOREAS·
CECIAS·APELIOTES·
SVBSOL ANVS·
VVLTVRNVS·EVRVS·
STER·VEL·NOTVS· EVRO·NOTVS·
CATAIO·PRO · SACARVM REGIO· · SOGDIANA · · ARIA · BACTRIANA · · PARTHIA · PRESIDIS DRAGIANA · CARMANIA · TAPROBANA · SINVS MAGNVS · INSVLAS·LAVRETII · IN·DICVM·MARE· · C·DE·BONA·SPER·ALA·

*Plate 14 in Battista Agnese's manuscript atlas of about 1544. From the collections of the Geography and Map Division.*

work 1564. It is significant of his want of care in registering the progress of geographical knowledge, that in this atlas of 1564 [a later type than the one in the Library of Congress], which is preserved in the Biblioteca Marciana at Venice, the Chilean coast is still undefined, though it had been known in Europe to have been tracked nearly thirty years. Cartier had established the insularity of Newfoundland at about the same time, and still in 1564 Agnese does not recognize its island character." [5]

Malavialle, writing in 1908, and Alberto Magnaghi, in a life of Agnese published in

*Enciclopedia Italiana di Scienze, Lettere ed Arti* (Milan, 1929), say nothing about Agnese's life except that he was born in Genoa and lived in Venice. These meager facts, of course, stem solely from the signatures on the dated atlases. A representative one reads: "baptista agnese Januēsis fecit uentijs anno Domini 1543 die 25 junij." This may be translated freely: "Baptista Agnese, a native of Genoa, made [this atlas] at Venice on June 25, 1543 A.D." There is no record of his ever traveling outside Italy.

Plates 5, 6, and 14 in the Library's Agnese are of particular interest, for they indicate the extent of European knowledge, when the atlas was made, of the territory now within the United States. No. 14, an attractive map of the world executed in red, green, blue, and gold, generalizes the Atlantic coast of the United States and the Pacific coast adjacent to southern California with an accuracy creditable in a period only half a century removed from the first voyage of Christopher Columbus. It shows no place names within the present United States. Plate 5 is on a larger scale than plate 14 and represents the same coasts in essentially the same manner. In eastern North America, north of the Caribbean and the Gulf of Mexico, some 30 place names are given for coastal features. Except *la florida,* none of these names is in use today.

To United States scholars, plate 6 is the most interesting for it shows the entire Atlantic Ocean, and thus presents both the eastern portion of continental United States and the Mediterranean basin. There are 42 place names in eastern United States and adjacent parts of Canada and Mexico. The coasts on the western border of the Atlantic are naturally much less complete and much more distorted than the coast lines of Europe, Africa, and western Asia.

All the maps in the atlas are vividly executed and in an excellent state of preservation. Plates 5, 6, and 14 leave North America without continental designation; on each of them South America is designated as *mvdvs novvs.* Study of the place names in this early manuscript atlas should make it possible for students of exploration to determine what source maps Agnese used in his compilation. Although he never visited any part of the New World, he probably knew more about its geography than did the navigators who had visited some of its coasts and mapped small portions of them.[6]

## AGNESE MANUSCRIPT ATLAS
## NOTES

[1] In *Nachrichten von der Koniglichen Gesselschaft der Wissenschaften zu Göttingen; Philologisch-historische Klasse; 1916, Beiheft* (128 p.).

[2] Henry R. Wagner, "The Manuscript Atlases of Battista Agnese," Bibliographical Society of America, *Papers,* 25:1–110 (1931).

[3] Ibid., p. 52, 75.

[4] Ibid., p. 2.

[5] Justin Winsor, "Baptista Agnese and American Cartography in the Sixteenth Century," Massachusetts Historical Society, *Proceedings,* 11:373 (May 1897).

[6] Other references to Battista Agnese and his work include the following:

Konrad Kretschmer, *Die italienischen Portolane des Mittelalters, ein Beitrag zur Geschichte der Kartographie und Nautik* (Berlin, 1909; reprinted 1962 by Georg Olms, Hildesheim, Germany).

"The Sea-Charts of the Renaissance," *The World Encompassed; an Exhibition of the History of Maps Held at the Baltimore Museum of Art October 7 to November 23, 1952* (Baltimore, Trustees of the Walters Art Gallery, 1952.) Items 88 to 91 describe manuscript atlases by Battista Agnese. Nos. 88 and 89 were lent by the Pierpont Morgan Library, No. 90 by Boies Penrose, and No. 91 by Henry C. Taylor.

Henry R. Wagner, "Additions to the Manuscript Atlases of Battista Agnese," *Imago mundi,* 4:28–30 (1947).

# Rosenwald Gift of 16th-Century Maps

## BY CLARA E. LEGEAR

Reprinted from the May 1949 issue of the *Library of Congress Quarterly Journal of Current Acquisitions*.

**F**IVE sixteenth-century maps of great Americana interest were presented by Lessing J. Rosenwald to the Library of Congress in 1949: maps of America by Diego Gutiérrez (1562), by André Thevet (1581), and by Franz Hogenberg (1589); a Gastaldo world map of 1565 engraved by Ferdinando Bertelli; and a map of the Pacific Ocean by Gabriel Tatton (1600).

GUTIÉRREZ's map of 1562 is the largest known map of the New World printed up to that time. Mr. Rosenwald's gift is one of two known copies of this map, the other being preserved in the British Museum. Entitled "Americae sive qvartae orbis partis nova et exactissima descriptio. Avctore Diego Gvtiero Philippi Regis Hisp. etc. Cosmographo. Hiero Cock Excvde. 1562," the map includes the eastern coast of North America, all of Central and South America, and portions of the western coasts of Europe and Africa. Although no coordinates are given, the area covered falls

*1562 map of America by Diego Gutiérrez. The maps illustrating this article are from the Geography and Map Division.*

39

roughly between 0° and 115° longitude west of Greenwich, and 57° north, and 70° south latitude. Six engraved sheets are neatly joined to form a single map which measures 93 x 86 cm. Because the map seems to end abruptly on the east and west and the ornamental border is only at the top and bottom, one might infer that a world map was planned, of which only this American part was completed. The British Museum copy has, however, an ornamental border on all four sides.

Paul Chaix published a description of the Gutiérrez map in the *Mémoires de la Société de Géographie de Genève* (1868, vol. 7, p. 237–242), but gave no indication of the location of the map he was describing. He concluded that the names on the map were originally written in somewhat Italianized Spanish and that the Dutch engraver made a number of errors in copying it, not only in the spellings of place names but also in place locations. Henry Harrisse, on the other hand, in his *Découverte et évolution cartographique de Terre-Neuve* (Paris, 1900, p. 160), expressed the belief that the map has a French-Italian origin.

Although the map is dated 1562, it shows none of the geographical discoveries made in the preceding decade. Drawn at a time when important explorations were increasing the geographical knowledge of the New World, it reflects neither the contemporaneous French explorations in North America nor those of the Spaniards in South America.

The following inscription on the map gives evidence, 70 years after 1492, of the popular belief that Americus Vespucius discovered America in 1497: "Quarta haec orbis pars geographis omnibus usque in annum 1497 incognita permansit, quo tempore iussu Regis Castellae ab Americo Vespucio inuenta est, a quo tanquam ab inuentore etiam nomen obtiunit[!]" [This fourth part of the world remained unknown to all geographers until the year 1497, at which time it was discovered by Americus Vespucius serving the King of Castille, whereupon it also obtained a name from the discoverer].

According to the findings of Ruth Putnam in her *California: the Name*,[1] the Gutiérrez map has the distinction of being the earliest on which "California" appears, for on it "C. California" is applied to the southern tip of Lower California.

The Gutiérrez map has been used as evidence in two South American boundary disputes. In this connection it was reproduced in part in (1) *Frontières entre le Brésil et la Guyane Française. Mémoire présenté par les États Unis du Brésil. Atlas* (Paris, 1899, nos. 7–8); and (2) *Judicio de límites entre el Perú y Bolivia. Prueba peruana presentada al gobierno de la República Argentina por Víctor M. Maurtua . . . Atlas* (Barcelona, 1906, vol. 2, no. 1). Tracings of it were made by Johann Georg Kohl for the Kohl Collection (nos. 184 and 359), now in the Library of Congress. The British Museum copy is reproduced by Leo Bagrow in his *A. Ortelii catalogus cartographorum* (1928, vol. 1, plate 10).

The copy of the Gutiérrez map now in the Library of Congress was formerly in the collection of the Duke of Gotha. It was sold at auction in Munich in 1932 and was subsequently acquired by an American book dealer.

40

About the map maker, Diego Gutiérrez, very little is known, and that little results largely from his association with Sebastian Cabot. Henry Harrisse [2] and Leo Bagrow [3] repeat the account of M. F. De Navarrete [4] that there were, a father and son with the same name. The senior Gutiérrez is said to have made a portolan chart of the Atlantic Ocean dated 1550 and the junior Gutiérrez, the 1562 map of America. José Toribio Medina, [5] however, disagrees with these earlier writers. He concludes from documentary sources that there was only one Diego Gutiérrez, that his son was named Sancho, and that both the known signed maps are the work of the same person.

Diego Gutiérrez was a chart and instrument maker as well as a pilot. He is believed by Harrisse to have been born at Seville in 1485, by Medina to have been born in Portugal in 1488, and by both to have begun making charts and nautical instruments in 1511. According to one of Gutiérrez' memorials he was first established in Cadiz, being there at the time the Magellan armada set out. Later he was established in Seville where he was associated with the pilots and cosmographers of the Casa de la Contratación. The Casa, also called India House, was established at Seville by royal order early in 1503 to control trade and navigation in American waters. It appears that Gutiérrez was closely allied with Sebastian Cabot as early as 1534. The latter represented him to the King as his partner in the sale of charts and nautical instruments, in order that Gutiérrez might be received as cosmographer and official map maker. It is interesting to note a decree of the King, dated February 17, 1540, restraining Cabot and Gutiérrez from requiring all pilots to buy charts and instruments from them alone.

Sebastian Cabot became pilot major to the Crown of Spain and official examiner of pilots on February 5, 1518. It was this office of pilot major to which he named Diego Gutiérrez as his substitute when he returned to England in 1547. The Casa de la Contratación, however, protested the substitution and required that Gutiérrez be examined regarding his professional abilities. Gutiérrez probably died early in 1554, since his son, Sancho, was named to succeed him on February 10 of that year.

Medina believes that the 1562 map was engraved by Hieronymus Cock some years after Gutiérrez' death. Of the 1550 chart of the Atlantic Ocean, preserved in the archives of the Dépôt de la Marine in Paris, A. Anthiaume [6] writes that it appears to be based upon that of Alonso de Chaves, that it omits the French discoveries in the Newfoundland-St. Lawrence area, and that its nomenclature is Portuguese.

The engraver, Hieronymus Cock, was a Flemish artist of considerable talent.[7] His father, Jan Wellens or Willems, alias Cock, and his brother, Mathias Cock, were both noted painters. Hieronymus Cock was born at Antwerp in 1510. He was admitted to the Guild of St. Luke as a master painter in 1545 but later engaged in engraving and print selling. Between 1546 and 1548 he traveled in Italy and produced several creditable engravings of Rome and of the Capitol there. Between 1550 and the time of

*Gastaldo map of 1565, engraved by Ferdinando Bertelli (see page 43).*

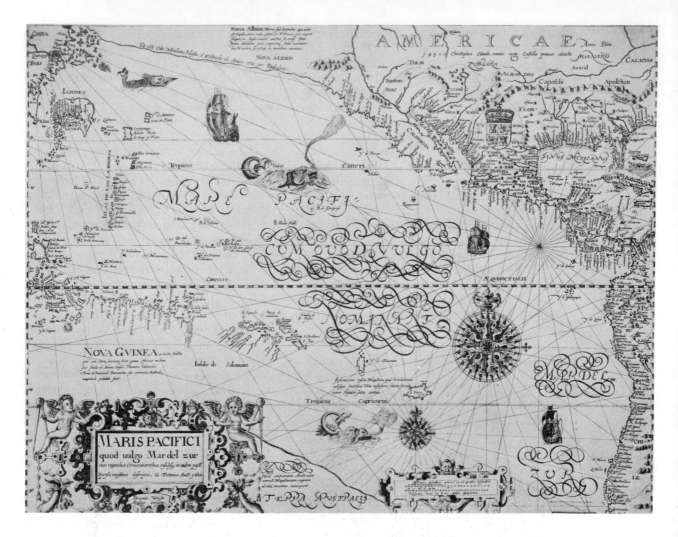

his death in 1570 he carried on a very
successful business in Antwerp, doing much
to popularize art by making available
through his engravings many of the finest
works of the Dutch masters.

Cock engraved several of the maps for
Abraham Ortelius' *Theatrum orbis terrarum,* which was published by the Plantin
Press at Antwerp, and a number of plans
of Antwerp as well as topographical views
of other cities. Engravings by him are included in Jacob van Deventer's *Nederlandsche Steden,* in Braun and Hogenberg's
*Civitates orbis terrarum,* in Sebastian Münster's *Cosmographia,* and other works.

In 1554, Hieronymus Cock engraved a
fine plan of the Antwerp fortifications
erected by Charles V of Spain. This very
early plan of Antwerp, drawn according to
the original design of Peter Frans and Virgil de Bologne, was engraved at the request
of Captain Francesco di Marchi of the

*Gabriel Tatton's 1600 map of the Pacific Ocean. Benjamin Wright,
engraver.*

household of Margaret of Parma, for presentation to Philip II of Spain at the time
of his marriage to Queen Mary of England.
In this connection it is interesting to note
that the map of America, 1562, was dedicated to Philip II by Diego Gutiérrez, and
to Margaret of Parma by Hieronymus Cock.

ANDRÉ THEVET's map is entitled "Le Nov-
veav Monde Descovvert et Illvstre de Nostre
Temps. A Paris, chez Guillaume Chaudiere,
Ruë S. Iaques, à l'enseigne du Temps & de
l'Homme Sauuage. 1581." The title appears
in the upper margin and the imprint in the
lower margin while the more generally
quoted title, "Qvarte partie dv Monde," is
given within the border. The name of
"Andre Thevet, Cosmographe du Roy" appears in a cartouche in the lower left portion of the map above his explanation to

the reader. The map measures 35 x 46 cm.

The only other copy known to us is in the collection of the Chicago Historical Society. An impression without the imprint in the lower margin is included in Thevet's *La Cosmographie universelle* (Paris, Chez Pierre L'Huillier, 1575, vol. 2).[8] Bagrow, in his biographical sketch of Thevet,[9] indicates that *La Cosmographie universelle* was published simultaneously both by L'Huillier and by Chaudiere, but he does not identify an impression of the map dated 1581. A. Anthiaume [10] does, however, mention a 1581 edition. Both the 1575 and 1581 editions of the map are woodcuts printed from the same block, the only difference being the explanation to the reader, the type for which was reset.

André Thevet was born in Angoulême in 1502 and died in Paris in 1590. He joined the Franciscan order and traveled widely in the interest of geographical science rather than for the propagation of the faith. He visited Italy, the eastern Mediterranean, and the Orient between 1537 and 1547. For several years thereafter he was engaged in preparing an account of his travels for publication. In 1555, he joined the expedition of Nicolas de Villegagnon to Brazil which arrived in Rio de Janeiro late that year. Because of ill health, he left Brazil the following year, sailing along the North American coast on his return voyage. His account of this voyage, *Les Singularitez de la France antarctique, autrement nommée Amérique,* published at Paris in 1558 contained no maps, although the epilogue refers to "Cartes de l'Auteur." Subsequently he was named "Cosmographe du Roy."

Thevet is believed by his contemporaries and by later writers to have been quite credulous and to have embellished his writings on the New World with accounts of others in addition to his own observations.

HOGENBERG'S map is entitled "Americae et proximarvm regionvm orae descriptio. Per Franc: Hogenberg: A° D. 1589," and measures 34 x 47 cm. H. R. Wagner [11] (*Sir Francis Drake's Voyage around the World*, 1926, p. 424) says that a map with this same title belongs to the German edition of the voyage of Drake to the West Indies in 1585, published in 1589, although it is seldom found in it. The map bears considerable similarity both to Abraham Ortelius' "Maris Pacifici" and to the anonymous map of America by Arnoldo de Arnoldi, 1582, being drawn on the same projection and having similar characteristics.

Franz Hogenberg, painter, engraver, and print seller, was born in Malines before 1540 and is believed to have died in Cologne about 1590. His father, Hans Hogenberg, also an artist-painter, migrated with his family from the Netherlands to England about 1555 because of religious persecution. Franz engraved a number of fine portraits and architectural drawings, as well as maps. He is believed to have remained in England only a short time. He probably was in Antwerp for a time before 1570, for he engraved some of the maps for the *Theatrum orbis terrarum* of Abraham Ortelius, first published in 1570. He settled in Cologne about that time.

With Georg Braun, he produced the six-volume *Civitates orbis terrarum,* a monumental work begun in 1572, comprising some 300 topographical drawings of the world's principal cities.

THE GASTALDO-BERTELLI map of 1565 is a delicately colored, well preserved impression, entitled "Vniversale descrittione di tvtta la terra conoscivta fin qvi." Drawn on an elliptical projection with windheads in the upper corners and inscriptions in the lower corners, it measures 44 x 78 cm. Like Gastaldo's original issue of 1546, which was drawn on a smaller scale, it shows North America joined to Asia. Gastaldo's name does not appear on this 1565 impression nor does that of Paulo Forlani. The inscription "Ferando berteli Exc. 1565" is in the lower left corner, and the dedication to Bartholomio Zacco in the lower right corner is inscribed "Fer. Bertelli libraro." Except for the omission of Forlani's name, it is like the facsimile reproduction in volume 4 of *Remarkable Maps.*[12]

Leo Bagrow [13] has identified a copy of this 1565 map in the Stadtbibliothek at Breslau (op. cit., vol. 1, p. 91). R. V. Tooley also mentions the Breslau copy in his list of "Maps in Italian Atlases of the Sixteenth Century." [14]

GABRIEL TATTON'S map of the Pacific Ocean is also quite rare. It is entitled "Maris Pacifici quod uulgo Mar del Zur cum regionibus Circumiacentibus, insulisque in eodem passī Sparsis, nouissima descriptio, G. Tattonus Auct. 1600. Beniamin Wright Anglus coelator," and measures 40 x 51 cm. Other copies of it are known to be in the British Museum and in the Institut de France. It is noted as no. 86 in the *Lowery Collection,* edited by P. L. Phillips, 1912, although neither Lowery nor Phillips had seen a copy. The latter took his description from Sidney Colvin's *Early Engraving & Engravers in England,* 1905, p. 32, where it is described as a most creditable engraving of Benjamin Wright.

Knowledge of Gabriel Tatton is fragmentary. He was English and is known to have spent some time in the Netherlands. In an article in *La Bibliofilia* Giuseppe Caraci describes an undated portolan chart preserved at the Biblioteca Nazionale in Florence.[15] It is inscribed "By mijn Gabriell Tatton uan London Englishman" and Caraci places it in the second half of the sixteenth century. It includes the eastern part of the Indian Ocean, the Pacific Ocean, and the Caribbean area with the lands surrounding them. The printed map shows much more detail in the North American continent than the portolan.

The engraver, Benjamin Wright, a resident of London, was engraving globes and celestial charts as early as 1596. Some of his later engravings were done at Amsterdam and at Bologna.

These five maps, all of which bear definite dates of publication (an estimable feature of sixteenth-century maps), greatly strengthen the Library's collection of maps in this period. A significant link in the chain of evidence concerning American discovery and exploration is represented by each of these maps.

## NOTES

[1] Issued as University of California Publications in History, vol. 4, no. 4 (Berkeley, 1917). See caption on the frontispiece.

[2] Henry Harrisse, *Discovery of North America,* (London, 1892), p. 720.

[3] Leo Bagrow, *A. Ortelii catalogus cartographorum* (Gotha, 1928), vol. 1, p. 103.

[4] M. F. De Navarrete, *Biblioteca maritima española* (Madrid, 1851), vol. 1, p. 342–343.

[5] José Toribio Medina, *El Veneciano Sebastián Caboto* (Santiago de Chile, 1908), vol. 1, p. 354 ff.

[6] A. Anthiaume, *Cartes marines* (Paris, 1916), vol. 2, p. 42 and 371.

[7] Biographical sketches of Cock are contained in Jean Denucé's *Oud-Nederlandsche Kaartmakers* (Antwerp, 1912), vol. 1, p. 118–139, and in Ulrich Thieme's *Allgemeines Lexikon der bildenden Künstler* (Leipzig, 1912), vol. 7, p. 143–144.

[8] A facsimile of *La Cosmographie* is included in *Frontières entre le Brésil . . . Atlas* (Paris, 1899), no. 23.

[9] Bagrow, *A. Ortelii,* vol. 2, p. 83–87.

[10] Anthiaume, *Cartes marines,* vol. 2, p. 470.

[11] Henry R. Wagner, *Sir Francis Drake's Voyage Around the World* (San Francisco, 1926), p. 424.

[12] *Remarkable Maps of the XVth, XVIth, and XVIIth Centuries, Reproduced in Their Original Size* (Amsterdam, 1894–99).

[13] Bagrow, *A. Ortelii,* vol. 1, p. 91.

[14] In *Imago mundi,* 3:16 (1939).

[15] Giuseppe Caraci, "Una nuova carta di Gabriele Tatton," *La Bibliofilia,* 26:240–247 (1924).

# Gerardus Mercator's Atlas of 1595

## BY CLARA E. LEGEAR

Reprinted from the May 1950 issue of the *Library of Congress Quarterly Journal of Current Acquisitions.*

Hic adeo promptas merces Mercator habebat,
Totus ut ex illis auxerit orbis opes.

**G**ERARDUS Mercator is best remembered for the map projection which bears his name, but his distinguished career was also marked by a number of other accomplishments which have earned for him the high esteem of posterity. Through his teaching and writing he did much to free geography from the Ptolemaic influence and to raise cartography from an art to a science, while his cartographic output added greatly to the geographic knowledge of his day. The culminating achievement of a long and active life was his world atlas of 1595 which introduced the designation "atlas" for a bound collection of maps.

A fine copy of this rare volume was presented in 1950 to the Library of Congress by the late Mr. Melville Eastham of Cambridge, Mass. The title page reads: *Atlas sive cosmographicæ meditationes de fabrica mvndi et fabricati figvra. Gerardo Mercatore Rupelmundano, Illustrissimi Ducis Julię Cliuię & Mõ:tis &c. Cosmographo autore. Cum privilegio. Dvisbvrgi Clivorvm.* The title might be translated as "Atlas, or the meditations of a cosmographer upon the creation of the world and the shape of that which was created." The colophon reads: *Dvsseldorpii excudebat Albertus Busius Illustrissimi Ducis Iuliæ, Cliuiæ, Montis, &c. Typographus, sumptibus hæredum Gerardi Mercatoris Rupelmundani, Anno 1595.*

*Portrait from Jean Jacques Boissard's* Icones quinquaginta virorum illustrium, *published at Frankfurt between 1597 and 1599. In the Rare Book Division.*

The engraved, illuminated title page is followed by a dedication to William, Duke of Juliers, Cleves, and Berg and his son, William John; a portrait of Mercator at the age of 62; and a detailed five-page biography by Gualterus Ghymmius. This biography by Mercator's friend and neighbor constitutes the principal source of authentic information concerning the great geographer. Several poems and eulogies in honor of Mercator also appear in the preliminary pages.

The volume contains 107 maps. Not included, however, is Mercator's 32-page account of the creation of the world, entitled *De mundi creatione ac fabrica liber* which is found in several known copies.

Of the 107 maps, 102 are inscribed "Per Gerardum Mercatorem." The first five maps are not Mercator's own, but they may have been made under his supervision. They are designated A to E as follows: (A) the world, and (B) Europe, by Rumoldus Mercator; (C) Africa, and (D) Asia, by Gerardus Mercator, Jr.; and (E) America, by Michael Mercator. These five maps, and the 28 which follow, appeared for the first time in the *Atlas* of 1595. They are preceded by a title page which reads: *Atlantis pars altera. Geographia nova totius mundi.* . . . The parts of the *Atlas* which had been published separately in 1585 and 1589 follow this new group of maps. The volume is bound in its original brown leather binding and is in an excellent state of preservation.

Mercator conceived the idea of a great cosmography about 1564, the year in which the Duke of Juliers, Cleves, and Berg bestowed upon him the title of Cosmographer. His first plan envisioned a work in two parts, one devoted to the heavens, the other to the earth. But recognizing that history should precede cosmography, the projected work was expanded to three parts: (1) the creation of the world; (2) the description of the heavens; and (3) the description of the earth. To these he added: (4) genealogy and history of the states; and (5) chronology. Mercator's description of the earth was to comprise three books. The first of these was to be devoted to modern geography; the second, to the geography of Ptolemy; and the third, to the geography of the ancients.

Mercator published the chronology in 1569 and the *Geographia* of Ptolemy in 1578 before devoting his energies to his modern geography. By 1585 the first part of the *Atlas* made its appearance. The volume contained 51 maps, with separate title pages for each of its three sections. Sixteen of the maps relate to France and Switzerland, 9 to the Netherlands, and 26 to Germany. The first title page reads: *Galliae tabulę geographicæ per Gerardum Mercatorem Illus-*

*Fifth map (E) from Gerardus Mercator's* Atlas *of 1595. From the Geography and Map Division.*

*trissimi Ducis Julię Cliuię Montis &c. Cos-
mographum Duysburgi Cliuorum editæ
cum gratia & priuilegio;* the second: *Belgii
inferioris geographicæ tabulę. Per Gerardum Mercatorem . . .;* and the third:
*Germaniae tabulę geographicæ. Per Ge-
rardum Mercatorem. . . .*

The second part of Mercator's *Atlas,*
and the last to be published in his lifetime,
was issued in 1589. It contained 23 maps

and was entitled: *Italiae, Sclavoniæ, et
Græciæ tabulę geographicę, Per Gerardum
Mercatorem. . . .*

Though in failing health, Mercator continued to work energetically toward his
goal. He succeeded in completing his description of the creation of the world, *De
Mundi creatione ac fabrica liber,* and in
adding 28 maps to the 74 already published.
These include a map of the polar regions,
one of Iceland, 16 of the British Isles, one of
Norway and Sweden, four of Denmark, and
one each of Prussia, Livonia, Russia, Lithu-
ania, Transylvania, and Crimea. Still lacking at the time of his death, on December 2,
1594, were maps of the world, the continents, and Spain and Portugal.

Mercator's youngest and only surviving
son, Rumoldus, was faced with the task
of completing and publishing his father's
voluminous work. With the help of his
nephews, Rumoldus supplied a map of the
world and one of each of the continents before publishing the *Atlas* in 1595.

Gerardus Mercator himself had selected
the name "Atlas" to entitle his great work.
As stated in the preface, the name was
chosen to honor the Titan, Atlas, King of
Mauritania, a learned philosopher, mathematician, and astronomer. The central
heroic figure on the title page, portrayed
with a celestial globe in his hand and a terrestrial globe at his feet, may be Atlas.

Mercator's *Atlas* was reissued in 1602 by
his heirs. No maps were added, possibly
because of the death of Rumoldus Mercator on December 31, 1599. All subsequent
editions of the *Atlas* were published by
Jodocus Hondius, his son Henricus Hondius, and their successor, Jan Janssonius.
Mercator's name, coupled with that of
Jodocus Hondius, continued to appear on
the title pages until 1639.

The Library of Congress has copies of the
first and second parts of Mercator's *Atlas,*
issued in 1585 and 1589; the complete editions of 1595 and 1602; as well as a representative number of later editions.

The many activities and achievements
of Mercator are chronicled in greatest detail by his biographers, Raemdonck and
Averdunk. The following brief biographical sketch is derived largely from these
sources. Gerardus Mercator, whose Flemish
name was Gerhard Kremer or De Cremer,
was born in the village of Rupelmonde,
East Flanders, on March 5, 1512. He spent

his early years in the village of Gangelt, in the Duchy of Juliers. To his uncle, Gisbert Kremer, chaplain of the Hospice of St. John in Rupelmonde, he was indebted for his education. After attending schools in Rupelmonde, and 's Hertogenbosch (Bois-le-Duc) in Brabant, he matriculated at the University of Louvain in August 1530. There he studied philosophy, mathematics, astronomy, and cosmography. There also, he met Rainer Gemma Frisius, noted professor of mathematics and medicine at the University of Louvain and former pupil of the cosmographer Petrus Apianus, of Ingolstadt. Although only four years older than Mercator, Gemma Frisius became his counselor and influenced him profoundly in his choice of a career in geography.

Mercator established his workshop at Louvain in 1534. One of his earliest cartographic efforts was the engraving of Gemma Frisius' terrestrial globe, in collaboration with Gaspare a Myrica, probably between 1534 and 1537. He developed considerable ability in making mathematical instruments and produced very creditable armillary spheres, astrolabes, astronomical rings, etc. He was commissioned by the Emperor Charles V to make a complete set of instruments of observation for the Emperor's military campaigns. When these were destroyed by fire in 1546, he was ordered to make another set. His skill in drawing, engraving, and coloring maps developed into a lifelong vocation.

Mercator engraved and published a map of Palestine in 1537, only one copy of which is known to have survived. It is entitled: *Amplissima Terrae Sanctae descriptio.* In the following year his first world map, on a double cordiform projection, was issued. This map has the distinction of naming the two Americas separately for the first time, that is "Americae prs sep:" and "Americae pars meridionalis." It demonstrates Mercator's belief that North America and Asia were not connected at any point and that Asia could be reached by the Northwest Passage above the northern extremity of North America. It also illustrates his belief in the existence of an Antarctic continent to balance the land masses of the world.

Another of Mercator's cartographic contributions is a large map of Flanders in four sheets, published in 1540 from his original surveys. It was made at the request of a

group of Flemish merchants and dedicated to the Emperor Charles V. In the same year, he published a brochure on the art of engraving, entitled *Literarum Latinarum quas italicas cursoriasque vocant, scribendarum ratio.*

Mercator's celebrated terrestrial globe made its appearance in 1541. Dedicated to Nicolás Perrenot, prime minister of the Emperor Charles V, the globe found such

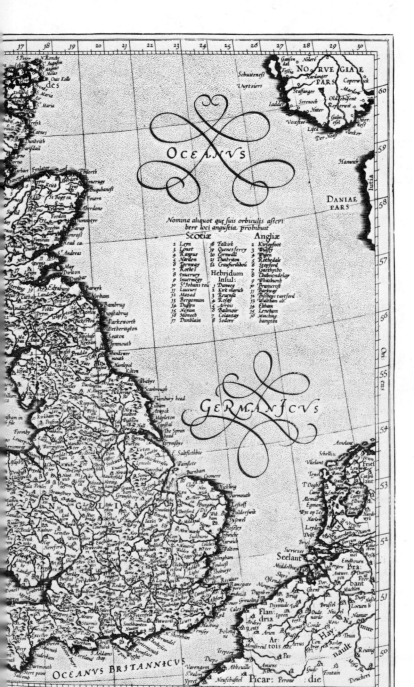

pleted the companion celestial globe and dedicated it to the Emperor Charles V. The following year, he made for the Emperor a special pair of small globes, which are described as works of art. The celestial globe of clear crystal had the constellations etched with a diamond and inlaid with gold. The terrestrial ball of solid wood contained all of the geographical data found on the larger globe, very finely executed. With this pair of globes, Mercator gave the Emperor a manuscript *Declaratio* on the use of the spheres.

Early in 1552, Mercator moved from Louvain to Duisburg, in the Duchy of Juliers, Cleves, and Berg, to accept the chair of cosmography at the university to be established there. Organization of this center of learning was, however, never completed during Mercator's lifetime.

Mercator, now settled on German soil, became Cosmographer to the Duke of Juliers, Cleves, and Berg. He returned briefly to the Netherlands to present to Charles V at Brussels the above-mentioned globes, in recognition of which the Emperor bestowed upon him the title of "Imperatorii Domesticus."

The next of Mercator's prodigious works to make its appearance was his map of Europe in 15 sheets, which had claimed much of his time for several years. With its publication in 1554, Mercator's stature as a cartographer was greatly increased. The map represented a marked departure from Ptolemy's cartographic conception of Europe, notably in the reduction of the length of the Mediterranean from 62° to 53°. A revised, second edition of the Europe map appeared in 1572.

From 1559 to 1563, Mercator taught geography and mathematics at the Latin school in Duisburg and then relinquished the post to his son, Bartholomeus, in order to devote himself to his consuming interests. It may have been during this period, after the title of Cosmographer had been bestowed upon him, that Mercator conceived his great plan. Convinced of the genuine need for a modern geographical atlas, he began laying the groundwork that culminated in his *Atlas* of 1595.

Mercator's large map of the British Isles in eight sheets was published in 1564, and

favor because of its fair size (41 centimeters in diameter), its accuracy, and its very attractive appearance that it had no real competitors for half a century. The fact that a number of fine examples are extant testifies to their sturdy construction, which Edward Luther Stevenson described in his *Terrestrial and Celestial Globes,* vol. 1, 1921, p. 133.

Ten years later, in 1551, Mercator comin the same year a large-scale map of Lorraine, based on his own surveys, was delivered to Duke Charles III of Lorraine.

The map of the world on the projection that has popularized the name of Mercator was issued in 1569. A seasoned mathematician and map maker, Mercator had tested every known map projection before he set himself the task of working out a projection useful to mariners. His aim was to devise one in which all parallels and meridians would meet at right angles and on which directions were true. On such a projection, a ship's course could be set in a straight line on the chart, and the mariner would be certain to arrive at his destination. He successfully laid out such a projection, but it remained for the English mathematician, Edward Wright, to work out (in his *Certain Errors in Navigation,* 1599) mathematical tables for calculating exact distances between ports. It was not until about 1630, when the chart makers of Dieppe began to prepare charts on the Mercator projection, that it came into popular use by mariners.

The year 1569 also brought forth Mercator's *Chronologia, hoc est supputatio temporum ab initio mundi ex eclipsibus et observationibus astronomicis et Sacrae Scripturae firmissimis testimoniis demonstrata.* This important work, which was the first part of Mercator's cosmography to be completed, was published at a time when the world was emerging from the Middle Ages and the Julian calendar was being revised. In his *Chronologia* Mercator sought to establish the beginning of the world and to reconcile the chronologies of the Hebrews, Greeks, Egyptians, and Romans with that of the Christian world.

Having completed his *Chronologia,* Mercator's next great work was an edition in 1578 of the *Geographia* of Claudius Ptolemaeus. With its 27 newly engraved maps, which are believed to be the finest ever prepared for this work, this Mercator edition of the *Geographia* is highly prized. Every subsequent edition has included maps either printed from the Mercator plates or re-engravings of such plates.

When Mercator sent a copy of his edition of Ptolemy's *Geographia* to Werner of Gymnich, he wrote that he was engaged in work on his new geography, which was to include 100 maps. In the 16 remaining years of his life, he very nearly completed this work. However, the remainder of the great plan was never carried out. One reason for his slow progress was his great difficulty in obtaining the latest maps, books, and other sources of information on geographical discoveries. Another impediment was the scarcity of skilled copper plate engravers. In the tedious and detailed work of engraving his maps, Mercator was assisted only by his grandson, Johannes, and occasionally by Hogenberg. A pertinent reason for his slow progress was the fact that he was compelled to do other work for a livelihood. In spite of many obstacles, Mercator persevered and gave to the world a work of lasting worth.

Much has been written about Mercator and his achievements. His principal modern biographers are Jean van Raemdonck, whose *Gérard Mercator, sa vie et ses œuvres,* was published in 1869, and Heinrich Averdunk and J. Müller-Reinhard, whose *Gerhard Mercator und die Geographen unter seinen Nachkommen* was published in 1914 (*Ergänzungsheft* Nr. 182 zu Petermanns *Mitteilungen*).

The writings of Mercator are described in bibliographical detail by Fernand van Ortroy in his "Bibliographie sommaire de l'oeuvre mercatorienne," *Revue des bibliothèques,* vol. 24, 1914, pp. 113–148; vol. 25, 1915, pp. 9–30; and vol. 25–26, 1915–16, pp. 119–141. Mercator's atlases and the maps they contain are described by Leo Bagrow in his *A. Ortelii catalogus cartographorum,* vol. 2, 1930, pp. 3–17 (*Ergänzungsheft* Nr. 210 zu Petermanns *Mitteilungen*) and by J. Keuning in his "History of an Atlas. Mercator—Hondius," *Imago mundi,* vol. 4, 1947, pp. 37–62.

# Sixteenth-Century Atlases Presented by Melville Eastham

## BY CLARA E. LEGEAR AND WALTER W. RISTOW

Reprinted from the August 1958 issue of the *Library of Congress Quarterly Journal of Current Acquisitions.*

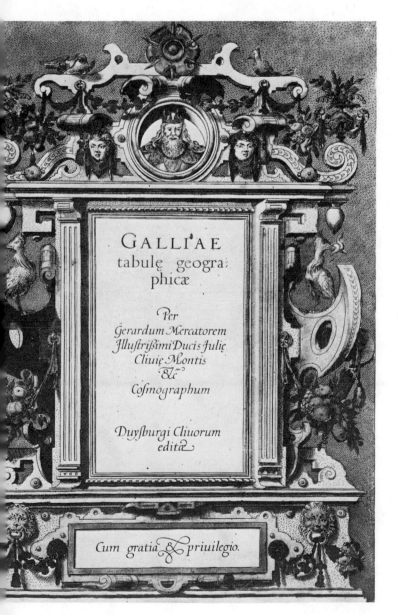

HERALDED AS "the most noteworthy gift of rarities ever received by the Map Division," nine sixteenth-century atlases were presented to the Library in 1958 by Melville Eastham.

Mr. Eastham, a retired industrialist of Cambridge, Mass., pursued over a number of years his hobby of collecting atlases and related works published in the sixteenth century. By discriminating and selective purchases (many of his volumes were acquired by personal visits to the shops of European dealers), he assembled a distinctive and representative collection of sixteenth-century cartographic works.

Five of the newly acquired atlases are the works of well-known cartographers of the period. The other four represent contributions of less renowned mapmakers.

Earliest in date of the first group is the Latin edition of Abraham Ortelius' *Theatrum orbis terrarum* (1571), with which is bound Braun and Hogenberg's *Civitates orbis terrarum* (1572). Plates for both works are uncolored. The volume is bound in contemporary brown calf and is in an excellent state of preservation. The spine is tooled and embellished with gold leaf. Engravings for all the maps in the combined volume are from the skilled hand of Franz Hogenberg.

This edition of Ortelius appears to be an earlier printing than the 1571 Latin edition previously acquired by the Library

*A colored engraving adorns this title page to the second part of the 1589 volume of Mercator maps. Illustrations in this article are reproduced from atlases in the Geography and Map Division.*

of Congress.[1] In the Eastham copy the map of Bavaria is entitled "Typus Vindelicae sive Vtrivsqve Bavariae." This map in subsequent issues is designated as "Bavariae olim Vindelicae delineationis compendivm." Furthermore, in the 1958 acquisition the "Catalogus Auctorum" accompanying the preface includes only 91 geographers, whereas 94 names are listed in the later printing. The type on a number of the maps in the earlier issue (notably plates 25, 27, 30, 31, and 35) is differently set.

With publication of the first edition of Ortelius' *Theatrum* in 1570, the modern atlas was born. The idea of assembling such a work apparently originated 10 years earlier, when Ortelius was commissioned to collect, for a merchant, maps of the several European countries printed on separate sheets. While the *Theatrum* was in production Ortelius refused to sell separately the maps he planned to include in the atlas.

The enthusiastic reception of the *Theatrum* is indicated by the publication of four separate issues in 1570. Forty editions of Ortelius' atlas had been published by 1612, and the number of maps had increased from 70 to some 170. The first edition of the *Theatrum*, and all editions of 1579, were printed by Aegidius Coppen Diesth, of Antwerp. In 1579 Christopher Plantin took over, and the distinguished printing firm which he founded issued editions in several languages through 1598. After Ortelius' death that year plates for the *Theatrum* were acquired by J. B. Vrients, who published several editions before 1612. Vrients' death and stiff competition from the popular Mercator *Atlas,* first published in 1595, contributed to the decline of the *Theatrum.*

Ortelius, born in Antwerp in 1527, was a promoter and distributor of the works of various cartographers rather than a producer of maps. The mapmakers whose works are incorporated in the *Theatrum* receive generous acknowledgment from Ortelius in the atlas. By listing their names in the "Catalogus Auctorum" he made possible the identification of a number of cartographers who might otherwise have remained unknown. Leo Bagrow's *A. Ortelii catalogus cartographorum* [2] contains a comprehensive analysis of the editions of the *Theatrum* and detailed biobibliographical data for the cartographers whose maps were incorporated in the atlas.

In the intervals between editions and printings of the *Theatrum* Ortelius issued supplemental collections of maps which were subsequently added to the atlas. Five such supplements, each identified as an *Additamentum,* are recognized, as follows: I, 1573; II, 1579; III, 1584; IV, 1590; and V, 1595. The first has 17 maps, and each of the remaining four 23 maps.

The French edition of *Additamentum* I, published in 1573 or 1574, is one of the nine gift atlases received from Mr. Eastham. Jean Denucé mentioned this volume in his *Oud-Nederlandsche Kaartmakers in Betrekking met Plantijn,*[3] but indicated that he had not been able to examine a copy. The maps in *Additamentum* I are listed in the

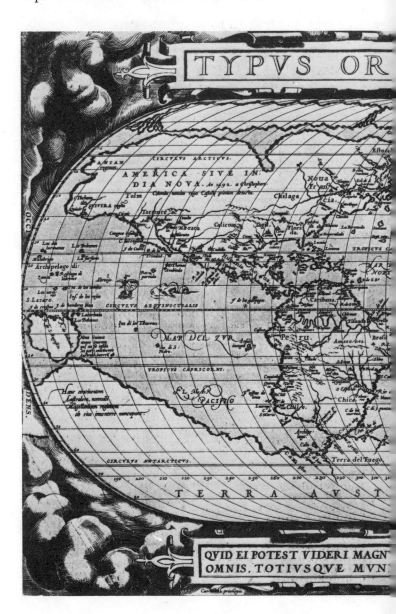

first volume (p. 16) of Bagrow's *A. Ortelii catalogus cartographorum,* mentioned above. The Eastham *Additamentum* I includes 16 double-page map plates, with descriptive material in French on the verso of one page of each. There are actually 26 individual maps, nine on double pages, 11 on single pages, and six on half pages. None of the maps are colored. The binding is modern half-vellum.

As noted above, the first part of Georg Braun and Franz Hogenberg's *Civitates*

*The oval world map from Abraham Ortelius'* Theatrum orbis terrarum *has been frequently reproduced. This copy is from the 1579 Latin edition printed by Christopher Plantin in Antwerp.*

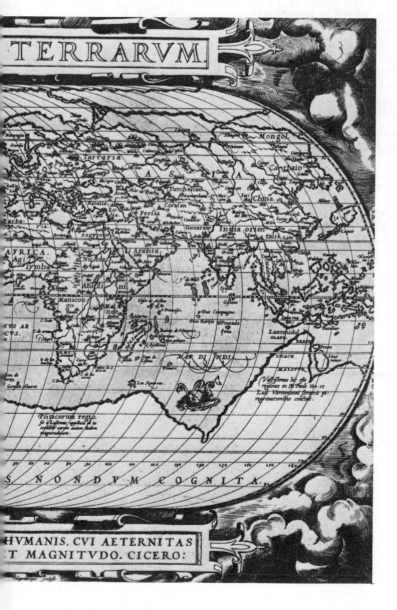

*orbis terrarum* is bound with the 1571 Ortelius presented by Mr. Eastham. The similarity in titles, in general execution, and in size of the two works suggests that it is no accident that they share a common binding. A note by Braun in the third part of the *Civitates* confirms that it was planned as a companion volume to Ortelius' *Theatrum.*

The *Civitates,* which was published simultaneously at Antwerp and Cologne in 1572, consists of 59 plates of views of the principal cities of the world, with descriptive data pertaining to them, in Latin, on the versos of the sheets. Included are plans of London, Istanbul, Jerusalem, and Cairo as well as of a number of cities in the Netherlands, France, Germany, Italy, and Spain, and a scattering of views of places in North Africa and the Middle East. America is represented by Cuzco, Peru, and by Mexico City.

Hogenberg is believed to have conceived the idea of a collection of city plans, and he is likewise responsible for the beautifully executed copper engravings from which the views were printed. There is considerable variety in the views. Some are bird's-eye perspectives on which individual buildings, streets, churches, fortifications, and walls are clearly pictured. Others are topographical drawings seemingly sketched from distant heights. Human figures in the foreground of a number of the views illustrate costumes, customs, activities, and occupations of the period. Another reason for including the figures, as Braun notes, was to discourage the use and defilement of the views by Turkish infidels, whose religion forbade representation of the human body.

Ortelius' relationship to the *Civitates* is not completely clear. Braun, who prepared and edited the textual parts of the book, acknowledges his indebtedness to Ortelius for providing descriptions of many of the cities. The dual purpose of the *Civitates,* Braun explains, was to provide for the traveler graphic views of the cities he might visit, and to enable the sedentary owners of the atlas to travel vicariously to the distant cities without experiencing the inconveniences and dangers associated with real journeys.

The book apparently met its objectives, for there was a popular demand for copies. French and German editions were published in 1574. Plates of the separate cities

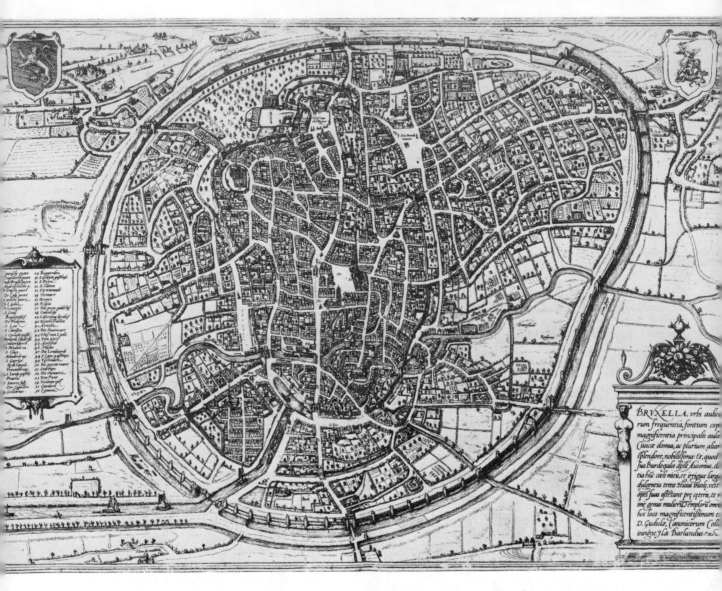

were also sold apart from the atlas. Five supplementary sections were issued before 1618. These were added to subsequent editions which also show minor changes on some of the original plates.

Jan Jansson of Amsterdam acquired the Braun and Hogenberg plates in 1653, and several years later he published an edition of the *Civitates* containing more than 500 plates.

Georg Braun, a Cologne scholar and theologian (ca. 1542–1622), is best known for the *Civitates,* but he also published a number of religious tracts. He was a great admirer of the cartographic publications of Ortelius and corresponded frequently and voluminously with him. It is quite possible that it was at Ortelius' suggestion that

Braun took on the assignment of preparing the text for Hogenberg's engravings.

Franz Hogenberg, a member of a renowned family of painters, engravers, and print sellers, was born at Malines about 1540 and is believed to have died in Cologne around 1590. Because of his religious beliefs he migrated from the Netherlands, settling successively in England, Antwerp, and Cologne. His output of engravings is phenomenal. In addition to the plates for the *Theatrum* and *Civitates* he is credited with more than 400 engravings of historical significance.

In *The Printed Maps in the Atlases of Great Britain,* Thomas Chubb wrote: "In the long list of compilers of British atlases the first name is also one of the greatest,

54

*Uncolored frontispiece in the second state from the Eastham copy of Christopher Saxton's atlas of the counties in England and Wales.*

*Facing page, plan of Brussels in the 1572* Civitates orbis terrarum, *by Georg Braun and Franz Hogenberg.*

Saxton are meager. It is known that he was born in Dunningley, Yorkshire, between 1542 and 1544, that he was a surveyor, and that he was still living in 1610. His great opportunity came about 1573 when he was engaged by Thomas Seckford, one of the Queen's Masters of Requests, to survey and map the counties of England and Wales.

About half the counties had been surveyed by 1577 when Saxton was licensed to print and sell his maps for a period of 10 years. The counties of England were completed in 1578 and by the following year Wales was fully mapped.

Although individual maps were sold earlier, Saxton's complete *Atlas* of the counties of England and Wales was not recorded in the Stationers' Register until 1579. It was reprinted and reissued a number of times and the maps served as prototypes for English county maps for the next century or more.

In addition to historical, geographical, and cartographical importance, Saxton's maps are valued for their artistic and decorative excellence. The atlas has no title page, but most copies include an ornamental frontispiece picturing Queen Elizabeth seated on a throne beneath an elaborately decorated canopy. Two different states of the frontispiece are recognized by scholars.

The Eastham Saxton has an uncolored frontispiece in the second state. Male figures representing Astronomy and Geography stand to the right and left of the seated Queen. Surmounting the canopy is the royal coat of arms, flanked by two cherubs holdings laurel wreaths in each hand. Two decorative cartouches below the pediment enclose two and six lines of Latin verse. Within the lower cartouche is inscribed the date "1579." In the lower right corner of the plate an astronomer peers through his telescope, and a mapmaker at work with a graver occupies the opposite corner. Arthur M. Hind [4] ascribes this plate to the engraver Remigius Hogenberg, a brother of Franz.

Indexes fill the two leaves following the frontispiece. The first is headed "Comitatvvm singvlorvmisto volv-/mine descriptorum index, ordinem quo cuiusque inueniatur carta gra/phica recte demonstrans." Three versions of this index are listed by Hind, but the plate in the Library's East-

the name of Christopher Saxton." Tooley affirms that "Saxton has rightly been called the 'Father of English Cartography.'" Saxton's *Atlas* of English counties, based on original surveys, introduced new standards of accuracy and established a pattern for atlases of a single country. It is truly the pioneer ancestor of the national atlases published by a number of countries in recent years and is thus an appropriate addition to the holdings of the Library.

Biographical data about Christopher

ham copy is identical with none of them. The following variations are noted: the third line of the heading is in italics; the list is set in Roman type, the plate carries no date, and *Anglia* heads the list of names, preceded in the numerical column by the symbol ⚜, in lieu of a number. The full list is set within ruled lines; the printed sheet is trimmed close to these lines and is mounted on the right inside page of the same sheet of paper that carries the frontispiece.

The second list of maps follows the one described above and is printed on a single unmounted sheet of paper, which is slightly smaller (40½ x 28 cm. compared with 42 x 29½ cm.) than the other pages in the atlas. This index conforms to Hind's fourth version, being printed in three columns, with the maps listed, (a) alphabetically, (b) as customarily arranged in the atlas, and (c) by judicial districts.

The Eastham copy does not include the coat of arms and "Catalogus" plates which are found in some Saxton editions.

All of the maps are printed on paper bearing the "bunch-of-grapes" watermark. The printed sheets are mounted on heavier paper cut to the same size. The paper on which is printed the first list described above also has the "bunch-of-grapes" identification. No watermark is visible on the sheet which carries the second list and the frontispiece.

The maps are arranged according to the first list, namely, ⚜ Anglia. 1. Herefordia. 2. Salopia. 3. Staffordia. 4. Wigornia. 5. Oxonium, Buckinghamia, & Berceria. 6. Hartfordia. 7. Northamptonia, Bedfordia, Cantabrigia, Huntingdonia & Rutlandia. 8. Warwicensis, & Lecestria. 9. Derbia. 10. Cestria. 11. Lancastria. 12. Westmorlandia, & Cumberlandia. 13. Northumbria. 14. Dunelmensis Episcopatus. 15. Eboraceusis: Comitatus. 16. Lincolnia & Nottinghamia. 17. Norfolcia. 18. Suffolcia. 19. Essexia. 20. Cantinum, Southsexia, Surria & Middlesexia. 21. Southamptonia. 22. Dorcestria. 23. Wiltonia. 24. Deuonia. 25. Cornubia. 26. Somersetensis. 27. Glocestria. 28. Monumetha. 29. Glamorgana. 30. Penbrok. 31. Radnor, Brecknok, Cardigan, & Caermarden. 32. Montgomeri, ac Mersonidh. 33. Anglesei, & Caernaruan. 34. Denbigh, ac Flnt [sic].

All maps are beautifully colored, with opaque reds and blues predominating. Each bears the Elizabethan coat of arms as well as that of Thomas Seckford and is inscribed "Christophorus Saxton descripsit."

One other copy of Saxton's *Atlas* is in the custody of the Geography and Map Division (Phillips 2913). The Rosenwald Collection, administered by the Library's Rare Book Division, includes three Saxtons, one of which is the only known copy printed on vellum. All three are listed under number 717 in *The Rosenwald Collection,* published by the Library in 1954.

The Saxton presented by Mr. Eastham may well be an earlier issue than the copy described in Phillips. In support of this belief the following evidence may be cited: the Eastham volume includes the earlier index; it lacks the plates with the coat of arms and the "Catalogus"; and latitude and longitude are not shown on its "Anglia" map.

The name Mercator is esteemed and renowned in the annals of cartography. To Gerardus Mercator and his heirs we are indebted for a number of contributions to cartographic science and terminology. In the latter category is the use of the name "atlas" for a bound volume of maps, which was introduced with the first edition of Mercator's *Atlas,* published in 1595. A fine copy of this edition presented to the Library by Mr. Eastham in 1950 is described earlier in this volume.

Supplementing the gift of 1950 in the present group of rarities are two Mercator volumes which predate the *Atlas* of 1595. Collectively the two new works include all the maps published by Mercator in 1585 and 1589. The arrangement of the maps within the volumes, however, follows a different sequence from that in any copy described by Averdunk, Bagrow, and Keuning, three of the most authoritative Mercator bibliographers.

Both volumes have matching contemporary vellum bindings with gold tooling on the front and back covers. The maps are printed from copper-engraved plates and are colored in the style of the period.

There are two parts, with separate title pages, in each volume. The first part of the 1585 edition includes nine maps preceded by a page reading *Belgii Inferioris geographicae tabule, Per Gerardum Mercatorem. . . .* Following this section is the title page for *Germaniae tabule geographicae, Per Gerardum Mercatorem . . .,* for which section there are 26 maps.

The first title in the 1589 volume reads *Italiae, Sclavoniae, et Graeciae tabule geographice, Per Gerardum Mercatorem . . .*, and includes 23 maps. There are 16 maps in the second part, which is preceded by a title page reading *Galliae tabule geographicae Per Gerardum Mercatorem. . . .*

In his authoritative "History of an Atlas, Mercator—Hondius," published in volume 4 of *Imago mundi* (1947), Keuning lists the four sections in the following sequence: edition of 1585, (a) Galliae, (b) Belgii Inferioris, and (c) Germaniae; and in the 1589 edition, Italiae, Sclavoniae, et Greciae.

The preliminary text of the *Germaniae* is not set like that in an uncolored copy of this work previously acquired. Slight variations, indicating type resettings, are also evident on the versos of some of the maps as well as in some of the tailpieces.

An uncolored copy of *Italiae* in the Library's collections seems to be identical (except for coloring) to the comparable work in the Eastham volume.

The mapmakers represented in the remaining four volumes presented by Mr. Eastham are less distinguished in the field of cartography than the producers of the works already described. Yet the volumes include several extremely rare items not previously among the Library's collections.

The earliest dated item is seemingly the earliest extant printed map of Greece, exclusive of those in Ptolemy's *Geographia*. In 1542 or 1543 Nikolaos Sophianos published in Rome a large map of ancient Greece entitled *Descriptio nova totius Graeciae*. There are no known copies of the original map, which was printed in eight sheets from wood engravings. Johannus Oporinus issued at Basel an edition of the Sophianos map in 1545. The plates were engraved on wood in Strassburg by Christoph, who also made engravings for Münster's *Cosmographia*. A preface and descriptive commentary in Latin by Nicolaus Gerbel accompanied the 1545 map.

The Gerbel-Sophianos work is entitled *Nicolai Gerbelij in descriptionem Graeciae Sophiani, praefatio* (Basel, 1545). This little volume has some 100 pages of text and index (31 x 21 cm.), which are bound with the folded map of Sophianos. The text is illustrated with 21 small brightly colored wood engravings of Greek cities. They are imaginative or fanciful sketches and not true portrayals of the places presented. The

map is preceded by a two-page table, prepared by Sophianos, which gives Greek and Italian names for places shown on the map.

The binding, in an excellent state of preservation, is contemporary bleached pigskin, blind-stamped with an ornamental design.

The map of Greece in the Eastham volume includes only five of the eight sheets which make up the complete map. Lacking are the sheets for the southeastern part of the Greek peninsula, the lower part of the Aegean Sea, and Asia Minor. If complete the map would measure 75 by 110 cm.

Relief is crudely portrayed by successions of "sugar loaf" mountain symbols. Pictorial representations of castles and fortifications locate a number of cities. Sailing vessels, mermaids, and sea monsters decorate the water areas.

Before Sophianos' work no separate map of Greece existed. Notwithstanding its inaccuracies, the map was enthusiastically received by contemporary scholars, and it remained the standard work on cartography of ancient Greece for almost 200 years. It is found in several editions of the *Theatrum* of Ortelius, beginning with that of 1579.

In 1550 Oporinus issued another edition of the map in Gerbel's revised and enlarged work, retitled *Nicolai Gerbelii Phorcensis pro delaratione picturae sive descriptione Graeciae Sophiani libri septem*. Sophianos personally also published a second edition of the map in Rome in 1552, which was printed on four sheets from copperplate engravings and is today exceedingly rare. It is the last known publication on which Sophianos' name appears.

Nikolaos Sophianos was born in Corfu, Greece, about the beginning of the sixteenth century. From 1515 to 1521 he studied at the Greek School in the Quirinal in Rome. When the school closed he remained in that city to work with Cardinals Marcello Cervini and Nikolas Ridolfi. With a fellow student he cataloged the latter's library of Greek manuscripts.

In 1533 the young Greek was reportedly engaged in copying manuscripts in Venice. Some time after this he was commissioned by Don Hurtado de Mendoza, the Ambassador of Charles V (Spain) to Venice, to visit monasteries in Greece and Asia Minor to purchase or copy Greek literary manuscripts. Travels in connection with this assignment, supplemented by a serious study of Ptolemy, provided the information for Sophianos map of Greece.

There is no evidence that Gerbel, who prepared the text for the 1545 and 1550 editions of the map, and Sophianos ever met. Nicolaus Gerbel was born in Pforzheim, Germany, about 1485. He studied Latin and Greek in that city before going to Vienna in 1502 for further schooling. The next 10 years he spent teaching and in additional study in Vienna and at the University of Bologna, Italy, where he was awarded a doctor's degree in 1514.

The early part of Gerbel's career was largely devoted to classical languages and in 1521 he published a Greek grammar. He was an intimate of Martin Luther and is reported to have prepared (anonymously and under various pseudonyms) a number of Reformation satires and dialogues.

During his later years Gerbel's principal interest was in history, and in the historical geography of antiquity. It was through these studies that he prepared himself for the two descriptive works which were published by Oporinus in conjunction with Sophianos' map of Greece.

Another volume presented by Mr. Eastham is a collection of city plans, with descriptive text, which predates Braun and Hogenberg's *Civitates*. By Antoine du Pinet, it is entitled *Plantz, povrtraitz, et descriptions de plvsievrs villes et forteresses, tant de l'Europe, Asie, & Afrique, que des Indes, terres neuues . . . avec plusieurs cartes generales & particulieres* and was published at Lyon in 1564 by Jean d'Ogerolles. It includes some 50 or more woodcut maps, views, illustrations, decorative initial letters, and headpieces and tailpieces. The 28 views are mostly of places in Europe, but they include also the cities of Istanbul, Cairo, Jerusalem, Acre, and Algiers, and Cuzco, Peru, and Mexico City in the New World.

A number of the city plans are printed on double pages; others occupy single pages in whole or in part. They are bird's-eye views which give details of buildings, landmarks, and the like. Sketches decorate the plans, and they are framed in elaborately ornamented borders. All the plates in the volume are colored. The name "Jean d'Ogerolles" appears on a number of the city maps. Printed beneath many of the views are lists of landmarks and places of interest. The map of Paris is one of the earliest printed maps of that city. It resembles somewhat the Paris plan in Münster's *Cosmographia*, and some authorities believe the two maps were derived from a common source. The Paris map in the *Plantz*, which is one of those bearing Jean d'Ogerolles' name, is considered to be transitional between the Münster and Braun views of the city.

Du Pinet's work also includes maps of the world, France, England and Scotland, Germany, Denmark, Italy, the Kingdoms of Naples and Sicily, Sardinia, and Greece. In the introductory part of the book the author lists some 15 of "Les meilleurs Chartes Geographiques du iourd'huy," among which are works of Gemma Frisius, Mercator, Orontius Fine, and Ruscelli.

The maps and views are accompanied by extensive descriptions (308 pages including maps) in French and an index of 21 pages. The book is in an attractive, modern, half-pigskin binding.

Antoine du Pinet, Sieur de Noroy, was born about 1513 at Besançon in the French Province of Franche-Comté. Much of his life, however, was spent in Lyon, and he died in Paris around 1584. Du Pinet was an archeologist, botanist, and linguist as well as a cosmographer and geographer. Like Gerbel, he was a zealous Protestant and an active participant in the Reformation movement.

Mr. Eastham's gift copy of Matthias Quad's *Europae totius orbis terrarvm partis praestantissimae, vniversalis et particvlaris descriptio* (Cologne, 1592) is possibly the earliest issue of this little book. It includes a title page and 42 engraved plates, 34 of which are maps. There are also several plates showing cities and battles, an incomplete portrait, and a mutilated drawing of Munich Cathedral, none of which are in other recorded issues of the atlas. These plates are of the same period and quite likely are also the work of Quad. The plates are unnumbered and none have text on the verso. Quad's name or his initial "Q" appears on 11 of the maps, and "Johannes Bussemecher" or a variant form of this name on 20 of the plates. The plate portraying an attack on the city of Grave (The Hague), is the only one which is colored. The book has a modern half-calf binding.

This 1592 issue of the *Europae* appears not previously to have been recorded by bibliographers, either under the name of

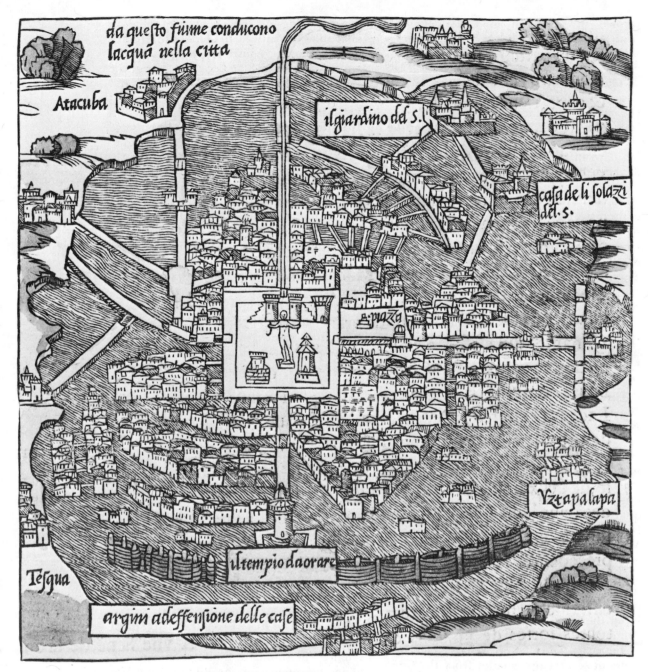

*Plan of Mexico City, partially colored, from Antoine du Pinet's* Plantz, povrtraitz, et descriptions de plvsievrs villes et forteresses.

Quad or of his publisher Bussemecher. Woltersdorf's *Reportorium der Land- und Seekarten* (1813), however, notes (p. 74) that in "1592. Joh. Bussemecher gab eine Sammlung von 40 allgemeinen und besonderen Karten zu Köln in quer Folio . . ." Because Quad's name does not appear on the *Europae* title page until the 1596 issue, this work is often attributed to Bussemecher.

The Library now has three issues of the Quad-Bussemecher atlas. The title of one is similar to that in the Eastham copy, and it likewise carries a 1592 publication date on the title page. However, it contains 54 maps (as compared with 34 in the Eastham copy), two of which are dated 1593. The third copy in the Library's possession is dated 1594 and contains 50 maps. Opposite the dedication, in the latter volume, is the coat of arms of Provost Philipp Kratz von Scharffenstein, to whom the atlas is dedicated. This copy is the identical one described in detail in F. I. Hildebrand's *Matthias Quad und dessen Europae universalis et particularis descriptio* (Leipzig, 1892).

The maps in Quad's atlas are largely based on those in Ortelius' *Theatrum*. If the author is indicated on a map in the latter the name is also included on the corresponding map in the *Europae*. Of the 50 maps in the 1594 issue of Quad's work, 23 bear his name or initial and 16 give credit to Heinrich Nagel (or Nagell) as the engraver. From the preface of the 1594 edition we learn that Quad's objective was to produce a small, inexpensive atlas for students and travelers, many of whom could not afford to purchase the larger, more elaborate world atlases published by Münster, Ortelius, de Jode, Waghenaer, and others.

Matthias Quad, engraver, author of historical and geographical works, and poet, was born in 1557 in Deventer, the Netherlands, of noble German parentage. He studied at Heidelberg, allied himself with the Reformed Congregation, and for some 10 years thereafter traveled in Germany, Norway, the Netherlands, England, and Scotland, sailing along the coasts or working in the establishments of gold and silversmiths. In 1587 he settled in Cologne; he married shortly thereafter and raised a large family. For a time he resided in the quarters that had formerly been occupied by the noted globemaker Caspar Vopel. Much of what is known about Quad is gleaned from his own writings.

Cologne was a well-known center of learning in the sixteenth century, where book-publishing flourished and where Quad enjoyed the friendship of numerous scholars. Among his early engravings was a fine plan of the city of Breslau, as well as plans and views of several other cities from the *Civitates orbis terrarum* of George Braun and Franz Hogenberg. In 1589 a leading Cologne publisher, Johann Bussemecher, engaged him to engrave a series of maps of the states of Europe. By 1592 Quad had completed some 50 maps, which formed the first edition of his *Europae . . . descriptio*. This was reissued in 1594 and in 1596 and subsequently was greatly enlarged to become his *Geographische Handtbuch,* published in 1600, with 82 maps. During his residence in Cologne, Quad is known to have produced at least 17 publications and numer-

ous engravings. In 1603, because of religious difficulties, he moved his family to Heidelberg, where he continued to ply the engraver's art. In 1608 he became rector of the Reformed Latin school in Weinheim, and in 1612 "Kollaborator" of the Reformed Latin school in Eppingen, where he died in 1613 at the age of 55. Quad produced his two most notable works after he left Cologne: *Fasciculus geographicus* (1608), a world atlas containing 86 maps, and the *Teutscher Nation Herrlichkeit* (1609), which is now quite rare.

The last of the Eastham gift items is a small volume of 30 leaves, in modern buckram binding, entitled *Königen Buch oder Register darinfein ordentlich erzehlt werden die Koenige aller fuernemsten Koenigreichen des Christenthumbs*. It was published at Cologne in 1598 and includes 14 double-page maps by Conrad Löw.

Printed from copper engravings, the maps portray France, Castile, Portugal, Aragon, England, Scotland, Denmark, Sweden, Poland, Hungary, Bohemia, Naples, Sicily, and Turkey. On the verso of each is a chronological list of rules which, in some instances, extend back to Roman times. The language is German.

Virtually nothing is known about the life and career of Conrad Löw except, as indicated by his writings, that he was a historian. In the same year in which the *Königen Buch* was published, 1598, his *Meer oder Sehanen Buch* also was issued. The latter is an account of the travels of the kings of Spain, Portugal, England, and France during the sixteenth century. In 1597 Löw published in Cologne a *Histoire von Navarra*.

The *Königen Buch* is very rare; no record of it has been found in the National Union Catalog, in standard bibliographic works, or in the catalogs of the Bibliothèque Nationale and the British Museum.

The rare atlases here described give evidence of Mr. Eastham's acumen as a collector and as a connoisseur of sixteenth-century cartographic works. In presenting these distinctive volumes to the Library of Congress he displayed, moreover, an uncommon degree of public interest and service. His generous gift has made available to the Nation's scholars a choice collection of maps and geographical works published in the sixteenth century.

In 1962 Mr. Eastham presented to the American Geographical Society, New York City, the balance of his collection of rare atlases. Included were a number of printed editions of Ptolemy, Ortelius, De Jode, Mercator, and other fifteenth- and sixteenth-century works, totaling more than 60 volumes. Mr. Eastham died on May 7, 1964, at the age of 79.

NOTES

[1] Described as number 375 in Philip Lee Phillips, *A List of Geographical Atlases in the Library of Congress* (Washington, 1909), vol. 1, p. 135.

[2] Published at Gotha in 1928–30 as *Petermanns geographische Mitteilungen*, Ergänzungsheft 199 and 210.

[3] In vol. 2, p. 102, published at Antwerp in 1913.

[4] Arthur M. Hind, *Engraving in England* (Cambridge, 1952), p. 73.

# BY WALTER W. RISTOW

Reprinted from the January 1967 *Quarterly Journal of the Library of Congress.*

THE EXCITING AND FAR-RANGING explorations and discoveries of the fifteenth and sixteenth centuries had a dramatic impact on all the arts and sciences in Europe. Mapmaking in particular was stimulated and revolutionized by the awakened geographical consciousness, the expansion of commerce and trade, and the development of new instruments and techniques for compiling and reproducing maps.

Until about the middle of the sixteenth century map publishing was largely concentrated in south and central Europe. Shortly after 1550, with the shift from woodcut to engraving, cartographic leadership moved to the Low Countries, where the craft of copper engraving had reached its highest development. For almost a century, beginning around 1570, Dutch mapmakers dominated the field, with the principal houses located, successively, in Antwerp and Amsterdam. This "Golden Age" of Netherlands cartography coincided with the period of the great Dutch artists. There were, in fact, close relationships between mapmakers and painters, and the two arts had reciprocal interests and influences.

Seventeenth-century Dutch cartography is especially renowned for its magnificent atlases, some of which were published in as many as 12 large folio volumes. Abraham Ortelius of Antwerp introduced the atlas format in 1570 with his *Theatrum orbis terrarum.* Atlas publishing, however, achieved its maximum development in Amsterdam during the middle of the seventeenth century. Here the large and efficiently organized cartographic workshops of Mercator-Hondius-Jansson, Willem and Joan Blaeu, Nikolaus Visscher, Frederik de

*Title cartouche of the 1669 Jaillot edition of Blaeu's map of Africa. Acquired in June 1966, it is one of two rare 17th-century wall maps in the Library of Congress.*

Wit, and others produced numerous editions of multivolume folio atlases. The beautifully decorated and illuminated atlases were purchased by prosperous merchants, traders, industrialists, and nobility of the Netherlands and of other European countries. Bound in vellum, leather, or velvet covers and preserved through the centuries in well-appointed private and public collections, a significant number of copies of seventeenth-century atlases have survived to bear witness to Holland's glorious age of cartography.

Less well represented today are the sheet and wall maps which were also produced in quantity by Dutch map publishers. Because they were exposed to all the processes and conditions of deterioration and wear, not many seventeenth-century wall maps survived. As Cornelis Koeman has noted, "Little is known as yet of the number and variety of these monumental items since only a few examples have been preserved. This is due to the fact that they were far more vulnerable than atlas maps. The historical significance of these maps, which decorated the walls of 17th century living and state-rooms, is great since their contents were, in most cases, the source of those of the atlas maps." [1]

Large wall maps commonly decorated the interiors of many private dwellings and public edifices in the seventeenth century, as is demonstrated by a number of art masterpieces which show maps as wall hangings. Jan Vermeer (1632–75) in particular made effective use of contemporary maps in his artistic compositions. At least a half dozen of his paintings include cartographic representations. Most readily identified is Nikolaus Visscher's large wall map of the Netherlands, which is prominent feature of Vermeer's *Artist in His Studio.* A map of Europe decorates the interior of the studio in his charming painting *Lady With a Lute.*

*Engraving of Blaeu by Jeremias Falck, reproduced from* Willem Janszoon Blaeu, *by Edward L. Stevenson, published by the Hispanic Society of America in 1914.*

Less easily distinguishable maps appear in other Vermeer canvases.

"With his superb translation of surface effects, ranging from brass and brocade to tapestry and ceramic tile, it was Vermeer," writes Elisabeth Walton, "who distinguished himself as the most accomplished portrayer of maps of his day." [2] Among Vermeer contemporaries whose paintings also testify to the popularity of wall maps in seventeenth-century Holland are Nicolaes Maes, Jacob Ochtervelt, Gerard TerBorch, and Pieter de Hooch. These "masters were not insensitive to the decorative value of maps or they might well have been satisfied to limit their back-wall devices to framed allegorical pictures. What the appearance of maps in scenes of comfortable Dutch domesticity affirms is that well-trimmed walls were settings for geographical art just as naturally as they supported portraits and landscapes. It is appropriate that maps, which were appreciated as works of art in their own right, should be recorded in the painted canvases of their time." [3]

Giant atlases, preserved in two of the world's notable libraries, provide further evidence of the significance of large wall maps in seventeenth-century cartographic publishing. In 1660 a group of Dutch merchants, among them Johan Klencke, presented to Britain's King Charles II, in recognition of the restoration of the Stuart dynasty following the Cromwell interregnum, a bound collection of some 35 large wall maps. The "Klencke Giant Atlas," now in the British Museum, measures 70 by 38 inches. It is mounted on casters to facilitate opening the covers. The individual maps, which were printed from engraved plates, are excellently preserved. Included are representative works of the leading Dutch cartographers of the period, some of which are the only extant copies.

A similar collection of Dutch wall maps, bound in leather-covered oak boards, was presented about 1661 by Johan Maurits van Nassau to Friedrich Wilhelm von Branden-

*Detail of Jan Vermeer's* Artist in His Studio, *with Nikolaus Visscher's map of the Netherlands hanging on the wall. In the collections of the Kunsthistorisches Museum, Vienna.*

burg. Identified as the *Maurits, Mauritius* or *Kurfürsten Atlas,* this large volume is now in the Deutsche Staatsbibliothek, Berlin.[4] Its 35 maps range in date from 1659 to 1661 and include works by Blaeu, de Wit, Hondius, Danckerts, Visscher, Ten Have, Colom, Jansson, and Allardt.[5] The *Maurits Atlas* was exhibited at the Chicago World's Fair in 1893. The giant volume was damaged on the return trip across the Atlantic but was restored in 1931.[6]

Apart from those preserved in the Klencke and Maurits atlases, fewer than 50 wall maps have been recorded, of the hundreds that were probably published in the seventeenth century. The high mortality rate reflects their decorative function. For display purposes the maps "were pasted on linen, often surrounded with edges, ornamental frames, series of views of cities, coats-of-arms, and cartouches, varnished and furnished with sticks and knobs, and made a very decorative effect with it all. The rather yellow varnish gave the maps a delicate and beautiful tone."[7] To which we might add that varnish, which becomes brittle and cracks with age, also contributed to the deterioration and destruction of the maps.

A number of surviving wall maps are products of the Blaeu firm, the foremost Amsterdam cartographic publishing house of the mid-seventeenth century. Willem Janszoon Blaeu (1571–1638), a native of Alkmaar, achieved fame as an instrument maker, surveyor, cartographer, globe maker, and publisher of maps, charts, and atlases. Shortly after 1600 he began making maps in his Amsterdam workshop. The Blaeu firm, which included sons Cornelis and Jan, published over the next 65 years some 400 maps, most of which were assembled in handsome folio atlases, in Dutch, Latin, French, German, Flemish, and Spanish editions.

Wall maps, a number of them of large size, were among the earliest Blaeu productions. Frederik C. Wieder, the distinguished Dutch cartobibliographer, recorded known copies of Blaeu wall maps in his "Descriptive Catalogue of Maps Published Separately by Blaeu."[8] Among them are wall maps of the four continents, Africa, America, Asia, and Europe, initially published in 1608. Wieder recorded first edition copies of only two of these—maps of Asia and Africa in the Bibliothèque Nationale, Paris —but he also listed editions dated 1612,

1624, 1655, 1657, 1659, 1669, and 1673 of one or more of the four maps. Some of the later editions bear imprints of other publishers and are obvious plagiarisms. Copying maps of other publishers was a common practice in this period, and the Blaeu firm itself was no exception.

The Africa, America, Asia, and Europe maps are similar in size and format. The maps proper measure about 83 by 109 centimeters ($32\frac{1}{2}$ by 43 inches). On the right and left margins are costumed figures representative of different countries, and at the bottom there is a series of city plans and panoramas. Some editions have a title, in large letters, across the top of the map, and there may be two or more decorative cartouches. A second, outer border found on several maps contains descriptive text, usually in three languages. Illustrations and descriptive notes are also inserted at various locations on the land or seas on the maps themselves. Some of the extant maps are undated. The wall maps were attractively designed, artistically executed, and beautifully and brilliantly colored. They were worthy companions of the art masterpieces with which they shared the interiors of Dutch homes and public buildings. Time and the processes of deterioration have unfortunately dimmed the luster and brilliance of most of the surviving wall maps.

In the collections of the Library of Congress are two rare seventeenth-century wall maps, one portraying America and the other Africa. Both are obvious plagiarisms of Blaeu maps, although neither bears the imprint of the distinguished Dutch firm. The provenance of the map of America, which has been in the Library's possession for at least half a century, is unknown, and it has not previously been described. The African map was acquired by purchase from a private owner in June 1966. Both maps are in fair condition, with only small pieces lacking, principally in the outer decorative margins. Both have recently been restored in the Library's preservation laboratory, where they were carefully and skillfully separated from the deteriorating linen cloth on which they were mounted, backed with pure rag paper, and remounted on cotton muslin.

*Following page, Pietro Todeschi's 1673 edition of Blaeu's map of America. The map, 38 by 54 inches, is in the Geography and Map Division.*

NOVA ET ACVRATA TO
GROENLANDI
AME R I CA SE
TRI O NALIS
TROPICUS CANCRI
MAR DE L
NOVA
GUINEA
MAGALLANICA
TERRA
AUSTRALIS INCOGNITA
MAR DI INDIA
TROPICUS
CAPRICORNI
REX et REGINA Florida
S. AUGUSTIN

# ˅S AMERICÆ TABVLA. au et. C

MENICANI

PERVIANI

BRASILIANA

BRASILIANI

BRASILIANA

INSVLANI DE LA MOCHE

ICONES PATACONVM

FRETI MAGALLANI INCOLÆ

OCEANVS ATLANTICVS

MAR DEL NOI

TROPICVS CANCRI

AMERICA MERIDIONALIS

EVROPA

HISPANIA PARES

AFRICÆ PARS

TERRA NOVA

TERRA CORTEREALIS

AMERICA

Fretum Magallanicum

TERRA DEL FVOGO

POTOSI

J. LA MOCHA IN CHILI

RIO IANEIRO

The two maps are similar in size and format to other Dutch wall maps of the seventeenth century. Drawings of inhabitants of different regions in typical dress form borders on the right and left, and across the bottom are vignettes of cities, forts, and landscapes. Sailing ships, sea cows, flying fish, mermaids, and decorative compass roses ornament the ocean spaces, and small sketches of native fauna and peoples are distributed over the land. Neither map has the outer border of descriptive text found on some surviving maps.

Across the top of the map of America is a banner title, in large capital letters, that reads "Nova et acvrata totivs Americae Tabvla. auct:" Only a part of the first letter of the author's name, "G. I. Blaev" (for Guilielmus), which is found on copies that have the marginal descriptive text, follows "auct:" in the banner. In the lower right corner the title "America" over a Latin

inscription appears in a cartouche flanked by figures representing Christopher Columbus on the left and Amerigo Vespucci on the right. Portraits of Magellan, Drake, Candisch, and Van der Noort are set in the base of the cartouche. The map carries no date or place of publication. Including marginal illustrations and title, it measures approximately 97 by 137 centimeters (38 by 54 inches).

Although Wieder, in his *Monumenta cartographica,* records that Blaeu published wall maps of all the continents in 1608, there is no known surviving copy of the map of America of this edition. He describes a 1624 edition, with the imprint of Henricus Hondius, under the title of *Nova totius Americae sive novi orbis auct: G.*

*Inset map of South Polar region on the Blaeu map of America. "Stretto lamairo" and "detecta 1667" features identify the Library of Congress copy as the Todeschi edition.*

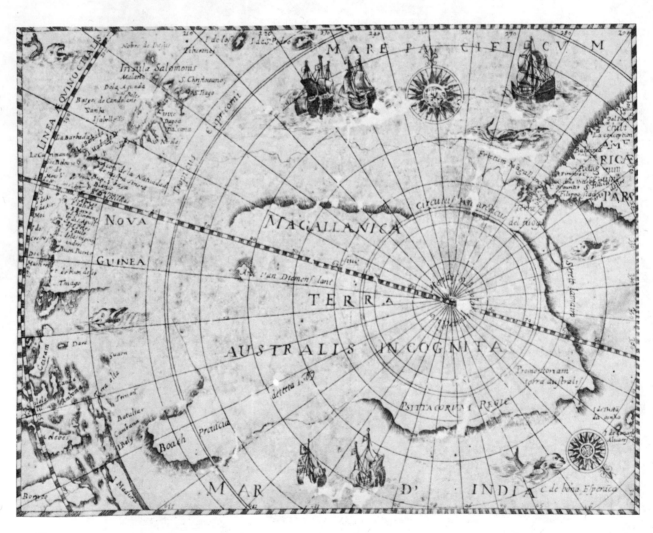

*Janssonio,* and a further state of the same title, with "auct: G. I. Blaeu," and with text reprinted and dated 1656.

Wieder assigns the date 1673 to an edition of four continent maps, engraved and published by Pietro Todeschi in Bologna, Italy. The Library's America map appears to be of this edition.

The four maps of the Todeschi edition are described by Wieder as of "the same size as the Dutch [1656] edition and have similar borders of views and aboriginal types . . . and a title printed in large type, running across the top of the map. The text [when present] is in Italian and Latin, the maps themselves and the pictorial borders are in Latin. . . . At bottom of the text: Bo[no]niae, M.D.C.L.XXIII." A distinguishing feature of the map of America, Wieder notes, is that "the Strait of Lemaire [southern end of South America] . . . is not drawn in the Italian edition. At the bottom of the

map are read the name only: Fretum le Maire. . . . On the inset-map of the Southern hemisphere the strait is not drawn either, but we find the name 'Stretto lamairo.' That same inset-map shows 'Ant [actually Aric] van Diemens land' and to the old name 'Boach' 'detecta 1667' has been added." The maps in the Todeschi edition described by Wieder were listed as "in private Dutch collection."

The Royal Geographical Society, London, acquired in 1922 a "series of [wall] maps of the four continents" which were described (apparently by Arthur R. Hinks) in the September 1922 issue of the *Geographical Journal* (p. 233–234). A footnote to the description states that "the Society's maps seem to have been re-engraved, perhaps in Italy, by one Pietro Todeschi."

*Columbus and Vespucci flank this title cartouche, while other explorers are represented in the base.*

In general character and contents . . . [the Royal Geographical Society maps] show (especially the America) a close resemblance to maps included by Hondius in the later editions of his Atlas, and dated 1631. But the productions of the two firms are so interwoven that it is impossible to say whether these maps of Hondius were copied from Blaeu's large maps, or were merely reductions of larger maps of his own copied by Blaeu. The present specimens appear to be later issues produced some time after the elder Blaeu's death, for on an inset of the South Polar region given (as in Hondius' atlas-map of 1631) in the lower corner of the America, an extremely rough indication of Van Diemen's Land (discovered by Tasman in 1642) has been added in a position originally covered by a part of the supposed southern continent. Also, while retaining the name "Boach Provincia" (more usually Beach) applied, as by Mercator and others, to the northernmost part of this continent in the Australian region, the words "detecta 1667" have been added. This would seem to be an error of the engraver, possibly for 1627, the date given on many maps of the period as that of Pieter Nuyts' voyage along the South Australian coast; for not only did no important voyage to this part of the world take place in 1667, but it is inconceivable that any map-maker who knew the results of Tasman's and other Dutch voyages to Australia in the first half of the seventeenth century should ascribe the first discovery to the year named.[9]

The Library of Congress acquired, in 1938, full-size photostat reproductions of the Royal Geographical Society's four wall maps. A comparison between the Library's wall map of America and the RGS copy indicates that they are identical in all respects. After Wieder and Hinks we can, therefore, ascribe the Library of Congress copy of *America* to the edition of Pietro Todeschi, published at Bologna in 1673.

The wall map of Africa, acquired by the Library in June 1966, appears to be a unique and hitherto unrecorded copy. In format and general appearance it resembles other editions of Blaeu's *Africa,* from which it is unquestionably derived. The Library's copy lacks the banner title but includes the border illustrations at the sides and bottom. With margins the map measures 93 by 135 centimeters (36½ by 53 inches). When received the map was backed with heavy linen and mounted in a hand-carved oak frame. As noted above, it has been remounted on rag stock paper and fresh cotton muslin.

The Library's map of Africa, unlike many seventeenth-century wall maps, includes the name of the publisher and the place and date of publication. It is also distinctive in having the title, inscriptions, and place names in French rather than Latin. The title, framed in a decorative cartouche, near the upper right corner of the map, reads: *Carte de l'Afrique Nouvellement Dressée sur les Memoires de Meilleurs Geographes de nostre temps et distinguée suivant les Royaumes, souverainetés et principales parties, qui se trouvent iusques apresent 1669*. Within a smaller, ornamental cartouche in the upper left corner is inscribed: "A Paris chez H Ialiot proche Les Grand Augvstin av bov dv Pō Nevf 1669."

In his *Monumenta cartographica,* Wieder recognizes editions of Blaeu's *Africa* for the years 1608, 1624, 1657, 1659, and 1673. He records no 1669 French map of Africa, but under that date he describes a map of Asia as "a French translation of Blaeu's large map, the date of publication being uncertain. It was published in France, judging from its general aspect, and perhaps at the same date as a similar map of America, dated 1669." Apparently neither the Asia nor the America map included the publisher's name.

Alexis Hubert Jaillot, or Hubert Jaillot, was born about 1632 in the hamlet of Avignon, near St. Claude, in Franche-Comté. Little is known of his early life or education. They were undoubtedly difficult years, for Franche-Comté was devastated by military invasions in 1637 and again in 1639, during the Thirty Years War. Through the middle decades of the seventeenth century there was a heavy exodus from Franche-Comté, particularly to Italy and Paris. In 1657 Hubert and his brother Simon, both of whom were sculptors, emigrated to Paris to seek their fortunes. They were probably stimulated to do so by the inducements offered by the regency of the young King Louis XIV to attract scientists, artists, and scholars to the French capital.

The Jaillot brothers worked as sculptors on various public buildings, and Simon continued in that profession until his death in 1681. Hubert became acquainted in Paris with a group of Dutch artists and engravers who had also been attracted by the favorable intellectual environment. Through these contacts Hubert Jaillot met Jeanne Berey, the daughter of a map illuminator and merchant. After his marriage to Jeanne in 1664, Hubert was increasingly drawn to the profession of his father-in-law, Nicolas

*Alexis Hubert Jaillot, after he was named Géographe Ordinaire du Roi. Engraving by Cornelis Vermeulen of Antwerp after a painting by J. Culin of Paris, from Jaillot's* Atlas français *of 1695. From the Geography and Map Division.*

Berey, whose cartographic shop was located "au Pont-Neuf, proche les Augustins, a la fontaine de Jouvence." Jaillot no doubt spent several years learning the skills of map drawing and engraving. Copying Blaeu's large wall map of Africa was apparently one of his earliest cartographic endeavors, for no map bearing his name is dated before 1669. In addition to the African map, Jaillot published in that year *Carte de Franche-Comté et du Comté de Montbeliard,* which was copied from a map by Nicolas Tassin. We do not know when Nicolas Berey died but, as recorded on the map of Africa, in 1669 Jaillot was established "proche les Grand Augustin au bou du pont neuf." It is possible that by this date Jaillot had fallen heir to his father-in-law's shop. For some of his early maps, Jaillot's biographer, François Roland, notes that "in substituting his name for that of his father-in-law, [Jaillot] had simply re-

vised and joined several old copper plates of which the majority were copies of Dutch maps for which there was no license in France." [10] Whether or not this applies to the map of Africa we do not know. Translating the place names from Latin to French and copying and engraving the large map obviously required considerable time. Jaillot may well have worked on the map for several years before it was published in 1669.

The foremost map publisher in mid-seventeenth century France was Nicolas Sanson, who was assisted by his sons Guillaume and Adrien. The Sansons were among Jaillot's professional colleagues and friends. Following the death of the firm's founder, in July 1667, Hubert Jaillot was invited by the sons to serve as editor for a new edition of Sanson's atlas. The *Atlas nouveau,* published in 1684, was dedicated by Jaillot to the Dauphin. Several subsequent editions of the atlas were published in Amsterdam by Pierre Mortier.

Jaillot, who was named Géographe Ordinaire du Roi in 1675, had a distinguished career as a publisher of maps and atlases. In 1693 he published for the French Government a volume of 29 navigation charts under the title *Le Neptune français.* Jaillot's last publication was the *Atlas français,* a summation of the cartography of France at the close of the seventeenth century. Jaillot's maps and atlases show a strong Dutch influence and are distinguished for their fine engraving, ornamentation, and color. Many of the plates in his atlases were, however, copies or reprintings of maps made some years earlier, and they show no influence of the scientific surveys which were carried out in France toward the end of the seventeenth century. Alexis Hubert Jaillot died in Paris in 1712 at the age of 80. Editions of the *Atlas français* were published over the next half century by his sons and grandsons.

Blaeu's original wall map of Africa, which Jaillot published in a French edition in 1669, was one of the first large-scale representations of the continent. An analysis of the sources used to compile it was made in 1938 by J. Denucé. [11] Denucé ob-

*Following page, the 1669 French edition, by Jaillot, of Blaeu's wall map of Africa. The map, 36½ by 53 inches, is in the Geography and Map Division.*

served that it was no accident that this early map of Africa was originally produced in the Netherlands, for "Antwerp and Amsterdam [were] centers of world trade, and particularly of commerce with Africa during the sixteenth and seventeenth century." Blaeu's map therefore reveals Dutch knowledge of Africa in this period.

For much of north and northwest Africa Blaeu, according to Denucé, derived his information largely from Ortelius. Dutch sources were used to draw the coastal regions southward of Sierra Leone. "We are also inclined to believe," wrote Denucé, "that Blaeu . . . had direct access to the distinguished maps of Africa made by the Portuguese Lopes and published by Pigafetta in Rome in 1591. In fact, Blaeu used, to embellish his map, the Congolese native types that illustrated the Lopes text."[12] South Africa, noted Denucé, was "not based on Lopes-Pigafetta. The Dutch names in this area, on Blaeu's map, were applied by his countrymen, precursors of Van Riebeeck, who initiated Dutch colonization in the extreme south of Africa in 1652." For east Africa the cartographer drew on Portuguese and Italian sources. Denucé concludes that the "wall map of Africa seems to have been an original work, independent of the maps in [Blaeu's] atlas."

An interesting and somewhat impassioned debate, concerning the publisher of the French edition of Blaeu's wall map of America, was published in several numbers of the *Bulletin de Société de Geographie* in 1891. The thoughts expressed by the participants may have some relationship to the wall map of Africa now in the Library of Congress. In 1880, according to the *Bulletin* report, Jules Marcou, a distinguished French geologist, purchased a French edition of a wall map of America, which bore the date 1669 but included no imprint or publisher. Marcou submitted it for examination and identification, in 1891, to Gabriel Marcel, then Curator of Maps at the Bibliothèque Nationale, Paris. Marcel found no copy of the map in the Bibliothèque Nationale, in the collections of the Foreign Office, or in any other French library. Marcel, after due study, concluded that "as the map does not bear the name of an author, or any address of engraver or publisher, it would be absolutely impossible to discover in what country it was engraved and from whose hand it came."[13]

But he added, "I would attribute the map of America belonging to M. Jules Marcou, a very rare and unique map, to Nicolas Visscher, after Willem Blaew."[14]

Marcel's conclusion and attribution were not acceptable to Professor Marcou. The latter theorized that his map of America was probably prepared at the direction of Jean Baptiste Colbert, who at that date was Minister of Marine, Controller General, and an influential figure in the government of King Louis XIV. Marcou's theory was supported by the fact that the monarch, pictured riding the horsedrawn barge in the north Atlantic Ocean, on the French map, bore the features of Louis XIV. On other editions of the map King Phillip IV of Spain is seated in the barge.

Professor Marcou further reasoned that, in 1669, the Dauphin was old enough to be studying geography. What could be more natural, he concluded, "than to prepare for him a map of America with the portrait of his father, King Louis XIV"?[15] "One can infer with reasonable certainty," continued Marcou, "that the map [of America] was quite likely made at Versailles for the education of the Dauphin, by one of the Géographes Ordinaires du Roi, most likely Du Val. For obvious reasons the map was sent for engraving to one of the large geographical houses in the Netherlands, long celebrated for the engraving and printing of maps." To explain its great rarity, Professor Marcou believed "that this map of America was not available to the public, that it was only placed in Versailles, either in the apartment of the Dauphin, or in the office of Colbert, probably in both."[16]

Subsequent studies have confirmed Marcou's belief that the French edition of the wall map of America was made by one of France's Géographes Ordinaires du Roi. It was not DuVal, but Jaillot, however, who published the map. Moreover, we now have confirmation that French editions of wall maps of all four continents were published "A Paris chez H. Ialiot proche Les Grand Augvstin av bov dv Pō Nevf."

A complete set of the Jaillot wall maps is preserved in the collections of the University of Bologna. They are described, and reproduced at reduced scale, in a catalog published by the university in 1959.[17] The maps are dated as follows: America, 1669, Africa, 1678, Europe, 1678, and Asia, 1679. Each map has a banner title as well as marginal text on the sides and bottom. The Library of Congress wall map of Africa, which is dated 1669 in both the title and imprint, is apparently an earlier state than the corresponding map in the University of Bologna.

## NOTES

1 Cornelis Koeman, *Collections of Maps and Atlases in the Netherlands, Their History and Present State* (Leiden, 1961), p. 30.

2 Elisabeth B. Walton, "Netherlandish Maps: a Decorative Role in the History of Art," *The Professional Geographer,* 14:33 (March 1962).

3 Ibid.

4 Berlin, Deutsche Staatsbibliothek, *Deutsche Staatsbibliothek 1661–1961* (Leipzig, 1962), vol. 1, Geschichte und Gegenwart, p. 406.

5 There is a list of the maps in the *Maurits Atlas* in F. C. Wieder's "Nederlandsche Kartenmusea in Duitschland," *Tijdschrift van het Koninklijk Nederlandsch Aardrijkskundig Genootschap,* 36:32–35 (January 1919).

6 Wilhelm Kohnert, "Der Riesenatlas des Grossen Kurfürsten und seine Restaurierung 1931," *Archiv für Buchbinderei* (Leipzig), 31:102–104 (1931).

7 P. T. A. Swillens, *Johannes Vermeer, Painter of Delft, 1632–1675* (New York, 1950), p. 82–83.

8 In text vol. 3 of his *Monumenta cartographica* (The Hague, 1929), p. 67–75.

9 "Large Maps of the Continents by Willem Jansz Blaeu," *Geographical Journal,* 60:233 (September 1922).

10 François Roland, *Alexis Hubert Jaillot, Géographe du Roi Louis XIV (1632–1712)* (Besançon, 1919), p. 11.

11 J. Denucé, "Les sources de la carte murale d'Afrique de Blaeu, de 1644 (Amsterdam)," in 15th International Geographical Congress, *Comtes rendus,* vol. 2, Sect. IV, Géographie historique et histoire de la géographie (Leiden, 1938), p. 172–174.

12 Ibid., p. 173.

13 Gabriel Marcel, "Note sur une carte d'Amerique de 1669," in Société de Géographie, *Bulletin,* Ser. 7, 12:256 (1891).

14 Ibid., p. 259.

15 Jules Marcou, "Carte d'Amerique dite de Louis XIV," in Société de Géographie, *Bulletin,* Ser. 7, 12:355 (1891).

16 Ibid., p. 356.

17 Bologna, Universitá, *La collezione delle antiche carte geografiche,* edited by Pietro Frabetti (Bologna, 1959).

*Jonathan Swift's* On Poetry: A Rapsody *contains a quatrain that well describes this detail of the equatorial region of the Africa wall map:*
*So Geographers in Afric-maps*
*With Savage-Pictures fill their Gaps;*
*And o'er unhabitable Downs*
*Place Elephants for want of Towns.*

# American Maps of the Seventeenth to Nineteenth Centuries

# Maps of Early America

## BY CLARA E. LEGEAR

Reprinted from the November 1950 issue of the *Library of Congress Quarterly Journal of Current Acquisitions.*

Few studies in the general history of American cartography have been carried on in the last 50 years without recourse to the rich collections in the Library of Congress. Here, one can find maps covering more American areas over a longer span of time than can be found in any other institution. When the Map Division, now the Geography and Map Division, was less than five years old, Philip Lee Phillips, its first custodian, stated: "The collection of maps relating to America is the largest single collection in existence. Its contents are set forth in the recently [1901] published *List of Maps of America in the Library of Congress*—a volume of 1,137 pages." Maps relating to early American history are especially well represented.

Unfortunately, maps directly connected with the Columbus voyages of discovery have been lost to posterity. American cartography, therefore, rightly begins with a map dated 1500 which was made by Juan de la Cosa and is generally conceded to be the earliest map showing the New World. Happily, this important map, made by the master and principal pilot of the flagship *Santa María,* is available to students in several excellent facsimiles. The islands of Cuba and Hispaniola, the Lesser Antilles, and part of the northern coast of South America are delineated on it, as well as the Cabot discoveries in the north. George E. Nunn, in his critical study, *The Mappemonde of Juan de la Cosa* (Jenkintown, Pa., 1934), believes it to have been augmented at least to 1510. The original colored manuscript on vellum is now in the Museo Naval at Madrid.

Though discovered by Columbus, the New World was nevertheless named for the explorer Amerigo Vespucci. It is likely that Martin Waldseemüller, a professor of cosmography in St. Dié, France, had much to do with impressing Vespucci's given name upon the new continent through his use of the name America in his *Cosmographiæ introductio* (1507) and on the world map which it accompanied. Printed in 12 sections from wood blocks and measuring about 54 by 96 inches, this map also depicts for the first time the extent of Spanish and Portuguese discoveries in the New World. For many years it was counted among the world's lost maps, but a copy was identified in 1901 by the great student of Ptolemaic geography, Father Joseph Fischer, who found it in the library of Prince Waldburg-Wolfegg at the Castle of Wolfegg in Württemberg. This map of outstanding historical importance to American history was made available in facsimile in the publication entitled *Die älteste Karte mit dem Namen Amerika aus dem Jahre 1507 . . .* edited by Joseph Fischer and R. von Wieser (Innsbruck, 1903). A new full scale reproduction of the Waldseemüller map, in 12 parts, was also published in 1959 by Carlos Sans of Madrid.

Information about America first appeared in the 1508 Rome edition of Claudius Ptolemy's *Geographia.* The New World map by Johann Ruysch included in this edition shows the extent of the American discoveries and indicates most accurately the Portuguese explorations. Until the Waldseemüller map came to light, the Ruysch map was considered a historical document of primary importance. At least three issues are known. It is first noted on the title page of the 1508 edition of the *Geographia,* although it has been found in several 1507 editions. According to Marcus Beneventanus, editor of the 1508 *Geo-*

*graphia,* Ruysch was a most painstaking geographer who was believed to have accompanied John Cabot on his famous voyage of discovery. The Ruysch map is the earliest original contemporary map relating to America in the collections of the Library of Congress.

Gerardus Mercator shares with Waldseemüller responsibility for naming the Americas. Whereas Waldseemüller applied the name America to South America, Mercator named the continents North and South America, respectively, on his first world map, published in 1538. On a double cordiform projection, this map embodies knowledge gained from explorations made along the American coasts in the intervening 30 years. There are original engraved copies of Mercator's world map of 1538 in the New York Public Library and in the American Geographical Society of New York.

Mercator derived his double cordiform projection from the world map by Orontius Finaeus in the publication *Novus orbis regionum* published in 1532 by S. Grynaeus and I. Huttich. The Finaeus map was the first to delineate a large "Terra Avstralis" where we now know the Antarctic continent to be. A separate copy of this map is one of the Library's treasures.

To Hernando de Soto we are indebted for the map of about 1544 showing his explorations. It is the earliest map to indicate geographical features—rivers, lakes, mountains, and settlements—in the interior parts of what is now the southeastern United States. Printed and photographic facsimiles of the manuscript original in the Archivo General de Indias at Seville are in the Library's map files.

To this period of discovery and exploration also belong the works of the Italian map maker, Battista Agnese, whose beautifully executed manuscript atlases on vellum are highly prized for their artistic as well as their cartographic merit. Henry R. Wagner says of the atlases, "My attention was first called to them in connection with historical and cartographical investigations of exploration on the northwest coast of America, by finding that he [Agnese] was the first cartographer in Europe now known to have depicted the discoveries of Francisco de Ulloa in 1539 and 1540." [1] Wagner describes 68 of the known Agnese atlases in considerable detail. It is thought that Ag-

nese made some 100 manuscript atlases between 1536 and 1564, 16 of which are in American institutions. The Library of Congress has a fine specimen on vellum, believed to have been drawn about 1544, since it shows Ulloa's explorations in the region of the Peninsula and Gulf of Lower California. (See the paper on one of the Agnese atlases in part one.)

Another atlas, the first devoted wholly to America, deserves special mention. Corneille Wytfliet's *Descriptionis Ptolemaicae avgmentvm* is as important to the study of New World cartography as Ptolemy's *Geographia* is to that of the Old World. This rare little volume, whose title is quite misleading, was published at Louvain in 1597. Six more editions, each containing 19 maps, appeared by 1615. Of these the Library of Congress lacks only the last.

The Library's important sixteenth-century maps illustrating the growing knowledge of America are too numerous to mention individually. Two collections, however, which relate primarily to the dawn of American cartography deserve special notice; these are the Kohl Collection and the Harrisse Collection.

The Kohl Collection comprises a series of 474 finely drawn copies of manuscript and rare printed maps in European archives, covering the period from pre-Columbian times to 1836. They were drawn by Dr. Johann Georg Kohl, a German student of American historical cartography, who came to this country in 1854, bringing with him copies he had made of many of the most important maps relating to the discovery and exploration of America. While here he was commissioned by the Congress of the United States to prepare copies of his drawings, both for the use of American scholars and as the nucleus for an elaborate catalog of the early maps of America. The maps are beautifully executed in black ink on fine white paper and vary considerably in size and in the inclusion of detail. Color is used sparingly. Each map was originally mounted on heavy gray paper of uniform size with copious notes in Kohl's fine handwriting mounted beside it. In 1963 all the maps in the Kohl Collection were removed from the deteriorating pulp paper and remounted on rag stock paper and laminated, with muslin reinforcement, between sheets of transparent acetate. The Collection was in the custody of the Department of State until July 1903, when it was transferred to the Library of Congress.

Justin Winsor, a former librarian of Harvard University, published an annotated bibliography of the Kohl Collection in 1886, as his Library's "Bibliographical Contribution No. 19." It was reprinted by the Library of Congress in 1904 with the addition of an author list and index as *The Kohl Collection (Now in the Library of Congress) of Maps Relating to America.* Many of the maps copied so painstakingly by Kohl have since become available in other forms, but Kohl's annotations have not outlived their usefulness.

The Harrisse bequest comprises 14 original manuscript maps and some 650 tracings of pertinent sections of old maps relating to the discovery and exploration of America in the fifteenth and sixteenth centuries. Many of the tracings were used by Henry Harrisse to illustrate his writings, notably his *Discovery of North America,* published in 1892. Among the original manuscripts are some of the Library's outstanding cartographic rarities, including the so-called Manatus map of 1639 by Joan Vingboons. This first topographic survey of America's most populous area covers Manhattan Island, Staten Island, a part of Long Island, and the adjacent mainland and gives the names and locations of some 45 Dutch boweries or farms. There are 11 other manuscript maps by Vingboons covering the Hudson River, Delaware Bay, Virginia, Florida, California, and the West Indies, all of value to the student.

The most historically significant map bequeathed by Harrisse is Samuel de Champlain's original manuscript of New England

*Hand-drawn facsimile by Johann Georg Kohl of the first survey of Gloucester-Harbor in Massachusetts, 1606, with his notes. Maps illustrating this article are from the Geography and Map Division.*

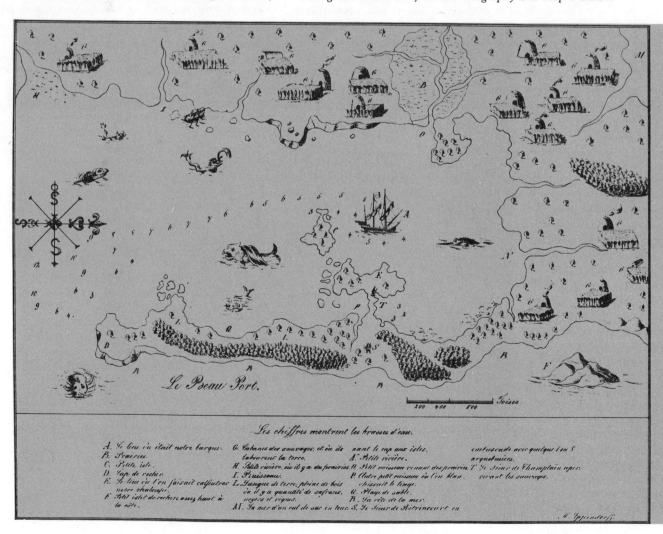

and Nova Scotia, drawn on vellum and dated 1607. It is the most important of Champlain's larger maps, giving in his own hand his explorations along these coasts in 1604, 1605, and 1606. It identifies without doubt the river he called St. Croix, a name that at the time of the establishment of our northeastern boundary was applied to no less than three rivers. The collection also contains an anonymous manuscript on vellum, entitled "Description dv pais des Hvrons, 1631," which is one of the very early surveys of the country between Georgian Bay, Lake Simcoe, and Lake Ontario, including the Saugeen Peninsula and part of Lower Ontario, evidently made to illustrate the extent of established missions.

Another of the division's special collections containing valuable material relating to the period of American discovery and Spanish exploration is the Woodbury Lowery Collection, received in 1906. In the course of writing *The Spanish Settlements Within the Present Limits of the United States,* Lowery examined and listed 740 maps, many of them original manuscripts in European archives. Some 300 of these, comprising contemporary printed maps, photocopies, or manuscript tracings, form the collection bequeathed to the Library. Some 200 additional maps had been acquired and about 180 were not available in 1912 when the Library of Congress published Lowery's catalog, edited and extensively annotated by Philip Lee Phillips (*The Lowery Collection; a Descriptive List of Maps of the Spanish Possessions Within the Present Limits of the United States, 1502–1820*). At the present time, fewer than 50 of the maps described are not represented in the Library's collections. As the catalog title indicates, the maps in the Lowery Collection relate principally to the parts of the country which had been under Spanish rule. The wealth of bio-

Gloucester harbor in Massachusetts was for the first time discovered, entered and surveyed on the 22d of Sept 1606 by Samuel Champlain, when he accompanied the Sieur de Poutrincourt on his exploring expedition along the coast of New England.

They thought it to be a very promising place and named it "Beau port" (the beautiful port) and Poutrincourt conceived the plan of making there his principal settlement They sounded in the bay and made a "plot" of it Champlain published this "plot" in his work "Les Voyages du Sieur de Champlain — Paris 1613".

Champlain's plan gives very exactly the principal features of our present Gloucester harbor The long stretched Peninsula of "East Point" is unmistakably indicated. Even in the interior of the bay our "Rocky Neck" and our "Ten Pound Island" is quite clearly drawn and likewise the site and the little peninsula, upon which at present stands our City of Gloucester. The soundings as given by Champlain are at the entrance of the harbor: 12, 10, 9 "brasses" (fathom) and shoal off in midchannel to 8, 7, 6, 5, 4, and this agrees completely with our present soundings, as given on the U S Coast Survey Charts.

bibliographical data contained in the notes, which relate to many significant maps, makes this catalog a most useful reference work to students of American historical cartography.

Many of the lacunae in the Lowery Collection were supplied through the tireless efforts of Louis C. Karpinski, who had photographs made of about 750 historically significant maps from originals in libraries and archives in France, Spain, and Portugal. These maps are distributed geographically throughout the Library's general map collection.

As permanent settlements followed explorations, more detailed maps of the Colonies began to appear. The John Smith map of Virginia is a notable example of the period. From its first printing in 1612 until 1632, it is known in 10 variant issues, of which the Library of Congress has five. The remaining five are represented in the collections by photostats. (See the article on John Smith's map of Virginia below.) John Smith's map of New England was first issued in 1616 and went through nine variant printings before 1634.

The first map printed in Colonial America was a woodcut included in William Hubbard's *Narrative of the Troubles with the Indians in New England* (Boston, John Foster, 1677). The pamphlet and the map were reprinted in London in the same year. The London issue of the map can be distinguished readily from the Boston printing by the designation "Wine Hills" for "White Hills." In a paper published in the September 1960 issue of *PAGA* (Printing and the Graphic Arts), Richard B. Holman presents the thesis that Foster may have cut

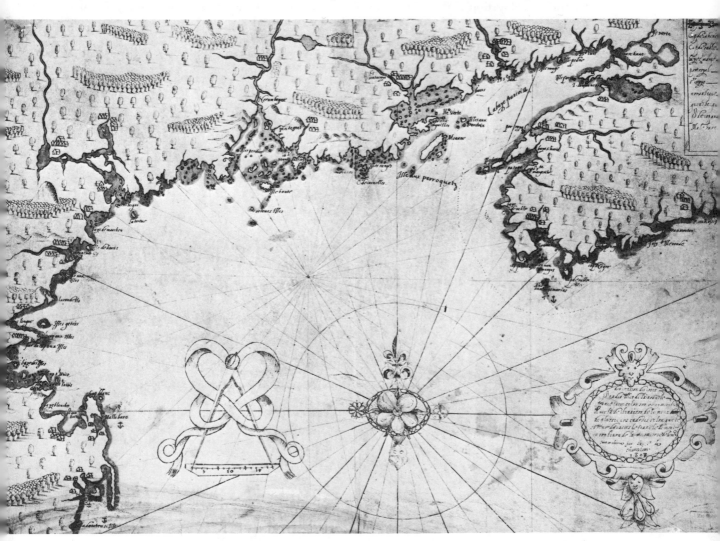

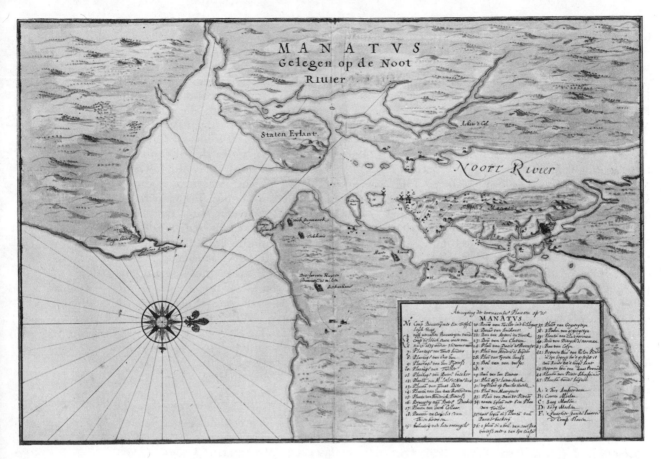

*Above, manuscript map of Manhattan by Joan Vingboons. (See page 80.)*

*Champlain's manuscript map of New England and Nova Scotia. (See page 80.)*

the blocks for both the London and Boston editions of the map. The Library of Congress has an original printing of the London issue of the map and several photostats and facsimiles of the Boston issue.

The John Smith map of Virginia served as a model for other maps until the appearance of Augustine Herrman's map of Virginia and Maryland in 1673. Herrman had offered to survey Lord Baltimore's domain in return for a manor. The resulting map was so well done that it superseded John Smith's map as a prototype until the publication of the Fry and Jefferson map of Virginia in 1751 and 1755. In 1960 the Geography and Map Division acquired an original engraved copy of the Herrman map. (See the article on it below.)

The first map of Maryland, *Nova Terrae-Maria tabula*, was included in *A Relation of Maryland*, published at London in 1635 to encourage settlement in the newly founded Colony. Although the map is anonymous, it is generally known as Lord Baltimore's, and while apparently founded on Smith's map, it is by no means a replica of it. A copy of the *Relation* containing the map is in the Library of Congress.

After the settlement of Pennsylvania, Thomas Holme, its surveyor-general, produced a *Map of the Improved Part of the Province of Pennsilvania in America,* about 1687, which showed the boundaries of some 800 tracts of land in the southeastern part of the Colony. The Geography and Map Division has an original engraved copy and photostats of several variants of this very rare large map.

The foregoing are but a few notable examples of the maps of individual Colonies, each of which was issued to satisfy a compelling need. Collectively, they serve to provide the geographical background for the early period of American history.

The Geography and Map Division has been steadily enlarging its collection of maps relating to the Colonial history of the United States. Where original printed maps are not obtainable, every effort is made to acquire reproductions of rare and unique items for reference use. The generous gifts of John D. Rockefeller, Jr., of a fund for acquiring source material for American history, and of the late James B. Wilbur in providing equipment, have made it possible for the division to obtain from the British Public Record Office and from the British Museum, photostats of hundreds of manuscript maps of the British Colonies in America. Many of these maps are on scales large enough to include detail especially useful to students of local history. The Library's marked copies of the *Catalogue of the Manuscript Maps, Charts and Plans, and of the Topographical Drawings in the British Museum,* vol. 3 (1861) and the *Catalogue of Maps, Plans, and Charts in the Library of the Colonial Office* (1910) provide keys to the maps thus acquired.

Reproductions of maps of French colonial possessions and of other maps important to American history in French archives, notably in the Bibliothèque Nationale and in the archives and library of the Service Hydrographique de la Marine, have been acquired from time to time. Many of them are listed in the *Catalogue général des manuscrits des bibliothèques publiques de France; bibliothèques de la marine,* by Charles de La Roncière (Paris, 1907), p. 143–270.

From the archives of the Dépot des Cartes et de la Marine, the Library of Congress has procured excellent hand-colored facsimiles of two very fine manuscript maps of North America, both entitled "Carte de l'Amérique septentrionale." One, believed to have been drawn about 1682, shows in great detail the territories claimed by the French, especially in the region of the Great Lakes and the Upper Mississippi. The other is Jean Baptiste Louis Franquelin's map dated 1688, which the American historian, Francis Parkman, described as the most accurate and complete map made in that period.

Similarly, photostats are being acquired of the manuscript maps in Pedro Torres Lanzas' list, *Relación descriptiva de los mapas, planos, &c. de México y Floridas, existentes en el Archivo General de Indias* (2 vols., Seville, 1900). Positive prints from microfilm copies of about 330 early manuscripts maps in Dutch archives have also been added to the Library's collections. These relate to the areas of Dutch interest in the Americas as well as in the Philippine Islands and were selected from volume 1 of the *Inventaris der verzameling Kaarten berustende in het Rijks-Archief* (The Hague, 1867).

The Library's atlases, notably those of the world and of America, contain a wealth of map material relating to the American Colonies. The indexes to the *List of Geographical Atlases in the Library of Congress* (1909–63), compiled under the direction of Philip Lee Phillips and Clara E. LeGear, provide the key to the American maps in the atlases. The rapidly growing knowledge of an area can often be traced by comparing a given map in the successive editions of an atlas. Thus, one might find the names of new settlements, streams, roads, and boundaries, or physical features more accurately located. The North American atlases in the Library's collections include those of Thomas Jefferys, William Faden, and George Louis Le Rouge.

The Spaniards and Portuguese were the principal chart makers of the early period of exploration, but the Dutch were making the majority of charts after the middle of the sixteenth century. The Library's collections contain many fine examples of Dutch charts, both in separate form and in the atlases of Waghenaer, Voogt, Goos, Loon, and many others. The British became their competitors after the middle of the seventeenth century and the French produced many creditable charts during the eighteenth century. British maritime atlases, hydrographic charts, and pilot guides, notably those of John Seller, John Thornton, William Mount, Thomas Page, and their successors, are also well represented in the Library's cartographic collections. The Service Hydrographique of France under the leadership of J. N. Bellin produced numerous excellent charts of American waters.

The *English Pilot, Fourth Book* served to guide British ships in American waters for more than 100 years. First issued in London in 1689, it appeared in at least 32 editions up to 1794; 17 of these are in the Library, ranging in date from 1706 to 1789. Successive editions were revised, and new maps were added from time to time.

The Library's *New England Coasting Pilot* by Cyprian Southack, published sometime after 1725, is one of two known copies, the other being in the British Museum. This series of eight very detailed maps of the northeastern coast from Sandy Hook to Cape Breton was based entirely upon observations Southack made while cruising the coasts between 1690 and 1712. The many descriptive notes found on the maps sandwiched in between the place names contain much useful information about these areas.[2]

Modern cartography was ushered in with the eighteenth century. British and French mapmakers, unlike their Dutch predecessors, produced simple unembellished maps based on the latest available information. Unexplored regions were no longer filled with pictures of Indians and wild animals but were left blank. By comparing De L'Isle's 1700 map of North America with Dutch maps of the same period, the trend in map making from the artistic to the utilitarian can readily be observed.

The period of the Colonial wars was another one of energetic map production. More maps of the Colonies and detailed plans of towns, harbors, and fortifications were produced than ever before by British, French, and Spanish mapmakers. Henry Popple's *Map of the British Empire in America* (1733), which is represented in the Library's files by three variants, deserves mention because of its size and rarity rather than for its importance in the sequence of American cartography. The last plate of the 20 comprising this map contains a statement that the map had been drawn with the approbation of the Lords Commissioners of Trade and Plantations and that the astronomer, Edmund Halley, had found it to have been drawn with great accuracy. In spite of its size, however, the map includes few details and was actually quite inadequate.

The need for a reliable map of the North American Colonies prompted the Lords Commissioners of Trade and Plantations to engage Dr. John Mitchell to prepare a new map. In compiling it, Mitchell had access to all available manuscript surveys and printed maps of the Colonies, and his *Map of the British and French Dominions in North America*, completed in 1755, went through more than 20 issues before 1792 in English, French, Dutch, and Italian. Because the boundaries of the United States were laid down on this map at the Treaty of Paris in 1783 it is of the utmost importance for the history of the Nation. The map had inadequacies, however, which gave rise to several boundary controversies along the northern border. The Library of Congress has copies of most of the known issues and full-scale photostats of those it lacks. (See the article on the Mitchell map below.)

The year 1755 also saw the first issue of another important map which was reprinted more than 25 times in the next half century. This was Lewis Evans' *General Map of the Middle British Colonies in America,* an expansion of his *Map of Pensilvania, New-Jersey, New-York, and the Three Delaware Counties,* published in 1749 and 1752. These maps were based largely on original surveys and the journals of Indian traders. The Library of Congress has an almost unbroken sequence of the issues of this map and several editions of the accompanying *Analysis* which was printed at Philadelphia by Benjamin Franklin.

To the pre-Revolutionary period belongs a rare little atlas entitled *Set of Plans and Forts in America* (1763). It contains 30 maps by Jean Rocque, geographer to the King of England at the time of his death in 1762. The volume also includes several important plans of fortifications, notably one of New York, based on the 1755 survey of Francis Maerschalck. The Library has two variant issues.

Among the Library's rare and important maps of the period may be enumerated Moses Park's map of Connecticut (1766), John Henry's map of Virginia (1770), and Captain John Collet's map of North Carolina (1770). Its copy of Bernard Romans' large map of Florida (1774) is the only one known to have survived. Romans mentioned on the title page of his *Concise Natural History of East and West Florida* (New York, 1775) that the work was accompanied by "Two whole sheet maps," but their existence was doubted for many years by the foremost bibliographers of Americana. Drawn on a scale of 1 inch to about $7\frac{1}{2}$ miles, the sheets measure respectively $24\frac{1}{2}$ by 87 and 58 by $66\frac{1}{2}$ inches. Philip Lee Phillips described the map in his *Notes on the Life and Works of Bernard Romans* (*Publications* of the Florida State Historical Society, no. 2, 1924).

Not so rare, but historically as important, are Blanchard and Langdon's map of New Hampshire (1761), Faden's map of New Jersey (1771), Claude J. Sauthier's map of New York (1776), Nicolas Scull's map of Pennsylvania (1759), and that of his son

William (1770), Thomas Hutchins' map of the western parts of Virginia (1778), Henry Mouzon's map of North and South Carolina and Georgia (1775), and Lieutenant Ross' survey of the Mississippi River from St. Louis to the Gulf of Mexico (1765), all of which are represented in the Library's collections by fine printed copies.

The Library's Faden Collection was brought together by the well-known British map publisher, William Faden, geographer to the King of England during the American Revolution, and by his predecessor, Thomas Jefferys. It was purchased by a Reverend Mr. Converse of New Haven at the sale of Faden's estate in 1836 and later acquired by Nathan Hale, from whose son, Edward Everett Hale, the Library of Congress obtained it in 1864. This collection comprises 101 items, more than half in manuscript. The maps illustrate various phases of the French and Indian Wars, as well as the American Revolution, and specifically the activities of Braddock, Burgoyne, Sir William Howe, Clinton, and Cornwallis. Some of the Library's most beautiful specimens of hand-drawn maps and some unique items are to be found in this collection. In 1862 Edward Everett Hale compiled a list of the maps entitled *Catalogue of a Curious and Valuable Collection of Original Maps and Plans of Military Positions Held in the Old French and Revolutionary Wars.*

The Geography and Map Division is remarkably rich in maps relating to the American Revolution. Besides the Faden Collection it possesses two other manuscript collections, several manuscript atlases, and upward of 2,000 separate manuscript maps to supplement those in the special collections. To facilitate the study of the manuscript maps, a great many photostats of significant original maps in other institutions have also been acquired.

The Rochambeau Collection was purchased by the U.S. Government in 1883 from the Marquis de Rochambeau. Its 67 maps and one manuscript atlas, which had belonged to the Comte de Rochambeau, Commander-in-Chief of the French Army in America, include some rare cartographic treasures. The manuscript atlas illustrates the exact locations of the Army's 54 encampments on its march from Yorktown to Boston, July 1 to December 2, 1782, after the surrender at Yorktown. Thirty-eight of the

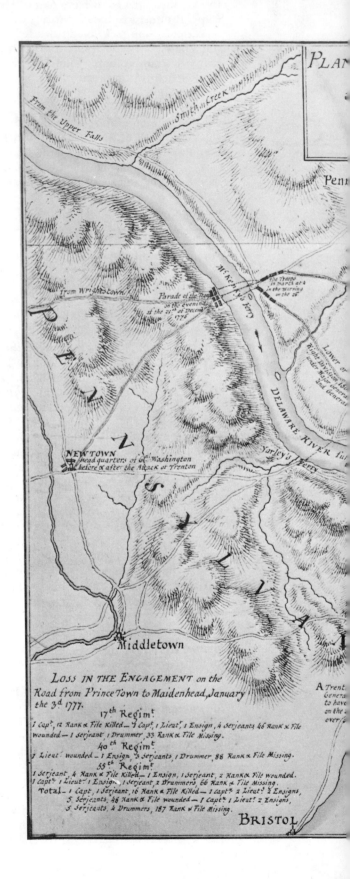

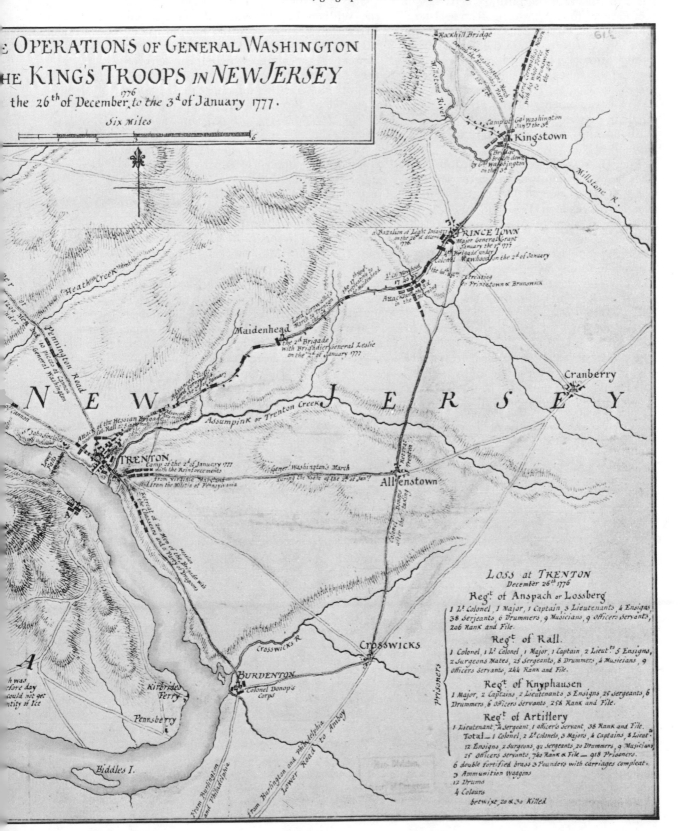

Hand-drawn map from the Faden Collection, assembled by William Faden, geographer to the King of England during the American Revolution.

87

maps are carefully drawn by French engineers to illustrate the military activities of the French forces between Rhode Island and Virginia. To supplement this collection the Library acquired from the Rochambeau family photographs of 34 maps from the Journal of the Vicomte de Rochambeau, son of the Comte. These represent the successive encampments of the French troops on their march from Providence, R. I., to Williamsburg, Va., between June 10 and September 26, 1781.

The Howe Collection was acquired in 1905 from the family of Admiral Richard Lord Howe, Commander of the British fleet in America in 1776 and 1777. It includes 72 manuscript maps of various parts of the American coast, the West Indies, and the Philippine Islands. Seven of the maps bear evidence of having been used by Lord Howe in his naval operations during the American Revolution in the New York and Philadelphia areas.

The activities of the British Army in New Jersey under Sir Henry Clinton between 1775 and 1782 are shown in a finely drawn set of 20 manuscript maps entitled "A Collection of Plans, etc., in the Province of New Jersey, by John Hills, Assistant

Engineer." Photostats of the 307 manuscript maps in the Clinton Collection of the William L. Clements Library at Ann Arbor, Mich., were acquired for the use of students in American Revolutionary War history. These maps, which form part of the headquarters papers of Sir Henry Clinton, are described in an annotated catalog prepared by Randolph G. Adams entitled *British Headquarters Maps and Sketches* (Ann Arbor, 1928).

Similarly, photostats of 10 manuscript maps bearing upon the American Revolution were acquired from the Scavenius Collection in the Dartmouth College Library. These show troop movements and fortifications between 1777 and 1782 at New London, Conn., Elizabeth, N. J., the Head of the Elk River, Md., Philadelphia, Yorktown, Va., and Charleston, S. C.

The *Atlantic Neptune,* published for the use of the Royal Navy of Great Britain under the direction of Joseph Frederick Wallet Des Barres (1774–84), is the outstanding collection of hydrographic charts covering the American Revolutionary War period. The charts constitute some of the earliest detailed surveys of our coastal areas and harbors and are highly prized for their

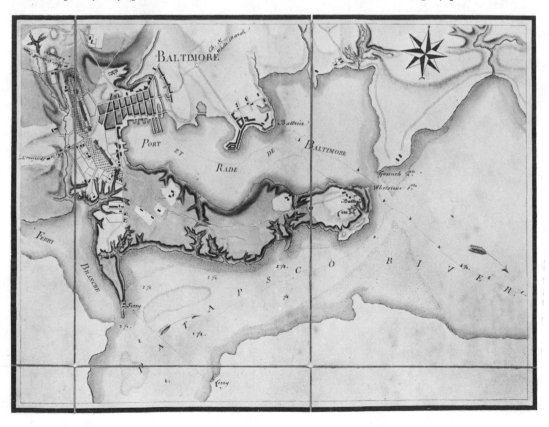

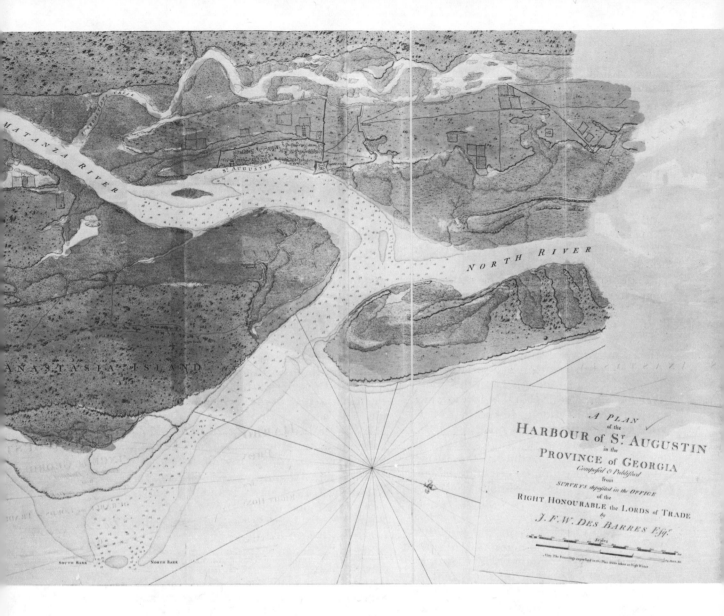

A PLAN
of the
HARBOUR of St AUGUSTIN
in the
PROVINCE of GEORGIA
Composed & Published
from
SURVEYS deposited in the OFFICE
of the
RIGHT HONOURABLE the LORDS of TRADE
by
J.F.W. DES BARRES Esqr.

*Above, harbor chart from the* Atlantic Neptune.

*Facing, 1781 map of Baltimore, No. 13 in the Rochambeau Collection.*

historical importance, as well as their attractive execution. Of the surviving volumes, no two contain identical series of charts. This may be explained by the fact that sets were assembled from the complete series of 250 charts and views as they were needed by British warships. The charts and views cover the eastern coast of North America from Cape Breton to the West Indies, including the Gulf of Mexico. Many of the charts, drawn on a fairly large scale, show topographic detail. This is especially true of the harbor charts, a number of which appeared in several variant issues. The Library has 19 sets of the *Atlantic Nep-*

*tune* in one, two, or three volumes, containing a total of 1,369 plates issued between 1774 and 1781.

All of the foregoing Revolutionary War maps were made either for British or French officers. In order to round out its collections, the Geography and Map Division has also acquired photostats of the American Army maps in the Erskine-DeWitt Collection at the New-York Historical Society. Robert Erskine was commissioned by General Washington as geographer and surveyor to make maps for the Army. Upon Erskine's death in 1780, Simeon DeWitt continued the task. The collection, which comprises more than 100 maps, covers parts of Connecticut, New York, New Jersey, Pennsylvania, Maryland, and Virginia. Roads, streams, and names of residents are given on many of the maps. Few have been reproduced although Christopher Colles copied relevant maps in compiling his *Survey of the Roads of the United States of America* (1789), two copies of which are in the Library's atlas collection. A facsimile edition, edited by Walter W. Ristow, was published by Harvard University Press in 1961. The Erskine-DeWitt Collection is noted in the *Proceedings of the New-York Historical Society for the Year 1845,* pp. 21, 38, and 55, and there is a partial list of its contents in *Noteworthy Maps No. 2, Accessions, 1926–27,* issued by the Library of Congress in 1929.

Photostats of a number of manuscript maps in the Jared Sparks Collection at the Cornell University Library are also in the Library's collections. They include plans of fortifications and encampments of the American Army during the Revolution. Many of them are closely associated with George Washington; in fact, the rough sketch of Fort Cumberland, Md., was drawn by Washington, and he is known to have used or annotated several others.

In consequence of the studies carried on in the Map Division during the George Washington Bicentennial celebration, some 164 maps drawn by Washington or annotated or used by him were brought together and listed in *The George Washington Atlas,* edited by Lawrence Martin and published by The George Washington Bicentennial Commission (Washington, 1932). These include the survey plats he made of lands belonging to Lord Fairfax in the Northern Neck of Virginia beyond the Blue Ridge. The division previously had nine original manuscript maps drawn by Washington, including those of his Mount Vernon lands and tracts along the Great Kanawha River in present West Virginia, and photostats of a few survey plats.

In the post-Revolutionary period, fairly detailed maps of most of the newly formed States were published, each of which marks a milestone in American cartographic development. They are represented in the Library's collection by Osgood Carleton's map of Maine and Massachusetts (ca. 1798), Samuel Holland's map of New Hampshire (1784), James Whitelaw's map of Vermont (1796), Reading Howell's map of Pennsylvania (1792), Dennis Griffith's map of Maryland (1794), John Churchman's map of Delaware and the Chesapeake Bay (1788), Manasseh Cutler's map of Ohio (1787), John Filson's map of Kentucky (1784), and many more.

Thomas Jefferson was the anonymous author of *A Map of the Country between Albemarle Sound and Lake Erie,* which accompanied his *Notes on the State of Virginia* (Paris and London, 1787). The map is a composite of Lewis Evans' map of the middle British Colonies (1755), Thomas Hutchins' map of the western parts of Virginia (1778), and the Fry and Jefferson map of Virginia (1775). The Geography and Map Division has two variant issues of this remarkable map.

In 1796 Abraham Bradley, geographer to the Post Office Department, published a quasi-official map of the United States showing post offices, post roads, and ports of entry. Several editions of it in the Library's collection bear witness to the rapid development of our early transportation system.

The original manuscript plan of the Capital of the United States is one of the division's rarest documents. Drawn by Major Pierre Charles L'Enfant in 1791 and quite brown with age, it still gives a clear view of the noble design that has made Washington one of the world's most beautiful cities. The L'Enfant plan was engraved both by Samuel Hill in Boston and Thackara and Vallance in Philadelphia. The latter engraving became the "official" plan of Washington. (See the articles below entitled "The Federal City Depicted, 1612–1801," and "The Federal City in 1793.")

Andrew Ellicott's manuscript survey of the boundaries of the District of Columbia's ten-mile square, completed in 1792, is another outstanding historical item. Besides indicating streams and general topographical features, it marks the exact location of each of the boundary stones.

## NOTES

[1] Henry R. Wagner, "The Manuscript Atlases of Battista Agnese," *Bibliographical Society of America, Papers,* 25:1 (1931).

[2] See "The New England Coasting Pilot of Cyprian Southack," by Clara E. LeGear, in *Imago mundi,* no. 11, 1954:137–144.

# Captain John Smith's Map of Virginia

## BY WALTER W. RISTOW

Originally published in 1957 as a leaflet accompanying a Library of Congress facsimile of John Smith's Map of Virginia.

AMONG THE SIGNIFICANT historical records of colonial America is Captain John Smith's Map of Virginia, first published in 1612.[1] Coolie Verner refers to it as "the most important map to appear in print during the period of early settlement and the one map of Virginia that has had the greatest influence upon map making for a longer period of time."[2] More than half a century ago Philip Lee Phillips concluded that "of all the Virginia maps the most interesting is that made by Captain John Smith under the most trying conditions owing to the enmity of the savage tribes. If we knew nothing of the famous Captain but what is conveyed to us in his map of Virginia it would alone entitle him to rank pre-eminently among great explorers and cartographers."[3] Worthington C. Ford described Smith's map as "an elaborate and detailed production of the highest historical importance and worthy to stand as a fine example of map making for that time."[4]

The surveys and explorations that are incorporated in the John Smith map constitute a vital and exciting phase of the Jamestown story. On May 14, 1607, a small band of adventurous men stepped off three small sailing vessels to establish on this "fruitful and delightsome land" the first permanent English settlement in North America. The names of few of that illustrious band are today remembered. Signifi-

*Portrait of John Smith from the map of New England in his* A Description of New-England, *published in 1616. The Library's copy of this tract is wanting the original map, which has been replaced by C. A. Swett's facsimile of the 1635 issue of the map. From the Rare Book Division.*

cantly, the one among them who was to achieve lasting fame and renown was under arrest on that memorable day and so in disfavor with the other leaders of the party that he was denied his rightful rank and position as a member of the governing Council.

Captain John Smith, happily, was not one to be lightly cast aside or disregarded, either by his fellow men or by history. Although only 27 years old when he arrived in Virginia, Smith was already a well-traveled adventurer and a seasoned soldier-of-fortune. His previous experience, coupled with his resourcefulness, strength, and courage, proved invaluable to the struggling colony in the difficult, bitter days following settlement. It was not long, therefore, before Smith was cleared of charges and admitted to the Council. In September 1608 he was elected Council President, a position he held until his return to London in the fall of 1609.

Not the least of Captain Smith's contributions to the survival of the colony, during its first two trying years, were his journeys to the Indian villages to barter for food. On one such expedition, in December 1607, several of his companions were killed and Smith himself was taken prisoner by unfriendly savages. His captors led him from one Indian village to another before finally delivering him to the great Chief Powhatan at Werowocomoco. It was here that, according to Captain Smith's later account, his life was saved by the timely intervention of Pocahontas, favorite daughter of Powhatan. This dramatic and romantic rescue, whether fact or fiction, won Smith a secure place among America's colonial heroes.

His more tangible and lasting contributions to our history have, unfortunately, been less well publicized. We are indebted to Captain Smith for some of the most vivid and detailed descriptions of the Virginia Colony. He was a zealous explorer and a keen observer of everything he saw on his various travels and expeditions. Moreover, he recorded these observations and experiences in letters and reports and in books and pamphlets written and published after his return to England. Of even greater value in picturing for us the Virginia of his day is the detailed and remarkably accurate map of Virginia, one of our treasured heritages.

The London Company, sponsor of the

*Sixth state of the John Smith map of Virginia, in the Geography and Map Division. The Rare Book Division has a copy of the fourth state, accompanying the 1612 tract* A Map of Virginia.

Jamestown Colony, was interested in settling and developing Virginia primarily as a commercial venture. To entice additional settlers to the New World and to determine the nature and character of the land and its resources, instructions to the colonists stressed the importance of explora-

of the ships which bore the settlers across the sea, set out with a party of 24 to explore the upper reaches of the James River. That first exploratory party, which included Captain John Smith, went up the river to about the site of Richmond before returning to Jamestown on May 27. Newport set sail for England on June 22, 1607, with the *Sarah Constant* and the *Godspeed,* promising to return within 20 months with more supplies and additional settlers. During the succeeding fall and winter Smith made a number of journeys up the several stream channels in search of food and provisions for the hungry colonists.

On June 2, 1608, Captain Smith, with a small party, set out in a barge to explore Chesapeake Bay and the Potomac River. The explorations continued over three months and extended some 30 miles up the Potomac to beyond Potopaco (present Port Tobacco), and up the Toppahanock (Rappahannock) as far as the present site of Fredericksburg. In the course of the surveys of Chesapeake Bay and the drowned streams which empty into it, Captain Smith and his men traveled more than 3,000 miles. The party returned to Jamestown on September 7, 1608, after which Smith busied himself in preparing a report in accordance with the further injunction of the London Company that "you shall do well to send a perfect relation by Capitaine Newport of all that is done, what height you are seated, how far into the land, what commodities you find, what soils, woods and their several kinds, and so of all other things else to advertise particularly." [6]

Smith's report and a draft map incorporating the findings of his several surveys were duly dispatched to England by Captain Newport. In an accompanying letter Smith informed the company officials that "I have sent you this mappe of the Bay and Rivers with an annexed Relation of the Counties and Nations that inhabit them as you may see at large." The original manuscript map unfortunately has not survived, but it is believed to have been used to prepare the copper plate from which was printed the map of Virginia which bears Smith's name.

The Smith map, engraved by William Hole, was published at Oxford in 1612. In the same year Joseph Barnes printed at Oxford a tract entitled *A Map of Virginia; With a Description of the Countrey, the*

tory surveys. The hope of finding a water passage to the Orient was also very much in their thoughts. "You must observe if you can," the settlers were directed, "whether the river on which you plant doth spring out of mountains or out of lakes. If it be out of any lake, the passage to the other sea will be more easy." [5]

In compliance with this directive, within one week after the landing at Jamestown, Captain Christopher Newport, commander

*Commodities, People, Government and Religion; Written by Captaine Smith, sometimes Governour of the Countrey, etc.* Later editions included a copy of the map. The tract was republished in 1624 in Smith's *The Generall Historie of Virginia, New-England, and the Summer Isles,* and in the 1625 edition of *Purchas his Pilgrimes,* volume 4.

A number of additions and modifications were made on the engraved plate during the next 20 years for successive printings of the map. Based on these variations, scholars recognize 10 different issues or states of the Smith map. They are identified in works by Eames [7] and Verner.[2]

Most scholars agree that Smith probably did not actually draw the map, as there is no evidence that he had skill as a draftsman. However, he undoubtedly provided the draftsman with all essential data and information based on his surveys and travels and his conversations with the natives. While the map was in preparation, Smith probably personally directed and instructed the draftsman, who some believe was Nathaniel Powell.

At first glance Smith's map bears little resemblance to one of present-day Virginia. This is partly because it is oriented with north to the right rather than at the top of the sheet. If the map is turned 90 degrees to the left, however, some of the familiar landmarks of tidewater Virginia can readily be recognized. Extending almost across the width of the sheet is Chesapeack Bay. Feeding into it from the west are the rivers Powhatan (James), Chickahomania, Patawomeck (Potomac), Patuxent, and Sasqusahanough (Susquehanna). At the mouth of the bay Cape Henry and Cape Charles may be located. Poynte Comfort at the entrance to the Powhatan is today known as Old Point Comfort. Some other names which can be identified on modern maps include Smyths Iles (Smith Island), Stingra Ile (Stingray Point), Nandsamund (Nansemond River), Appamatuck (Appomattox), Potopaco (Port Tobacco), and, of course, Jamestowne.

Many of the names (of which there are about 200) on Smith's map locate Indian villages and settlements, with the result that this is one of the best sources for Indian names and localities for pre-English Virginia. Names such as Gosnolds Baye, Sharpes Ile, Fetherstones Baye, Wiffins

Poynte, and Russells Ile honor members of Smith's survey parties or leaders of the Jamestown Colony. The origin of some English names is uncertain, as they are not noted in any of Smith's writings.

Smith's map includes the coastal region between the North Carolina-Virginia border and the head of Chesapeake Bay. The Atlantic side of the Delmarva Peninsula (at the bottom of the map) is not clearly delimited. Inland the map extends for approximately 150 miles to include headwaters of the coastal plain streams. The western reaches, however, are vague and based largely on information Smith received from the Indians. In the tract published with the map Smith notes: "in which mappe observe this, that as far as you see the little Crosses on rivers, mountains, or other places, have been discovered, the rest was had by information from the Savages, and are set downe according to their instructions."

When we consider the difficulties under which the surveys were made, the relatively brief periods the parties were in the field, and the almost complete lack of scientific instruments, the accuracy of Smith's map is truly amazing. For example, it shows Cape Henry, located on modern charts at latitude 36°56′, as 37°02′. Determining correct longitude was especially difficult in Smith's day, for the chronometer did not come into use for another hundred years. Even so the longitude error for Cape Henry is less than eight minutes. Longitude (marked on the right and left borders) is reckoned east of Ferro in the Canary Islands. Cape Henry is thus shown at about 309°30′ east longitude.

Characteristic of seventeenth-century cartography, the Smith map is adorned with illustrations, sketches, scrolls, and ornamental lettering. In the upper left corner is pictured the interior of Powhatan's lodge, where the Indian Chief "held this state and fashion when Capt. Smith was delivered to him prisoner." The portrait at the upper right is of the most impressive of the Sasquesahanocks, whom Smith described as "great and well proportioned men . . . for they seem like Giants to the English . . . yet seemed of an honest and simple disposition. . . . The picture of the greatest of them is signified in the Mappe. The Calfe of whose leg was 3 quarters of a yard about, and all the rest of his limbs so answerable to that proportion, that he seemed the goodliest man that ever we beheld."

The royal coat of arms decorates the top central part of the map, immediately below the title scroll. Near the lower right corner is Captain Smith's own coat of arms, which was granted him by the Duke of Transylvania. The three heads on the shield are of Turks "which with his sword before the town of Regall, he did overcome, kill, and cut off, in the Province of Transylvania in 1602." The scroll below the shield carries the Latin motto *Vincere est Vivere* (to conquer is to live). Smith's coat of arms is not found on the first or second states of the map, and the third includes the arms without the motto. The fourth and subsequent states include both arms and motto.

The sea monster and sailing vessel in "The Virginia Sea" are typical of early seventeenth-century map ornamentation. The ship is not identified as one of the three which carried the first settlers to Jamestown, but it undoubtedly resembles them. The scale, in leagues, is given in the decorative cartouche in the lower center of the map. Note that the fleur-de-lis on the 32-point compass rose points to the right, which is north on the Smith map. Below the scale is the inscription "Discovered and Described by Captayn John Smith 1606." The significance of the date, which does not appear on the first state of the map, has never been satisfactorily explained. As noted above, Smith's draft map was sent to England in November 1608 and the printed map was first issued in 1612.

Although several earlier maps of Virginia had been published, Smith's map has been described by Ford as "the most authoritative survey of the country yet furnished and had no real predecessor." It continued to be so regarded for a number of years and was reproduced in many of the magnificent atlases (for example, those of Blaeu, Mercator, and Jansson) published in the Netherlands during the seventeenth century. Smith's Virginia "greatly influenced every map of the area made after its publication," according to Verner, "and the names of the places given on it have in many instances survived to the present."

John Smith never returned to Virginia after 1609, but in 1614 he spent about five months exploring and mapping the coast of New England. The results of this expedition he incorporated in a book, *A Description of New-England,* which described the natural resources of the lands between Cape Cod and the Penobscot River in Maine. Published in 1616, the tract included an outline map of the coast and islands between these two points. This map became the standard chart of the northern coast of English America. It helped attract the Pilgrims to that area and was instrumental in guiding them to "Plimouth," which first appears on Smith's chart. The style, ornamentation, and lettering are similar on the Virginia and New England maps.

The two maps of colonial America with which Captain John Smith's name is indelibly linked are irrefutable evidence of his contributions in exploration, observation, and cartographic recording. The map of Virginia, in particular, is unique in portraying for us the geographical landscape of pre-English America.[8]

### NOTES

[1] The Library of Congress has published a full-sized facsimile reproduction of John Smith's map of Virginia. Identified as "Library of Congress Facsimile No. 1," it may be ordered at $1.75 per copy from Library of Congress, Information Office, Navy Yard Annex, Building 159, Washington, D.C. 20540.

[2] Coolie Verner, "The First Maps of Virginia, 1590–1673," *Virginia Magazine of History and Biography,* 58:3–15 (Jan. 1950).

[3] P. Lee Phillips, "Some Early Maps of Virginia and the Makers, Including Plates Relating to the First Settlement in Jamestown," *Virginia Magazine of History and Biography,* 15:71–81 (July 1907).

[4] Worthington C. Ford, "Captain John Smith's Map of Virginia, 1612," *Geographical Review,* 14:433–443 (July 1924).

[5] Instructions of the London Company, in *Captain John Smith's Works,* edited by Edward Arber, vol. 1 (Birmingham, 1884), p. xxv. (English Scholar's Library, No. 16.)

[6] Ibid., xxxvii.

[7] Wilberforce Eames, description of John Smith's maps of Virginia, in *Bibliotheca Americana,* edited by Joseph Sabin and others, vol. 20 (New York, 1928), p. 227–231.

[8] Other references to the Smith map of Virginia include the following:

Fairfax Harrison, *Landmarks of Old Prince William,* vol. 2 (Richmond, 1924), p. 601–652.

R. R. Lukens, "Captain John Smith's Map," *Military Engineer,* 23:435–438 (September–October 1931).

Justin Winsor, *Narrative and Critical History of America,* vol. 3 (Boston, 1884), p. 211–212.

# Augustine Herrman's
# Map of Virginia and Maryland

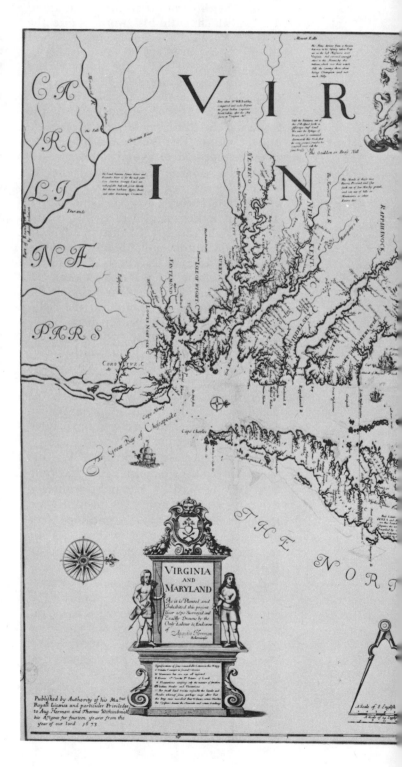

N O MATTER HOW RICH and comprehensive may be its collections, it is a rare library which does not lack significant historical documents. Decades and even generations may sometimes pass before certain elusive items are acquired. High on the desiderata list of the Map Division, since its establishment in 1897, was Augustine Herrman's rare map of Virginia and Maryland, published in 1673. Less than a century ago the Herrman map was virtually unknown in this country, even among scholars, and not until 1929 was an original copy acquired by an American library.

Proudly reporting its accession by the John Carter Brown library in that year, Lawrence C. Wroth described the Herrman map as "of such rarity as to be almost the subject of legend."[1] He further observed that "with the notable exception of the fundamental John Smith Map of Virginia of 1612, it is the most distinguished map of the early colonial period of English America."

Such a noteworthy historic document, obviously, should be in the collections of the Library of Congress. It was with a real sense of satisfaction and gratitude, therefore, that the acquisition of this outstanding cartographic and historic treasure was reported in 1960.

Herrman's map, which bears the lengthy title "Virginia and Maryland As It Is Planted and Inhabited This Present Year 1670 Surveyed and Exactly Drawne by the Only Labour & Endeavour of Augustin Herrman Bohemiensis," covers the Atlantic coast from Barnegat, on the Jersey shore, southward beyond Cape Henry in Virginia. Parts of Carolina, New Jersey, and Pennsylvania as well as Virginia, Maryland, and the present State of Delaware are included.

The long-sought map was acquired through the generosity of Arthur A. Houghton, Jr., of New York City, long a friend and benefactor of the Library of Congress, and with the much appreciated

# BY WALTER W. RISTOW

Reprinted from the August 1960 issue of the *Library of Congress Quarterly Journal of Current Acquisitions.*

*From the Geography and Map Division.*

cooperation of the Bibliothèque Nationale in Paris. When members of the Map Division staff learned that France's national library possessed two copies of the Herrman map, a letter promptly went off to its Curator of Maps and Charts inquiring whether an exchange or purchase might be negotiated for one copy. The reply was disappointing: Both copies were in special collections which could not be violated.

Hope was revived several months later when the Bibliothèque Nationale reported finding in its collections a third copy of the Virginia and Maryland map. Officials of that institution would, moreover, consider making this copy available to the Library of Congress on an exchange basis. Agreement was reached whereby the Library of Congress would purchase from a French dealer, at a specified price, a map desired by the Bibliothèque Nationale, a fifteenth-century manuscript chart of the Mediterranean region. This the French library would accept in exchange for the Herrman map.

But a new roadblock was now encountered. All the Library's purchase funds for the year were already allocated. Would plans for acquiring the rare historic map have to be abandoned? Fortunately, the Library was able to turn to its friend Mr. Houghton, who readily offered to provide the funds for completing the transaction with the Bibliothèque Nationale. Thus one of the truly noteworthy maps of colonial America is in the Library of Congress, where it is available for examination and study by the Nation's scholars.

Augustine Herrman, author of the map, was one of the most lusty and colorful personalities of seventeenth-century America. In addition to surveying and mapping, he was occupied at various times in industry, engineering, fur-trading, privateering, land speculation, commercial enterprises, slave-trading, public administration, diplomacy, law, finance, and farming.

Concerning Herrman's early years in his

native Europe, we have only meager information. He was born in Prague, Bohemia, probably in 1605, of well-situated parents. Seemingly he had his early education in Prague, where he studied geology, surveying, languages, and classical literature. The elder Herrman was a follower of the pioneer Protestant reformer Jan Hus, and with the return to power of the anti-Hussite forces the Herrman family fled Bohemia, about 1618. They went first to Germany, then settled in Amsterdam, where Augustine probably continued his studies.

Some accounts indicate that young Herrman spent several years in the army, serving under the Protestant hero Gustavus Adolphus around 1628. If this is true, he may have acquired engineering and surveying experience while in military service.

By the third decade of the century Amsterdam had become a leading center of commerce and trade. Almost every day ships entered the port with cargo from remote and fascinating parts of the world. The large trading companies sought bright young men to serve as their foreign agents, and Herrman was among those engaged by the Dutch West India Company.

When the young adventurer first went to America we do not know. There is record of his presence at the site of Philadelphia in 1633, when those lands were purchased from the Indians. During the next 10 or 12 years Herrman undoubtedly carried on trading activities in various parts of the West Indies and the North American colonies. In later years, he was to boast of having been the "beginner of the tobacco trade in Virginia."

By 1644, perhaps earlier, Herrman was an agent in New Amsterdam for the Dutch trading firm of Peter Gabry and Sons. Shortly thereafter he established his own trading company and also engaged in farming, fur-trading, and land speculation. By the middle 1650's he was one of the leading merchants and citizens of New Amsterdam, and a close, though not always friendly, associate of Governor Peter Stuyvesant. The latter found it expedient to utilize Herrman's talents and experience on several missions involving relations and differences with neighboring colonies. One such assignment resulted in the Virginia and Maryland map.

In 1655 the Dutch in America extended their possessions to the south by taking over the Swedish settlement on Delaware Bay. This accession of territory, however, opened up new problems, for it placed the Dutch in contact with the British lands of Lord Baltimore. Because of the vague and uncertain limits of the original grants it was inevitable that jurisdictional differences would develop.

Governor Josiah Fendall of Maryland, noting the increasing Dutch colonization on the Delaware, dispatched a military expedition in 1659 to inform the settlers that they were encroaching upon British territory. This in turn incensed the Dutch Governor Peter Stuyvesant, who appointed Augustine Herrman and Resolved Waldron as special ambassadors to discuss the matter with the Maryland Governor. Herrman ably presented the Dutch claims, but no definite agreement was reached regarding the disputed territory. The report on the conference was carried back by Waldron, while Herrman repaired to Virginia to spend the winter with relatives and to negotiate trade treaties between that colony and New Amsterdam.

Herrman's travels through Maryland for the meeting with Governor Fendall and his experiences at the conference impressed upon him the need for a good map of the region. Consequently, in October 1659, he wrote to Governor Stuyvesant: "But first of all, the South River (Delaware) and the Virginias, with the lands and kills between both, ought to be laid down on an exact scale as to longitude and latitude, in a perfect map, that the extent of country on both sides may be correctly seen, and the work afterwards proceeded with, for some maps which the English have here are utterly imperfect and prejudicial to us. The sooner this is done the better, before Baltamoor whispers in the ears of the States of England, and thus make the matter much more difficult." [2]

Herrman obviously enjoyed his winter in Virginia and Maryland and decided to settle permanently in this region. Whether or not Stuyvesant's lack of interest in the proposal to make a map had any influence on his decision we do not know. Among other factors, he may have foreseen the end of Dutch rule in New Amsterdam and decided to cast his lot with the British. Undoubtedly, too, he was impressed with the beauty of Maryland and its great expanses of unsettled land and fancied the more gracious social life in the southern colonies.

Whatever his reasons, sometime late in 1659 Herrman made an application to become a "denizen" of the territory of Maryland, in order to be able to hold property. On January 14, 1660, the denizenation order was signed by Lord Baltimore. Herrman had already approached the Maryland proprietary with reference to mapping the territory and apparently had even shown him a preliminary manuscript map. Inasmuch as Herrman, the order read, "for our satisfaction and the bennefitt of Trade hath drawne a Mapp of all the Rivers Creekes and Harbours thereunto belonging KNOW YEE that wee willing to give due encouragement to men of his profession . . . hereby Declare him the said Augustine Herman to be a free Denizen of this our Province of Maryland." [3]

In August 1661 Herrman received from Lord Baltimore the first of several extensive grants of land, which subsequently totaled between 20 and 25 thousand acres. Bohemia Manor, where he established his manorial residence, was named after his native land and included some 6,000 acres, located on both sides of the Elk River in what is now Cecil County. It was first surveyed in August 1661 and was granted to Herrman by patent of June 19, 1662, "for making the Mapp of this province." [4]

Some time in 1661 or 1662 Herrman transferred his family and servants from New Amsterdam to Bohemia Manor. He and his wife, the former Janneken Verlett of New Amsterdam, whom he married in 1651, had two sons and three daughters. Janneken apparently died shortly after the family moved to Maryland, for only the names of Herrman and his five children appear on the "Acte of Naturalization" papers which were submitted in 1663. [5]

Herrman conducted surveys for more than a decade, from 1659 to 1670. Preliminary surveys were made during his ambassadorial journey in 1659, and during that winter he undoubtedly did some mapping in Virginia. The map shows the greatest detail along the borders of Chesapeake Bay, and Herrman probably personally explored and surveyed this area. In addition to his own explorations, he undoubtedly consulted various printed and manuscript maps, including the one published by Captain John Smith in 1612.

The decade between 1660 and 1670 was a busy one for Herrman, and surveying often had to be halted for other pressing tasks. A manor house and other buildings had to be constructed, land cleared, and new settlers located. For several years Herrman still maintained interests and property in New Amsterdam, and he also carried on some trading activities there as well as in Maryland. The death of his wife and his remarriage in 1666 also delayed completion of the map. Moreover, he was not long resident in his new home before he was heavily involved in administrative and magisterial responsibilities.

Consequently, it was not until 1670 that the surveys were completed, and during the next several years Herrman was occupied in plotting, drafting, and ornamenting the map. The finished manuscript was sent to London, where it was engraved in 1673 by William Faithorne. It is suggested by some authorities that the engraver may have been recommended by Herrman's fellow Bohemian and probable boyhood companion, the artist Wenceslaus Hollar. The latter, it is noted, had some years earlier resided in the same London house as Faithorne. Herrman was not pleased with the engraved map; he is said to have remarked that it "was slobbered over by the engraver Faithorne defiling the prints by many errors."

Although no publisher's name appears on the map, it was published and sold by John Seller, well-known London map printer of the period. A notice in the *London Gazette* for 1674 (no. 873) states that "there is now Extant a new Map of Virginia and Maryland in four Sheets, describing the Countries, and the scituation of the Plantations in the said Countreys, with the Rivers, Creeks, Bayes, Roads and Harbors on the Sea-Coasts. Published by His Majesties especial Licence, and are sold by John Seller, Hydrographer to the King." [6] On the John Carter Brown Library copy of the Hertman map (the only other known copy in this country) there is a pasted slip which bears the imprint: "Sold by John Seller, Hydrographer to the King at his shop in Exchange ally in Cornhill, London."

The Virginia and Maryland map is on four sheets which, if joined, measure 31 by 37¼ inches. The two top sheets are 15⅜ by 18⅝ inches, and the bottom ones 15⅝ by 18⅝ inches. The Herrman map, like that prepared by John Smith in 1612, is oriented with west at the top. Chesapeake Bay, with its numerous embayments and tributary streams, occupies the central portion. Settlements, plantations, and Indian villages are named along the shores, and soundings are given for many of the bays and harbors. On the northwestern (top right) sheet, hills and mountains are indicated by pictorial hill symbols and hachuring.

Notwithstanding Herrman's personal disappointment with Faithorne's craftsmanship, the map is an outstanding example of seventeenth-century drafting and engraving. The lengthy title and inscription are set in an ornate plate on the lower left sheet. The bottom of this plate is a pedestal, flanked on either side by an acanthus and faced with the legend or list of symbols used on the map. Standing on the pedestal, with the title inscription between them, are the figures of an Indian boy and girl. An ornamental shield, surmounted by a Neptune head and trailing clusters of leaves and fruit, decorates the top of the plate.

Other embellishments include the British royal arms, the shield of Lord Baltimore, a mariner's compass, a mason's compass, an Indian canoe, several sailing vessels, and a bust of Herrman. The latter, very likely a self-portrait, is set in an oval frame within which is lettered "Augustine Herrman Bohemian." (It is interesting to note that two different spellings of both the cartographer's surname and given name are found on the map. There are actually some dozen or more variations of Herrman's name in different documents and reports. The form "Herrman" is most commonly accepted today.)

Herrman apparently did not survey the area comprising the western part of the map. Printed descriptions give information (some of it legendary) about these regions and also serve to fill in the blank portions of the map. Thus, on the southwest sheet we are informed that "The Land between James River and Roanoke River is for the most parts Low Suncken Swampy Land not well passable but with great dificulty. And therein harbours Tygers Bears and other Devouringe Creatures."

Although the 1673 map was apparently Herrman's only cartographic work, he is credited with having drawn the earliest view of New Amsterdam. It first appeared on Nikolaas Jan Visscher's map of New

*Portrait of Augustine Herrman, from his map.*

*Right, title cartouche from the Herrman map.*

Netherland (1650), and later (1655) illustrated Adriaen van der Donck's *Description of the New Netherlands*. Some Herrman biographers believe it likely that he may have helped Visscher in preparing his map.

The Herrman map ranks with that of John Smith (1612) as one of the major cartographic publications of seventeenth-century America. Mathews has noted that "when compared with its predecessors Herrman's map shows a marked increase in detail and evidence of much greater time and labor spent in its preparation. Compared with the Smith map it shows that while Herrman was a more skillful draftsman and a better surveyor, he did not possess the geographic sense shown by Smith." [7]

Mathews believed that the "influence of Herrman on later works seems to have been about equal to that of Smith, since in the minds of the prominent map and atlas publishers of the last of the seventeenth and the first of the eighteenth centuries, these two men stand as the chief authorities for the cartographic representation of the territory on each side of the Chesapeake Bay."

The Virginia and Maryland map was copied and adapted by mapmakers for more than a century after its publication. It was especially important in helping to solve the boundary differences between Maryland, Virginia, and Pennsylvania. "Indeed," says Lawrence C. Wroth, "the usefulness of the map has been extraordinary from the earliest days, for in the ninety years of Privy Council and Chancery proceedings that resulted in the running of the Mason and Dixon line between Maryland and Pennsylvania in 1763, the Herrman map was always looked upon as an important exhibit between the Baltimores and the Penns." [8]

Wroth notes that "it is an ironical reflection that, in spite of Lord Baltimore's pleasure and satisfaction in this delineation of his province, the Herrman map should have been used successfully against the interests of his colony, and of the State of Maryland, in every boundary dispute from the day of its construction to the present generation." [9]

The Library's acquisition increased to five the number of known copies of Augustine Herrman's map. In addition to that in the John Carter Brown Library, there are three in Europe: one in the British Museum, and two in the Bibliothèque Nationale in Paris. In the latter library one copy is in the collection of d'Anville and the other in the collection of the Service Hydrographique de la Marine.

Through the years a number of facsimiles and reproductions of the map have been made. P. Lee Phillips, first Chief of the Map Division, published a monograph in 1911 entitled *The Rare Map of Virginia and Maryland by Augustine Herrman; Bibliographical Account With Facsimile Reproduction From the Copy in the British Museum* (Washington, 1911). Still available is a facsimile first published in 1941 by the John Carter Brown Library, of the copy in its collections.

The Geography and Map Division copy is in an excellent state of preservation. Each of the four sheets had been folded in half, apparently for some time, and there are several wormholes along the folds. For permanent preservation the map was laminated, with cloth backing, retaining the four-sheet format.

## NOTES

[1] John Carter Brown Library, *Annual Report, 1929–30* (Providence, 1930), p. 10.

[2] *Archives of Maryland,* vol. 3 (Baltimore, 1885), p. 398.

[3] Ibid., vol. 1 (Baltimore, 1883), p. 398–399.

[4] Donnell M. Owings, "Private Manors: An Edited List," *Maryland Historical Magazine,* 33:332 (December 1938).

[5] *Archives of Maryland,* vol. 1 (Baltimore, 1883), p. 462.

[6] Quoted in P. Lee Phillips, *The Rare Map of Virginia and Maryland by Augustine Herrman* (Washington, 1911), p. 9.

[7] E. B. Mathews, *Maps and Map-Makers of Maryland* (Baltimore, 1898), p. 385–386.

[8] John Carter Brown Library, *Annual Report, 1929–30* (Providence, 1930), p. 10.

[9] Ibid., p. 13.

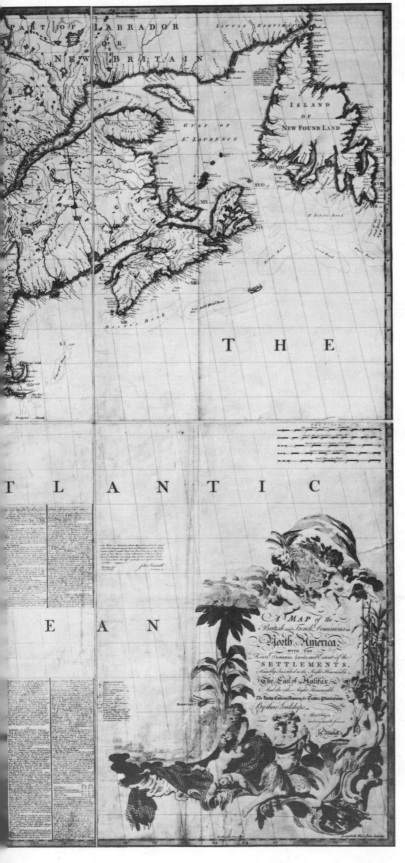

# John Mitchell's Map of the British and French Dominions in North America

## COMPILED AND EDITED BY WALTER W. RISTOW FROM VARIOUS PUBLISHED WORKS OF LAWRENCE MARTIN

**D**URING HIS TENURE as Chief of the Library of Congress Map Division (1924–46), Col. Lawrence Martin made detailed studies of several maps especially significant in the history of the United States. Among those to which he gave particular attention were John Mitchell's *Map of the British and French Dominions in North America* (1755), John Melish's *Map of the United States* (1816–23), and John Disturnell's *Map of the United Mexican States* (1847).

*Second English edition of John Mitchell's map. Maps illustrating this article are from the Geography and Map Division.*

Each of these maps was used to delimit boundaries in treaty agreements between the United States and its neighbors. Martin's studies were undertaken to determine which of several variants of the respective maps were consulted by the boundary arbiters. This information was initially sought by David Hunter Miller, Historical Advisor of the Department of State and Editor of *Treaties and Other International Acts of the United States of America* (8 vols., Washington, 1931–48). Summaries of Martin's findings on the Mitchell and Disturnell maps were published in volumes 3 and 4 and volume 5, respectively, of the *Treaties* series.

Of the three maps, Martin was perhaps most interested in Mitchell's *British and French Dominions.* Over a period of two decades he sought to acquire for the Library's collections originals or photoreproductions of variant issues of the several editions and impressions of the map. By careful and minute examination of many copies he developed a code for identifying the variant states. Newly acquired copies of the map were described by Martin in his annual reports. Certain of the descriptions were included in the published *Report of the Librarian of Congress* for selected years, and in reprints and separates distributed by the Map Division.[1] A brief article by Martin, entitled "John Mitchell's Map," was published in the April-May-June 1944 issue of the *Library of Congress Quarterly Journal of Current Acquisitions* (p. 36–38). Martin also extensively researched the life and activities of John Mitchell. He used some of his findings in compiling the biographical sketch of Mitchell he contributed to the *Dictionary of American Biography* (vol. 13, 1934, p. 50–51).

Before his retirement from the Library in 1946, Martin had completed, in preliminary typescript form, a comprehensive study on John Mitchell and his important historical map. Because of failing health he was not able to revise and edit the projected book, which was never published. Martin died on February 12, 1955. The Mitchell typescript is known to have been in his possession as late as March 1954, but whether it disappeared before or after Mrs. Martin's death in 1956 is unknown.

Because of the historical and cartographical significance of Mitchell's map, and Martin's extensive research on the map and its maker, a summary of his findings is here presented. The information is derived primarily from Martin's published works that have been cited above.

In concluding his biographical sketch of John Mitchell in the *DAB,* Martin emphatically stated: "Without serious doubt Mitchell's is the most important map in American history." There is impressive support for this evaluation. Most conclusive, perhaps, is the fact that it was the cartographic document consulted by official representatives of Great Britain and the United States at Paris in 1782 and 1783 in negotiating the treaty that terminated the Revolutionary War and recognized the independence of the United States. Although there is no mention of Mitchell's map in the treaty and no copies of the map were signed by the plenipotentiaries, there is strong evidence that it was consulted by the delegates. For example, Hunter Miller cited a letter from John Adams to James Sullivan, written on August 2, 1796, in which Adams affirmed that "Mitchell's map was the only one which the ministers plenipotentiary of the United States and the minister plenipotentiary of Great Britain made use of in their conferences and discussions relative to the boundaries of the United States, in their negotiation of the peace of 1783, and of the provisional articles of the 30th of November, 1782. Upon that map, and that only, were those boundaries delineated." [2]

On April 8, 1790, nine days before his death, Benjamin Franklin wrote to Thomas Jefferson, then Secretary of State, as follows: "I now can assure you that I am perfectly clear in the Remembrance that the Map we used in tracing the Boundary was brought to the Treaty by the Commissioners from England, and that it was the same that was published by Mitchell above 20 Years before." [3]

In the *DAB,* other historical uses of Mitchell's map are noted. It is thought, Martin stated, "to have been in use in the British House of Commons during the debate on the Quebec Act of 1774; it is known to have hung in the halls of Congress in 1802 and several times subsequently. It was used . . . in the discussions of British land grants in the Ohio and Mississippi valleys, and in scores of controversies involving the boundary lines existing at the time of its publication. Great Britain and the United States agreed to its official status in the

Convention of September 29, 1827; the King of the Netherlands made one of his conclusions, albeit an erroneous one, after using it in 1831; it exerted substantial influence in the negotiation and ratification of the Webster-Ashburton Treaty of 1842, and serious argument was based upon it by Great Britain before the Court of Arbitration at The Hague in 1910 in connection with the North Atlantic Coast Fisheries Arbitration. It was submitted in evidence before the Law Lords of the British Privy Council in 1926 in the appeal of Price Brothers & Company, Limited, from a judgment of the supreme court of Canada, and in 1926–27 in the Canada-Newfoundland (Labrador) boundary case. It was used as evidence before the Supreme Court of the United States in 1926 in the Wisconsin-Michigan boundary case, in 1926–27 in the Great Lakes level case, and in 1932 in the New Jersey-Delaware boundary case."

Who was John Mitchell, and how did he come to make a map that so vitally influenced the history of the Nation over a period of almost two centuries? Regrettably, facts about Mitchell are exceedingly scarce. After two decades of diligent research, Martin could summarize in a few hundred words all he had learned about the life of the famous mapmaker:

Dr. John Mitchell, of Virginia and England, was a distinguished and learned man of his time; he was a physician whose treatment of yellow fever became famous in 1793, a botanist of repute, the author of numerous works, and the maker of one map; but our knowledge of his life and career is strangely incomplete.

The place and date of Mitchell's birth are unknown. Although a Swedish authority, a contemporary, understood that Mitchell was born in Virginia, it seems that he was born in the British Isles, since his more intimate friends said in 1746 that he "returned" to England and spoke of that return as his voyage "home." His ancestors and descendants have not been identified. He was married, but we do not know to whom. Where he was trained in medicine is not recorded. He is known to have received part of his botanical education at the University of Edinburgh, and he may have studied botany and medicine either at Leiden in the Netherlands or at Oxford or Cambridge in England. He probably had no formal training in the making of maps.

It cannot even be said when Mitchell came to America, though the unsupported statement that he reached Virginia in 1700 has often been printed. He spent some years (six at least) in Virginia, collecting plants, according to Linnaeus; his residence was at Urbanna on the Rappahannock River. In October, 1735, the vestry of Christ Church parish gave him eight hundred pounds of tobacco for caring for the sick; on December 19, 1738, he was appointed a justice of the peace in Middlesex County, Virginia; in 1744 he visited Philadelphia, where he became a friend of Benjamin Franklin, with whom he corresponded thereafter. His writings were in part in Latin and, aside from those regarding botany, zoology, and medicine, bore chiefly on the theme that America should be British rather than French. His travels in America were limited to Virginia and the region north to Philadelphia. There is some ground for believing that Mitchell was a Quaker, but this is not at all certain.

Mitchell returned to England in 1746; hence we cannot actually prove that he spent more than eleven years in America.

After his return to England, he seems to have lived mostly in London; he was elected a Fellow of the Royal Society in 1747; he did not practice medicine and gradually gave up his botanical studies; but he wrote a number of scientific and historical papers; and he made Mitchell's Map.

Dr. Mitchell died on February 29, 1768, in or near London.[4]

Notwithstanding his numerous other professional contributions, John Mitchell is best known for the map that bears his name. As Martin observed, "it is very aptly called Mitchell's Map, for not only was John Mitchell its author, but he made no other." [5] Mitchell was concerned at the active French expansion throughout the northwestern part of North America and the seeming disinterest of the British authorities in enlarging and solidifying their colonial possessions. The map and an unsigned pamphlet attributed to Mitchell, entitled *The Contest in America Between Great Britain and France by an Impartial Hand,* are expressions of that interest.

Mitchell commenced work on the map in 1750 and he was occupied in compiling it for the next five years. Through his intimacy with George Dunk, Earl of Halifax, he had access to the extensive collection of manuscript maps and geographical reports in the archives of the British Board of Trade.[6] Mitchell's map was issued in 1755 with the approval and at the request of the British Government; it was dedicated to the Earl of Halifax, who was then President of the Board of Trade; it bears the endorsement of John Pownall, Secretary of the Lords Commissioners for Trade and Plantations, dated February 13, 1755; and in the printed text of the map is this statement:

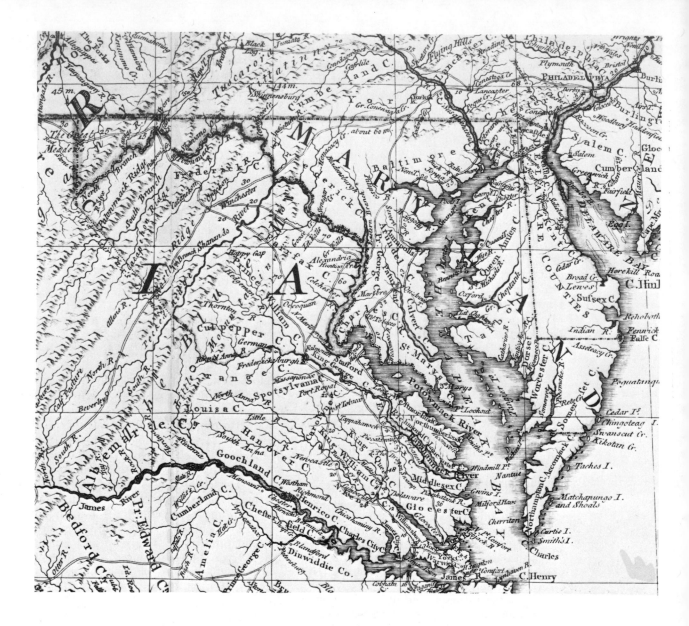

*Virginia-Maryland border, from the first English edition, third impression, of the Mitchell map.*

This Map was undertaken with the Approbation and at the request of the Lords Commissioners for Trade and Plantations [the Board of Trade]; and is Chiefly composed from Draughts, Charts and Actual Surveys of different parts of his Majesties Colonies & Plantations in America; Great Part of which have been lately taken by their Lordships Orders, and transmitted to this Office by the Governors of the said Colonies and others.

"It appears, moreover," notes Martin, "from the text printed on the second edition of his map, that Mitchell had access not only to the records of the Board of Trade, but also to those of the British Admiralty, which he speaks of as 'the Journals of our Ships of War kept in the Admiralty Office.'"

In general, Mitchell's Map is a political map, showing the division of eastern North America between the British and the French and the administrative subdivisions of the British North American Colonies. The map also has roads, however, and gives the positions of the principal Indian tribes, as well as extensive notes regarding the dates of various settlements, the nature of the country, and so forth. Topographic features are roughly indicated, particularly in the Appalachian Mountains. It is especially worthy of note that, although a considerable portion of the territory of Louisiana is included, the boundaries of the maritime colonies are extended westward across the Mississippi River to the western border of the map. This is deliberate, for the parallel of 40° north latitude in the position of the present boundary between Nebraska and Kansas is denominated, "Bounds of Virginia and New-England by Charters, May 23. 1609 and Nov[r] 3. 1620, extending from Sea to Sea, out of which our other Colonies were granted." Northwest of Lake Superior, in the present State of Minnesota, the same claim is repeated along the forty-eighth parallel in the words, "Northern Bounds of New England by Charter Nov[r] 3 1620, extending to the South Sea's." Just off the present coast of Texas and just off the east coast of Florida the twenty-ninth parallel is marked "Bounds of Carolina by Charter" and "Bounds of Carolina by their Charter." North Carolina is carried westward beyond the Mississippi River to the western edge of the map by specific boundary symbols.[7]

The ornately decorated title, set in the lower right corner of the map, reads as follows on the first three editions: *A Map of the British and French Dominions in North America With The Roads, Distances, Limits, and Extent of the Settlements, Humbly Inscribed to the Right Honourable The Earl of Halifax, And the Other Right Honourable The Lords Commissioners for Trade & Plantations, By their Lordships Most Obliged and very humble Servant Jn°. Mitchell.*

The map is impressive in size, measuring approximately 52 by 75 inches. It is at the scale of 1:2,000,000, or about 32 miles to an inch. Printing was from engraved plates on eight separate sheets. The coast from Newfoundland and southern Labrador to Florida and Texas is shown, and the map extends on the west to what is now Oklahoma, Kansas, and Nebraska, and on the north to Hudson Bay. An inset map in the upper left corner, entitled "A New Map of Hudson's Bay and Labrador," includes part of the west coast of Greenland, and the Mississippi River extends up to and disappears beneath the neat line of the inset map. Thus the position of its supposed headwaters is omitted. Mitchell's map was most favorably received, and a number of editions and plagiarisms of it were issued over a period of 30 or more years. Because the several versions were published at different dates and in a number of places, it is difficult to identify the specific copies of Mitchell's map that were consulted in treaty negotiations.

After years of detailed research Martin differentiated seven English impressions; two Dutch editions, with English titles, published in Amsterdam; ten French impressions, several with titles and notes in German as well as French; and two Italian piracies published in Venice. All of the above are at the scale of the initial edition. While the publication dates are not known for all variants, except for the latest French and Italian editions all were published before 1782.[8]

Thanks to Lawrence Martin's diligent and persistent acquisition program, the Library of Congress has a most comprehensive collection of the several editions and impressions of Mitchell's map. For 19 of the 21 impressions the Library possesses originals, and it has photocopies for the other two. It also has photocopies, from originals in other repositories, of variants for which the Library has printed editions.

By painstaking study and comparison of many copies, Martin devised a code for identifying variant editions and impressions, based upon points of difference between successive issues. The code for the English editions was published in volume 3 of the *Treaties* series. It is reprinted as a supplement to this paper, along with codes for identifying the several French, Dutch, and Italian editions and impressions.

Martin believed that two existing copies of Mitchell's map are, with some certainty, to be identified as directly connected with the negotiations of 1782.

One copy of Mitchell's Map which was certainly used during the earlier part of the negotiations of 1782 is that which is now in the archives of the New York Historical Society; that annotated copy of Mitchell's Map (the first impression of the third English edition), was continuously in the possession of the Jay family up to the year 1843. That map is colored to show Canada according to the Quebec Act, and it gives the whole boundary of the United States as proposed on October 8, 1782 (Wharton Diplomatic Correspondence, V, 805–7) . . . .

On the boundary line of this copy of Mitchell's Map in thirteen places are written the words "Mr. Oswald's Line," and it was said in 1843 by Albert Gallatin ("A Memoir on the North-eastern Boundary," 19) that those words had been "recognised by Mr. William Jay as being in the handwriting of his father, the Hon. John Jay." . . . Moreover, John Jay's name is written, in his own hand, on the back of this map. . . .

Perhaps the most famous copy of Mitchell's Map is the King George Map [a photocopy of which, from the original in the British Museum, is in the Library of Congress]. . . . It is the fourth English edition and is known as the "King George Map," as it was in the library of George III. . . .

This King George copy of Mitchell's Map is of

undoubted authenticity; whether it was used at Paris during the 1782 negotiations or whether it was a map of reference used by George III and his ministers, as supposed by White ("Boundary Disputes and Treaties," 823), does not affect its evidentiary value.[9]

## NOTES

[1] See *Noteworthy Maps*, No. 1 (1925–26), No. 2 (1926–27), and No. 3 (1927–28).

[2] Hunter Miller, Ed., *Treaties and Other International Acts of the United States of Amreica*, vol. 3 (Washington, 1933), p. 330.

[3] Ibid., p. 329.

[4] Ibid., p. 349–350.

[5] Ibid., p. 349.

[6] *Dictionary of American Biography*, vol. 13, p. 50.

[7] Miller, *Treaties*, vol. 3, p. 330–331.

[8] Ibid., p. 331.

[9] Ibid., p. 341–345.

*Eastern North America, with Canadian border, from the dual impression of the third French edition of Mitchell's map.*

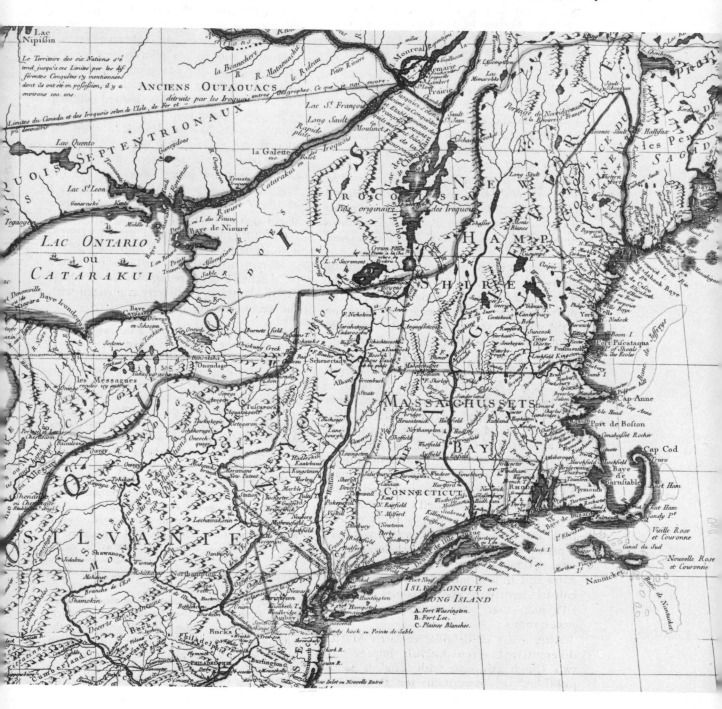

# TABLE FOR IDENTIFYING VARIANT EDITIONS AND IMPRESSIONS OF JOHN MITCHELL'S MAP OF THE BRITISH AND FRENCH DOMINIONS IN NORTH AMERICA

*Compiled by Richard W. Stephenson*

## ENGLISH EDITIONS

### First edition, first impression

*A Map of the British and French Dominions in North America with the Roads, Distances, Limits, and Extent of the Settlements, Humbly Inscribed to the Right Honourable The Earl of Halifax, And the other Right Honourable The Lords Commissioners for Trade & Plantations, By their Lordships Most Obliged and very humble Servant Jnº Mitchell. Tho: Kitchin Sculp. Clerkenwell Green. Publish'd by the Author Febʳʸ 13ᵗʰ 1755 according to Act of Parliament, and Sold by And: Miller opposite Katherine Street in the Strand.*

In the imprint, Millar's name and Katharine Street are misspelled Miller and Katherine.

Two cities in Massachusetts are named Leicester, and none is named Worcester.

Library of Congress holdings:

A colored original mounted on cloth, sectioned in 32 parts to fold to 13½ x 9½ inches. In a buckram-covered box with binder's title: Map of North America—Mitchell—1755. Division stamp: Mar 31 1939. Handwritten note on verso of map reads: Amerique Carte En anglais.

### First edition, second impression

"Millar" and "Katharine" are correctly spelled in line of print outside neat line in the lower right corner.

Two cities in Massachusetts are named Leicester, and none is named Worcester.

Library of Congress holdings:

An original mounted on cloth, sectioned in 8 parts to fold to 27½ x 20 inches. Brightly colored. Division stamp: Oct 5 1916.

### First edition, third impression

One of the two towns in Massachusetts identified on the two preceding impressions as "Leicester" has been correctly redesignated "Worcester."

Library of Congress holdings:

a) An original mounted on cloth, sectioned in 8 parts to fold to 27½ x 19½ inches. Lightly colored. Division stamp: Oct 5 1916.

b) A lightly colored original mounted on cloth, covered with crepeline, sectioned in 10 parts to fold to 27½ x 18 inches. This discolored copy was transferred to the Library of Congress by the State Department. Division stamp: Jan 30 1926.

c) An imperfect original mounted on cloth, sectioned in 6 parts, each 18 x 39 inches. The top border and a 6 to 8-inch adjoining strip of the map are wanting. Lightly colored. Division stamp: Gift Jun 30 1950.

### Second edition

Tables of text have been added in the Atlantic Ocean.

Retains the name "And: Millar" as map seller.

Library of Congress holdings:

a) An original mounted on cloth, sectioned in 8 parts to fold to 28 x 20½ inches. Lightly colored. Division stamp: Jun 27 1930.

b) A brightly colored original mounted on cloth, sectioned to fold to 14 x 10 inches. Annotations, in ink, concern the French surrender of Canada to Jeffery Amherst. The map is in its original slipcase with handwritten label on one side which reads "North America by Dʳ Mitchell," and a printed advertisement on the other which states "Bought of Thomas Jefferys Engraver, Geographer to His Majesty . . ." The Library of Congress purchased this copy in London in 1937.

### Third edition, first impression

Millar's name no longer appears outside the neat line.

"Printed for Jefferys and Faden Geographers to the King at the Corner of Sᵗ Martins Lane Charing Cross London" has been added inside the neat line near the lower right corner.

Engraver's statement has been shortened to "Tho: Kitchin Sculp."

Library of Congress holdings:

a) An original mounted on cloth, sectioned in 8 parts to fold to 28½ x 21½ inches. It was purchased in London and accessioned by the Library on January 3, 1900. Lightly colored. Stamped in lower right corner: Library of Congress Maps & Charts. No. 3438.

b) An imperfect original mounted on cloth and faced with crepeline, sectioned in 8 parts to fold to 28½ x 19½ inches. Large pieces are missing from the northern portion of the map. It is lightly colored, but the paper is badly discolored. Two handwritten short titles are mounted below the bottom neat line: Mitchell's Map of North America. 1755 [and] Map of the British & French Dominions in North America, North America N° 10.

## Third edition, second impression

An engraved boundary has been added in Lake Ontario.

Library of Congress holdings:

A colored original mounted on cloth, sectioned in 32 parts to fold to 14 x 10 inches. Division stamp: Jul 30 1932. Transferred to the Library of Congress from the Department of State on June 30, 1932. Handwritten title on verso: Map of the British & Franch [sic] Dominions in North America.

## Fourth edition

Title has been changed to read *A Map of the British Colonies in North America* . . .

Library of Congress holdings:

A lightly colored original mounted on cloth, sectioned in 8 parts to fold to 27 x 21½ inches. Division stamp: Dec 6 1928.

### DUTCH EDITIONS

## First edition

*A Map of the British and French Dominions in North America with the Roads, Distances, Limits, and Extent of the Settlements, by D^r Jn° Mitchell. at Amsterdam Printed for I. Cóvens and C. Mortier.*

Library of Congress holdings:

Positive photostat, mounted on cloth, sectioned in 8 parts to fold to 27½ x 19 inches. From original in the William L. Clements Library, Ann Arbor, Mich.

## Second edition

Author and publisher's statement changed to read "By Jn° Mitchell D. F. with Improvements—at Amsterdam Printed for I. Cóvens and C. Mortier."

Library of Congress holdings:

a) A lightly colored original mounted on cloth,

*Title cartouche from the fourth English edition of the Mitchell map, in which the title has been changed.*

sectioned in 6 parts to fold to 18½ x 39 inches. Division stamp: Jan 30 1926.

b) Brightly colored original mounted on cloth, sectioned in 8 parts to fold to 28 x 20½ inches. This copy was removed, in December 1927, from the Library's copy of Johannes Cóvens and Cornelis Mortier's *Atlas nouveau, contenant toutes les parties du monde* . . . A Amsterdam, Chez Jean Cóvens et Corneille Mortier [1683–1761] v. 9, no. 47–50. (G1015.C68 1761 Cage; Phillips no. 3448).

### FRENCH EDITIONS

## First edition

*Amerique Septentrionale avec les Routes, Distances en miles, Limites et Etablissements François et Anglois. Par le Docteur Mitchel Traduit de l'Anglois a Paris Par le Rouge Ing^r Geographe du Roy rue des Grands Augustins 1756.*

Includes the word "Limites" in the title rather than "Villages," which appears in all subsequent editions.

Title given only in French.

Library of Congress holdings:

An original mounted on cloth, sectioned in 8 parts to fold to 28½ x 21 inches. Lightly colored. Division stamp: Oct 23 1907.

## Second edition, first impression

*Amerique Septentrionale avec les Routes, Distances en miles, Villages et Etablissements François et Anglois Par le Docteur Mitchel Traduit de l'Anglois a Paris Par le Rouge Ing^r Geographe du Roy rue des Grands Augustins 1756. North America So Doctor Michel zu London im 1755: ten jahr ausgegeben jetzt aber in das franzosische ubersetzet. zu Paris. durch h. le Rouge in der grosen augustiner Strasse 1756.*

The word "Villages" replaces "Limites" in the French title.

Title in German appears below French title. This is found on all subsequent French issues.

An index to sheets is reproduced in lower left corner of French title.

The headdress of the Indian lady on the right of the cartouche has five feathers.

Library of Congress holdings:

a) An unmounted original in 8 sheets (each 30 x 22 inches) in Georges Louis Le Rouge's *Atlas général contenant le detail des quatre parties du monde principalement celui de l'Europe* . . . A Paris, Chez le S^r Le Rouge [1741–62] no. 143–

A MAP of the BRITISH COLONIES in North America WITH THE Roads, Distances, Limits, and Extent of the SETTLEMENTS, Humbly Inscribed to the Right Honourable The Earl of Halifax, And the other Right Honourable The Lords Commissioners for Trade & Plantations, By their Lordships Most Obliged and very humble servant Jno. Mitchell.

Longitude West from London.

Map Division
DEC 6 1928
Library of Congress

150. (G1015.L43 1762 Cage; Phillips no. 5975). Lightly colored.

b) An unmounted original, in 8 sheets (each 31½ x 22 inches) in Roch Joseph Julien's *Le théatre du monde contenant les cartes générales et particulières des empires, royaumes et états qui le composent*. Paris, le S<sup>r</sup> Julien, 1768. v. 1, no. 57–57g. (G1015.J8 1768 Cage; Phillips no. 641). Lightly colored.

### Second edition, second impression

The headdress of the Indian lady on the right of the cartouche contains only four feathers.

Library of Congress holdings:

An original mounted on cloth sectioned in 8 parts to fold to 27 x 20 inches. Lightly colored. Formerly in the collection of the French geographer Henri Vignaud. Acquired in 1926, on exchange, from the William L. Clements Library, Ann Arbor, Mich.

### Third edition, first impression

Retains the original date 1756.

The following statement has been added to cartouche: Corigée en 1776 par M. Hawkins Brigadier des armées du Roi.

Library of Congress holdings:

An original in 8 sheets (each 21½ x 29½ inches) bound as an atlas. Book plate: Library of Congress, United States of America (Force Collection) Chap. 4, Shelf 3112a. Map is lightly colored.

### Third edition, second impression

Retains the original date of 1756.

Includes the statement "Corigée en 1776 par M. Hawkins Brigadier des armées du Roi."

The conventional sign for the fort at Ticonderoga has been added.

The name of the fort is misspelled "Ticonderago."

A new lake has been drawn connecting two small lakes, one called "Lac George," the other, unnamed, on the New York-New Hampshire boundary. The dual lake is represented as flowing into "Wood Creek ou Creek du Bois."

Library of Congress holdings:

An original mounted on cloth, sectioned in 16 parts to fold to 14 x 20 inches. This copy was acquired in 1943, on exchange, from the Catholic University of America, Washington, D.C. Map is lightly colored. Division stamp: Jul 31 1943.

### Third edition, third impression

Retains the date 1756.

Includes the statement "Corigée en 1776 par M. Hawkins Brigadier des armées du Roi."

"Lac George" has been changed to "Fo<sup>t</sup> George."

Below "L. S<sup>t</sup> Sacrement" is added "ou L. George."

Library of Congress holdings:

An original mounted on cloth, sectioned in 8 parts to fold to 28 x 20 inches. Lightly colored. It was removed from Georges Louis Le Rouge's *Atlas Amériquain Septentrional . . .* Paris, le Rouge, 1778–[1792] and mounted separately. no. 5–8. (G1105.L4 1792 Cage; Phillips no. 1212).

### Third edition, fourth impression

The date 1756 in the cartouche has been changed to 1777.

Library of Congress holdings:

Positive photostat, mounted on cloth, sectioned in 9 parts to fold to 19½ x 27½ inches, and negative, in 16 parts, each 18 x 23 inches, of original in the John Carter Brown Library, Providence, R. I.

*Title cartouche from the second impression of the second French edition. The headdress of the Indian lady has been reduced from the usual five plumes to only four.*

## Third edition, fifth impression

Includes the date 1777 in the cartouche.

The phrase "A. German-Town, Carré. M. 28" has been added south of Long Island.

Library of Congress holdings:

> An original mounted on cloth, sectioned in 8 parts, 4 of which are 27 x 20 inches and 4 of which are 28 x 20 inches. Brightly colored. This copy was obtained, by exchange, from Tracy McGregor in 1934. Division stamp: Mar-5 1934.

## Third edition, sixth impression

Includes the date 1777 in the cartouche.

The boundary between the United States and Canada is indicated by a dashed line.

Following statement is added east of New Hampshire: En Mars 1783 on a tracé sur cette Carte Les Limites des Etats unis et des autres puissances selon le dernier Traité de paix.

Library of Congress holdings:

> An original mounted on cloth, sectioned in 45 parts to fold to 11 x 9 inches. Lightly colored. Division stamp: Oct 31 1905. Label pasted on verso: Oskar Gerschel Buchhandlg. u. Antiquariat, Stuttgart, 16. Calwerstrasse 16.

## Third edition, dual impression

The date has been revised to 1777, indicating that it is the cartouche to the fourth, fifth, or sixth impression of the third edition.

Sheet "3e" covering New England is from the second impression of the third edition. It shows the new lake on the New York-New Hampshire boundary connecting a small unnamed lake and one identified as "Lac George."

Library of Congress holdings:

> An unmounted original. Lightly colored. Eight sheets have been joined in four parts, each measuring 55 x 21½ inches. This copy was obtained by exchange from the William L. Clements Library, Ann Arbor, Mich., in 1926. It was formerly in the collection of the French geographer Henri Vignaud.

## First edition

*Le Colonie unite dell' America settentr^le di nuova projezione a ss.ee. li Signori Riformatori dello Studio di Padova. Venezia, 1778. Presso Antonio Zatta Con Privilegio dell' Eccellentissimo Senato.*

Title in Italian.

John Mitchell's name does not appear as author.

Library of Congress holdings:

> a) An unmounted, colored original in 12 sheets, each 16 x 22 inches. It is bound with three other maps of North America by Antonio Zatta. (G1105.Z3 1779 Cage).

> b) An unmounted, colored original in 12 sheets, each 16½ x 21½ inches, in Guillaume Thomas François Raynal's *Storia dell' America Settentrionale del signor abate Raynal* . . . In Venezia, Dalle stampe di Antonio Zatta, 1778. (G1105.R3 1778 Cage).

> c) An unmounted, colored original in 12 sheets, each 14½ x 19 inches, in Antonio Zatta's *Atlante novissimo*. Venezia, Antonio Zatta, 1779–85. v. 1, no. 56–67. (G1015.Z3 1785 Cage; Phillips no. 650).

> d) An altered original in 10 sheets, each 13½ x 17½ inches. This copy has had the cartouche skillfully added to sheet XI and includes numerous pen and ink annotations, among them the name, location, and date of many engagements of the French and Indian and the Revolutionary Wars. The 10-sheet map and Antonio Zatta's map, *Le Isole di Terra Nuova e Capo Breton*, are in a brown paper wrapper with handwritten title "Kanada und die Vereinigten Staaten, zugleich Indianerkarte, um 1778." The maps are unmounted and brightly colored. They were presented to the Library on May 15, 1943. Division stamp: Jun 30 1943.

## Second edition

The date 1778 has been changed to 1791.

"Con Privilegio dell' Eccellentissimo Senato" has been omitted.

Library of Congress holdings:

> An unmounted, colored original in 12 sheets, each 14½ x 19½ inches, in Antonio Zatta's *Atlante novissimo*. Venezia, Antonio Zatta, 1779–85 [i.e. 1799] v. 4, no. 27–38. (G1015.Z3 1799 Cage; Phillips no. 651).

# The Walker-Washington Map

## BY PAUL G. SIFTON

Reprinted from the April 1967 *Quarterly Journal
of the Library of Congress.*

ON OCTOBER 5, 1770, George Washington wrote in his diary that he was going "on a journey to the Ohio." [1] His mission was to survey the lands between the Little and Great Kanawha Rivers for the veterans of the French and Indian War. As far back as 1754, Governor Dinwiddie had promised 200,000 acres of western land to the regiment Washington commanded in the Great Meadows campaign.[2] After innumerable delays the Executive Council of Virginia promised, on December 15, 1769, that Washington and his regiment might take up the grant in 20 surveys.[3]

Acting in a characteristically selfless fashion, Colonel Washington took upon himself the trouble and expense involved in making an extended trip and survey in behalf of the men under his command. It should be added, however, that the Colonel did not hesitate to purchase quite a number of the surveyed grants for his own use.[4] Although Washington had access to several contemporary maps of British North America, it is probable that he would have taken advantage of any opportunity to obtain an up-to-date one before setting forth into the relatively unknown northwest of his native Virginia.

The Manuscript Division of the Library in 1966 received as a gift from Miss E. Penissa Wills, a descendant of John Augustine Washington, a holograph map in George Washington's hand. On the verso is the docket notation "Aligany/Copied from a Map of/Doct.ʳ Walkers/laid before the Assembly." [5] It is entirely possible that Colonel Washington used this map on his "journey to the Ohio."

The map that Washington copied was undoubtedly the map that Dr. Thomas Walker presented to the Virginia House of Burgesses on December 13, 1769, to accompany his memorial about the boundary between the western settlements and the Indians. The present whereabouts of the original Walker map is not known. Thomas Jefferson's contemporaneous printed copy of the Burgesses' *Journals* failed to indicate its location.[6] And the authoritative printing of the *Journal* in 1906, taken from the careful transcriptions made for the Virginia State Library in the Public Record Office, London, likewise failed to locate it.[7]

To understand Walker's memorial and the maps, it should be remembered that the land rivalry among influential Virginia factions extended as far back as 1745.[8] Each group sent out surveyors to stake out and map the land they proposed to occupy and sell. One such survey involved Dr. Walker, who with his associates organized the Loyal Land Company of Virginia to counteract the Ohio Company, which, in 1749, had wrested from the Executive Council of Virginia a grant of 200,000 acres near the Forks of the Ohio.[9] In March 1750 Walker and his companions made a wide-ranging survey of the area west of Virginia, reaching as far as the headwaters of the Cumberland River in present-day Kentucky.[10] The accuracy and import of Walker's work were gracefully acknowledged by Lewis Evans in the *Analysis* accompanying his renowned "General Map of the Middle British Colonies" (second edition, 1755):

As for the Branches of the Ohio, which head in the New Virginia, I am particularly obliged to Mr. Thomas Walker, for the Intelligence of what Names they bear, and what Rivers they fall into Northward and Westward.[11]

For the next 18 years, the Virginia land companies continued to wield their power-

*"Washington as a Surveyor," an engraving after Felix Octavius Carr Darley, a noted early American illustrator. In volume 1 of Washington Irving's* Life of George Washington, *published in 1857 by G. P. Putnam and Company.*

ful influence to wrest grants from the House of Burgesses, the Executive Council, the Governor, the Colonial Secretary, and the Board of Trade.[12] In a countermove the Board, in a 1763 proclamation, set up a definitive western boundary not only to reassure the Indian nations but also to hold in check the expansionist ambitions of the coastal land companies. The northern Indian Superintendent, Sir William Johnson, and his southern counterpart, John Stuart, were directed to survey and establish such a line. Stuart, by far the more zealous of the two, had completed the western boundaries for the Georgia and Carolina settlements at the end of 1766 and was ready to perform the same service for Virginia. Stuart's pace was slowed down, however, by changes in both London and Williamsburg.

John Blair, who was made president pro tempore of the Executive Council after the death of Governor Fauquier,[13] appointed Dr. Walker and Andrew Lewis, two of the most influential of the Loyal Land Company's grantees, to represent Virginia in fixing the boundary.[14] Stuart and the Southerners were charged by London to make a treaty with the Cherokees. Acting with a speed which must have astonished the Virginians, Stuart arrived at Hard Labor, N.C., 11 days before Governor Blair's projected arrival, and made a treaty with the Cherokees on October 14, 1768. Stuart and the Indians agreed upon the "Hard Labor Line," which was to run from Chiswell's Mine near the North Carolina border to the mouth of the Great Kanawha River.[15] This is the line designated on the Washington map as "The Line proposd by the Superintendant."

The Virginians' reaction was one of outrage and shock since, as they took pains to point out, settlers had already moved into the area beyond the Great Kanawha River as far west as the Holston River. The outgoing Colonial Secretary, Hillsborough, had already agreed to a more advantageous line running directly northward from the Holston River to the mouth of the Great Kanawha.[16] And, in fact, the Board of Trade had agreed, on March 12, 1768, to a straight line running from the Holston to the Kanawha.[17] This line was therefore known in the colonies as "The Line proposd by the Lords of Trade & approvd of by His Majesty."

The memorial presented to the House of

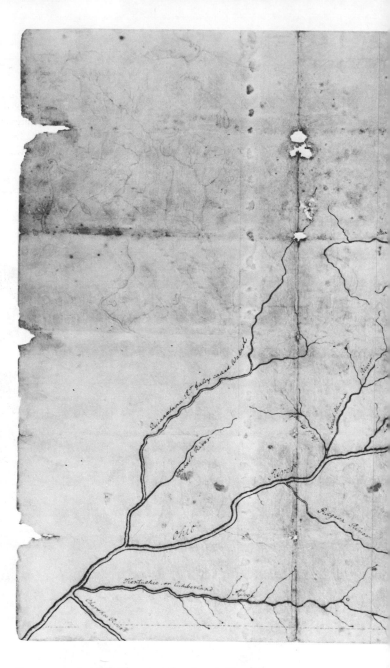

Burgesses by Walker made the following points:

That the Hard Labor Line would expose settlers in the Kanawha-Holston area to Indian attacks.

That both Virginia and Pennsylvania would themselves be exposed to Indian attack by the absence of a buffer-zone of western settlements.

That if the Holston-Kanawha Line were not allowed, all land patents and grants in the area would be overturned and rendered invalid.

That the physical difficulties and expense involved in running the line could be obviated if the legislature permitted a survey to run due westward from the existing North Carolina-Virginia boundary to the Ohio River.[18]

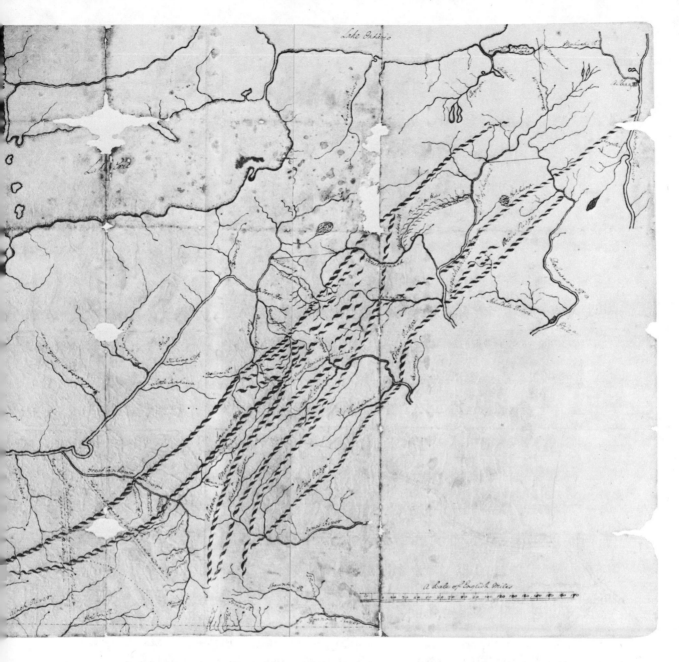

*A map of the "Aligany" region, hand copied by George Washington from a map made by Dr. Thomas Walker in 1769. In the collections of the Manuscript Division.*

It may be said that the House of Burgesses found the latter contention particularly difficult to accept.

The part of the Washington map most closely concerned with the main points of the memorial is the center area, north of the Virginia-North Carolina boundary line. Here the cartographer has depicted six prominent features:

"The Line proposd by the Superintendant."

"The Line proposd by the Lords of Trade & approvd of by His Majesty."

A dotted line covering the southwest quadrant of the area between these two lines.

"Extent of yᵉ Inhabitants 1769."

A thorough representation of the rivers in the area of the two boundaries.

A dotted line extending the North Carolina-Virginia boundary to the Ohio River.

"The Line proposd by the Superintendant," or the Hard Labor Line, and the "Line proposd by the Lords of Trade & approvd of by his Majesty," or the Holston-Kanawha Line, were the heart of the matter. "Extent of yᵉ Inhabitants 1769" was

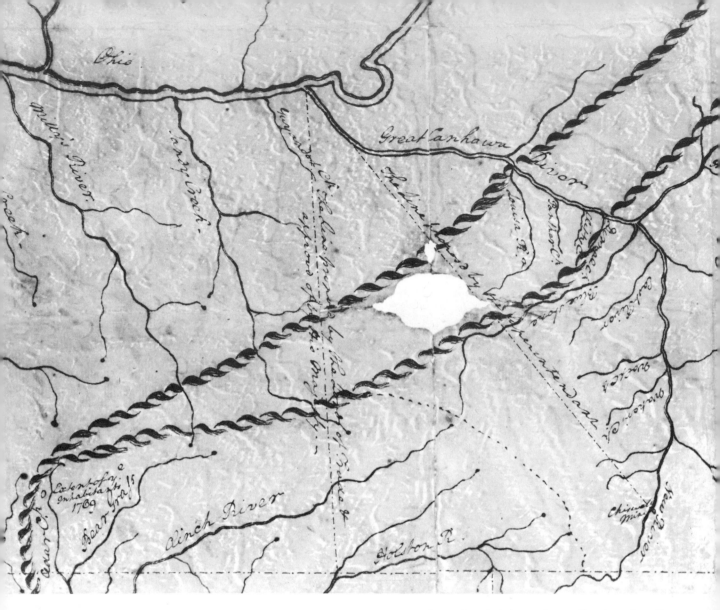

*Center area north of the Virginia-North Carolina boundary line on the Walker-Washington map.*

also included to convince the legislators of the de facto settling of the western lands as far west as the Cedar River.[19] The large number of rivers named in the area between the Roanoke River and the Kanawha River points, however, to the long experience of Dr. Walker in the transmontane area.

It might reasonably be asserted that a map presented by Walker and his associates to advance the claims of the Loyal Land Company of Virginia need not have included as much as the map which Miss Wills presented to the Library. One such feature is a line made of straight sections alternating with dotted ones, extending from "Kilianing" (Kittanning), above Fort Pitt (Pittsburgh), to the eastern end of "Onoyda Lake" (Lake Oneida). It marks the northern section of the Indian boundary

proposed by the Board of Trade in March 1768 and negotiated by the master tactician, Sir William Johnson, and the Wharton-Franklin coterie in Philadelphia. It is possible that Washington may have added this line from his own knowledge.

Washington had a good opportunity to copy the map when he was in Williamsburg to attend the Burgesses' meetings from November 6 to December 22, 1769.[20] On December 13, the day Walker presented his memorial, Washington was in the Burgesses' Chamber to present a bill to "Dock the Intail" of one Daniel M'Carty.[21] In fact, Washington's action was the third piece of legislative business after the presentation of the map. Further proof of Walker's close connection with Washington, during the Burgesses' second 1769 session in Williamsburg, is a postscript Washington attached to his petition on behalf of his Virginia regiment, addressed to Governor Botetourt on December 8, 1769. The postscript indicates that Walker corrected some details of land transactions in the Kanawha region after Washington had begun writing the petition.[22]

A comparison of Washington's map with Lewis Evans' 1755 map, with which Washington was acquainted, reveals several striking similarities of expression: "Mineami River," "Burnetts Hills," "Onoyda Lake," "Onondag^a. Riv.," and "Quiaaxtana R^r. falsly called Wabash." Did Walker copy Evans, or did Washington fill in these de-

copied almost too exactly the work of another.

Washington's use of the term "The Line Proposd by the Lords of Trade & approvd of by His Majesty" help to date his map before October 5, 1770, when he left on his journey to the Ohio. Upon the formal signing of a treaty with the Cherokees at Lochaber, S.C., on October 18, 1770,[26] this line became known as the Lochaber Line. It seems likely that soon after Washington returned from the West on December 1 he would have learned of the new name and would have substituted it for the old had he been copying it then.

All these factors lead to this conclusion about the map Miss Wills presented to the Library: It represents a holograph map, in Colonel Washington's hand, made for his

*Washington's inscription on the back of the map.*

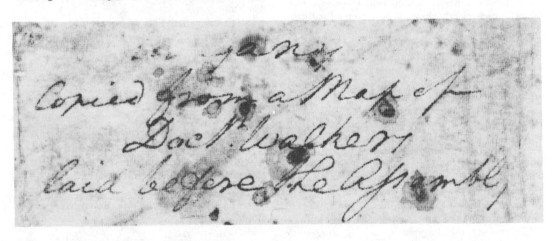

tails of his map from Evans? Washington had in his library over 90 other maps and was constantly seeking out geographical information as when, for example, he obtained the mileages along the Ohio and Mississippi Rivers while he was at Fort Pitt on November 6, 1770.[23]

The misspellings on the map, such as the use of "Canhawa" twice, might throw some light on the source of Washington's cartography. On December 15, 1769, we find him, in his formal petition to the House of Burgesses on behalf of his regiment, mentioning the "Canhawa" River,[24] but on October 16, 1770, he correctly wrote in his diary of passing the "little Kanawha." [25] The other misspellings on the map such as "Blew Ridge," "Schulkill," and "Miama" indicate that the usually meticulous Washington had, in fact,

own use on the survey trip to the Little and Great Kanawha Rivers area. And it was made after December 13, 1769, when Dr. Walker's map was presented to the Virginia House of Burgesses, and before October 5, 1770, when Washington started on his journey.

In the absence of the Walker map, Washington's copy is a unique pictorial representation of a pre-Revolutionary Indian boundary and western land dispute. After the successful American Revolution, this vexing problem was to rise up to confound the framers of the Articles of Confederation. The Walker-Washington map reminds us that the western lands question did not arise full-blown at the close of the rebellion but had its roots in the manifold skirmishes of the colonial period of American history.

# NOTES

[1] George Washington Papers, Manuscript Division, Library of Congress, 1st series, 13:76. Cited hereafter as GW.

[2] Thomas P. Abernethy, *Western Lands and the American Revolution* (New York, 1937), p. 70.

[3] Journal, Executive Council of Virginia, Public Record Office, Colonial Office (cited hereafter as PRO, CO) 5:1440, December 15, 1769. See also Washington's lengthy petition to Governor Botetourt, December 8, 1769, GW, 4th series, 11:1404 A–B.

[4] Abernethy, p. 69. The Geography and Map Division in the Library of Congress holds three of Washington's Kanawha land plats: "Copy of a survey return'd by M$^r$ Sam$^l$ Lewis . . . Surveyed for George Washington . . . on the NE Side of the Great Kanawhy . . . Novemb$^r$ 1774," with holograph notes by Washington; "Plan of the tracts of land on the Great Kanawha River covering the interests of George Washington in that district," map and notes, 1771–75, in Washington's hand; and Nicholas King's "A map of lands situate on the Great Kanawha River, near its confluence with the Ohio," which clearly shows Washington's holdings. The writer is indebted to Richard W. Stephenson of the Geography and Map Division for his knowledgeable assistance. Kanawha maps and plats in the Manuscript Division are listed in *The George Washington Atlas* (Washington, 1932), items 58–62, 96–102.

[5] The spelling "Aligany" appears in Washington's December 8, 1769, petition to Botetourt, GW, 4th series, 11:1404A, and in *The George Washington Atlas,* plate 11 (Washington's sketch of his trip from Cumberland, Md., to Fort Le Boeuf, Pa., 1753–54). The subject of this article was apparently unknown to the compilers of the *Atlas.*

[6] In the Jefferson Collection, Rare Book Division, in the Library of Congress.

[7] *Journal of the Virginia House of Burgesses, 1766–69,* edited by John Pendleton Kennedy (Richmond, 1906), p. 336.

[8] Abernethy, p. 7.

[9] Archibald Henderson, "Dr. Thomas Walker and the Loyal Company of Virginia," American Antiquarian Society, *Proceedings,* 41, pt. 1 (April 1931), 88–89; Abernethy, p. 5.

[10] The manuscript journal of the survey and various privately printed versions of it are in one of the eight containers of Walker material in the William C. Rives Papers, Manuscript Division. See also Henderson, p. 91–92, and Abernethy, p. 7.

[11] Evans' *Analysis,* p. 11; facsimile reprinting in Lawrence H. Gipson, *Lewis Evans* (Philadelphia, 1939).

[12] Abernethy, p. 8–13, 59–66.

[13] Ibid., p. 60ff.

[14] Journal, Executive Council of Virginia, PRO, CO 5:1435, June 15, 1768.

[15] Abernethy, p. 64.

[16] Hillsborough to Stuart, PRO, CO 5:70, May 13, 1769.

[17] See map 2, Abernethy, following p. 34.

[18] Paraphrased from the Burgesses' *Journal,* p. 335–336.

[19] The Cedar River figures in the 1771 survey of John Donelson, made after the Lochaber Treaty. Abernethy, p. 75.

[20] GW, 1st series, 12:56–60. Washington again went to Williamsburg, May 22 to June 23, 1770, for the next session; GW, 1st series, 13:31–45.

[21] *Journal,* p. 336.

[22] GW, 4th series, 11:1404B.

[23] Computations, in Washington's hand, of the Ohio and Kanawha distances appear in his diaries, GW, 1st series, 12:6 and 13:118, and in his correspondence, GW, 4th series, 11:1450.

[24] GW, 4th series, 11:1405.

[25] GW, 1st series, 13:78. The Kanawha plats (see footnote 4) also use the correct spelling.

[26] Abernethy, p. 71.

# John Ballendine's Eighteenth-Century Map of Virginia

## BY ARTHUR G. BURTON

## AND RICHARD W. STEPHENSON

Reprinted from the July 1964
issue of the *Quarterly Journal
of the Library of Congress.*

U NIQUE HISTORICAL MATERIALS may rest unnoticed in library collections for years before some special need leads to their rediscovery. A search in the map collections of the Library of Congress for items to be used in the exhibit commemorating the centennial of West Virginia's statehood in 1963 led to the rediscovery of a manuscript map considered for almost 30 years to be of little apparent historical significance. Entitled "A Map of Potomack and James Rivers in North America Shewing their several Communications with the Navigable Waters of the New Province on the River Ohio," it was purchased from Goodspeed's Book Store in Boston on January 11, 1934, for the nominal sum of

$25. The Map Division's annual report of that year includes no reference to its acquisition.

Ballendine's map, it was learned recently, was once in the possession of the London map publishing firm of Thomas Jefferys. Evidence of this is found in a manuscript inventory, entitled *Catalogue of Drawings & Engraved Maps, Charts & Plans; the Property of Mr. Thomas Jefferys; Geographer to the King* (1775). In the catalog, now in the collections of the Royal Geographical Society, London, the map is cited, in folio 9, part 3, as "A Drawing of the Potomack & James Rivers: shewing their several Communications with the Navigable Waters of the New Province on the Ohio by John Ballendine." Thomas Jefferys, one of the most distinguished of Britain's eighteenth-century geographers and mapmakers, died on November 20, 1771.

Neatly drawn in pen and ink on a scale of about 15 miles to the inch, the map shows that part of Colonial Virginia from the Potomac River south to the James and from the Chesapeake Bay west to the Ohio River.[1] It has been carefully designed to emphasize the principal river systems of Virginia and their relationship to one another. The James, Potomac, and Ohio, together with their tributaries, are tinted in green, blue, and yellow, respectively, while the principal mountain chains are lightly colored with a gray wash. The "seaport" towns of Alexandria, Georgetown, and Richmond are represented, as are such frontier military posts as Fort Pleasant on the South Branch of the Potomac, Fort Cumberland at the mouth of the North Branch, and Fort Pitt at the confluence of the Allegheny and the Monongahela. Included also are a few land routes, one of which is the famous "Road from the Yadkin," shown at the point at which it crossed the James. Of more significance to the purpose of the map, however, are an "11 Miles Portage" between the North Branch of the Potomac and the Cheat, a tributary of the Monongahela; a "Waggon Road 20 Miles" joining "Luneys Creek," a tributary of the South Branch, with the Cheat; and a "4 Miles Portage" connecting the "Gapin," a tributary of the "Great Kenhawa," with "Carpenters Creek," a tributary of the James.

In many of its details the map is remarkably similar to the famous eighteenth-century printed map by Joshua Fry and Peter Jefferson entitled *A Map of the Most Inhabited Part of Virginia* (London, Thomas Jefferys, 1755). It differs, however, in the placement of some of the rivers and mountain ranges of the western region.

The map is undated. The date "c. 1802," penciled in the lower margin—possibly by a dealer—is obviously in error, for John Ballendine, to whom the map is ascribed,[2] died on October 14, 1781.[3] Furthermore, it is clear from the reference in the title to the "New Province on the River Ohio," that the map belongs to the period immediately preceding the American Revolution when plans were being developed in Great Britain for the creation of a fourteenth colony in western Virginia to be called "Vandalia." This was an undertaking promoted by the Walpole or Grand Ohio Company, whose shareholders included such leading personages on both sides of the Atlantic as Thomas Walpole, Benjamin Franklin, Samuel Wharton, and Thomas Pownall.

John Ballendine was a man of considerable energy and ability, a promoter of numerous enterprises[4] which frequently brought him into contact with prominent men of his day. Some of his projects involved him rather closely with George Washington. One, to which the map relates, was a scheme[5] for connecting the eastern seaboard via improved river navigation with the unfolding West. Washington, who for some years had been keenly aware of the commercial and military advantages of an inland waterway, in 1772 secured passage by the Virginia Assembly of an act providing for "opening and extending the navigation" of the Potomac by private subscription.[6] At this time also he was instrumental in enlisting support for Ballendine's plan to improve the Potomac. He wrote on May 5 to Thomas Johnson in Annapolis, "Mr. Ballendine has a natural genius to thing's [sic] of this sort, which if properly encouraged may lend much to publick utility." He added "I wish to see him encouraged."[7]

By 1773 Ballendine was in London where he published a set of *Proposals*[8] in which he stated that having entered into an agreement on May 9, 1772, with the Governors of Maryland and Virginia, Lord Fairfax, and "most of the principal gentlemen of the said provinces," he had proceeded, "in conformity to his engagement," to England to make a study of the British system of canals and locks.

In the same document he invited subscriptions from potentially interested parties, such as the members of the Walpole Company, who for commercial reasons were vitally concerned in the possibility of improved transportation between the "new province" and the seaports of the east. The sums of money subscribed were to be "solely applied to, and disposed of, for removing the obstructions in, and rendering more open and extensively navigable, than

are at present" the Potomac and James Rivers "from the tide waters of the same, (or, as far as sea vessels do now sail up these rivers) to such parts of the heads of the said rivers; as from thence, the shortest and most convenient wagon roads can be made, to the rivers Great Kanhaway and Monongahela, in the intended new colony." The proposals provided also that all "accounts of the costs, expenditures, and charges" incurred by the project were to be

*Tinted map accents river systems. From the Geography and Map Division.*

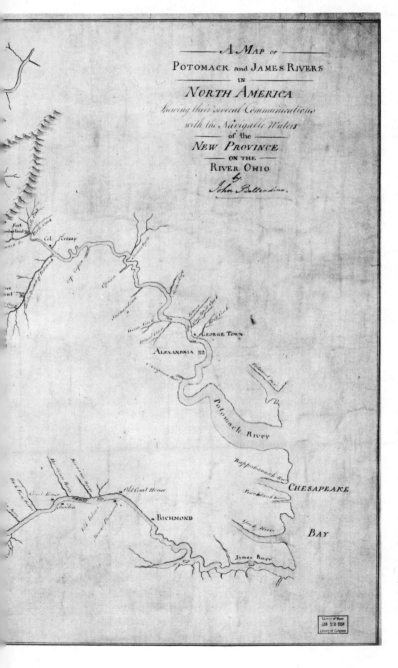

submitted "to the examination and final adjustment of six gentlemen," to be appointed by the Governors of Maryland and Virginia and by Thomas Walpole, the principal stockholder in the Grand Ohio Company.

As early as February 25, 1773, Ballendine also published in London a prospectus [9] which, together with the map, he undoubtedly used in explaining his plans to potential subscribers. In it he related that in August 1772 he made an exploratory trip to the upper reaches of the Potomac and the James. He found that the distance between the "Head of the North Branch of the navigable Waters of Potowmack" and the Monongahela "is not, at most, more than Ten or Eleven Miles." He further "ascertained the Distance between the navigable Head Waters of James River, and those of the Great Kenhawa, and found it not to exceed Four Miles." Ballendine's map, since it incorporates these same distances, must have been prepared at about this time. The presence of the manuscript in the estate of the publisher, Thomas Jefferys, in 1775, suggests that there may have been plans to publish it.

The inclusion on the map of a "Waggon Road 20 Miles" suggests that Ballendine may also have had in mind an alternate route to the Cheat, via the South Branch rather than the North. Washington, a year later, may have been referring to the same road when he wrote to Henry Riddell, on February 22, 1774: "This Land Carriage if the Inland Navigation of Potomack should be effected, than which I think nothing easier, will be reduced to sixty miles as matters now stand; some say 40; and others are of Opinion to twenty miles." [10]

Ballendine was not entirely successful in raising the funds he had hoped for in England. He returned to Virginia in August 1774 and publicly announced [11] that he had "just arrived from Great Britain, with a number of engineers and artificers, in order to remove the obstructions to the navigation of Patowmack river, at and above the Lower Falls." He desired a meeting of his principal subscribers to lay before them "an accurate plan, and estimate of the expence; also an act of the Virginia assembly, and likewise a subscription from some of the principal proprietors, &c. of the province of Vandalia, now residing in England, for the further encouragement of the proposed

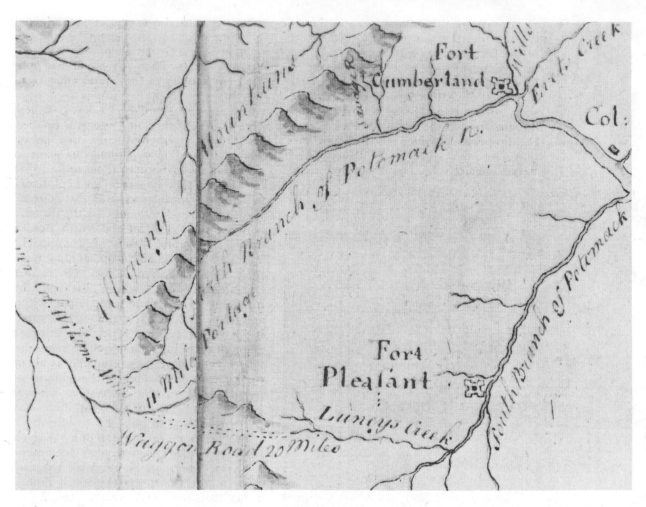

*Detail showing "11 Miles Portage" and "Waggon Road 20 Miles."*

*Facing page, "4 Miles Portage" on the Ballendine map.*

undertaking." The meeting, which was attended by George Washington, Thomas Johnson, and other notable men of the day, was held at Georgetown on October 10. Ballendine's plan and estimate were approved, trustees were appointed,[12] and additional funds were subscribed.[13] Subsequent meetings relating to Ballendine's progress at Little Falls and other locations were held on November 16 at "Frederick Town," [14] on December 1 at Georgetown, and on December 19 at Alexandria.[15]

Owing to a combination of factors, which included the opposition of legislators in Maryland and central Virginia, the Potomac venture was abandoned. In October 1775 Ballendine announced that he had been "at considerable Expence in Preparation, &c. to forward that useful Work," but that "the Necessity of a Maryland Act of Assembly co-operating with one passed in Virginia, and which I have not yet been able to obtain, has obliged me to decline it for the present." He continued that he

had therefore removed himself to the falls of the James River above Richmond, where he planned to devote himself to "opening and extending the Navigation of James River, which, though a Work less interesting to me, is of equal Utility to the Public." [16] Unfortunately six years later, with the project on the James largely incomplete, Ballendine died.

A man whose "genius" Washington admired, Ballendine has generally been ignored by the writers of history or simply regarded "like many a man of vision a failure." [17] Though they failed, his were the first serious attempts to improve the Potomac and the James. Even under the impetus of a rapidly expanding West, similar ventures of a later date also fell short of success. His map survives as a reminder of the rugged individualism that helped to open the West and mold a Nation.

[1] The map measures 23½ x 32 inches and has been mounted on muslin and faced with crepeline for better preservation. It is quite legible, with the exception that the ink used in two lines of the title, the signature, and some of the place names has faded. The ink on the remainder of the map shows no evidence of fading.

[2] Ballendine's signature follows the title. Comparison with signed letters, written by Ballendine to Washington on January 24 and November 18, 1760 (now in the Washington Papers in the Library's Manuscript Division), confirms the authenticity of the signature on the map.

[3] See Randolph W. Church, "John Ballendine, Unsuccessful Entrepreneur of the Eighteenth Century," *Virginia Cavalcade*, 8:46 (Spring 1959).

Ballendine's will is recorded in the Clerk's Office, Fairfax County, Va., in Will Book D 1, p. 247–256. It is dated June 3, 1781, and was presented in court on March 19, 1782.

[4] For a general discussion, see Church, op. cit., p. 39–46; and, especially for documentation, Fairfax Harrison, *Landmarks of Old Prince William* (Richmond, 1924), vol. 2, p. 435, n. 23, and p. 556, n. 9.

[5] See the section on the Ballendine scheme in Corra Bacon-Foster's "Early Chapters in the Development of the Potomac Route to the West," *Records of the Columbia Historical Society*, 15:117–123 (1912). See also Harrison, op. cit., p. 556, n. 9.

[6] "An act for opening and extending the navigation of the river Potowmack from Fort Cumberland to tide water." In the same year the Assembly also passed "An Act for opening the Falls of James River by Subscription, and for other Purposes."

[7] *The Writings of George Washington From the Original Manuscript Sources, 1745–1799*, edited by John C. Fitzpatrick (Washington, 1931), vol. 3, p. 82, 83.

[8] John Ballendine, *Proposals for Opening the Navigation of the River Potomac*, reprinted in George Armroyd's *A Connected View of the Whole Internal Navigation of the United States* (Philadelphia, 1830), p. 209–213. Although not so indicated in the title as rendered by Armroyd, the "Proposals" actually relate to both the Potomac and the James Rivers.

[9] John Ballendine, *Cost of Carriage From the Sea Ports of George Town in Maryland, and Richmond, and Alexandria in Virginia, to the Proposed New Colony on the Ohio in North America* (London, 1773). Copy consulted is in the New York Public Library.

[10] This letter is in the Washington Papers in the Library's Manuscript Division.

[11] *The Maryland Gazette* (Annapolis), no. 1513, September 8, 1774.

[12] Ibid., no. 1522, November 10, 1774, and *The Virginia Gazette* (Williamsburg), no. 444, November 10, 1774. A meeting of trustees was also requested to take place at Georgetown on November 12 in order to elect "a small and convenient number of the trustees, who shall be a committee to act for the whole."

[13] See subscription paper published in Hugh T. Taggart's *Old Georgetown (District of Columbia)* (Lancaster, Pa., 1908), p. 59–60.

[14] See the section on the Ballendine scheme in Grace L. Nute's "Washington and the Potomac: Manuscripts of the Minnesota Historical Society, [1754] 1769–1796," *The American Historical Review* 28:516 (April 1923).

[15] On the December meetings, see *The Virginia Gazette* (Williamsburg), no. 1223, January 14, 1775.

[16] Ibid., no. 1264, October 28, 1775.

[17] Opinion of John C. Fitzpatrick, editor of *The Diaries of George Washington, 1716 1799* (Boston and New York, 1925). See vol. 1, p. 109, n. 6.

# The Federal City
# Depicted·1612-1801

## BY NELSON R. BURR

Reprinted from the November 1950 issue
of the *Library of Congress Quarterly
Journal of Current Acquisitions.*

ALTHOUGH the region now occupied by the Nation's Capital was known to Englishmen shortly after 1600, popular histories of Washington generally pass over events before 1790 as if they were almost negligible. But the area was well settled generations before Congress created the "Ten Mile Square," and Captain John Smith had sailed up the Potomac as far as Indian Head in 1608. Four years later appeared the first map by an Englishman, the famous *Virginia Discouered and Discribed by Captayn John Smith, 1606,* on which one can recognize familiar features of the region, such as the Eastern Branch (Anacostia River) and the nearby Indian village of "Nacotchtanck." The first book containing this map is Smith's *A Map of Virginia. With a Description of the Covntrey* (Oxford, 1612). The map was published later in the first and second editions, 1624 and 1626, of the Captain's *Generall Historie of Virginia.* (See the article on the map above.)

Smith's map was the prototype of many others until late in the seventeenth century. It appeared in the 1625 edition of *Pvrchas His Pilgrimes* and was used by Henricus Hondius for his *Nova Virginiae tabula* which was included in a 1642 edition of Mercator's *Atlas.* A map bearing the same title occurs in Arnoldus Montanus' *Die unbekante neue Welt* of 1673 and an "impudent plagiarism" is found in John Ogilby's *America* (London, 1671), with the decorated cartouche featuring the tobacco leaf which adorns many later maps of the Potomac region. The pervasive influence of Smith is evident even on Peter van der Aa's *D'Engelze Volkplanting in Virginia,* a handsome engraving made at Leyden early in the eighteenth century.

The cartography of Washington remained hazy, however, before Augustine Herrman, "the Bohemian," issued his fine *Virginia and Maryland as It Is Planted and Inhabited This Present Year 1670* (London, 1673). As a settler on the Eastern Shore, Herrman knew the country at first hand, and his detail surpasses that in all previous maps. It includes the Eastern Branch and "Turky Bussard Point" near its mouth, "Anacostien Ile" (later Mason's, now Roosevelt Island) with an Indian village, Rock Creek, and "Potowmeck" Falls. (See the article on the Herrman map above.)

For about 75 years, Herrman's work was practically copied by cartographers who usually included the Great Falls, Anacostien Island, and Turkey Buzzard Point. A number of small streams, generally not named, are obviously intended to be Rock Creek, St. James' Creek, and the one immortalized by the traveling Irish bard, "Tom" Moore: "And what was 'Goose Creek' once is 'Tiber' now." The family resemblance is obvious in James Lancaster's manuscript map of Maryland in the Blathwayt Collection at the John Carter Brown Library, and a similar contemporary one issued anonymously, which is in the British Colonial Office records.[1] Other Herrman progeny are maps by John Senex (1719), Johann Baptist Homann of Nuremberg (1720), Pieter Mortier of Amsterdam (c. 1730), and Herman Moll's map of Virginia and Maryland in his *Atlas Minor* (London, 1736).

Another era in cartography began about 1736, with surveys by John Warner and William Mayo of Lord Fairfax's princely estate on the Northern Neck of Virginia. Their manuscripts crossed the ocean and eventually reached the Public Record Office, whence photostats made the return trip to the Library of Congress. Warner indicates Four Mile Creek, Alexander's Island, the Eastern Branch, Goose Creek, and Rock Creek. Mayo adds Mason's Island, the Little Falls, "Watson's" place on the Potomac in the present city, and McGee's ferry west of Rock Creek. This accurate work was lost upon some cartographers, including the drafter of the *New Map of Virginia* (published in Sir William Keith's *History of the British Plantations in America,* London, 1738), who located the Great Falls and "Anticostin" Island below the Eastern Branch!

Such a convulsion of nature would have discomposed the planters and merchants who were already dreaming of a great trading center at the head of tidewater. Their ambitions appear in the location of the new town of "Belhaven" (Alexandria) on the first scientifically accurate map to include the area of the future District. This is the famous *Map of the Inhabited Part of Virginia . . .,* drawn by Joshua Fry and Peter Jefferson and published at London in 1751 by Thomas Jefferys.[2] Its origin

*Aquatint of George Town and Federal City, or City of Washington, 1801, from George Beck's drawing. From the Prints and Photographs Division.*

127

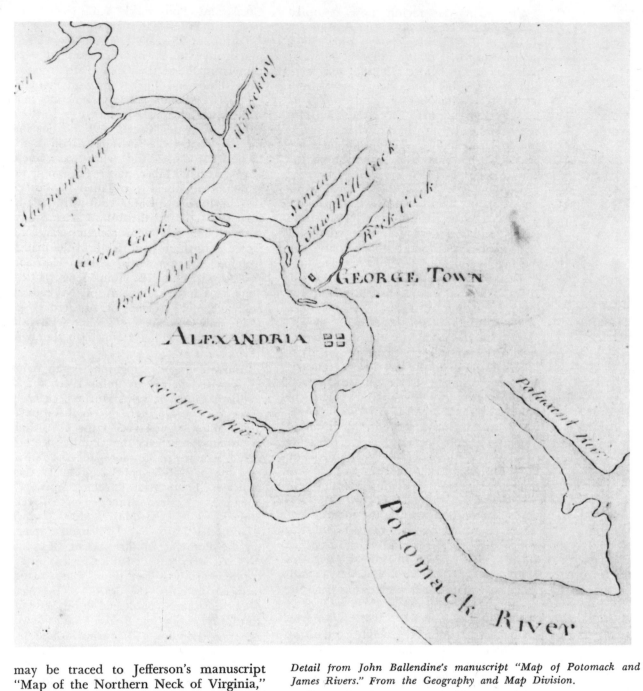

*Detail from John Ballendine's manuscript "Map of Potomack and James Rivers." From the Geography and Map Division.*

may be traced to Jefferson's manuscript "Map of the Northern Neck of Virginia," completed in 1746 according to surveys of the preceding decade.[3] Peter Jefferson was the father of the famed Thomas, who helped to plan the "metropolis" at the point where roads began to converge significantly at the Potomac ferries, as indicated on the 1755 and 1775 editions of the Fry and Jefferson map.

When France joined the Maryland and Virginia gentry in their war for independence, the head of tidewater became a con-

venient road junction and crossing place for the armies. The demand by French and British commanders for more accurate maps illustrates how the region was becoming a center of trade and population. A fine example is a manuscript atlas, "Amerique campagne 1782," made by order of the Comte de Rochambeau. Its 54 colored plans of camps include three, dated July 17–19, at Alexandria, near Georgetown, and at

Bladensburg, respectively, embodying considerable local detail.

The American cartographers, Robert Erskine and Simeon De Witt, performed an inestimable service in preparing maps depicting roads. The Library has photostats of these maps from the originals in the New-York Historical Society's collection. Christopher Colles' *Survey of the Roads of the United States of America* (New York, 1789) includes maps engraved by Cornelius Tiebout, based in part upon Erskine and De Witt. (See the facsimile edition of this publication, edited by Walter W. Ristow and published by Harvard University Press in 1961.) Two of these maps show roads from Annapolis to Bladensburg and Alexandria, with topographical features of the future District and small sharply cut plans of Alexandria and Georgetown.

Military activities helped commercial interests in calling attention to the possible site of an emporium for the Western trade. And on both sides of the Potomac, gentlemen of vision were catching the internal improvement fever as they scanned charts. John Ballendine's manuscript "Map of Potomack and James Rivers . . . ," about 1772 or 1773, emphasized communication with the Ohio and the Northwest. (See the article on this map above.)[4] One may guess what was in the collective mind of the Executive Council of Virginia, in requesting William Tatham in February 1790 to draw a manuscript "Map of the Parts of Virginia and Maryland Bordering on the Potomac River above Alexandria."[5]

By that time Congress was already considering the Potomac site for a capital city, and none followed the debate with keener interest than the owners of large tracts of land. After the establishment of Prince Georges County in 1695–96, speculators had taken up patents for thousands of acres along the Potomac and the Eastern Branch. Among them were Col. John Addison, Col. Ninian Beale, the Carrolls, and Notley Rozier, who owned Duddington Manor, which eventually descended to the second Daniel Carroll of Duddington, nephew of one of the original Commissioners of the District.

Long before 1790 this area was dotted with mansions, slave cabins, tobacco warehouses, and mills turned by Rock Creek and lesser streams. The owners formed a select society and sometimes gave their estates fanciful names, such as Widow's Mite, Queen's Hazard, Rome, Jamaica, and New Troy. The locations, dates, and areas of these estates appear on Dr. Henry J. Berkley's manuscript maps entitled "Early Large Estates in the District of Columbia and Neighboring Territory," and "Prince George County, 1696."[6] They are based primarily upon minute study of the surveys of 1692–1714 by Clement Hill, Surveyor General of Prince Georges County, and of the Lord Baltimore rent rolls of 1720–30.

One may construct a fairly complete real estate map of Washington before 1795 from these maps, and from the many extant plats of individual estates.[7] The plats include some outside the old city bounds but within the District, such as Friendship, St. Phillip and Jacob, Philadelphia, and Frogland. A typical plat is one of "Cerne Abby Manor," patented in 1760 by Charles Carroll, Jr.[8] Made supposedly by John F. A. Priggs, it extends from the Eastern Branch to Rock Creek and includes Duddington Manor and Pasture, and New Troy. Other "views" of Washington in embryo comprise two interesting undated pencil tracings of surveys by Charles Beatty and Archibald Orme, displaying George Beall's mill, the lands of Anthony Holmead, James M. Lingan, Edward and William Pierce, Robert Peter, and David Burnes, the Threlkeld property, and the old Frederick, Bladensburg, Eastern Branch, and Church roads. Three anonymous maps show properties from 1687 to 1694, including names and dates, along the old northern limit of the city from Rock Creek to the Bladensburg Road. Another comprises tracts along the Potomac from Foxhall to the Great Falls, probably after 1795, since it includes the Chesapeake and Ohio Canal.[9]

Most of these surveys are interesting only to local historians and iconographers, but occasionally the searcher comes upon a real display piece. Such is the delicately traced, black and yellow plat of the Carroll lands, made in 1793 by John F. A. Priggs for Daniel Carroll of Duddington. Another shows the site of Duddington Manor at E and 2nd Streets, S. E., with square 736 in pale green tint and the buildings erected before and after 1791 in yellow and red. It does not include the famous house on New Jersey Avenue, which Major L'Enfant summarily demolished because it interfered with his street plan. A third tinted show-piece is an anonymous and undated "Plan, Exhibiting the Squares on Which Robert Peter's Buildings Stood . . . ," bounded by the Potomac, New Hampshire Avenue, and H and K Streets, N. W. This is the oft-mentioned "Mexico" tract, with the house and tobacco barn, which appear in George Beck's beautiful view of Georgetown and Washington in 1800.

To the foresight and good taste of Robert Peter we owe one of the finest records of Washington iconography. When the proprietors agreed with the District Commissioners in 1791–92 about the disposition of their lands, Peter commissioned Nicholas King to compile an atlas of his "Mexico" and "Mount Pleasant" estates. This contains finely tinted maps of the tracts, and plats of squares variously colored to show lots assigned to Peter and to "the public." King likewise compiled a superb atlas of Samuel Davidson's "Port Royal," from 15th to 18th Streets, N. W. and New York Avenue to M Street, including the north part of "President's Square." [10] Most of the plats in these volumes are signed and dated by James R. Dermott, maker of the famous "Tin Case Map" of Washington.

Through study of such records Dr. Joseph M. Toner (1825–96) became an authority on the history and iconography of the District. One of the most useful results of his research is the well-known "View of the City of Washington in 1792," believed to have been made for him. This manuscript, without scale, date, or signature, comprises the city within its original bounds and specifies limits and names of estates, names and homes of proprietors, plans of Georgetown, Hamburgh, and Carrollsburg, and the location of Jenkins (Capitol) Hill. The U. S. Geological Survey used it in 1914 to prepare a *View of the City of Washington in 1792 and 1911,* illustrating the relation of the old estates to the modern city. Dr. Toner's painstaking labor also provided the groundwork for Ernest F. M. Faehtz and Frederick W. Pratt's *Washington in Embryo* (Washington, 1874), showing the estates before L'Enfant's survey and indicating by dotted lines his avenues and such early "improvements" as reservations and bridges. J. W. Stewart's *Map of the City of Washington* (Washington, 1884) displays in colors, with plat numbers, the estates at the time of division, with the original owners.

The landowners had long been planning to devote their acres to something besides tobacco and dreamed of making the brown Potomac a thronged highway of commerce. Until late in the eighteenth century, the only evidences of such activity were "rolling towns," clusters of wharves and warehouses from which hogsheads of tobacco were rolled to the ships. Cartouches of quaint old maps depict planters and merchants lounging, gossiping, and whiffing the "sot-weed" among bales and barrels, with a Negro boy bearing a cup, as Hebe did when Jove grew languid. Similar designs later enlivened the fascinating handkerchief maps of Washington.

A "rolling town" called Belhaven sprang up after 1730 near the mouth of Hunting Creek. Its romantic name persisted until 1748, when a group of enterprising Virginians founded Alexandria, named for the Alexanders who owned a large share of the land. As the projected emporium was included in the original District, special interest attaches to its cartography. The trustees had the site laid out by John West, Surveyor of Fairfax County, whose plats are in the county land records.[11] His "Plat of the Land Where on Stands the Town of Alexandria" (1748) and "Plan of Alexandria Now Belhaven" were copied by George Washington, a youth of 17, who had recently returned from surveying the lands of his patron, Lord Fairfax. Alexandria so prospered that by 1790 it was a formidable contender for the honor of being the national capital. Its backers were probably familiar with James Dermott's manuscript survey for the proprietors in 1791 and the anonymous "Plan of Alexandria in the Territory of Columbia . . ." (c. 1798) in the Alexandria land records.[12] The masterpiece of local cartography before 1801 is Col. George Gilpin's large *Plan of the Town of Alexandria in the District of Columbia, 1798,* engraved by T. Clarke of New York and published by John V. Thomas of Alexandria in 1799. Besides the beautiful original, the Library has a reproduction published in 1944 by Mangum Weeks, who bought Thomas' original copper plate.

Marylanders could not long endure being outdistanced by Virginians, so in 1751 a group of the former secured permission to "erect a town on Potomack River above the mouth of Rock Creek in Frederick

County," which they loyally named "George Town." The Commissioners appointed Alexander Beall to survey and lay out the site, and his plat appears in the "Georgetown Commissioners Minutes," 1751–89. A finer one, "The Plat AD [1758] of the Divisions of GeorgeTown . . . ," was drafted by the well-known surveyor John F. A. Priggs. This plat, which is bound into the "Georgetown Journal," 1751–1801, shows the landings and the rectangular street plan. More detailed is the linen tracing of part of the town, made in 1900 by S. R. Seibert according to notes on surveys of lots in 1752. An addition to Georgetown, laid out about 1755 for Charles Beatty and George F. Hawkins, was platted by William Smith for the land records at Rockville, Md.[13] Zachariah

White's plat of this area (1769) is bound into one of Beatty's mercantile account books, with the courses of lots, assessments, and valuations, and a neat table dated 1770, including owners, dates of conveyance, lot numbers, areas in acres, and rents.

The success of Alexandria and Georgetown provoked the jealous rivalry of other landowners. Among them was Jacob Funk, an up-country "Dutchman" who lived near Frederick. In 1768 he decided to have his own trading town and laid out a site on the pleasant southward slope from 19th to 23rd Street, N. W. and from H Street to the Potomac. His "emporium," complete with sites for a market and a tobacco warehouse, was hopefully named Hamburgh, but the crude and common tongue christened it "Funkstown." It is depicted on a browned manuscript survey of the streets, unsigned and undated, but probably drawn between 1791

*This map showing estates and original bounds of Washington was probably made for Dr. Joseph M. Toner. From the Geography and Map Division.*

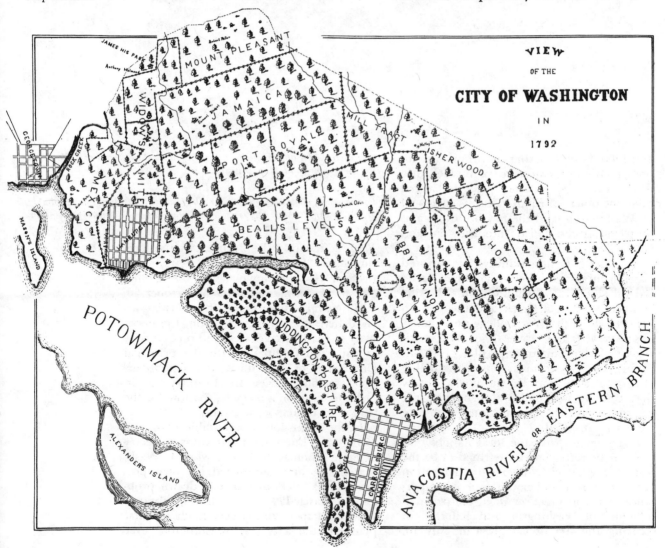

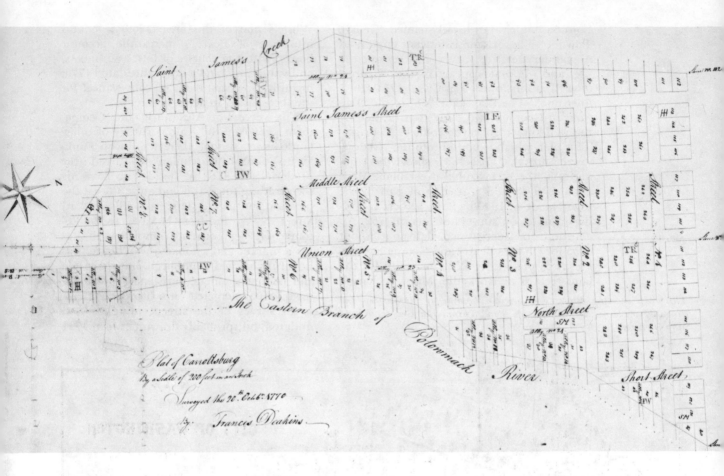

*Manuscript plat of Carrollsburg by Francis Deakins, October 1770. From the Geography and Map Division.*

*Facing page, Jefferson's plan for the City of Washington, probably drawn by him in March 1791. The Jefferson Papers, Manuscript Division.*

and 1800. Funk's soaring ambitions came to nought, however. Most of the lots fell into the hands of speculators who exchanged them for others of equal value, as suggested by Washington, and the few buildings and projected streets faded into the "Federal City."

A somewhat more kindly fate favored Carrollsburg, established in 1770 by Charles Carroll (1729–73) of Duddington. The site, between St. James' Creek and the Eastern Branch where the War College now stands, was surveyed in October 1770 by Francis Deakins, whose manuscript plat gives full details. Local newspapers report the lading of ships at this "port" in the 1790's, but by that time it was being absorbed by the greater city which the ambitious proprietor had partly inspired.

Many agreed with the local nabobs that their rustic retreats were destined to be the seat of a great city. The region's location between North and South and its importance as a road junction aided the personal influence of Washington and Jefferson in securing the Act of Congress of July 16, 1790, designating the Potomac as the location for a "Federal Town." Bets ran high in favor of Georgetown, when *The Times, and the Patowmack Packet* of October 20, 1790, gravely announced, "Last Friday arrived here from Mount Vernon, the PRESIDENT of the United States, and on Saturday morning, in Company with the principal Gentlemen of this town and neighbourhood, set out to view the Country . . . in order to fix upon a proper situation, for the GRAND COLUMBIAN FEDERAL CITY. . . ."

In the discussion of a suitable plan, one of the most interested parties was Secretary of State Thomas Jefferson, who, at Washington's request, submitted his own proposal. This celebrated sketch, drawn probably in March 1791, is now in the Library's Jefferson Papers and is very likely the first plan of the city of Washington ever

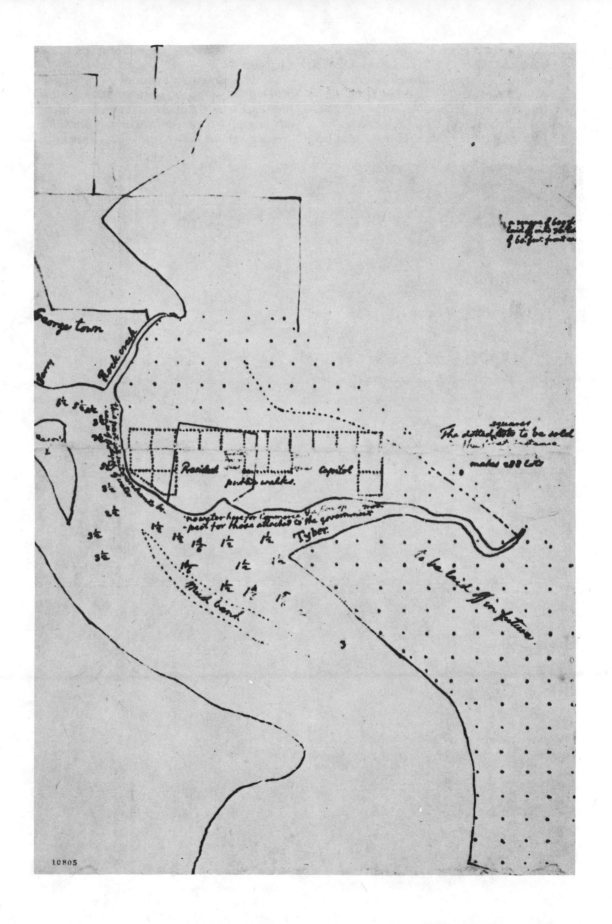

George town

Rock creek

President

public walks.

Capitol

Tyber.

The dotted lots to be sold

makes 288 Lots

squares

Mud land

10805

drafted. It comprises a roughly rectangular site between Tiber Creek and Rock Creek, divided into squares by dotted lines, and a larger dotted area to be laid out later. The details, showing Jefferson's foresight and study of foreign city plans, include sites for the Capitol, a President's House, "public walks" (the Mall), a market, and space for wharves.

While the master of Monticello arranged his own ideas, Washington appointed Maj. Pierre Charles L'Enfant to conceive a splendid city and forwarded to him Jefferson's "rough sketch," with the suggestion that the

Note.) All the Lines coloured red are Finished and thos coloured yellow are intended to be compleated this Season.

city extend from Rock Creek to the Eastern Branch, including "as much ground (to be ceded by individuals) as there is any tolerable prospect of obtaining." [14]

Combining his own vision with the European city plans Jefferson sent him, the testy Frenchman surveyed the site, battling snow squalls, rough wind, and high water, while he slowly perfected his grand "Plan of the City Intended for the Permanent Seat of the Government of the United States. . . ." [15] He wanted "to delin[e]ate on a new and orriginal way the plan the contrivance of which the president has left to me without any restriction soever." [16] The browned original manuscript, many details of which are almost obliterated, is a cherished possession of the Library. With it is his "Doted Line" map, an incomplete manuscript of the plan, untitled, unsigned, and undated, but delicately executed in ink and water color tints. Dotted lines indicate the proposed avenues and streets, and other details include squares, elevations, and the proposed western and northern limits. The only note on the manuscript reveals the progress of L'Enfant's survey: "All the Lines coloured red, are finished and those coloured yellow are intended to be compleated this Season."

The major literally interpreted his own phrase "without any restriction" and became so cocky toward the Commissioners that Washington firmly told Jefferson, *"he must know,* there is a line beyond which he will not be suffered to go," or, "we shall have no Commissioners." [17] L'Enfant did overstep the line, and early in 1792 he was dismissed. He had promised to have the plan ready for the engraver in the spring of 1791, but months slipped away, and Jefferson wrote anxious letters while Washington fumed in angry impatience. Finally, Andrew Ellicott, the surveyor of the District lines, prepared a copy, and Samuel Blodget, the speculator and builder of Blodget's Hotel, wrote to Jefferson that Samuel Hill of Boston had contracted to engrave it for $150, promising to forsake all other work until its completion, which he hoped would be no later than June 1792.[18] But it was October before Hill gave to the world his large and elaborately detailed *Plan of the City of Washington in the Territory of Columbia . . .*, generally called the "Boston" or "Hill" engraving, with "Observations explanatory of the Plan," a note on "Breadth of the Streets," and the latitude and longitude of the Capitol.

Philadelphians were intensely jealous of the new Capital, but probably were proud when their local engravers, Thackara and

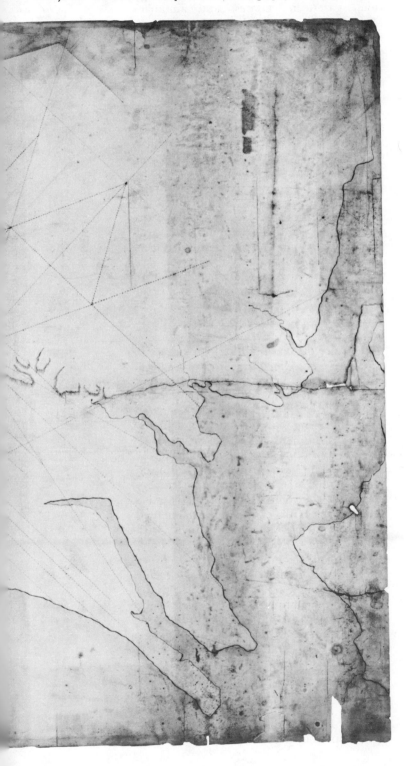

*L'Enfant's "Doted Line" map. From the Geography and Map Division.*

Vallance, issued the second large plan of the city in November 1792. It is based upon Ellicott's drawing, has the same title and descriptive texts as Hill's plan, and is generally known as the "Philadelphia engraving" or the "official plan." As it was issued to promote sales of lots, it bears details not found on previous maps, such as numbers of squares, depths of water, wharves, projected bridges over the Potomac and the Eastern Branch, the proposed city canal, and the ornamental planting along the Mall.

Early plans were so popular that in June 1797 the District Commissioners informed Timothy Pickering, Secretary of State, that their stock of plans of the city and the "Territory of Columbia" was exhausted. They requested him to forward any stock remaining in his office, so that the plans might be sent abroad and distributed in the United States.[19]

Especially attractive were the handkerchief plans, which anticipated the cloth maps of World War II by a century and a half. The Library has two beautiful examples, printed about 1792 in red and in brown on cotton cloth about two feet square, entitled *Plan of the City of Washington in the Territory of Columbia.* The red one is from the Hill engraving, but with the descriptive texts differently placed; it has an ornamental border of leaves and fruits and allegorical figures in the corners. The brown one, bordered with stars, reproduces the Philadelphia engraving and adds a medallion portrait of Washington.

Before 1801 public attention was focused on the new Capital by insets in maps of other regions. Of special interest are three which call the city "Columbia" instead of Washington. These are: *Map of the Middle States of North America* (1791), *A Map of the Genesee Tract . . .* (1791), and *Map of the Middle States . . . Showing the Position of the Geneseo Country* (1800). The last two were made for promotional pamphlets. Improved maps of Maryland promoted knowledge of the "Federal Town"—and the sale of lots. Samuel Lewis' map, in Mathew Carey's 1795 edition of Guthrie's *Geography,* is a curiosity, as it omits the name and bounds of the District. The most impressive of these maps is Dennis Griffith's *Map of the State of Maryland . . . 1794* (Thackara & Vallance, Philadelphia, 1795), which contains a handsome inset, *Plan of the City of Washington and Territory of Columbia,* based on the Philadelphia engraving and including most of the detail.

Meanwhile, the public became familiar with Washington through many descriptive articles and variations of the two early engravings of L'Enfant's plan in books, magazines, gazetteers, atlases, and almanacs. Many if not most of these were skillfully "planted" to catch the eye of people with cash or credit to invest in lots.

The first American description was an essay by "A Spectator" in the *Maryland Journal* for September 30, 1791. Others quickly followed in the *New York Magazine* (November 1791), the *Massachusetts Magazine* (December 1791), and the Philadelphia *Gazette of the United States* (October 8, 1791, and January 4, 1792). These were also the sources of many later descriptions, which were sometimes accompanied by maps. *Massachusetts Magazine* (May 1792) was one of the first periodicals to publish L'Enfant's plan.[20] It is a simpler form of Hill's engraving, with a graceful oval wreath encircling a shortened title. An interesting small map derived from the L'Enfant plan was engraved by Cornelius Tiebout for the *New York Magazine* of June 1792.[21]

Accounts of Washington soon began to circulate in cultivated and liberal circles of western Europe, which probably saw their own sentimental republicanism reflected in the new rustic Capital. A plan derived from Hill's engraving was appended to a highly patriotic *Oration on the Discovery of America* (London, 1792) by Elhanan Winchester, a liberal American Universalist minister. The London *Literary Magazine* for January 1793, in a descriptive article, presented a reduction of Hill's engraving, ornamented with a key, a spread eagle and shield, with the city squares tinted pink and the Potomac a highly imaginary green. Not to be outdone, the London *Universal Magazine* for July included a plan [22] derived from the Philadelphia engraving, which was also the source of maps in J. Stockdale's edition of Jedidiah Morse's *American Geography* (London, 1794) and in William Winterbotham's *Historical . . . View of the American United States* (London, 1795; New York, 1796).[23] The Commissioners' efforts to get a loan from Amsterdam financiers probably inspired the *Plan der Stad Washington* in the *Algemeene vaderlandsche*

*Letter—Oefeningen* for 1793. Highborn gentlemen and ladies who perused the *Gothaischer Hofkalender* and the *Almanac de Gotha* for 1795 must have studied a small, delicately engraved *Plan de la Ville de Washington en Amerique* and used the key to locate the points of interest.

The surveyors who made the plans a reality were still tramping through quagmires and getting their noses scratched by brambles, as did Benjamin H. Latrobe near the Navy Yard. The first was Andrew Ellicott, who in February 1791 began to run the lines of the "Ten Mile Square" at Jones' Point at the mouth of Hunting Creek, near Alexandria. On New Year's Day, 1793, he wrote to the Commissioners, "With this [report] you will receive a map of the four

*Handkerchief map of Washington based on Andrew Ellicott's plan as engraved by Samuel Hill of Boston. Ellicott executed this detailed version of L'Enfant's plan after the major was dismissed from his appointment by the Commissioners of Washington. Thackara and Vallance's engraving of Ellicott's work, issued in Philadelphia one month after the Hill edition, also appeared in a cloth version. From the Geography and Map Division.*

lines, with a half mile on each side, to which is added a survey of the waters in the Territory and a plan of the city of Washington." On February 11 the Commissioners sent to Jefferson "the plat of the Territory, executed according to the President's request." [24] Ellicott sent the copper plate to Washington, assuring him that "the accuracy of the work is infinitely superior to any thing of the kind heretofore executed. . . ." [25]

This is a reference to his beautiful topographical map, *Territory of Columbia . . .*, probably engraved by Thackara and Vallance in 1793–94 and printed by Joseph T. Scott. It is about 21½ inches square, the title being curved around the north corner in accordance with Jefferson's "idea of doing it on a square sheet to hang corner upwards." A characteristic little sketch in the text of Jefferson's letter describes just what he wanted. [26] Ellicott's own estimate of his work proved to be no idle boast, as it was the first of its kind for the District and the standard until 1861. Drawn on a scale of two inches to one mile, it includes the boundary stones, sites of the Capitol and President's House, "grand Avenues and principal Streets," the Potomac islands, many streams and roads, and plats of Georgetown and Alexandria. The stone piers which marked Ellicott's lines at one-mile intervals appear in Ernest A. Schuster's 40 small photographs entitled "The Original Boundary Stones of the District of Columbia, 1791–92," taken in 1908. The locations of 32 of the stones are given on Fred E. Woodward's neat black ink "Chart Showing the Original Boundary Milestones of the District of Columbia."

Before 1801 other patient surveyors battled undergrowth, mud, and mosquitoes to lay out the streets and squares. The Library has fascinating original records of their work. One is "Survey Notes, 1793–5, Washington, D.C.," a manuscript volume supposedly by Robert King, which contains detailed memoranda on the streets and many references to important landmarks. [27] Robert or Nicholas King probably made a similar undated manuscript book, "Calculations of Squares, Washington, D.C.," with surveyor's descriptions of Squares 1–1149, including lands of many original proprietors. [28] Robert King, Sr. (father of Nicholas), bequeathed to posterity a most valuable guide to early Washington iconography.

While in charge of records in the Surveyor's office, he compiled a six-page "Inventory of Books, Plans, Instruments &c. Belonging to the Public in the Surveyor's Office—May 31st 1802," which contains numerous entries for plats essential to constructing a "view" of the city before 1801. [29]

Many surveys before that date were embodied by James Dermott in his *Map of the Public Appropriations of the City of Washington,* which the District Commissioners sent to President John Adams on June 21, 1798. From the manner of protecting it, this has always been called the "Tin Case Map." The Library has a reproduction made in 1854 from the original in the office of the Commissioner of Public Buildings and a photolithograph of 1888, by the U. S. Coast and Geodetic Survey.

Indispensable to a study of early Washington are 21 plats made by Nicholas King, who surveyed for the Commissioners in 1796–97 and was Surveyor of the City of Washington from 1802 until his death in 1812. Much of his work was done before 1801, as a letter from Samuel Davidson to the Commissioners in 1797 praises "Mr. King's elegant and descriptive work, now going forward in your office." The U. S. Coast and Geodetic Survey in 1888 issued a folio atlas, *The King Plats of the City of Washington . . .*, embracing L'Enfant's plan, Ellicott's and Dermott's maps, and King's plan of the city, 1803. The handsome plats bear names of streets and avenues, numbers, measurements, and bounds of original estates.

Ellicott was still busy with his instruments when Jefferson, on March 6, 1792, reminded the dawdling Commissioners to advertise a prize for the best plans of a Capitol and a President's House. The notice, dated March 14, caught the eye of Dr. William Thornton, an amateur architect from Tortola in the West Indies. In October he requested permission to submit his drawings for a Capitol, which the Commissioners were glad to receive, as most of those submitted were impractical or ridiculous. [30] Washington was delighted, praising "The Grandeur, Simplicity and Beauty of the exterior—the propriety with which the apartments are distributed—and the œconomy in the mass of the whole structure. . . ." [31]

Thornton's plan of the Capitol was accepted in March 1793. This was not his first one, which appears in his drawings.[32] An incomplete draft shows a portico, an entrance hall, and three large assembly rooms with semicircular apses. The complete plan, attractively tinted in salmon pink, follows the same general idea but adds an office wing. Thornton did not enter this design in the competition, as he was acutely aware of its defects. After seeing Stephen Hallet's plans, he prepared a new one, according to rough sketches which he had made from Hallet's plans on the back of one of his own. The revised plan adopted the tall central dome, first proposed by Hallet, and was the concept of Thornton's winning design, which has not survived. This is outlined in his "Description of the Plan of the Capitol to Be Erected at the City of Washington . . ."[33] and is the subject of James Hoban's critical memorandum to Thomas Jefferson, "On Drawings Delivered by Doctor Thornton. . . ."[34]

When Thornton was appointed a Commissioner in 1794, he resented changes made by Hallet and wanted to draw another set of plans, to correct "some wilful Errors which have been fallen into, by those jealous men who objected to my Plan, because I was not regularly brought up an architect."[35] George Hadfield succeeded Hallet as superintendent in 1795, and at his demand, Thornton furnished a complete set of working plans. The "revised design" of 1795–97 is represented by an east elevation, handsomely tinted in buff, with a blue dome; a west elevation with a semicircular portico surmounted by statues and a blue dome supported by columns; a tinted floor plan with a central rotunda and three assembly rooms; a roughly sketched section; and an elevation of the North Wing, the only part completed before 1801. These drawings were given to Benjamin H. Latrobe when he became Architect of the Capitol in 1802, and they were later presented to the Library by his family.[36]

Washington somewhat testily observed in 1795 that the Capitol plan represented nobody's ideas, "but a compound of everybody's." That situation was due largely to Etienne Sulpice (Stephen) Hallet, the French "Architecte Expert," whose major contribution was not fully appreciated for over a century.[37] After he was invited by the Commissioners to criticize plans submitted in the competition, he drafted his own, which they liked but did not accept. Greatly chagrined, he was soothed by an appointment, at Washington's suggestion, to study Thornton's plans and to estimate costs.[38] The President soon repented, however, when quarrels began to thicken.

Hallet's designs, exquisitely drafted and tinted, were given to the Library in 1873 by Edward Clark, Architect of the Capitol, 1865–1902, who received them from a son of Latrobe. The earliest, drawn for Jefferson in 1791 before the competition, he called his "Fancy Piece" or "original." It consists of a floor plan and elevation, showing his basic concept of a central dome and wings (Plans "B" and "B2"). His first competitive design ("A1") has floor plans for two stories surrounded by a colonnade, and two sections. Plans "C" and "D" (1792) are the first and second adaptations of the original, the former rather severe and economical, the latter elaborate. Plan "C," from which Thornton evidently made his second design, consists of a domed central hall and large wings, with offices, for the Houses. Plan "D," laid before the President in January 1793, was based upon the Pantheon in Paris, as suggested by Washington and Jefferson, and has a large central portico, a circular domed hall in the center, a west wing with a conference room, and wings containing elliptical halls for the Houses. Early in 1793 Hallet made his last series of competitive designs, Plan "E," with sections and elevations and a floor plan consisting of three halls.

Following the announcement of the prize, Hallet drew additional plans in an attempt to bring Thornton's to practical use. The final plan included a great rotunda with an interior peristyle, a conference room, an elliptical Hall of Representatives, and a semicircular Senate Chamber. Hallet's drawings include later variations of this design with the square central court which he favored so obstinately that he was dismissed.

After seven years of debate, the North Wing was completed. It is pictured in a charming ink and water color sketch made about 1800 by William Russell Birch, an Englishman who was well known as an engraver and painter of enamel miniatures. This, the earliest contemporary view of the Capitol, with elegant red draperies in the windows, shows it as it looked when Congress assembled in November 1800.

The building's unfinished state is suggested by two men cutting stone, and the waiting hacks and gossiping bystanders imply that a session is in progress. The layout of the grounds about that time is illustrated by three manuscript sketches, apparently made before 1801 and including "Capitol circle."

In the decade before 1801 grandiose plans for public works were conceived in enthusiasm but were doomed by indifference, poverty, or bad construction. One such was the first Rock Creek bridge, proposed in a handsome ink and tinted design, which was drafted for the Commissioners in 1792 by Leonard Harbaugh of Baltimore.[39] Plans to develop Tiber Creek as a canal appear in a design of the Mall from Seventh to Fifteenth Street and a drawing of a bridge over the creek.

Private building absorbed most of the speculative interest, while public works languished. A manuscript "Enumeration of the Houses in the City of Washington . . .," prepared in November 1801 by Robert King, Jr., lists over 700, mostly of wood.[40] Many were simple cottages like David Burnes' home, romantically pictured in an anonymous engraving and in a woodcut of 1876, by Eliza Greatorex. Others probably built before 1801 appear in two pale water colors of 1874–75 by James R. Alden. One depicts the home of James Hoban, architect of the White House, on the north side of F near Fifteenth Street; the other portrays houses seen from the N. E. corner of Seventeenth and H Streets.

Photographs and measured drawings of buildings erected before 1801, in the archives of the Historic American Buildings Survey, include the old Stone House in Georgetown, Dumbarton House, old North Building of Georgetown University, Samuel Davidson's "Evermay," the Octagon House, Wheat Row, Thomas Law's home, and William M. Duncanson's "The Maples." The Pictorial Archives of Early American Architecture contain valuable supplementary material, including references to pictures in books and magazines. William Thornton's fascinating tinted designs for the Octagon House and Tudor Place illustrate the contemporary classical taste and the vogue of oval rooms.[41]

The result of this enterprise was not a city, but a project where surveyors and speculators still tramped through marshes and around stumps. The air of improvisa-tion and incompleteness, the piles of lumber, brick, and uncut stone, as well as the avenues leading nowhere, are reflected in accounts of travelers who observed the inchoate "metropolis" with appraising eyes. One of the earliest, an English clothier named Henry Wansey, arrived in the summer of 1794 and described the city at some length.[42]

Perhaps the acutest observer was the cultured Duc de La Rochefoucauld Liancourt, a refugee from the French Revolution, who ranged over the United States during the years 1795–97 and wrote an entertaining account of the "Federal City," Georgetown, and Alexandria.[43] He had ample time to gather impressions during a visit with Thomas Law, who was deeply involved in the speculative mania which the Duke regarded as the city's evil genius and the cause of the slow growth lamented by Jefferson. "In this place," wrote Liancourt, "all the strength of the community is lost. There is no common effort, because the interests of the several individuals are really different. . . . After the plan of the city had been for a while admired for its beauty and magnificence, people began to perceive that it was too extensive, too gigantic, for the actual circumstances of the United States. . . . The number of its inhabitants is at present very inconsiderable, and they are so scattered, that if they were less occupied with their speculations, rivalry, and hatreds, they could still form no society. They visit like people in the country. . . ." He counted about 150 buildings, thinly sown over the vast area or clustered in hamlets at Georgetown, on the Potomac and the Eastern Branch, at Greenleaf's Point, and near the unfinished Capitol and President's House, between which stood Samuel Blodget's "handsome tavern."

The duke's observation is confirmed by George Isham Parkyns' view, *The City of Washington in 1800,* engraved by Heath and published in 1804 by R. Phillips of London. Looking from a wharf on the Virginia side of the Potomac, one sees a panorama of thinly scattered buildings and public works from Georgetown to William Mayne Duncanson's house, including Rock Creek bridge, Lear's wharf, Wheat Row, Thomas Law's house, the Capitol, Conrad's boarding house, Duddington Manor, and Tunnicliff's Hotel, where (according to Mrs. William Thorn-

*William Birch's sketch of the north wing of the Capitol, ca 1800. From the Prints and Photographs Division.*

ton's diary) President John Adams stayed when he arrived in 1800.[44]

Isaac Weld, a Briton, visited Washington about the same time as Liancourt and described the Capitol, the President's House, Blodget's Hotel, and the private houses. He could not take Washington's urban pretensions seriously. "Were the houses that have been built situated in one place all together, they would make a very respectable appearance, but scattered about as they are, a spectator can scarcely perceive anything like a town. Excepting the streets and avenues, and a small part of the ground adjoining the public buildings, the whole place is covered with trees. To be under the necessity of going through a deep wood for one or two miles, perhaps, in order to see a next door neighbor, and in

the same city, is a curious, and, I believe, a novel circumstance." [45] Early editions of his *Travels*, published between 1799 and 1807, contain a plan originally engraved by J. Stockdale of London in 1798. It is a small copy of the "Philadelphia engraving," with the street plan, sites of the Capitol and President's House, the proposed canal, Mall, and wharves.

A hint of real growth appears in a book of travels by the Englishman, John Davis, dedicated to President Jefferson.[46] He mentions the Navy Yard, Marine Barracks, Treasury, and War Office and admires the diagonal streets, radiating from important points. He thought they prevented "the monotony that characterises *Philadelphia*. We here perceive the superiority of taste in a travelled Frenchman, over a homebred

141

Englishman." He preferred L'Enfant to William Penn. But the White House distressed him so that he invoked against poor James Hoban the dreadful epitaph which a wit conceived for the architect Vanbrugh:

"Lie heavy on him Earth;—for he
Has laid a heavy load on thee!"

Modern "planners" should take counsel from his praise of the scattered government buildings. ". . . Some have objected, that the public offices are so remote from each other as to obstruct the business of state. A shallow, gothic remark! The symmetry of the city would have been destroyed, had these buildings been more contiguous." [47]

Several other notable descriptions of the city appeared before 1801, but few approach those mentioned above in charm and critical judgment. Some borrowed heavily from Jedidiah Morse's *American Geography,* like the French Swiss, Charles Pictet, who used other "best" American writers to describe the plan, the sites of the public buildings, and the planting along the streets.[48] Christoph Daniel Ebeling, professor of history and librarian of the Hamburg Gymnasium, compiled a scholastic treatise with many valuable iconographic notes and references to contemporary books, pamphlets, magazines, and newspapers.[49]

The disappointing dearth of illustrations in early travel books is relieved by two beautiful views executed by wandering artists. The earlier one is *Washington* by George Isham Parkyns, a somewhat obscure Englishman who came to Philadelphia in 1795 and worked for T. B. Freeman, a publisher and engraver. It is a black and white print, published by J. Harrison of New York in 1795, and in London by Parkyns. The view, southeast from Georgetown heights, frames the scattered embryo city between huge trees. Its romantic and rather lonesome atmosphere is heightened by a single cart descending the hill, birds wheeling above the trees, and wooded Mason's Island in the distance.

The city as it looked to Congressmen coming to the first meeting there in 1800 is portrayed in George Beck's lovely colored print, *George Town and Federal City, or City of Washington.* It was reproduced from his sketch in 1801 by T. Cartwright of London and published in that city on June 1 by Atkins & Nightingale, and at Philadelphia, presumably in the same year. Beck

(1748?–1814), a Philadelphian, drew many sketches of Potomac River scenery. His view from the wooded heights of Georgetown has often been reproduced. It pictures buildings in Georgetown, the road descending the hill towards the stone-arched bridge over Rock Creek, Robert Peter's house and tobacco shed, distant buildings on the heights and water front of Washington, and two on the sylvan hump of Mason's Island. A weary traveler sitting by the road and patting his dog adds the romantic and sentimental note of the period. This is Washington, as it was when government clerks arrived from Philadelphia, wondering (like many later ones) where they would live. This is the new Capital which President John Adams viewed with mingled feelings, when Mrs. Thornton wrote in her little diary how she saw him rolling along in his "Chariot and four," over the magnificent distances from which time alone could evoke the city of L'Enfant's majestic vision.[50]

## NOTES

[1] Photostats from the John Carter Brown Library and the British Public Record Office.

[2] Photostats made from the first edition in the Alderman Library, University of Virginia, and the New York Public Library.

[3] Photostats from the British Public Record Office.

[4] The Library has photostat copies.

[5] The Library has photostat copies.

[6] The Library has blueprints.

[7] Owned by Charles Beatty, Samuel Blodget, David Burnes, Daniel Carroll of Duddington, John and Samuel Davidson, Joseph Deakins, George Fenwick, James M. Lingan, Lynch and Sands, Robert Peter, William Prout, Benjamin Stoddert, Elizabeth Wheeler, Mrs. Ruth Young, and Abraham and Notley Young.

[8] Photostats from the original MSS, Land Office, Annapolis, Maryland.

[9] Photostat from the original MS, War Department.

[10] Photostat by courtesy of H. H. Dodge, Mount Vernon.

[11] The Library has photostat copies.

[12] The Library has photostat copies.

[13] The Library has a photostat copy.

[14] Washington to L'Enfant, April 4, 1791. L'Enfant-Digges-Morgan Coll., vol. 1, Manuscript Division.

[15] L'Enfant to Jefferson, March 10, 1791. D. C. Letters and Papers, vol. 1, Manuscript Division.

[16] L'Enfant to Jefferson, Apr. 4, 1791, ibid., vol. 1.

[17] Washington to Jefferson, Nov. 30, 1791, ibid., vol. 1.

[18] Blodget to Jefferson, May 3, 1792, ibid., vol. 1.

[19] Gustavus Scott and Alexander White to Pickering, June 16, 1797, ibid., vol. 3, pt. 2.

[20] Has note, "Massa. Mag. 1792."

[21] Has note, "N. York Mag."

[22] Engraved by B. Baker, published by W. Bent.

[23] The New York edition has a map engraved by Rollinson of that city. The Library has separate copies of the Bent and Rollinson maps, and of the John Russell and J. Reid ones made for Winterbotham's book.

[24] Commissioners to Jefferson, Feb. 11, 1793. D. C. Letters and Papers, vol. 2.

[25] Ellicott to Washington, Feb. 28, 1794, ibid., vol. 2.

[26] Jefferson to L'Enfant, Aug. 18, 1791. L'Enfant-Digges-Morgan Coll., vol. 1.

[27] District of Columbia Miscellany, Manuscript Division.

[28] Ibid.

[29] Ibid., box 1791–1832.

[30] Daniel Carroll to Thornton, Nov. 15, 1791. Thornton Papers, vol. 1, Manuscript Division.

[31] Washington to Commissioners, Jan. 31, 1793. Letters of Presidents to Commissioners of the D. C., Manuscript Division.

[32] Thornton Papers, Manuscript Division, portfolio.

[33] Thornton Papers, letterbook.

[34] D. C. Letters and Papers, vol. 6, pt. 1, July 10, 1793.

[35] Thornton to John Trumbull, Jan. 6, 1795. Thornton Papers, vol. 1.

[36] "William Thornton and the Design of the United States Capitol," by Fiske Kimball and Wells Bennet, in Art Studies, vol. 1, 1923. Based upon the Thornton, Latrobe, District of Columbia, and J. Henley Smith Papers in the Manuscript Division.

[37] "Stephen Hallet and His Designs for the National Capitol, 1791–94," in The Journal of the American Institute of Architects, July–Oct. 1916.

[38] Hallet to Jefferson, Sept. 21, 1792. D. C. Letters and Papers, vol. 1. Washington to the Commissioners, Jan. 31, 1793. Letters of the Presidents to the Commissioners.

[39] District of Columbia Letters and Papers, vol. 6, pt. 2, Manuscript Division.

[40] Ibid.

[41] Thornton Papers, Manuscript Division, portfolio.

[42] Journal . . . Salisbury, England, 1796, p. 220–225.

[43] Travels . . . 2d ed., London, 1800, vol. 3, p. 613–667. Quotations, p. 628, 640, 650.

[44] Copy annotated in pencil, Batchelder Coll.; Marshall's Life of George Washington (London, 1805), vol. 3, frontis.; (Paris, 1807), pl. 16.

[45] Travels . . . 4th ed. (London, 1807), vol. 1, p. 86.

[46] Travels of Four Years and a Half in the United States . . . 1798–1802 (London, 1803), p. 168–185.

[47] Ibid., p. 169, 172.

[48] Tableau de la situation actuelle des États-Unis d'Amérique (Paris, 1795), vol. 2, p. 143–146.

[49] Erdbeschreibung und Geschichte von Amerika (Hamburg, 1799), vol. 5, p. 641–679.

[50] Manuscript diary of Mrs. William Thornton, June 3–4, 1800.

In 1904 the Library received as a gift from William Kent the personal papers of his grandfather, James Kent (1763–1847), better known as Chancellor Kent—a title he bore after his appointment to the New York Court of Chancery on February 24, 1814. Among the papers are a number of journals and diaries. Chancellor Kent, in accordance with the general practice observed during the eighteenth century by literate people, kept detailed accounts of his travels.

Almost half a century later, in 1951, Arthur A. Houghton, Jr., gave the Library a first edition of Tobias Lear's *Observations on the River Potomack* (New York, 1793), which bears copious annotations in Chancellor Kent's handwriting. This acquisition has a close relationship to one of Kent's journals in the earlier gift, which commences:

Between 5th December 1793 & the 3d January 1794 both Inclusive I performed a Journey from New York to the City of Washington & Alexandria on the Potomack—the Distance to Alexandria as the Post Road runs being 251 Miles. I went in the public Stage with James Greenleaf Esq. and Mr. Charles Lagarenne a French Gentleman, & the following Facts and Observations are the result of the Tour—

The author comments in considerable detail about every important town and city which he encountered en route—Newark, Elizabethtown, New Brunswick, Princeton, Perth Amboy, Trenton, Philadelphia, Chester, Darby, Wilmington, Havre de Grace, Baltimore, and Bladensburgh—as well as many smaller communities. His notes possess a fascination for the modern historian. For example, his account of his stay in Philadelphia includes the following:

I visited the President at one of his public Levees—They are every Tuesday from 3 to 4 oc. p. m.—You enter, make a Bow—The President & Company all stand with their Hats in their hands, & after exchanging a few words you retire *sans ceremonie*. I saw Mr. Adams, the British Minister Mr. Hammond, & several members of Congress. The President was dressed in a Suit of plain cloth of a snuff color with Silk Stockings & a Sword by his Side. His manners were easy but distant & reserved. His Eye was expressive of mildness & Reflection. His Person was tall & full of Dignity. no Person can approach him without being penetrated with respect & Reverence. Without the brilliancy of Caesars Talents, or the daring exertions of Frederick, such has been his Steadiness, Discretion, good Sense & Integrity that no man ever attained a greater ascend-

# The Federal City in 1793

## BY FREDERICK R. GOFF

Reprinted from the November 1951 issue of the *Library of Congress Quarterly Journal of Current Acquisitions*.

ancy over free Minds, or ever reigned so long & so completely in the Hearts of a sober & intelligent People.

Later on near the end of the journal the writer states:

As I have pretty fully described the result of my visit to George-Town, the city of Washington & Alexandria in *Notes* to Mr. Lear's Pamphlet on the Potowmac, & to which I refer, I conclude this memorandum with some *Miscellanea*.

Mr. Houghton's gift constitutes therefore the missing portion of the journal, united once more with the main part. The annotated copy of Lear's *Observations* is itself an extraordinarily interesting pamphlet. The title page carries the date 1793, the autograph of James Kent, and the note "From James Greenleaf Esq."

On the verso of the flyleaf preceding the title page Chancellor Kent has made two annotations: "The Notes I have added to

*Portrait, by an unknown artist, of James Kent as a young man, illustrating an article on "Society in the Early Days of the Republic," in the February 1893 issue of the* Magazine of American History.

this Pamphlet were done in George–Town Dec[r] 1793" and "The following Observations were made by *Tobias Lear* Esq. late Secretary to the President, & under his Inspection—[1] The Pamphlet came out late in the Fall of 1793 just before Mr. Lear embarked for Europe,[2] & large Numbers were sent over to facilitate the Sale of Lots in the City of W. & to invite emigrants to it from Europe, not only for the Interests of the City, but to import goods & to establish a commercial Connection. He & *Tristam Dalton* Esq. are to commence Trade at the City of Washington next Season = "

Chancellor Kent has made brief marginal comments on Lear's text, but the primary notes relating to Georgetown, Alexandria, and Washington are found on six blank pages at the end. These are so informative and entertaining that a generous sampling has been quoted:

In December 1793 I visited the City of Washing-

ton, George-Town & Alexandria on the Potomack, & the following Notes I made in addition to the Information in the Pamphlet. *George-Town* which as well as Alexandria is included in the federal District tho neither belong to the City of Washington is a pleasant Village situated on the waving Hills on the N. side of the Potomack & about 1 mile W. of the President's House in the City—a small stream called Rock-Creek seperating this Town from the City. This Town has a fine view of the Potomack. It has a beautiful appearance from the S. side of the River, & the Hills on the back of the Town which are improved & improving with handsome Country Seats & which in some Situations will now sell for 50 guineas an acre, command a noble View of the Town, of the City of Washington & of the Potomack quite down to Alexandria. Mason's Island in front of the E. End of the Town adds much to the Beauty of the view. The Houses are exceedingly well built of Brick. The Town may contain 150 families & between 30 & 40 very good brick Buildings. At the Peace this Place had not above 1 doz. Houses. Tho the Wharfs are few & indifferent I observed 2 ships here, & am told that George-Town on an average ships annually 8,000 HH[ds] of Tobacco—From 150 to 160,000 bbls. of Flour, & between 3 & 400,000 Bushels of Wheat, & that Alexandria doubles it as to both the latter articles, tho in Tobacco George-Town more nearly rivals it, as its Inspection is better &c. = George-Town is incorporated—has a Goal & small market, the Streets are pretty regular, tho the Hills are waving. There is a little Presby. Church partly finished, & a plain brick Roman Chapel at the W. End with a clumsy Steeple to it. They have an Academy here under the Direction of a President & vice-President who are Romish Priests. The House now used is a large square 2 Story brick building on a most salubrious & commanding Eminence at the W. End of the Town—a new Building is begun near the same place—Tho the Academy is but of two years old they have now between 80 & 90 Scholars drawn from all quarters, & principally from Roman Catholic families. The Protestants don't relish it. 3 Boys came with me from Phil. This academy contemplates to give Degrees. It gives great attention to the Scholars. A Physician visits them daily, & it is growing rapidly. George-Town is larger now, & has more trade than Baltimore had in 1775. A view from George-Town up the Potomack is as rugged as up the Hudson from Poghkeepsie. The little Falls are 2 miles west. The 3 Locks there will be finished next Spring. The canal which is compleated is 2-¾ miles long. I was on the spot = At the Great Falls a Canal is already cut near a mile thro a Solid Rock, 8 feet deep—£20,000 already expended on these upper falls, the Locks will be completed in 2 years &

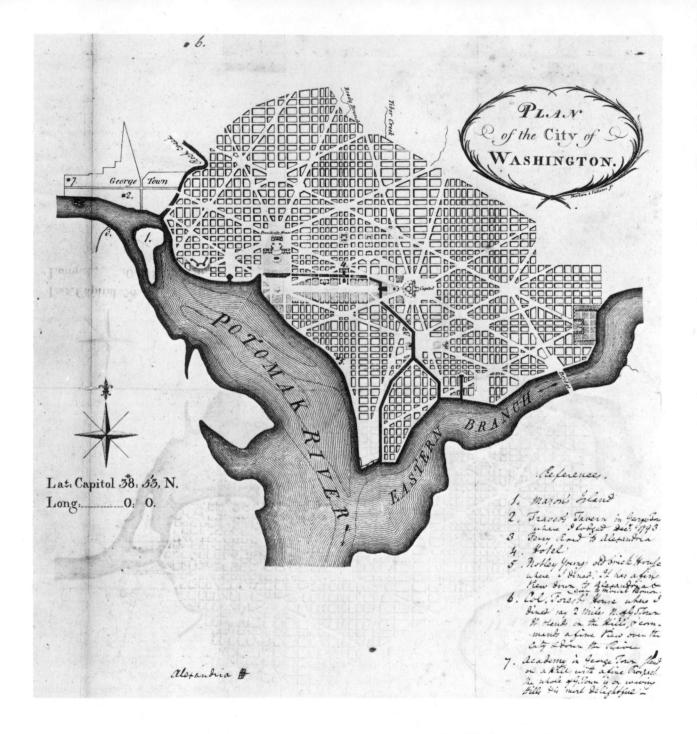

PLAN
of the City of
WASHINGTON.

George Town

Lat. Capitol 38: 53, N.
Long. 0: 0.

References.

1. Mason's Island
2. Travers Tavern in Georgetown where I lodged Dec.r 1793
3. Ferry Road to Alexandria
4. Hotel
5. Notley Young old brick House where I Dined. It has a fine View down to Alexandria & even to Mount Vernon.
6. Col. Forest's House where I Dined say 2 Mile N. of G.Town it stands on the Hills, & commands a fine View over the City & down the River.
7. Academy in George Town stands on a Hill with a fine Prospect the whole of G.Town is on waving Hills & is most delightful.

Alexandria

beyond them the Navigation is clear to Fort Cumberland. One night while I was at George-Town the Potomack from being free of Ice was shut next morning. A Causeway wide 2-¼ mile long & a Stone Bridge of 3 arches leads from George-Town to the *City of Washington*. They were built by the commissioners of the federal district, & cost £13,000. The President's House in ¾th of a Mile E. of the Creek dividing the City from George-Town & ½ a Mile from the River on a Hill yielding a gentle declivity to the River & commanding a fine view for several miles down the River. The Basement Story was laid & built of greyish white free Stone handsomely polished, & brought from a quarry near 50 Miles down the River. But quarries of the same Stone are now found at Mount Vernon & also on the S. of the Potomack opposite the Eastern Branch. The House is 272 feet long—112do broad—spacious Cellars—the Front is a circular Room projecting from the House. The *Hotel* is ¾th of a Mile E. Basement Story also erected of the same Stone. Front even, no circular Room. 120 feet long—60do deep—

*Thackara and Vallance engraving of Andrew Ellicott's plan for the Federal City from James Kent's copy of* Observations on the River Potomack *by Tobias Lear, with notations by Kent. From the American Imprints Collection, Rare Book Division.*

¾ᵗʰ of a mile Further E. is the Ground chalked out for a most magnificent *Capitol,* & this is the highest Ground in the City—¾ᵗʰ of a Mile further E. is the eastern Branch—40 Stone Cutters were now at work on the House & Hotel. The President's House presages to be the grandest & most elegant Palace in the world. The *Avenues* are all cut thro the woods, & these, together with the Basement Stories I have mentioned, & here and there a House & Hut scattered, being *excepted,* this City, so splendid already in the exaggerating Tales of Fame consists of *woods, Swamps & naked Hills* of apparently thin sandy Soil. But great Improvements are contemplated next Spring. House Lots (not water Lots) are now held up high, say £100 & are offered for Sale in Europe at £150. Ster. Mr. Greenleaf & Mr. Morris purchased 6000 Lots at £30 each. There is Ground chalked out for a national University, & subscriptions now on foot for a free School. No ground for Church-yards in the City. Ground left for a national Church. Major L Enfant is the principal Projector of the Plan of the City. 8 miles from George-Town to *Alexandria.* Country poor between —large unfenced & sterile plains surround Alex. It stands on a plat with a fine view of the River flowing E. of the City, & in that Point resembles Chester on the Delaware. The country back is fine for wheat. The Streets are wide & as regular as at Phil. A few excellent brick Houses. The best one is an Inn. It has upwards of 300 Houses. In general the Houses are indifferent—most every House appears to have a Store of Goods—a greater number of Shops for a town of its Size is not to be found—sidewalks paved—Streets not, & extremely muddy. They were crowded with covered waggons from the Country, & it appears to be a very commercial Town. 2 Ships & several Brigs were here. The water here is very bad, & the Town liable to fever & ague. The wharfs are expensive & liable to be carried away by the Ice. A saw a Presby. Church—a plain brick Building, & a Bell hung on a paltry Scaffold out from the Church. The court House was contemptible, & the lower Story was a market. The Bell for this was on a Scaffold near the Court House. I observed such a Scaffold near the fine Epis. Church at Baltimore—contrary to N. England the People here seem to view Steeples as a Deformity. Mount Vernon is 10 miles below Alex. Land has fallen in Alex. 25 per cent in 3 months owing to the bright Prospects of the federal City.

The purpose of Kent's visit of course was these "bright Prospects." Mr. Greenleaf had made an extensive purchase of lots in the Federal City during September 1793. He took young Mr. Kent along to aid him in legal work; from the conclusion of the manuscript journal in the Manuscript Division we learn that Mr. Greenleaf not only bore the young lawyer's expenses but paid him 7⅓ dollars a day "in consideration of the deeds & Contracts . . . [drawn] for him on the Journey—total £ 88."

The Lear pamphlet contains as a frontispiece a "Plan of the City of Washington," engraved by Thackara and Vallance. Neither of the other two copies in the Library contains this plan, nor is it present in the two copies located by the National Union Catalog at the Massachusetts Historical Society and the University of Virginia.[3] It is evident, however, that the map accompanied the copy which Kent annotated. In fact he has marked the map at seven places and identified them through a table of references:

1. Mason's Island
2. Traver's Tavern in George-Town where I lodged Decʳ 1793
3. Ferry Road to Alexandria
4. Hotel [4]
5. Notley Young's Old Brick House where I dined. It has a fine View down to Alexandria & even to Mount Vernon [5]
6. Col. Forest's House where I dined say 2 miles N. of G-Town. It stands on the Hills, & commands a fine View over the City & down the River
7. Academy in George Town stands on a Hill with a fine Prospect. The whole of G. Town is on waving Hills & is most delightful

The Thackara and Vallance plan which derives from Maj. L'Enfant's original drawing is of itself of considerable interest. While Pierre Charles L'Enfant was responsible for the design of the Federal City, he experienced irreconcilable difficulties with the Commissioners. By September 1793 his work in the Federal City terminated completely, and earlier, in 1792, he had been suspended. The Library of Congress has in its possession L'Enfant's original manuscript map of Washington, which the designer is believed to have taken with him to Philadelphia for submission to President Washington on August 28, 1791.[6] Somewhat later Andrew Ellicott, an assistant to L'Enfant and an early surveyor of the District of Columbia, went to Philadelphia for the purpose of preparing, with the assistance of his two brothers, a plan of the city of Washington, using as a basis a copy of L'Enfant's plan since L'Enfant himself apparently withheld his original plan. Mr. Ellicott wrote from Philadelphia to the

Commissioners about this situation on February 23, 1792, saying:

> On my arrival at this City, I found that no preparation was made for an engraving of the plan of the City of Washington.—Upon this representation being made to the President and Secretary of State, I was directed to furnish one for an engraver; which with the aid of my Brother was compleated last monday, and handed to the President.—In this business we met with difficulties of a very serious nature.—Major L'Enfant refused us the use of the *Original!* What his motives were, God knows—The plan which we have furnished, I believe will be found to answer the ground better, than the large one in the Major's hands. I have engaged two good artists, (both americans,) to execute the engraving, and who will begin the work as soon, as the President comes to a determination respecting some small alterations.[7]

The Ellicott plan was turned over both to Messrs. Thackara and Vallance, Philadelphia engravers, and to Samuel Blodget, Jr., who arranged for its engraving by Samuel Hill in Boston. Mr. Hill sent a proof sheet to Secretary of State Jefferson in Philadelphia, who wrote to the Commissioners on July 11, 1792:

> I now send a proof sheet of the plan of the town engraving at Boston. I observe the soundings of the creek & river are not in it. it would be well to know of Mr. Ellicot whether they were in the original sent to Boston. if not, you will probably think it adviseable to insert them in this proof sheet, and send it to Boston, addressed to Mr. Blodget, under whose care the engraving is going on.[8]

The next day Mr. Jefferson wrote to Mr. Blodget informing him of these facts.[9] Apparently the recommendations did not reach Boston in time, for the Hill engraving does not contain the soundings. As a matter of fact, from correspondence exchanged between George Taylor, Jr., and Thomas Jefferson during August 1792,[10] we learn that the plate engraved by Samuel Hill was shipped to Philadelphia on the Sloop *Juno* and arrived there on July 20. The steward at Jefferson's residence in Philadelphia laid it aside and Mr. Taylor did not receive it until August 16. On that date Taylor wrote to the Commissioners of his plans to have a Mr. Scott print the necessary edition of 4,000 copies. Since Mr. Scott was not able to begin printing for a week, he probably did not start until August 23, providing of course that the Commissioners forwarded their approbation. Mr. Scott agreed to undertake the printing of about 100 a day.

At this rate the printing of the edition would not have been completed until early in October. We know from William Tindall's *Standard History of the City of Washington* (Knoxville, Tenn., 1914) that "the Boston Plate was completed in time to be exhibited at the second sale of lots on October 8, 1792."

Meanwhile Thackara and Vallance were preparing at Philadelphia their engraving of Ellicott's map measuring $21 \times 29$ inches. It was much larger than the Hill engraving, which was $17 \times 22$ inches, and cost 4 shillings, $8\frac{1}{2}$ pence—2 shillings and $2\frac{1}{2}$ pence more than the Hill engraving. The Thackara and Vallance plan did not reach the Commissioners until November 13, according to Tindall. However, on September 15, 1792, identical advertisements appeared in two Philadelphia newspapers, *Dunlap's American Daily Advertiser* and the *Gazette of the United States,* announcing that "Plans of the City of Washington" are "to be sold by the booksellers, viz Dobson, Carey, Young and Crukshank." In the former newspaper the advertisement appeared at least four times in October and November and twice in December. This notice quite probably refers to both plans, not to the one engraved in Philadelphia alone.

Several smaller engravings of Washington were made during 1792, three of them before the larger engravings appeared. Messrs. Thackara and Vallance, apparently using Ellicott's plan as a prototype,[11] engraved a plan measuring $8\frac{1}{4} \times 10$ inches (the plate is slightly larger). This appeared as the frontispiece in *The Universal Asylum, and Columbia Magazine* for March 1792, printed at Philadelphia—"for the proprietors by William Young." The engravers' names appear beneath the wreath enclosing the title of this map, which was prepared expressly to accompany a two-page "Description of the City of Washington . . .," based upon a short article which appeared in *The New-York Magazine* for November 1791.[12]

The next American periodical to contain a plan of the Federal City was the May 1792 issue of *The Massachusetts Magazine,* published by Thomas and Andrews. This map measures $8 \times 10$ inches and was engraved by S. Hill, who was undoubtedly working at this time on the larger "Boston" engraving of Ellicott's plan. In the upper left-hand corner there is engraved the phrase "Massa. Mag. 1792."

A similar plan, except for the substitution of the name Tiebout as engraver beneath the frame for the title and the phrase "N. York Mag." in the upper left-hand corner, appeared in the June 1792 issue of *The New-York Magazine,* printed by Thomas and James Swords. On the verso of the title page is a statement requesting the reader to turn to the November 1791 issue of the magazine for a description of the city of Washington. Originally this account was published in *The Maryland Journal* for September 30, 1791. A map of Washington similar to the Thackara and Vallance small engraving appeared in London late in 1792 or early in 1793 in Elhanan Winchester's *An Oration on the Discovery of America Delivered in London, October the 12th 1792.* The title of the plan is not within a wreath and no engraver's name is mentioned, but a rather detailed key covering letters A-Y on this engraving appears within the text.

The Thackara and Vallance small engraving based upon Ellicott's original plan is also used as the frontispiece to Chancellor Kent's copy of Tobias Lear's *Observations,* dated 1793; it was again used as a frontispiece to the edition of 1794. All the foregoing information [13] is presented to show that the frontispiece to the Lear pamphlet, in the Library's Rare Book Division, is a copy of the earliest engraved map of the city of Washington, first published in the March 1792 issue of *The Universal Asylum.*

As a matter of incidental information the paper on which it is engraved bears the watermark "S. L." (Samuel Loudon?). A copy of the map in the Batchelder Collection carries the same watermark. One of the other copies in the Rare Book Division is without watermark, and another is watermarked with a large fleur-de-lys. Two additional copies in the Geography and Map Division are without watermarks. Since this article was first published (in the November 1951 issue of the *Quarterly Journal*), a number of these maps—apparently representing an unused remainder—have come to light.

Nearly 50 years later Chancellor Kent annotated the back of the map in the Lear pamphlet by citing advertisements in the *National Intelligencer* for August 1841 for tax sales on lots owned by James Greenleaf and the heirs of Notley Young. "Thus,"

Kent writes, "terminates Mr. Greenleaf's visionary & fatal Speculations in 1793 in lots in the City of Washington." In view of present realty values in Washington one wonders what these same lots would bring at public sale today.

### NOTES

[1] See *Observations on the River Potomack, etc.* by Tobias Lear. *Unpublished Correspondence of George Washington and Tobias Lear about the Observations. Published Text Compared with an Autograph Copy Sent to George Washington.* Edited by Samuel T. Chambers. Baltimore, 1940. Lear's original manuscript of the *Observations* is now owned by the Library of Congress.

[2] According to Washington's letter to Lear, dated 8 November 1793, Lear was scheduled to sail two days later.

[3] A second edition appeared at New York in 1794 with a slightly different imprint and with the Thackara & Vallance plan. Copies are located here and at the Boston Athenaeum, the American Antiquarian Society, Harvard University, the New-York Historical Society, the New York Public Library, and the Pennsylvania Historical Society.

[4] Located on the north side of E Street between Seventh and Eighth Streets, N. W.

[5] Located near Seventh Street and Maine Avenue, S. W.

[6] See *District of Columbia, Sesquicentennial of the Establishment of the Permanent Seat of the Government;* [Catalog of] *An Exhibition in the Library of Congress, Washington, D. C., April 24, 1950 to April 24, 1951* (Washington, 1950), item No. 60; and *The Grand Design;* [Catalog of] *An Exhibition Tracing the Evolution of the L'Enfant Plan and Subsequent Plans for the Development of Pennsylvania Avenue and the Mall Area, Organized Jointly by the Library of Congress and the President's Temporary Commission on Pennsylvania Avenue* (Washington, Library of Congress, 1967).

[7] Quoted from the original in the National Archives: Miscellaneous Letters Received, No. 81 of 1792, in the Records of the Commissioners of Public Buildings and Grounds. Cited in William Tindall's *Standard History of the City of Washington* (Knoxville, Tenn., 1914), p. 148. Tindall also quotes Washington's letter of March 6, 1792, in which Washington states that Ellicott recently prepared a plan for engraving but that the engravers cannot complete their work under three months.

[8] Jefferson MS 13235 in the Library's Manuscript Division. On the same day Jefferson had received a letter from President Washington in Tobias Lear's handwriting informing the Secretary of State that the President retained one of the proof sheets but returned the other with Mr. Blodget's letter which he recommends be sent to the Commissioners. The letter concludes:

Tobias Lear Esqr:

My dear Sir,

I arrived at this place at the time appointed to wit — the 5 inst but did not receive your letter of the 3d until yesterday for want of a regular communication with the Post office, and this too at a time when as you have well supposed I was immerced in the consideration of Papers from the different Departments after seperation from the heads of them almost two months. —

I have, however, run over your observations on the Potomac Navigation &c &c — and in a hasty manner, as I went along at the first reading made the notes & remarks which are returned with one of the copies. — The statement made by you in all other respects accord with my ideas of facts as far as a recollection of them will enable me to pronounce nor can I controvert, by evidence even those which it would seem that I had queried by my remarks and especially if I could have had recourse to my papers.— Had I more leizure I might have been more exact in some things but as the 10th is the day appointed for your sailing & that happening to be on a sunday a chosen day by Sailors for commencing their Nautical movements I did not incline to miss the Post of the day to return your observations and furnish the title you have asked for. —

It gives me sincere pleasure to hear that Lincoln continues well as I am sure it will do the family at Mount Vernon who must remain there until it is known what Congress will

do;

Tobias Lear was George Washington's private secretary from 1786 to 1793. Upon his return to New York from Georgetown in 1793, Lear wrote down his "observations respecting the river Potomack, the Country about it and the City of Washington" and sent them to Washington on November 3. In the letter accompanying the manuscript, Lear asked that Washington look it over, correct any errors, and return one copy with "your sanction of the statement being founded in truth, if you shall feel yourself perfectly free to do so." His lengthy letter then went into other matters, such as an acquaintance who had expressed interest in employment as a servant. Reproduced on these pages is a copy of the original reply, dated November 8, 1793, from volume 18 of Washington's letterbooks. Lear's letter, the copy of the "observations" retained by Washington, and the letterbooks are in the George Washington Papers, Manuscript Division.

do; for till then I move like a snail with every thing
on my back. —

I do not yet know whether I shall get a
substitute for William: nothing short of excellent qualities and a man of good appearance, would induce me
to do it. — and under my present view of the matter
too, who would employ himself otherwise than William
did — that is as a Butler as well as a Valette, for my
wants of the latter are so trifling that any man ( as
William was) would soon be ruined by idleness who
had only them to attend to — Having given these ideas—
if your time will permit I should be glad if you would
touch the man upon the strings I have mentioned —
probe his character deeper — say what his age, appearance & country is — what are his expectations and how
he should be communicated with, if, upon a thorough investigation of matters you should be of opinion he would
answer my purposes well for Kennedy is too little acquainted with the arrangement of a Table, and too stu-
pid for a Butler, to be continued if I could get a better. —

Once more, and I suppose for the last
time before you sail, bid you adieu; my best wishes
wherever you go will accompany you, for with much
truth I am

your sincere friend &
Affect! Servant —

German Town
8 November 1793

G.º Washington

Excerpt of letter from Tobias
Lear to George Washington.
*In the copies I may have
printed, or otherways I shall
make no improper use of the
sanction you may be pleased to
give of the truth of the statement.—I wish it only for my
own satisfaction, that I may feel
confidence in what I relate; for
altho it will not be mentioned
in the printed copies by whom
the observations are made; yet
as that may hereafter be known,
and possibly while I am at a
distance from this Country,
the truth of the statement may
be questioned by persons who
may be interested in depreciating
the subject of these notes. I shall
feel gratified by having it in my
power to convince those who
may be interested in obtaining
the truth, that they have been
inspected by one whose situation has given him the best
opportunity of knowing the
circumstances of the Country,
and who would not suffer a
statement to have his sanction
unless supported by truth.*

"The President observes that the soundings of the River & Branch are not noted either in this or the other proof sheet, which he thinks would be very satisfactory & advantageous to have done."

[9] Jefferson MS 13249 in the Manuscript Division. The text is as follows:

Philadelphia July 12. 1792.

Sir

I have duly rec^d your favor of June 25. & forwarded the letter it inclosed for the Commissioners. I am setting out tomorrow for Virginia, & therefore in the midst of hurry have only time to say that I suppose it will be well to retain a few copies of the plan of the town, disposing of them where they will be most seen. I observe the soundings are not in the sheets you sent me. I have written to the Commissioners recommend^g to desire Mr. Ellicott, if they were not in the original, to insert them in one of these proof sheets & forward it to you that they may be put into the plate. some good plans of buildings have been proposed.

I am sir

Your most obed^t humble serv^t<br>Th: Jefferson

Mr. Blodget

[10] Jefferson MSS 13309–11, 13317–20 in the Manuscript Division.

[11] See H. Paul Caemmerer, *The Life of Pierre Charles L'Enfant, Planner of the City Beautiful* (Washington, 1950), p. 219. The author reproduces the text of a letter L'Enfant wrote to Tobias Lear on February 17, 1792, in which he refers to Ellicott's plan in uncomplimentary terms and to Mr. Young's interest in a reproduction on a reduced scale of this plan for his monthly magazine.

[12] P. 656–658.

[13] For this section the author has drawn heavily upon the late Philip Lee Phillips' unpublished list of maps and views of Washington and the District of Columbia. This typewritten descriptive list, prepared in 1916, is now in the custody of the Geography and Map Division.

Reprinted from the July 1966 issue of the *Quarterly Journal of the Library of Congress.*

*The great seal of the State embellishes the title of John Melish's map of Pennsylvania published in 1822. Maps illustrating this article are in the Geography and Map Division.*

# From an Actual Survey
# Early Maps
# of Pennsylvania and Virginia

## BY WALTER W. RISTOW

**W**ITH THE ESTABLISHMENT of peace and the adoption of the Constitution, the leaders of the young United States were confronted with urgent and difficult problems. At both national and State levels, good maps were essential, and pre-Revolutionary maps, most of which were published in Europe, were inadequate for the needs of the youthful and vigorous nation. Because State budgets could not support surveying and mapping programs in the early years of the Republic, the initiative in preparing State maps was taken by enterprising and public-spirited individuals, who received encouragement, and often some financial aid, from State legislatures. How effective these individual and cooperative efforts were is evident in some 30 State maps that were published in one or more editions before 1840. All the former colonies were mapped at least once, and in addition maps were published for Vermont and Maine, which had been part of the Colonies of New Hampshire and Massachusetts, respectively, during the colonial period.

The State maps are among the earliest examples of truly American cartography. Based on original surveys made by Americans, the maps were compiled, drafted, engraved, printed, and published in the United States and were specifically designed to meet the cartographic needs of the officials and citizens of the several States. Above all, in the methods, techniques, and procedures used to produce State maps, American ingenuity and resourcefulness were abundantly demonstrated. Commercial map publishing, which attained a high degree of excellence and productivity during the nineteenth century, was largely built upon the cartographic foundations laid by the several State maps and their makers. This indebtedness was acknowledged in 1829 by Henry S. Tanner, one of the foremost map engravers and publishers of his day, who affirmed that "important accessions to the stock of knowledge on the geography of the United States have recently been made, by the publication of excellent local and State maps." [1]

"From an actual survey," or some variant phrase, is included in the title inscriptions of most early State maps. Crude though they were, the surveys represented a distinct advance over cartographic practices of the colonial period. Surveying was an essential and honored profession in early America; virtually every town or county had its official surveyor who located and determined areas and boundaries of private and public land holdings. The manuscript plats or maps, on which these data were recorded, were filed in county, district, town, or city archives. For the earliest compilers of State maps they constituted a major source of data. Through notices in the press, some mapmakers solicited supplemental and more current data, but efforts to secure information on a voluntary basis, were generally unfruitful. At the request of some of the more vocal mapmakers, legislatures were moved to pass laws requiring county, town, or district officials to supply the State with up-to-date surveys of their jurisdictions. Such local surveys were, of course, independently made, and there was no common geodetic or geographic frame of reference. The State map compilers therefore experienced considerable difficulty in matching roads, administrative boundaries, and property lines along county and town borders.

Nonetheless, this proved to be the most expedient and economical procedure for assembling the essential survey data. By 1830, mandatory survey and deposit laws for county maps had been enacted in many of the States. The work of compiling, drafting, engraving, and printing the State map usually was contracted or entrusted to private individuals or to commercial map publishers; in only a few instances was the map published by official State agencies or personnel. Financial aid or subsidies were often provided to the private mapmaker, and there was at least the assurance that a number of copies of the map would be purchased for use by State officials and offices.

The 1822 *Map of Pennsylvania Constructed From the County Surveys Authorized by the State; and Other Original Documents, by John Melish,* is a model of its type. In the planning and production stages the Pennsylvania map enjoyed a larger measure of official support and direction than did most of the other State maps. The map also benefited from the experience, knowledge, and skill of its compiler, John Melish, one of the most energetic and competent commercial map publishers of his day. Melish, who began his mapmaking career around 1810, was thoroughly familiar with State maps. He drew upon a number of them to compile his large *Map of the United States,* the first edition of which was published in 1816.[2] In *A Geographical Description of the United States . . . Intended as an Accompaniment to Melish's Map,* the compiler acknowledges "recourse . . . to the . . . various State maps, from actual survey, so far as these surveys have extended." [3]

Melish early recognized the respective spheres of interest of private and official cartography. The maps produced by commercial publishers, he noticed, were on small scales, of a generalized character, and compiled from original survey maps and other source data. In his *Geographical Description,* he acknowledged that "the basis on which the whole of the geography of the country rests, is maps from actual survey, and its political subdivisions is highly favourable to the bringing them forward in the character of State Maps." It was quite obvious to Melish "that every State should have its own map. It should be State property," he asserted, "subject to the control of no individual whatever." Their production, Melish believed, should be an official responsibility. "Individuals," he observed, "are not equal to the task of bringing them forward, and keeping them correct. Wherever they have embarked in the business, they have lost much time and money; and unless the states embark in it, the geography of the country cannot be brought to maturity." [4]

Melish's thoughts regarding official sponsorship and support of State maps were transmitted to influential members of the Pennsylvania Legislature. In its session of 1814, as reported in the *Geographical De-*

*The cartographic detail and excellence of the Pennsylvania map are apparent from this segment showing Philadelphia County.*

scription, "Mr. Isaac Weaver, of Green County, . . . moved a resolution that measures might be taken to bring forward a new map of the State. This resolution passed both houses unanimously; and, during the summer, the preparatory steps were taken by the secretary of the commonwealth to ascertain the best plan of procuring the materials, and publishing the map." [5]

Because of his interest in the proposed map and his recognized competence as a geographer and map publisher, Melish's advice was solicited, early in 1816, by Pennsylvania officials. Melish recognized in the request for information "an excellent opportunity for the introduction of his favourite theory," and decided, therefore, "to take a journey to the seat of the state government on the subject." He found the State officials and legislators most receptive and "it soon appeared that the disposition towards the map was favourable throughout both branches of the legislature." [6] Together with members of a legislative committee, Melish drew up plans for the proposed map and act. With slight modifications, it passed both houses and, with the Governor's signature, was enacted into law, in March 1816, as "An Act Directing the Formation of a Map of Pennsylvania." Its clear, precise, and detailed provisions, specifications, and instructions could only have been formulated by a professional mapmaker.

Section one of the act directed the Surveyor General "to contract with the deputy surveyors . . . for the formation of a map of each of the counties . . .; which maps shall be on a scale of two miles and a half to an inch." [7] The physical and cultural features to be included on the map were prescribed in detail. With reference to roads, the surveyor was instructed to note "particularly such as are turnpiked, and the distances in miles between the principal towns and remarkable places." The completed maps were to be "sent, as soon as convenient, to the office of the surveyor general." The expense per map was "not [to] exceed two hundred dollars for each county, unless the information . . . cannot be had in any of the public offices of the state, or of the proper

155

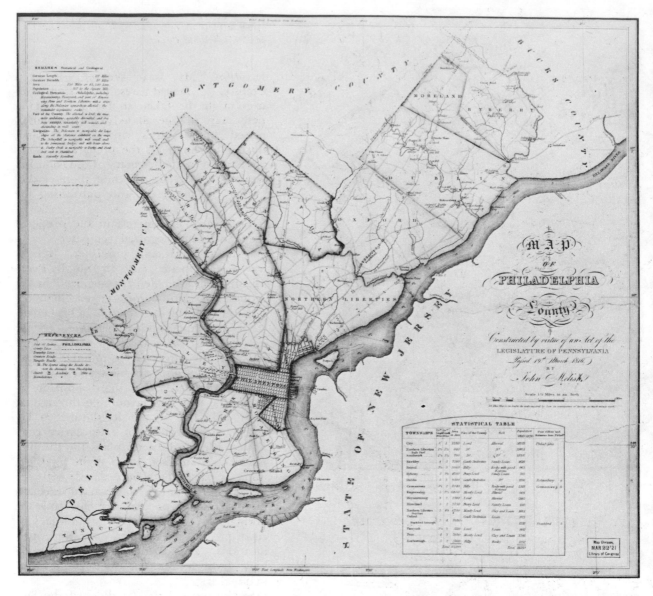

*John Melish surveyed Philadelphia County and prepared this map for engraving, which was published in 1819.*

county," in which case, the Surveyor General was authorized to obtain the desired data "by actual survey . . . at [an] expense not exceeding in the whole six hundred dollars for each county."

In section two of the act the Surveyor General, following receipt of the county maps, was directed to "contract for the publication of a Map of Pennsylvania, with some suitable person." There was no more "suitable person" in Pennsylvania than John Melish, and the map contract was accordingly awarded to him. The Surveyor General, in the third section of the act, was instructed to have hand-drawn copies of the county maps prepared for his office.

In 1965, through the courtesy and cooperation of the Bureau of Land Records,

Department of Internal Affairs, Harrisburg, the Library of Congress acquired photoreproductions of 44 manuscript maps of Pennsylvania counties. Dated chiefly 1816 or 1817, the maps were prepared by county surveyors under provisions of an act of the Pennsylvania Legislature enacted March 19, 1816. All carry the inscription "Copied from the original under the direction of the Surveyor General" over the signature of Jno. C. Whiteside.

After copies were made of the original maps, the latter were transmitted to Melish, who was instructed to use the data to "make a connected map of this commonwealth, on a scale of five miles to an inch, marking thereon so many of the particulars specified in the first section of [the] act . . . and shall cause the same to be engraved on copper, in a handsome and workmanlike manner, and shall cause . . . a number to be printed . . . whereof one hundred, duly coloured, mounted, and finished, shall be delivered . . . to the surveyor-general for the use of the commonwealth."

Melish and his assistants spent more than six years compiling the map of Pennsylvania. A preliminary copy was completed late in 1820 and submitted for examination. A report, dated December 15, 1820, and signed by S. D. Ingham, Secretary of the Commonwealth, and Jacob Spangler, Surveyor General, notes that Melish's map "has undergone a rigid examination in all its parts . . . and we have the satisfaction to say, with much confidence, that the Map promises to be one of uncommon excellence. The whole design is in our opinion judiciously arranged and well executed, and, should the engraving be done with neatness, it cannot fail to give general satisfaction." [8]

Benjamin Tanner, a leading Philadelphia engraver and elder brother of Henry, prepared the plates for the map, a task that required another 15 months. Advance copies of the printed map, examined by the Joint Committee of the Legislature and the Surveyor General, were most favorably received. The committee's report, dated March 23, 1822, noted that "the engraving is executed in a very strong, clear, and neatly finished manner, peculiarly suited to maps of this class, and equal, if not superior, to the style of any other map of the same class ever heretofore published." [9] The Surveyor General and the Secretary of the Commonwealth likewise testified that "they feel no hesitation in declaring that, in their view, the whole work, embracing the plan, the drawing, the engraving, and the colouring, are all evincive of the great exertions of the contractor to comply with his engagement, and that the map is worthy the expense [more than $30,000] which the State has incurred in bringing it to perfection." [10]

To ensure that the published map might be as accurate and up to date as possible, proof copies were sent to officials of all counties for criticisms, corrections, and possible additions. The compiler also secured from State authorities information on the latest road surveys, and the engraved plates were corrected to incorporate these data.

In late summer of 1822 the map was released for public sale and distribution and was very favorably received. *Niles' Weekly Register* announced, in its September 28, 1822 issue, that "the long expected map of [Pennsylvania] by Mr. Mellish [sic] has at length appeared. It may be called a magnificent work, worthy of the great commonwealth which has so liberally furnished the means to produce it. Greater accuracy could not well have been expected than is assured in this map; made up chiefly of county surveys, taken by experienced persons, resident in the respective counties and responsible to their immediate friends and neighbors for the truth of their presentations." When assembled and mounted the six sheets, printed from engraved plates, formed a map of Pennsylvania measuring $4\frac{1}{2}$ by $6\frac{1}{2}$ feet. It was available in several formats, colorings, and mountings, which ranged in price from $9 to $12.50.

The *State Map of Pennsylvania* has been described as John Melish's greatest published work. This is high praise, indeed, when we note the many excellent maps and geographical publications bearing his name that were published in the period 1812 to 1822. The 1816 act empowered the Secretary of the Commonwealth and the Surveyor General "to contract with the publisher of the . . . state map, or other persons, from time to time, for new editions of the map . . ., on such terms as they deem just and reasonable." No subsequent editions were compiled by Melish, for he died on December 30, 1822, at the peak of his publishing career. Revised editions of the Pennsylvania map were issued by the State, however, in 1824, 1826, and 1832.

The 44 photocopies acquired from the Pennsylvania Department of Internal Affairs relate to 44 of the 51 counties within the State of Pennsylvania in 1822. For three counties (Union, Venango, and Warren) there are two separate maps. On each of three maps two counties (Erie and Crawford, Northampton and Lehigh, Wayne and Pike) are shown. Counties not included in the photocopies acquired are Adams, Cumberland, Dauphin, Franklin, Lebanon, Perry, and Philadelphia. The names of 21 surveyors or mapmakers appear on the different maps and 12 maps are unsigned.

About half of the surveyors named were associated with more than one map, and it is possible that they were deputy surveyors on the staff of the Surveyor General who were assigned to map counties that had no official surveyor. For two of the counties, Delaware and Montgomery, the maps were personally drawn by John Melish.

As prescribed in section one of the act authorizing the map, all counties were mapped at the scale of 2½ miles to an inch. In an effort to secure maps of uniform quality and execution Melish prepared for the local surveyors "Directions for Constructing the County Maps in Terms of the Act of Assembly." The first of these instructed the surveyor to "ascertain as near as possible, the latitude of the seat of justice [i.e., the county seat], and its longitude from Washington, and run a true meridian line, and an east and west line through it, as in the specimen." [11] The various physical and cultural features to be shown on the map were specified. The surveyors were also advised to "delineate the border exactly as on the model exhibited in the specimen, and graduate the scale on the inner margin in miles of latitude and longitude." The "model" was a small (10 by 7 inches) "Specimen of the County Maps to be Constructed by virtue of an Act of the Legislature directing the formation of A Map of Pennsylvania." This sample map included a section of the Susquehanna River to the northwest of Harrisburg with the several adjacent mountain chains indicated with hachures. A legend picturing "Characters and Writing to be used in delineating the County Maps" occupied the upper right corner of the "specimen."

Most of the surveyors seem to have followed Melish's "Directions" and the county maps are fairly uniform in appearance and format. Some few maps do not have marginal lines; their makers obviously did not heed the carefully outlined instructions. Manuscript descriptive notes supplement the cartographic data on several county maps. Hachures or crude shading depict generalized relief for a number of counties. Township boundaries, towns and cities, churches, roads, bridges, and grist mills are among the cultural features mapped. The general format laid down by Melish served as a pattern from which evolved the larger-scale county maps, showing property owners and the extent of private land holdings,

published in great numbers in the years immediately before and after the Civil War.

In addition to using them as compilation data for the *Map of Pennsylvania,* Melish expected to publish the county maps individually. To this end section nine of the act empowered the Surveyor General "to authorise the publisher of the state map to publish the *County Maps or any number of them separately,* provided the same shall be done without any expense to the state." In a "Prospectus of the State Map & County Maps of Pennsylvania," published as an addendum to the 1816 edition of the *Geographical Description,* Melish announced that "The County Maps will be published on the large scale on which they are originally delineated, provided there be a sufficient number of subscribers to defray the expense." He suggested that they would "be exceedingly useful as pocket maps, affording at all times the means of obtaining a correct knowledge of the respective counties." The price of the county maps, printed "on fine vellum paper, or bank note paper" was not to exceed "One Dollar to One Dollar and a half, according to the size of the counties."

Reporting on the progress of the Pennsylvania map, in the third edition (1818) of the *Geographical Description,* Melish listed a number of counties for which manuscript maps had already been received. "Of these," he noted, maps of "Montgomery, Luzerne, Dauphin, Lebanon, and Huntingdon are in the hands of the engraver, and will be speedily published." Maps of Montgomery, Dauphin and Lebanon, and Huntingdon, as well as of Philadelphia, Chester, Berks, Somerset, and Wayne and Pike Counties were listed for sale in Melish's 1822 *Catalogue.* Of these, the Library has in its collections printed copies of all but the Chester and Montgomery maps. The Somerset map, dated 1830 and published by H. S. Tanner, bears the credit "prepared for engraving by John Melish." County maps for York and Adams (1821), Lancaster (1824), Wayne (1828), and Schuylkill (1830), also in the Library's collections, may be based on surveys for the 1822 map of Pennsylvania although none of them bear Melish's name.

Melish fervently hoped that the Pennsylvania map would serve as a model that other States would emulate. In his 1822 *Catalogue* (p. 22) he wrote:

The state of Pennsylvania has now set the example, and a map of that state has been produced on a plan that has met with general approbation, and as perfect in its details as can reasonably be expected from a work of such magnitude, embracing such a vast variety of objects, and being necessarily the work of so many hands. This work is respectfully submitted to the inspection of the several state governments, as a specimen of what State Maps ought to be, and the publisher is in great hopes that be-

fore the next census is published, many of the states will follow the example set by Pennsylvania.

Maps of a number of other States were published within the next decade, but only a few were prepared on as systematic and orderly a plan as the Pennsylvania map. One that compared favorably in quality was the 1826 *Map of the State of Virginia Constructed in Conformity to Law From the Late Surveys Authorized by the Legislature and Other Original and Authentic Documents by Herman Böÿe*. Like Melish's Pennsylvania map, it is at the scale of one

*This small section of Böÿe's "Nine-Sheet Map" beneath the title cartouche illustrates the use of hachures to represent relief.*

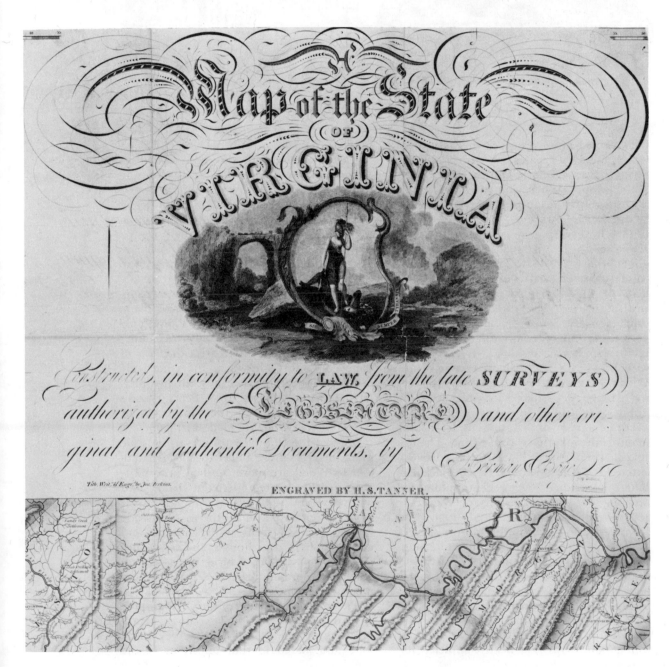

*The University of Virginia campus, laid out by Thomas Jefferson, as shown on the Böÿe map.*

inch to five miles. Because it was printed from engraved plates on nine separate sheets, it was popularly known as the "Nine-Sheet Map." When joined the separate sheets formed a magnificent map of Virginia 60 by 93 inches in size.

The Böÿe map had its inception in an act passed by the Virginia General Assembly on February 27, 1816, "to provide an accurate chart of each county and a general map of the Territory of this Commonwealth." [12] The law directed the county courts "to contract with some fit person or persons for making an accurate chart of their respective counties," in accordance with provisions set forth in precise detail. Within one year the manuscript surveys were to be deposited with the Board of Public Works. The initial suggestion for a scientific survey of Virginia under official sponsorship may have come from Thomas Jefferson. On April 19, 1816, in a lengthy letter to Governor Wilson C. Nicholas, Jefferson outlined suggested procedures for carrying out the provisions of the act.[13] Jefferson also was instrumental in engaging John Wood to supervise the county surveys and to direct compilation of the State map.

Wood, a native of Scotland, emigrated to the United States shortly after 1800. Before he was selected to direct the county surveys, he was employed as an instructor at Petersburg Academy. He worked on the surveys from 1816 until his death in May 1822, by which time maps had been completed for most of Virginia's counties. Herman Böÿe, a German engineer who had settled in Richmond, succeeded Wood as director and carried the project to completion.

Photostat reproductions of manuscript county maps prepared under the direction of John Wood and now in the Virginia State Library and the National Archives were acquired by the Library of Congress in 1965. The 38 reproductions from the State Library include maps of 36 separate counties. Wood's name appears on 30 of them, including a small chart of Piankitank, dated 1817, which is the only noncounty map in the group. There are two maps of Henrico County, drawn at the same scale and showing similar features but in different hands. One, dated 1819, bears Wood's name; the other has no title, inscription, or date, but was probably made in 1820.

Most of the county maps are at the scale of an inch to a mile. Those specifically credited to Wood are more finished in appearance, with ornately lettered titles and decorative north-pointing compass roses. Features portrayed on all the maps include streams, roads, taverns, mills, churches and meetinghouses, courthouses, and towns and cities. A few property owners are named. Hachures represent generalized relief in the mountain counties.

Through the courtesy of the Cartographic Records Branch, National Archives, reproductions of five Wood-Böÿe survey maps were also added to the collections of the

Geography and Map Division in 1965. Maps of Culpeper (1821), Hardy (1822), Harrison (1821), and Sussex (1819) counties were prepared under Wood's direction. Surveys for the Pocahontas map, dated 1825, were directed by Herman Böÿe.

Maps of Hardy and Harrison Counties (now in West Virginia) were received in both groups of reproductions. The titles and inscriptions are the same for the maps from both institutions, the originals are at the same scale, and the data they present appear to be identical. Slight variations in spelling and in the placement of geographical names, however, suggest that the manuscript maps of these two counties in one depository may be contemporary copies of the maps in the other. For example, on the Archives' Hardy County map the upper fork of the Potomac River is spelled with a final "k," but the "k" is omitted on the map in the State Library. On the western part of the Hardy County map there is the inscription "Corner of Maryland and Hardy in the Randolph line at Fairfax Corner Stone." Hardy is misspelled "Harardy" on the reproduction received from the Archives. There are similar variations on the two Harrison county maps.

Photostat copies of Wood maps of Frederick and Nansemond Counties have for some years been in the Library's collections. These counties are also represented in the 1965 accession from the Virginia State Library. Comparison of the old and more recent photocopies indicates that they were reproduced from the same manuscript originals.

The earlier Nansemond County reproduction was made in 1926 from a manuscript original then in the Office of the Clerk of the Circuit Court, Nansemond County. On the copy a number of place names, illegible or faded on the original, have been relettered in a modern hand, while only the original names appear on the reproduction received from the State Library. Lettered on the Nansemond County map in the State Library is the statement "Map owned by J. Walter Hosier, Suffolk, Virginia."

The Geography and Map Division has reproductions of 38 county maps in the Wood-Böÿe series, less than 40 percent of the counties listed in the statistical table on the border of the "Nine-Sheet Map."

Although Herman Böÿe directed the final compilation and drafting of the *Map of the State of Virginia,* John Wood is given credit for directing the county surveys in a "Memoranda Relative to the Plan materials and construction of this Map" printed within the map border. Henry S. Tanner of Philadelphia was the engraver. Engravings of the University of Virginia campus and a view of Richmond from the west decorate the upper corners of the map and the ornately lettered title encircles the Virginia seal and views of Natural Bridge and Harpers Ferry.

The photocopies of the Melish and Wood-Böÿe surveys supplement a group of reproductions of Massachusetts and Maine town plans acquired in 1932. The latter were prepared in 1794 and 1795 in response to an act of the Commonwealth of Massachusetts, passed on June 18, 1794, requiring local officials to deposit with the Secretary of State, within one year, surveys of the several towns. The 265 Massachusetts town plats and some 100 for the Province of Maine (then administered by Massachusetts) were used by Osgood Carleton to compile maps of the two jurisdictions. As finally approved and accepted by Commonwealth officials, the Massachusetts map was published in 1801 and the Maine map in the following year.

### NOTES

[1] Henry S. Tanner, *Memoir on the Recent Surveys, Observations, and Internal Improvements in the United States . . . Intended to Accompany His New Map of the United States* (Philadelphia, 1829), p. 8.

[2] See "John Melish and His Map of the United States," below.

[3] *A Geographical Description . . . by John Melish* (Philadelphia, 1816), p. 9.

[4] Ibid., p. 172.

[5] Ibid., p. 175.

[6] Ibid., p. 175.

[7] As printed in Melish's *Geographical Description,* p. 176.

[8] Reprinted in *A Catalogue of Maps and Geographical Works Published and for Sale by John Melish, Geographer and Map Publisher* (Philadelphia, 1822), p. 5.

[9] Ibid., p. 6.

[10] Ibid., p. 5.

[11] From "Directions" as printed in Melish's *Geographical Description* (1816), ff, p. 178.

[12] As quoted in Earl G. Swem, *Maps Relating to Virginia in the Virginia State Library* (Richmond, 1914), p. 102.

[13] Ibid., p. 104.

## BY WALTER W. RISTOW

Reprinted from the September 1962 issue of the *Library of Congress Quarterly Journal of Current Acquisitions.*

*1816 edition, fifth state, from the Geography and Map Division.*

JOHN MELISH'S *Map of the United States* (1816–23) is one of three noteworthy historical maps that were intensively studied by the late Col. Lawrence Martin when he was Chief of the Library's Map Division. His interest in these maps was related to their use in various international boundary arbitrations and treaties. As indicated in the paper on the Mitchell map, Martin's researches were coordinated with studies of David Hunter Miller, editor of the Department of State's *Treaties and Other International Acts of the United States of America* (8 vols., Washington, 1931–48).

In volume 3 of Miller's *Treaties,* mention is made of John Melish's *Map of the United States,* on which was laid down the United States-Mexican boundary, as described in the Adams-Onis Treaty, signed at Washington, February 22, 1819, and proclaimed February 22, 1821. When this volume of the *Treaties* was published in 1933, Martin had not yet begun his detailed examination of Melish's map.

About 1935 Philip Coolidge Brooks embarked on a scholarly analysis of the Adams-Onis Treaty and enlisted Martin's help in seeking to determine which of several possible variants of Melish's map was used in drawing the treaty boundary. During the next five or six years, Martin devoted considerable attention and effort to the Melish map and its many editions and states. By 1939, when Brooks' *Diplomacy and the Borderlands, the Adams-Onis Treaty of 1819* was published by the University of California Press, Martin had identified 20 different states or, as he chose to call them, "editions" of Melish's *Map of the United States*. With only the meager references to the map in the treaty as a guide, Martin and Brooks were not able to determine which of the four variants published in 1818 was used in drawing the boundary.

In his endeavor to unravel the chronology of the Melish map, Martin engaged in an

# John Melish and His
# Map of the United States

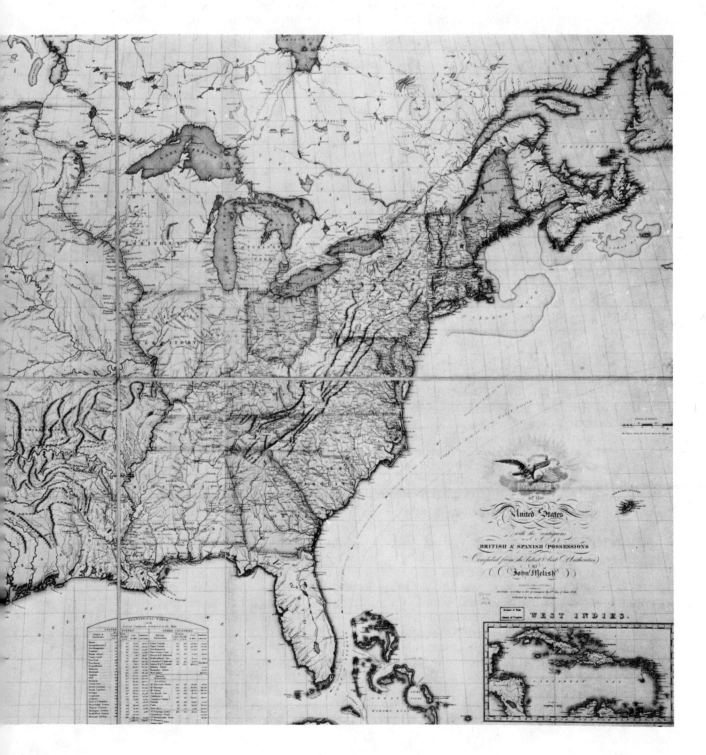

intensive acquisitions program. By purchase, exchange, transfer, and photocopy during the period 1936–42, he added some 20 or more originals and reproductions of the map to the Library's collections. The acquisitions were briefly described in the annual reports of the Map Division for those years. In 1942 Martin reported that a newly acquired 1818 edition "represents the tenth of the twenty-two identified editions and the Library of Congress has originals of sixteen of these editions and photostats of the other six. Our census of the examples of this map in the United States and abroad now includes 64 copies which we have examined, and eight others to which we have reliable references." [1]

World War II interrupted Martin's research, and the 1942 *Annual Report* is the last that refers to the Melish map. During the next two years Martin and his staff were swamped with wartime requests for maps and cartographical information, and in April 1944 Colonel Martin took leave from the Library to accept an assignment in the Map Division of the Office of Strategic Services.

When World War II ended, Martin had completed 30 years of Federal service, 22 of which were in the Library's Map Division, and, having reached the age of 66 years, he applied for retirement. The request was officially granted in April 1946, when the Librarian of Congress named Martin Honorary Consultant in Geography.

During the next year or two, Colonel Martin sought to resume work on the several studies that had been halted by World War II. His workshop was now in his home, and he removed from the Library the typescripts and notes of his Melish studies. Failing health, however, prevented him from carrying the project to completion or adding appreciably to the data he had compiled before 1942.

After Lawrence Martin's death on February 12, 1955, members of the staff of the Map Division assisted Mrs. Martin in examining his effects. No trace was found of the Melish materials or of several other incomplete and unpublished studies. Various clues and possible repositories were subsequently investigated but none of the missing data were recovered.

The need to assemble in an orderly arrangement the several editions and states of the *Map of the United States* and to fill requests for the Melish identification code prompted this writer to reconstruct and complete Martin's study. He had as source material at least one original or photocopy of each of the 22 "editions" of the map identified by Martin up to 1942. For many of the maps the "edition" numbers were revised three or four times as Martin's studies revealed new variants.

The brief references to Melish's United States map in the annual report of the division from 1936 through 1942 were also of assistance in establishing identifications. To reconstruct the table it was necessary, however, to examine and to compare in detail (as did Martin) the separate maps in order to ascertain what data were added or deleted from the engraved plates between printings.

The reconstructed table and an accompanying text relating to Melish and his contributions to early 19th-century map publishing were forwarded to the editor of the *Quarterly Journal* in April 1962. Several weeks later the notes and unedited draft of Colonel Martin's study of the Melish map were located. They were carefully examined, then compared and collated with the identification table prepared by this writer; and the composite data were rechecked against all copies of the Melish map in the Library of Congress. This resulted in enlarging the list of recognized variant states from 22 to 24 and in expanding the lists of identification data. The augmented table is appended to this paper. An additional state of the map was identified in 1963, expanding to 25 the list of recognized states.

Rather than consider each variant a separate "edition," as did Martin, it was decided to limit that designation to maps dated the same year. Variants within a given year are designated as "states." Should additional states be identified, renumbering will be minimal. As an aid to more exact identification, Martin's "edition" numbers (amended in some instances) are given for each state.

It should perhaps be noted that, like most maps published from the seventeenth through the mid-nineteenth century, Melish's *United States* was printed from engraved copper plates. To correct or add to a map the engraver could polish off selected parts of the plate and reengrave on it the newly acquired information. As geographical knowledge increased during the several decades after the United States Constitution was ratified, alert map publishers frequently revised their plates.

In *A Geographical Description of the United States,* published as a supplement to his large map, Melish noted that in accordance with his general plan "editions of moderate size, only, are prepared, so as to afford frequent opportunities of bringing forward new matter. The map is printed off 100 at a time, and before a new hundred be printed, the plates are carefully revised, and if there be room for corrections or improvements, these are made accordingly."

The criteria listed for each of the 25 different states do not necessarily include all the differences between it and the preceding state but rather serve to identify the ascertained states. In compiling the identification code, only changes made on the engraved plates have been recognized. Between plate modifications, Melish, or members of his staff, at times indicated boundary changes by relocating the colored lines that were added by hand after the maps were printed.

John Melish, author and publisher of the *Map of the United States,* established the first company in the country devoted solely to the publication of maps and geographical works. He played a leading role in bringing together, from many and varied sources, the geographical knowledge of the period and in presenting it in an attractive and orderly manner for the edification and enlightenment of citizens and visitors alike during the expanding and formative years of the young Nation. Proudly advertising his profession as "Geographer and Map Publisher," Melish is recognized as one of the founders of American commercial cartography.

Orphaned at an early age, John Melish was apprenticed to a leading textile manufacturer in his native city of Glasgow. During his leisure hours he studied at the University of Glasgow, and in due course his enterprise and ability were rewarded by admission to partnership in the textile company.

Company business took Melish to the West Indies in 1798, and eight years later he paid his first visit to the United States. Georgia was his primary goal, but personal interests also took him through most of the other seaboard States before he returned to Scotland in 1807. A careful and intelligent observer, he reported in the journal of his travels that he "used every diligence in [his] power in making observations and committing them to writing."

Through various short-sighted policies, the British Government at this time was hampering commercial relations between Great Britain and the United States. With the hope of salvaging some of his commercial outlets and investments, John Melish returned to America in 1809, accompanied by his son. As the political and economic situation had not improved by 1810, Melish decided to sever his commercial and personal ties with Scotland and to settle in the United States. Toward the close of the year his wife joined him in New York, and together they reviewed future economic and professional prospects.

Melish's lifelong interest in farming suggested a tour of the western lands to appraise their agricultural potential. The trip covered more than 2,400 miles and extended west to Ohio and north to upper New York State. The information collected, Melish reasoned, might also be of value to others. Consequently he decided to publish his journal of the western tour along with the reports of his earlier travels. The fact-filled two-volume work, entitled *Travels in the United States of America in the Years 1806 & 1807, and 1809, 1810, & 1811,* was published at Philadelphia in 1812. It contains many excellent descriptions of the physical and cultural landscape, as well as shrewd personal observations.

Probably of greater significance, however, were the eight maps that illustrated the two volumes, for they launched Melish on a career as cartographer and map publisher, which he followed for the rest of his life. In the preface to *Travels,* Melish reported that he had "spared no labour, nor expence, to have a good set of maps to illustrate this work. They have been drawn with great care from the best materials to which I could get access, aided by much local information, and the engraving has been executed by the first artists in Philadelphia." James Thackara and John Vallance, established map and print engravers, prepared the plates.

Melish settled in Philadelphia after his western tour. Plans to engage in agriculture were apparently abandoned as he became more deeply involved in geography and cartography. His next project closely fol-

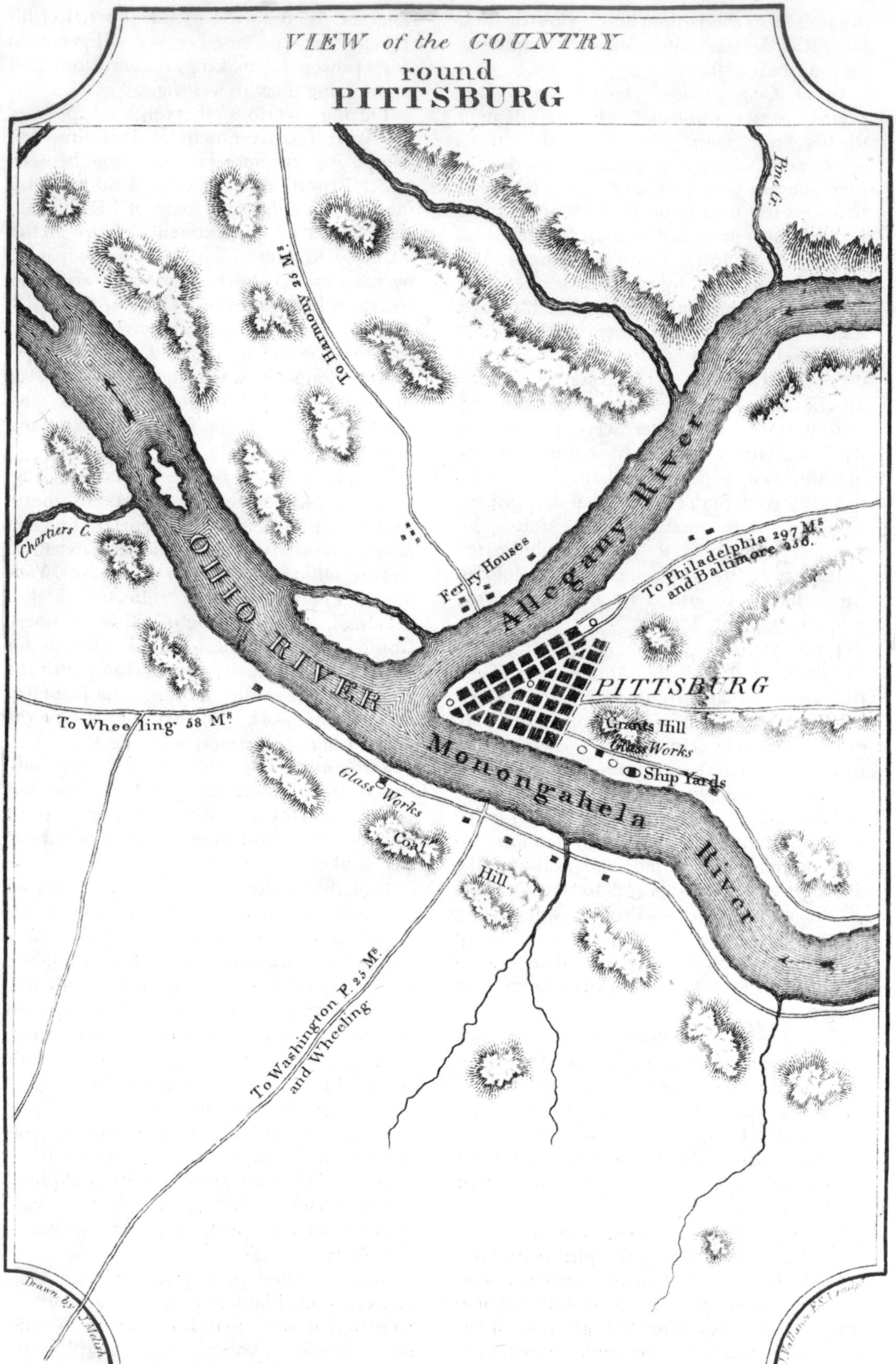

VIEW of the COUNTRY
round
PITTSBURG

Pine G<sup>r.</sup>

To Harmony 25 M<sup>s</sup>

Allegany River

Chartiers C.

OHIO RIVER

Ferry Houses

To Philadelphia 297 M<sup>s</sup>
and Baltimore 256.

PITTSBURG

To Wheeling 58 M<sup>s</sup>

Monongahela

Grants Hill
Glass Works
Ship Yards

Glass Works

River

Coal

Hill

To Washington P. 25 M<sup>s</sup>
and Wheeling

Drawn by J. Melish

lowed publication of the *Travels*. "While engaged in drawing [the maps for the *Travels*]," Melish informs us, "a much valued friend suggested the propriety of drawing a general map of the seat of war [*i.e.* the War of 1812], and proferred the use of a very ample set of maps in his possession." The resulting publication, Melish's first exclusively cartographical work, was *A Military and Topographical Atlas of the United States,* published at Philadelphia in 1813 by G. Palmer. Six of its eight maps were engraved by Henry S. Tanner, who shares credit with Melish, as both associate and competitor, for establishing commercial map publishing in the United States. For the enlarged 1815 edition of the *Military . . . Atlas,* Tanner engraved eight of the 12 maps.

Perhaps because his own travels disclosed a need for a guidebook of the country, Melish published in 1814 *A Description of the Roads in the United States,* a 54-page booklet. It includes no maps but lists in tables the major roads leading from Washington to various parts of the country, the most important lateral or crossroads, and the principal State roads. Mileage between cities is also indicated.

With the War of 1812 still of major public interest, Melish observed in the preface to the *Description of the Roads* that "the events of war, though often distressing in their nature, produce at least one good effect: they excite curiosity, and become subservient in a high degree to the dissemination of useful information." To the task of compiling and disseminating geographical information Melish devoted his energies during the next eight years. A revised and enlarged edition of the *Description of the Roads* was published in 1816 as *The Traveller's Directory Through the United States.* Melish also published an 1822 edition of the *Directory,* and an 1826 version was issued under the imprint of A. T. Goodrich of New York.

Except for revisions of earlier items, Melish published no major geographical works in 1815. Most of his time and energy during that year were employed in compiling the large *Map of the United States With the Contiguous British & Spanish Possessions.* The June 1815 issue of the *Analectic Magazine* reported that "Mr. John Mellish has issued proposals for publishing by subscription, a six sheet map of the United States, and contiguous British and Spanish possessions."

A year later, on June 15, 1816, the editor of *Niles' Weekly Register* announced: "The indefatigable Mr. Mellish is about to furnish us with a new and very interesting map of the United States and their territories, with the adjacent British and Spanish possessions. . . . A proof impression was shewn to the editor a few days ago."

For the suggestion to publish a large map of the United States, Melish also gives credit to a friend. In a prospectus published in 1818 the cartographer wrote:

During the progress of the war [of 1812], a very respectable *Friend* in Philadelphia, when talking of the Map of the Seat of War, said "I wish friend John, thee would make a Map of the Seat of Peace." The hint was not lost. The author had seen the good effects of maps, particularly when accompanied by descriptions, and he resolved to condense into one grand view the *whole of the United States territory,* including the *British Possessions* and *Spanish Possessions* contiguous to it, to be ready as soon as possible after these regions became the "Seat of Peace."

The Author accordingly constructed the Map and Description of the United States With the Contiguous British and Spanish Possessions, accompanied by a Geographical Description, which, being one link in the chain for the dissemination of geographical science among the citizens of the United States, will be more particularly described hereafter.[2]

Melish emphasized in the prospectus that his map was to cover the whole of the United States territory. Colonel Martin believed, however, that the cartographer's original plan envisioned a map in four sheets, each approximately 25 by 20 inches, and limited to the territory east of the Pacific watershed. This belief is supported by a statement in the 1816 edition of Melish's *Geographical Description:* "It was intended to carry the map no farther west than the ridge dividing the waters falling into the Gulf of Mexico, from those falling into the Pacific Ocean. A subsequent view of the subject pointed out the propriety of adding the two western sheets so as to carry it to the Pacific Ocean."

As published, the six-sheet map measured approximately 3 by 4¾ feet. Six of the seven states of the map published in 1816 carry the notice "Entered According to Act of Congress the 6th day of June 1816." The note in *Niles' Register* indicates, however, that no copies of the map were distributed at this early date. Colonel Martin believed that the first copies of the map were not offered for sale until November 1816.

The United States map apparently found a ready market, and early printings were quickly sold out. In Martin's opinion, at least three states of the map were published before the end of 1816. No copies of Melish's map are dated 1817. The last four states of the 1816 edition, however, were probably not distributed until the succeeding year.

The *Map of the United States* is one of John Melish's major publications and is a noteworthy milestone in the development of American private cartography. The early editions were printed from six engraved copper plates prepared by the well-known craftsmen John Vallance and Henry S. Tanner. Published at the scale of one inch to 60 miles, the map was one of the first to show the full east-west extent of the United States from the Atlantic to the Pacific.

As mentioned above, Melish prepared as a supplement to his large map a booklet entitled *A Geographical Description of the United States*. A particularly valuable and useful feature is the section that summarizes the source materials consulted in compiling the United States map. "The various state maps, from actual survey" supplied data for the more settled areas of the country, while "information regarding the territories was principally procured from the land office at Washington." The travel reports of Zebulon Pike, Lewis and Clark, and other explorers and surveyors furnished data about the western lands. Summing up, the *Description* affirms that "the author has been most generously supplied with information from every quarter; and he has used every exertion to avail himself of it, so as to produce a view of the country, which he hopes will be as valuable to his fellow citizens as it is gratifying to himself." The *Geographical Description* proved to be as popular as the map, and a second 1816 edition was published.

The "various state maps from actual survey," which were basic source material for the large United States map, were highly regarded by Melish. The United States map, he emphasized, was intended for general reference and "as a key to the local maps of the several states and territories from actual survey." For more detailed information, the State maps were recommended.

Most State maps published before 1816 were privately produced, but some subsidy was provided by the State governments in certain instances. Melish strongly advocated that such maps "should be state property, subject to the control of no individual whatever. Individuals are not equal to the task of bringing them forward, and keeping them correct. Whenever they have embarked in the business, they have lost much time and money; and unless the states embark in it, the geography of the country cannot be brought to maturity."

Largely because of the insistence of Melish and other enthusiasts, the Pennsylvania Legislature adopted in 1814 a resolution to sponsor preparation of a State map. Early in 1816 Melish appeared before a legislative committee to outline ways and means to produce the map, and shortly thereafter an act was passed by the Legislature authorizing compilation. The act provided that surveys be carried out in each county by qualified local surveyors.

Instructions for drawing the county maps, along with a sample format, were printed in the *Geographical Description;* the specifications were very probably drawn by Melish. County maps, based on the surveys, at the scale of $2\frac{1}{2}$ miles to an inch, were deposited with the Pennsylvania Secretary of State. The latter was authorized to contract with "some suitable person" to use the county surveys in compiling a map of Pennsylvania at the scale of five miles to an inch. The contract was awarded to John Melish, and he was occupied with the map for the next five or six years.

A number of other cartographic works were also produced by Melish and his staff during this period. The large *Map of the World on the Mercator Projection,* published in 1818, was described as "one of the most beautiful and best finished maps we have seen published in the United States." [3] *A Geographical Description of the World, Intended as an Accompaniment to the Map of the World on Mercator's Projection* was issued in the same year.

A third edition of the *Geographical Description of the United States* was also an 1818 publication. Melish notes therein that

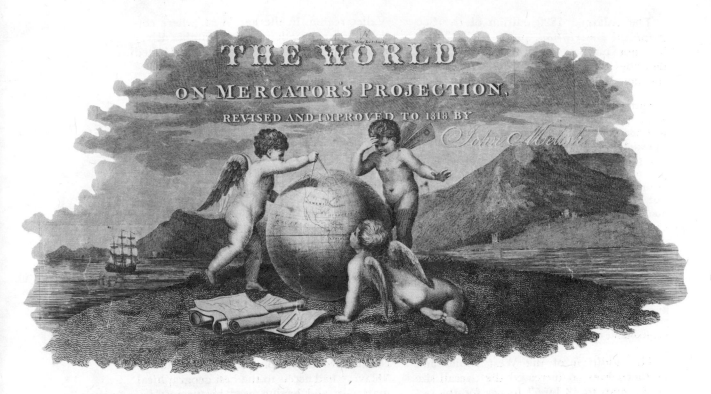

*Title cartouche from John Melish's world map. From the Geography and Map Division.*

"it is about fifteen months since the first edition of this work issued from the press. Two whole editions have been disposed of, and the demand continues unabated." He hoped that "a new edition of the description will be made annually, and every thing new that occurs in the course of the year, will be inserted in the new edition." This goal was not achieved, and only one subsequent edition of the *Description,* published in 1826 after Melish's death, is known.

In 1818 Melish also published a new edition of the United States map. Five variants have been identified, each of which carries the note "Improved to the 1st of January 1818." It is the 1818 edition that was consulted by the official arbiters in laying down the boundary between the United States and the Spanish possessions in 1819. Article III of the Adams-Onis Treaty, concluded at Washington on February 22, 1819, notes:

The boundary line between the two countries, west of the Mississippi, shall begin on the Gulf of Mexico, at the mouth of the River Sabine, in the sea; continuing along the western bank of the river to the 32d degree of latitude: thence by a line due north to the degree of latitude where it strikes the Rio Roxo of Natchitoches or Red River; thence, following the course of the Rio Roxo westward to the degree of longitude 100 west from London and 23 from Washington, thence crossing the said Red River, running thence by a line due north to the River Arkansas; thence following the course of the southern bank of the Arkansas to its source, in latitude 42° north; and thence in that parallel to the South Sea. The whole being as laid down in Melish's Map of the United States, published at Philadelphia, improved to the first of January, 1818.

Two states of an 1819 edition of the *Map of the United States* were also published, both bearing the designation "Improved to the 1st of April, 1819." The earlier of the two is the first to show, by means of a dash-dot engraved line, the United States-Mexican boundary as fixed by the Adams-Onis Treaty.

Eight identified variants of the map are dated 1820. The first two carry the notice "Entered according to Act of Congress the 6th day of June 1820"; on the other six the date is given as the "16th of June." Only the southeast sheet (of six) is known for the first state. It is uncolored and may have been deposited for copyright in this incomplete form. No published maps of this state were distributed as the publisher apparently decided to make major modifications shortly after the proofsheet was deposited.

The enlarged 1826 edition of the *Geographical Description,* prepared by Melish but not published until after his death, describes the basic changes and the reasons for them. He wrote:

When the late treaty was negotiated with Spain which had reference to the map in fixing the southwest boundary, it was determined to bring forward *an entire new edition of the Map,* exhibiting Florida as a part of the United States, and making all alterations that had taken place in the country, up to the time of publication; and from a conviction that Mexico would soon become independent, and would eventually be of great importance to the United States, it was determined to add another sheet exhibiting a complete view of that very interesting country, with all the most important West India Islands. This was accordingly executed, and the supplement was so enlarged as to exhibit a view of the whole West Indies, with Guatimala [sic], the Isthmus of Panama, and the northern provinces of South America, now forming part of the Republic of Colombia.

The addition of the West Indies and southern Mexico increased the overall size of the map to 43 by 57 inches for the second state of the 1820 edition, which was the first to be published in the enlarged format. The change in the imprint date from the 6th to the 16th of June is the only recognizable alteration on the third state of the 1820 edition. Subsequent variants published in 1820 are distinguished primarily by additions and corrections in the Latin American portions of the map.

There is no 1821 edition of the United States map, and no other major work was published by Melish in that year. Very likely, he and his associates were busily engaged in completing the compilation and engraving of the State map of Pennsylvania. Prepared on contract for the Pennsylvania Legislature, this map is one of Melish's most distinguished contributions. It was published in 1822 and was enthusiastically received. It is the subject, together with the Wood-Böÿe map of Virginia, of a separate article in this volume.

With the Pennsylvania map in the hands of the engraver, Melish was able to devote further attention to revising and improving his *Map of the United States.* A new edition was published in 1822, of which two states are identified. Both bear the notice "Improved to 1822" at the bottom of the title cartouche. The principal modifications and additions are found in the upper Mississippi

Valley region, in the Far West, where corrections were made in the Columbia River drainage system, and along the United States-Mexican border.

Work on a revised and enlarged edition of the *Geographical Description* also engaged John Melish during this period. Expanded to more than 500 pages, the revision was published in 1826 by A. T. Goodrich of New York. In the preface, written in July 1822, Melish noted that "the *Description* having answered a valuable purpose, it was determined to bring forward a new and improved edition as soon as possible after access could be had to the United States census of 1820. This, it was presumed, could be comprised in a work of 250 pages; but, on arranging the necessary details, it has swelled out to more than 500 pages .... To this has been added 12 local maps, so as to illustrate some of the most important positions in the country."

The closing paragraph of the preface could serve as an epitaph to John Melish. "Having had access to the best geographical materials, and having used his utmost endeavours to put them into a form calculated to instruct his fellow citizens, the author respectfully consigns this work to their care, believing that his labour will not have been in vain."

Death came suddenly to John Melish while he was still vigorously engaged in "promulgating geographical information." Publisher Goodrich notes in his preface to the 1826 edition of the *Description:* "A memoir of the late John Melish was intended to have been inserted in this edition, but unforeseen circumstances have prevented it, and confines this brief note to the single remark that he closed his active and valuable life in the city of Philadelphia, on the 30th of December, 1822." It is to be regretted that the memoir was never written, for our information about Melish is derived almost exclusively from his own publications.

The final chapter on John Melish is not a happy one. Within a week after his death, newspapers announced an auction at which was offered "all the entire stock in the trade of the late John Melish, comprising a valuable collection of Engraved Copper Plates, with the copy rights and impressions from the said plates." A fortnight after his interment there was auctioned "all the neat household furniture of

John Melish, deceased, comprising sideboard, breakfast and dining tables, chairs, carpets, bedsteads, beds and bedding, with a variety of other articles not enumerated as well as kitchen furniture."

Thus, the Melish map firm, like its founder, came to an abrupt end. The plates and stock of publications were purchased by A. T. Goodrich of New York City, who issued the third edition of Melish's *Geographical Description* in 1826. A small United States map carries the note "Improved to 1824 by Jno. G. Melish and published by A. T. Goodrich & Company, New York." This appears to be the sole cartographic contribution of John G. Melish, who was probably the son of the distinguished map publisher.

The final edition of Melish's large *Map of the United States* was published in 1823. There appear to be no geographical or cartographical changes from the second state of the 1822 edition; however, the phrase "Published by John Melish Philadelphia," was removed from the title cartouche and replaced by "Published by James Finlayson, Agent Philad^a Successor to John Melish," and beneath the cartouche is the note "Improved to 1823."

With these few exceptions and except for later editions of the Pennsylvania map, previously noted, Melish's name does not appear on maps published after 1823. The position he held as the leading map publisher of Philadelphia and of the United States was very shortly assumed by Henry S. Tanner. During the next several decades, Tanner raised American commercial map publishing to new levels of excellence.

An obituary, in a Philadelphia paper, attested that Melish's "works in the sciences of geography and political economy are universally known, and their importance has been acknowledged by the highest characters in our country." [4] Five Presidents of the United States are known to have possessed copies of Melish's large map of the country,[5] and Melish was personally acquainted with several of these gentlemen.

The variety and number of Melish's publications are truly remarkable, especially when it is recalled that he accomplished all this within scarcely more than a decade. For his significant cartographic contributions John Melish merits recognition as one of the founders of American commercial map publishing.

### NOTES

[1] *Annual Report of the Librarian of Congress . . .* 1942, p. 117.

[2] *Geographical Intelligence, Including a Prospectus of the Map and Description of the World, Map and Description of the United States . . .* (Philadelphia, 1818), p. 4. Photostat in Martin's notes.

[3] In *Niles' Weekly Register*, June 6, 1818, p. 241–242.

[4] *Democratic Press*, Jan. 1, 1823.

[5] John Adams, John Quincy Adams, Thomas Jefferson, James Madison, and James Monroe.

## TABLE FOR IDENTIFYING VARIANT EDITIONS AND STATES OF JOHN MELISH'S MAP OF THE UNITED STATES

*Reconstructed and Edited by Walter W. Ristow*

*After Original Studies by Lawrence Martin*

### 1816 EDITION

Seven states of this edition are recognized. All but the first carry, at the bottom of the title cartouche, the printed notice "Entered according to Act of Congress the 6th day of June 1816."

### First state (Martin's "first edition")

This incomplete proof copy was probably deposited for copyright by Melish before finished copies were available for sale. Martin believed that Melish's original plan envisioned a map, to be printed from four engraved plates, that extended west only as far as 108°15′ west of London. This plan was apparently abandoned by Melish in favor of the six-sheet map that extends from the Atlantic to the Pacific coast. The copyright deposit copy in the Library of Congress Geography and Map Division is the only known copy of this state. It has the following unique features:

Lacks imprint date below "John Melish" in title cartouche.

Engravers' names are lacking.

The design of the eagle, shield, and box around the word "Map" at the beginning of the title are not completely filled in as on all subsequent states.

Lacks scale of miles.

Except in the margin of the south central sheet, there are no printed latitude and longitude figures.

A manuscript notation in the lower right margin reads: "Entered According to Act of Congress the [blank] day of June 1816, and published by John Melish."

The Gulf of Mexico is not named.

The U.S.-Canadian boundary (Great Lakes to the Pacific) is an engraved line of dashes and dots, labeled "Northern Boundary of Louisiana," that curves broadly along the watershed.

Library of Congress holdings:

An original (mounted) and a photostat negative (4 parts only, of 6) of same.　　G3700 1816.M4

## Second state (Martin's "second edition")

Copyright notice, "Entered according to Act of Congress the 6th day of June 1816," is printed on the title cartouche.

"Engraved by J. Vallance & H. S. Tanner" added.

"Published by John Melish Philadelphia" added.

Eagle, shield, and box around "Map" at the top of the title cartouche are filled in.

Scale of miles added to right of cartouche.

Longitude and latitude figures are printed on the outer margins of all six sheets of the map.

A "Statistical Table" is added in the Gulf of Mexico.

The Gulf of Mexico is named.

West of the headwaters of the Rio del Norte (*i.e.*, the Rio Grande) are added the words "The Limits of Louisiana in this quarter are undefined."

At the head of "Marias R.," the northernmost branch of the Missouri, the word "Northern" is inserted before "Point of observation."

There has been deleted all but a fragment (2 dots and 2½ dashes due east of Lake Yuntas) of the dash-dot line that, on the first state, extended from B. S. Joseph on the Gulf of Mexico, passed east of San Antonio, then followed the mountain range east of the Rio Puerco. This fragment remains on all subsequent states of the map.

The dot boundary line along the east border of Coahuila Province, Mexico, has been changed to a dash-dot line.

The hand-colored boundary of the Spanish possessions is shifted to the lower Rio Grande and the

Rio Puerco, but parts of the names "Coahuila," "New Santander," and "Intendency of San Louis Potosi" are left astride the Rio Grande.

In the State of Louisiana are added the words "Grant to Maisonrouge," "Derbane R.," "Bastrops Claim," and "R. Bon Idee."

In Georgia a boundary and the words "Genl. Jackson's Treaty Line" are added.

"Indiana Territory" is changed to "Indiana."

The names "Northwest Territory," "Michigan Territory," and "Illinois Territory" are added.

The curved line of dashes and dots from the Gulf of Georgia to the Lake of the Woods (designated as "Northern Boundary of Louisiana" on the first state) is deleted.

From the Gulf of Georgia to the Lake of the Woods an engraved dash-dot line is added along the approximate parallel of 49°37′30″ north.

Note: Relative to the northwest boundary of the United States, Melish gives the following explanation in the first edition of the *Geographical Description:*

"So far as the northwest corner of the Lake of the Woods, there can be but one opinion on the subject of the northern boundary. The boundary as exhibited on the map, is expressly in the terms of the treaty. When the line comes to be accurately run by the commissioners, there may be some deviations from the views here given, but the principle will remain unchanged.

"As to the country west of the Lake of the Woods, it is evident that the commissioners were of opinion, that it should be part of the territory of the United States, as high as a line to be run due west from the north-west corner of that lake until it reached as far west as the Mississippi, which was at that period the western boundary of the United States. Subsequent events have annexed the whole of Louisiana to the country, so that the northern boundary behoves to be ascertained, as it was possessed by France; but the country never having been settled, the boundary has not been accurately defined. The best course as regards this map, has appeared to run the boundary line *due west from the north-west corner of the Lake of the Woods* to the Gulf of Georgia, and thence along that gulf, and the Straits of Juan de Fuco, to the Pacific Ocean. In colouring the map, however, we have deviated a little from that line. From the view of the head waters of the Missouri, as exhibited on the map, which is the result of all the information we have been able to procure, it appears that they extend beyond this line, and so does the head waters of Clark's River. It is presumed, by some, that both ought to belong to the United States, and the map is coloured accordingly, that both views of the subject may be seen."

Library of Congress holdings:

a) Original, mounted on cloth sectioned to fold,

in red buckram case, 9½ x 6½ inches, labeled "Melish Map U.S. 1816 2nd issue." "TWS" bookplate on cover of map when folded. Photostat negative (in 6 parts) of same. The original was acquired from the Streeter Collection in April 1969. Thomas W. Streeter died on June 12, 1965, and his collection of rare books and maps was sold in a series of auctions from 1966 to 1969. Five of the Melish maps in the collection were acquired by the Library of Congress.

b) Photostat negative (in 6 parts) from an original in the New York Public Library ("Mrs. Thomas Gordon's copy"). G3700 1816.M4a

### Third state (Martin's "third edition")

"Mansfield" and "Wooster" are added in Ohio.

"Vevay or" is inserted before "Swiss Vineyards" in southeastern Indiana.

Library of Congress holdings:

a) Original (mounted) acquired on exchange in 1940 from the Historical Society of Pennsylvania.

b) Photostat positive (mounted) and negative (in 8 parts) acquired on exchange, in 1937 from the Historical Society of Pennsylvania. (Not a copy of (a) above). G3700 1816.M4b

### Fourth state (Martin's "third [actually fourth] edition")

The town of Adelphi is added in Ohio.

A new trail has been introduced in Ohio between Athens and Chillicothe by way of Adelphi.

Library of Congress holdings:

a) Original ("James Monroe copy"). Photostat positive (mounted) and negative (in 6 parts) of same.

b) Photostat negative (in 6 parts) from original in collections of the Maryland Historical Society.

c) Photostat positive (mounted) and negative (in 10 parts) from original in the Bibliothèque Nationale.

d) Photostat positive (mounted) and negative (in 6 parts) from original in the New York Public Library. G3700 1816.M4c

### Fifth state (Martin's "fourth [actually fifth] edition")

Towns of Cadiz and Cambridge appear for the first time in Ohio.

"Frankfort" in Ohio is renamed "Washington."

"Charleston" replaces the letters "C.H." in western Virginia (present West Virginia).

Newly added place names in western Virginia are Great Falls, Salt Works, and Coal R.

Olympian Springs is added in eastern Kentucky.

A trail is added from G. Kenhawa in western Virginia to Mt. Sterling, just west of Olympian Springs.

In southwestern Pennsylvania "N. Geneva" is deleted and reengraved near Union.

The road between Steubenville and Zanesville in Ohio is relocated. The mileage numeral 35 is deleted, and the numerals 19, 42, 10, and 25 are introduced.

Library of Congress holdings:

a) Original (mounted).

b) Photostat negative (in 6 parts) from an original formerly in the collection of Thomas W. Streeter. G3700 1816.M4d

### Sixth state (Martin's "fifth [actually sixth] edition")

The following new place names are introduced in southern Indiana: Brookville, Blackford, Brownstown, Busserow C., Centreville, Darlington, Fredericksburg, Lawrenceburg, Loughery Cr., Madison, Orleans, Paoli, Princeton, Salem, Shaker T., Troy, Vernon, and White Water R.

In southern Indiana "Harmonist Society" is changed to "Harmony" and "Clarksville" to "New Albany."

A dotted line is added in eastern Indiana to enclose a land grant west of Centreville.

The name "Charleston" is added in northern Kentucky.

Library of Congress holdings:

An original (mounted). G3700 1816.M4e

### Seventh state (Martin's "sixth [actually seventh] edition")

The designation "Mississippi Territory" is removed, and the former area of the Territory is divided to form the State of Mississippi and Alabama Territory, which are so named. A dash-dot boundary divides the two new units.

Jacksonville is added in east central Louisiana.

Also in Louisiana, the words "Amite or" are introduced before "Manshak R.," and the new stream names Tangapaho R., Tickfah R., and Thompsons C. are added.

Buttahacky Cr. and Tukaloosa R. are deleted in Alabama. The streams are redrawn and renamed, respectively, Black Warrior R. and Cahawba R.

Course of Bear Cr. has been rerouted so that the stream enters the Tennessee River farther west than on the previous state.

The circle locating the city of Mobile, Ala., has been replaced by a new symbol.

A trail has been introduced extending from Mobile northwestward to east central Mississippi.

a) Original, mounted on cloth sectioned to fold, in red buckram case, 9½ x 6½ inches, labeled "Melish Map U.S. 6th issue." "TWS" bookplate on cover of map when folded. Photostat negative (in 6 parts) of same. Original acquired April 1969 at Streeter Collection auction. After Streeter had case made and labeled, an earlier state was identified, making this the seventh state or issue.

b) Photostat positive (mounted) and negative (in 4 parts) of southern half of map only, from an original in the Historical Society of Pennsylvania.

G3700 1816.M4f

## 1818 EDITION

Five states of this edition have been identified, each of which carries the note "Improved to the 1st of January 1818." Most of the changes on all five states are found in the upper Mississippi Valley and in the Gulf States.

### First state (Martin's "seventh [actually eighth] edition")

Near the mouth of Black Warrior R., in western Alabama Territory, is added the designation "French Settlement."

In the sea, off the coast of southeastern United States, is added the name "Atlantic Ocean."

Library of Congress holdings:

An original (mounted).     G3700 1818.M4

### Second state (Martin's "eighth [actually ninth] edition")

The Illinois-Indiana dash-dot boundary has been moved slightly west to approximately the 10°25′ meridian west of Washington, D.C. It touches the S in "Illinois."

The upper course of the Illinois River in northern Illinois has been relocated, and the following names that were present on the previous state have been removed: Illinois R., Fox R., L. Illinois, Old Fort, March R., Semi Quan R., Demi Quan L., Sagasnon R., and Mine R. To replace some of them, these names are introduced: Illinois R., Lake Illinois or Peoire, Ft. Clark, R. Micouenne, R. of la Mine, and R. Mauvaise Terre.

These names are deleted along the Mississippi River in western Illinois: Sand Bank, Steep Bank, Sand Bank Cr., U.S. Agricultural Establishment, Rapids des Moines, Indian Vil., and Hurricane I. In the same general area these new names are introduced: Edward R. and Hendersons R.

West of the Mississippi River near its junction with the Missouri, these new names are introduced in uppercase letters: Arkansas District, Cape Girardeau

*One of 12 local maps added to the 1826 posthumous edition of Melish's A Geographical Description of the United States.*

District, Howard District, Lawrence District, and St. Louis District. Dash boundary lines enclose them.

The name "Missouri River" is moved from the north to the south side of the stream in its lower course.

In Howard District the phrase "Army Lands 500,000 Acres" is introduced, with a dotted boundary around the tract.

The designations "Indian Boundary" and "Osage Boundary" are introduced on the north and west borders of Howard District, respectively.

The words "Army Lands 500,000 Acres" are deleted in St. Louis District.

These new names appear in Alabama Territory: Eagleville, Ft. Mimes, Ft. Montgomery, and R. Aux Pierres.

The Black Warrior River has been relocated slightly to the east and now cuts through the L in "Alabama."

Murder Cr. is deleted in south central Alabama Territory.

In the north central part of that Territory Madison County is introduced and is outlined with a dotted border, and Huntsville is moved and relettered.

The Wabash River is relocated on the southwestern border of Indiana, and "F. Harrison" is relettered "Ft. Harrison."

In southeastern Illinois "L. Water" is changed to "L. Wabash R."

Library of Congress holdings:

a) Original of east half of map only (mounted), transferred from U.S. Geological Survey in April 1936.

b) Photostat negative (in 8 parts), made from a copy in the Streeter Collection in 1963. It resembles (a) above in that the Illinois-Wisconsin boundary has been extended northward by a colored line, but the engraved dark line boundary has not been removed.

c) Photostat positive (mounted) and negative (in 8 parts) of an original in the collection of Dr. William E. Wrather.     G3700 1818.M4a

### Third state (Martin's "ninth [actually tenth] edition")

The northern boundary of Illinois has been relocated farther north, near the parallel of 42°30′ north. This places Chicago within Illinois rather than in the Northwest Territory as on earlier states.

Illinois appears as a State for the first time with the word "Territory" deleted. (Inasmuch as Illinois was not admitted as a State until December 3, 1818,

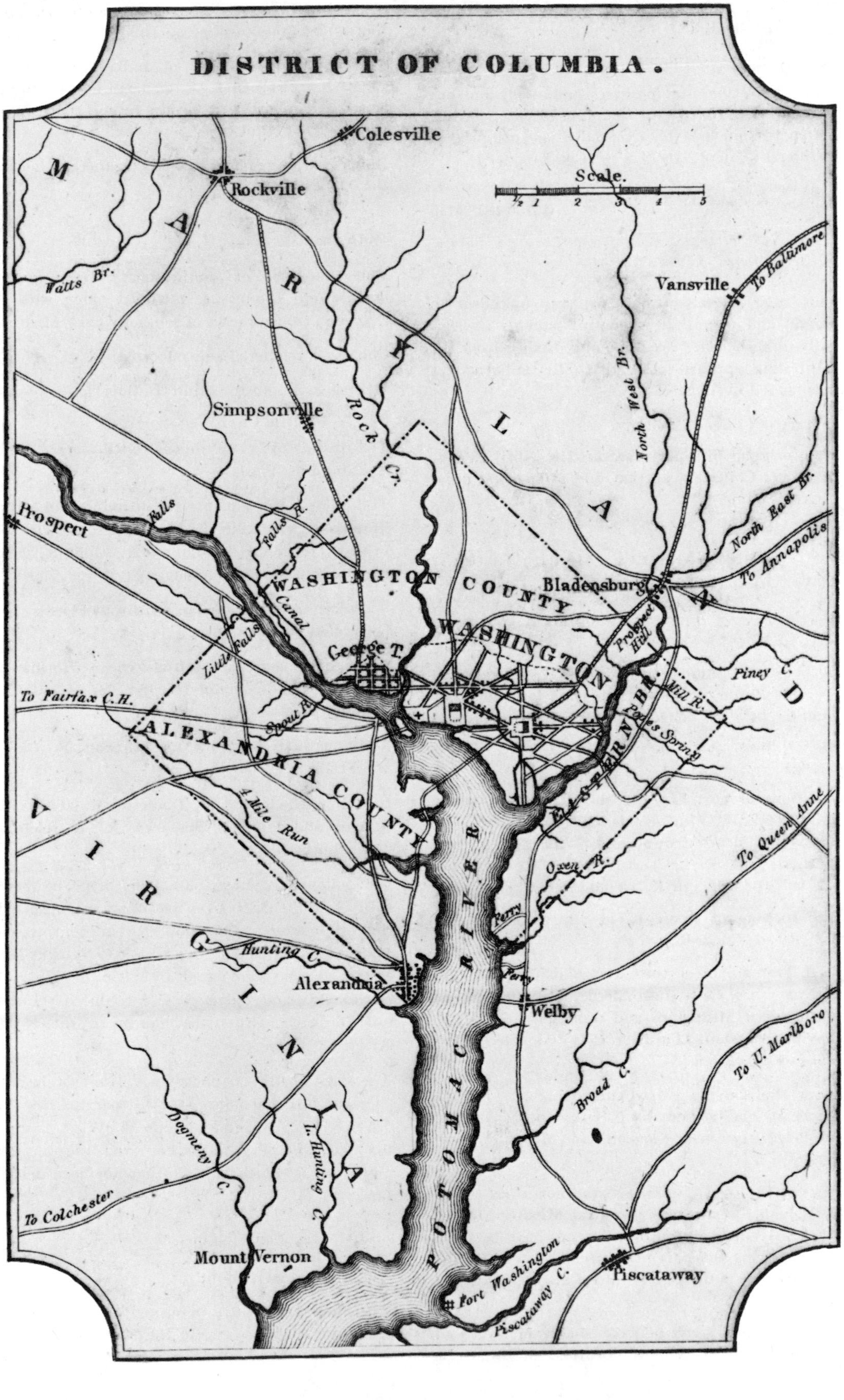

# DISTRICT OF COLUMBIA.

Colesville

M
A
R
Y
L
A
N
D

Rockville

Scale.
½ 1 2 3 4 5

Watts Br.

Vansville

To Baltimore

Simpsonville

North West Br.

Rock Cr.

North East Br.

To Annapolis

Prospect

Falls

Falls R.

WASHINGTON COUNTY

Bladensburg

Canal

WASHINGTON

Prospect Hill

George T.

Piney C.

To Fairfax C.H.

Little Falls

Mill R.

Spout R.

Powders Spring

ALEXANDRIA COUNTY

E
A
S
T
E
R
N
B
R.

V
I
R
G
I
N
I
A

4 Mile Run

M
D

Owen R.

To Queen Anne

Hunting C.

Ferry

Alexandria

Ferry

Welby

P
O
T
O
M
A
C
R
I
V
E
R

Broad C.

To U. Marlboro

Dogueny C.

L. Hunting C.

To Colchester

Mount Vernon

Fort Washington

Piscataway C.

Piscataway

this state of the map may not have been published until after that date.)

Library of Congress holdings:

a) Three photostat positives (mounted) and one negative (in 8 parts) from an original in the Department of State. (Reproductions acquired at different dates.)

b) Reduced photographic print.

G3700 1818.M4b

## Fourth state

This state, identified in 1963, was unknown to Martin and to author when this paper was originally published in 1962. The only change from the third state appears to be that Ft. Claiborne has been added in Alabama.

Library of Congress holdings:

An original in 5 parts, acquired in April 1969 at Streeter Collection auction, and a photostat negative of same. G3700 1818.M4

## Fifth state (Martin's "tenth [actually eleventh] edition")

After "Scale of miles" there is added "60 to an inch."

In Louisiana "Amite or Manshak R." is renamed Iberville Bayou. A tributary flowing into the latter from the north is named Amite R.

In northwest Alabama Territory "Watts T." is deleted.

Additions in northern Alabama Territory include Paint Rock R., Flint R., Second Cr., Cotaco Cr., Florence, Turkey Town, and Wills Cr. In the southern part of the Territory, Ft. Crawford, and a branch of Conecah R. are added.

The spelling of Koose R. in central Alabama is changed to "Coosa R."

From Florence in northwestern Alabama a straight highway has been introduced, extending across southeastern Mississippi and terminating at Madisonville in eastern Louisiana. It is designated "General Jacksons Road."

From Madisonville a new, curved highway extends northeast, via Jacksonville C.H., to the ford across the Pearl River near the Louisiana-Mississippi border.

Parts of the road that crossed the northwest corner of Alabama Territory and central Mississippi, with a general northeast-southwest trend, have been rerouted. Along the part of the road in central Mississippi appears the phrase "Road made by order of Government."

The shape and trend of Lake Michigan have been altered; the new trend is northeast-southwest. Its name has been relettered from south to north (north to south on earlier states).

The northern boundary of Indiana is relocated slightly to the south. Lake Michigan now washes the State at the northwest corner rather than on the north central border.

Illinois has been relettered, closing the gap between the N and the O.

The Ohio-Michigan boundary has been moved south about 12 miles.

The shorelines of southeastern Wisconsin and northeastern Illinois are modified along with the change in configuration of southern Lake Michigan.

Chicago is relettered and relocated.

Melwakee is added within Illinois to a position north of Chicago.

The spelling of Lake Peoire in north central Illinois is changed to "Pioria."

The following new names are introduced in central Illinois: Edwardsville, F. Russel, Grand Kickapoo Village, Janoanong R., Manitou R., Monk R., Saline Fork, Sanguemon R., and Sugar Cr.

Pensacola and St. Marks, in northwest Florida, have been relettered and moved.

These new names are introduced in Florida: Ft. Gadsden, Oke-lockeonne R., St. Marks R., and Suwaney R.

Additions in Georgia include Ft. Scott, Ft. Gaines, and Ft. Early.

In Tennessee Holston R., Tennessee R., and Tellico R. are added and Notahacky R. is relettered "Natachucky R."

The following changes have been made in the vicinity of the U.S.-Mexican boundary established by the 1819 treaty: Carcasiou R. in southwestern Louisiana is relettered "Carcasui R."; Natchez R. in eastern Texas is replaced by "Rio de nieves or Neches R."; and Galveston is introduced about 45 miles upstream from the mouth of the Neches River.

The U.S.-Canadian boundary is shown as a dash-dot engraved line that follows the 49° parallel from the Lake of the Woods to longitude 36° W of Washington, D.C. The old dash-dot engraved line (approximately 49°37' north latitude) has not been deleted, however.

Library of Congress holdings:

a) An original (mounted).

b) Photostat positive (mounted) and negative (in 6 parts) of an original in the Harvard University Library. G3700 1818.M4c

Both of the two identified states of this edition carry the note "Improved to the 1st of April 1819."

## First state (Martin's "eleventh [actually twelfth] edition")

This is the first state to show (with a dash-dot engraved line) the U.S.-Mexican boundary, as established by the Adams-Onis Treaty. The boundary begins on the Gulf of Mexico and follows successively the Sabine River, the 93°55' meridian (w. of London), the Red River, the 100° meridian, the Arkansas River, and the 42° parallel. Along the latter parallel, between the Rocky Mountains and the upper course of the Multnomah River, the dash-dot symbols are omitted. They are also lacking in the middle course of the Arkansas River. A dash line in this section, designated as "Pikes route," is found on states of the map dated as early as 1816.

West of the Arkansas River and south of the parallel of 42° the phrase "The Limits of Louisiana in this quarter are undefined," which was first introduced on the second state of the 1816 edition, is removed.

Alabama is shown as a State for the first time with deletion of the word "Territory"; notwithstanding the fact that Alabama was not officially admitted to the Union until December 14, 1819.

"Arkansaw Territory" is added to embrace Lawrence District and Arkansas District. The spelling of the latter is changed to "Arkansaw."

The dashed boundary between Lawrence District and Cape Girardeau District, near latitude 36°10' north, is deleted.

A new northern boundary of Arkansaw is introduced as a line of dashes and dots following the parallel of 36° east of St. Francis River and the parallel 36°30' west of the stream. Between these two parallels the new engraved boundary follows the east bank of the St. Francis.

The word "Territory" of "Missouri Territory" is moved from a position near 35°30' north latitude to a position near 39°15' north.

A new western boundary of Texas is introduced as a dotted line extending from the Arkansas River at Pikes Block House to the Rio del Norte north of Santa Fe, near the 38° parallel.

A new dash-dot boundary is engraved along the 49° parallel from the Lake of the Woods to the Rocky Mountains, but the older dash-dot engraved line along the parallel of 49°40' from the Lake of the Woods to the Gulf of Georgia is not deleted.

A northward curving dash-dot boundary crossing the Rocky Mountains around 50°20' north latitude is introduced.

Library of Congress holdings:

An original (mounted).　　　G3700 1819.M4

## Second state (Martin's "twelfth [actually thirteenth] edition")

In the statistical table "Territory" is dropped following Illinois and Mississippi.

Alabama is added at the bottom of the first column of the table with no figures for length, breadth, area, or population.

Missouri is shown as a State for the first time, with dash-dot engraved borders.

New place names in Missouri include Herculaneum, Rogers T., Potosi, and Franklin.

The eastern boundary of Illinois is extended northward (as a dash-dot line) to separate the Northwest Territory and Michigan Territory; thus the Green Bay Peninsula and the western shore of Lake Michigan are placed in Michigan Territory.

The southern 90-mile segment of the Mississippi-Alabama boundary is relocated so that the southern end is 10 miles east of the mouth of the Pascagoula River.

The West Indies inset map has been extended southward to 7°30' and westward to the 92° meridian.

On the inset Yucatan, Guatemala, New Granada, Venezuela, and a number of other place names in northern South America have been added.

Library of Congress holdings:

An original (mounted), acquired from Godfrey F. Eyler in 1937, and a photostat negative (in 8 parts) of same.　　　G3700 1819.M4a

## 1820 EDITION

There are eight identified states of this edition. Except for the first state, which is incomplete, most of the modifications are in the Latin American regions. The first two states are designated as "Entered according to Act of Congress the 6th day of June 1820." The date on the other six states is "the 16th day of June 1820."

## First state (Martin's "thirteenth [actually fourteenth] edition")

Of this state only the southeast sheet, including the title cartouche and the West Indies inset map, exists. On the copyright notice the numeral 1 has been inserted in ink before the 6, so that it appears to read "16th of June 1820."

As on earlier states, the southern border of the map extends to approximately 23° north latitude.

Nickojack, which on earlier states was located in

northwest Georgia, has been moved across the border into Tennessee.

Spiritu Santa Bay in Florida has been renamed "Tempa Bay."

The dash-dot boundary between Alabama and Georgia has been moved slightly to the east and now passes between the E and R of Cherokees, rather than between the C and H as on the previous state.

The dot locating Turkey T. is therefore within Alabama, although the name is on the Georgia side of the border.

A portion of the Tennessee River in southern Tennessee near the Georgia boundary has been slightly altered.

The western extent of the northern boundary of South Carolina has been relocated.

Library of Congress holdings:

An uncolored original (mounted), the southeast sheet only (of 6). G3700 1820.M4

## Second state (Martin's "thirteenth [actually fifteenth] edition")

This is the first state of Melish's map to be published from nine plates. It extends southward beyond 16° north latitude and embraces the southern half of Mexico, part of Guatemala, all of Cuba, Jamaica, Hispaniola, Puerto Rico, the Virgin Islands, and the southern Bahamas. The inset map has also been extended southward to 6° north latitude.

A second "General Statistical Table" has been added in the southwest corner of the main map, in which the total of the population column is incorrectly given as 81,629,903.

In the old statistical table the following changes are noted: Arkansas Territory is added below Alabama; "Ceded to U.S. by Treaty" is inserted before "Florida"; "Territory" is dropped after "Missouri"; and a new "Missouri Territory" is inserted.

The Tennessee-Kentucky border east of the Tennessee River has been moved northward.

Christian C.H. in southern Kentucky is changed to Hopkinsville.

"Philadᵃ" is added in north central Kentucky.

In Illinois the following are deleted: "Ceded by the Sac & Fox Indians 3 Nov. 1804" "Indian Boundʸ", "Indian Bʸ", "I. Boundary," and three dotted boundaries adjacent to these designations.

Place names added in Illinois are Alton, Vandalia, Carlisle, Covington, Browns Ville, Vienna, Hamburg, America, Golconda, Carnir, Palestine, and Harrisonville.

In Missouri the names Jackson, Boonville, and Bluff Town are added, Herculaneum is relocated, Bonhomme R. is deleted, and the final Y in Missouri

Territory is moved westward beyond the limits of the State of Wisconsin.

The oblique name "Arkansaw Territory" is replaced by Arkansas Territory, lettered horizontally; "Arkansaw District" is changed to Arkansas District; and Cedran and Lawrence are introduced as new names in Arkansas Territory.

In Indiana "Ceded at Fᵗ Wayne Sept. 1809" is deleted along with eight dotted Indian boundaries; Fredonia, Mt. Carmel, Palmyria, and Terre Haute are added; Ft. Harrison is relocated; and several roads and trails in the southern part of the State are rerouted.

Additions in Ohio include N. Haven, Huron, Mecca, Putney, Woodsfield, Burlington, Hillsboro, Wilmington, Washington, Xenia, and Troy. A dotted Indian boundary is deleted in the western part of the State.

Deletions in Mississippi include "Yazoo Lands," "Ceded by the Choctaws," "Indian Boundary," and several dotted boundaries. In the same State the names Warrenton, Monticello, Holmville, Meadville, Shieldsborg, and Cotton Gin Pt. are added, Huntsville is replaced by Greenville, and a trail is added from Natchez to Stephens.

An unnamed canal (obviously the Erie Canal) is added in north central New York State.

The designation Gulf of Mexico has been moved slightly southward.

On the inset map are added the names Merida and Caribes, latitude numbers 8, 9, and 10, and three unnamed tributaries to a southern branch of the Orinoco River.

The following modifications are noted along the U.S.-Mexican boundary, established by the 1819 treaty: the dot-dash boundary line has been completed along the 42° parallel between the Multnomah River and the headwaters of the Arkansas; and the boundary line is moved and reengraved on the west bank of the Arkansas between the junction of parallel 42° with the 34° meridian (west of Washington, D.C.) and the intersection of the 41° parallel with the 32° meridian.

Library of Congress holdings:

Original, mounted on cloth sectioned to fold, in red buckram case, 9½ x 6½ inches, labeled "Melish Map U.S. 1st ed. June 6." "TWS" bookplate on cover of map, when folded. Photostat positive (mounted on cloth) and negative (in 9 parts) of same. Original acquired April 1969, at Streeter Collection auction. In the revised, updated identification this is the second state of the 1820 edition, not the first edition as on the Streeter label. G3700 1820.M4a

## Third state (Martin's "fourteenth [actually sixteenth] edition")

*Inset from the 1820 edition of Melish's map of the United States, second state. From the Geography and Map Division.*

The only apparent change from the second state is in the copyright notice which on the third state reads "Entered according to Act of Congress the 16th day of June 1820."

Library of Congress holdings:

a) An original.

b) Photostat positive (mounted) and negative (in 9 parts) of an original in the Library of Harvard University.     G3700 1820.M4b

## Fourth state (Martin's "fifteenth [actually seventeenth] edition")

There is a single apparent modification from the third state. In the general statistical table (southwestern corner) the total of the population column is corrected from 81,629,903 to 18,629,903.

Library of Congress holdings:

Photostat positive (mounted) and negative (in 9 parts) of an original in the collection of Thomas W. Streeter.     G3700 1820.M4c

## Fifth state (Martin's "sixteenth [actually eighteenth] edition")

In eastern Michigan Territory the phrase "Ceded by Treaty at Detroit 17 Nov$^r$ 1807" is deleted; and the following streams are added: Huron R. of L. Erie, R. Rouge, Huron R., Belle R., and Pine R.

In Louisiana the lower course of the Sabine River has been relocated so that its mouth is near 94° (west of London) rather than near 93°45' as on the previous state; the small lagoon near the mouth of the Sabine River is named "Sabine Bay"; and the international boundary (dash-dot line) is not shown running through Sabine Bay as it did on the fourth state.

The following deletions have been made in eastern Texas: Galveston, Trinity River, Arcokissas Bluff, Culebras I., Carancoways, S. Bernards B., B.S. Joseph, R. San Antonio, I. St. Francisco, Passo Cavallo, Pass of Aranjuez, and the sentence "Here LaSalle landed in 1685 and built F. Matagarda."

Also in eastern Texas, "Galueston B." has been relettered to read "Galveston Bay."

Some 300 miles of the Texas coast, west of the mouth of the Sabine River, have been redrawn.

The following have been added in eastern Texas: R. de la Trinidad, R. Brassos, Fort (unnamed), Pasa del Caballo, S. Bernards Bay, I. de S. Luis, R. Colorado, R. de Flores, R. de S$^n$ Marcos, R. de S$^n$ Antonio, R. de S. Jose, R. Frio, and the designation "LaSalles Establishment in 1683."

The following roads are introduced or extended in Texas and Mexico: From Nacogdoches to San Antonio along the course of "Pikes route" and con-

179

tinuing through Loredo and Saltillo to Fresnillo; Vera Cruz westward via Mexico City to Ascuaro; Acapulco to Mexico City, via Cuernavaco; north and northwest from Mexico City through Guanaxuato, Fresnillo, Durango, and Chihuahua and continuing along the trail designated as "Pike's route through the Interior Provinces."

The following name changes are noted in Mexico: "Valadolid" is respelled "Valladolid"; "Yurirupundaro" becomes "Puruandiro"; in Guanaxuato Province "Guan" is corrected to "Guanaxuato" and "Leon" to "Villa de Leon"; "Cuernevac" is corrected to "Cuernavaca"; "Potosi" is added to "S. Louis" for the province of that name; the city name "S. Louis de Potosi" is changed to "S. Luis Potosi"; "Valles" becomes "Valle de Maiz"; "Altamiria" is corrected to "Altamira"; "R. Hua Sacualco" is relettered "R. Guasaqualco."

"Part of" is deleted before "Guadalaxara" in west central Mexico.

Additions in Mexico are Calpico, Zacapo, Xauxilla, and Huango in Valladolid Province; Zelaya, Salamanca, Irapuato, San Miguel, Los Remedios, Tlachiquera, and "Comanjao or Sombrero" in Guanaxuato Province; Arroyo Sarco, Pachuca, and Real del Monte in Mexico Province; Tampico, Tampico Bay, Tamiagnao Lake, Nautla, Punta de Piedras, R. de la Antigua, S. Juan de Ulua, Xalopa, Fortress, Rio del Paso, and Paso de la Fabrica in Vera Cruz Province; and R. Chimalapa and the designation "Proposed Canal" in Oaxaca Province.

Library of Congress holdings:

An original (mounted), transferred from the Department of State in 1937, and photostat positive (mounted) and negative (in 9 parts) of same.

G3700 1820.M4d

## Sixth state (Martin's "seventeenth [actually nineteenth] edition")

The word "Northern" is deleted from "Northern Point of Observation" east of the Rocky Mountains, near the U.S.-Canadian boundary.

Rio des Monie is deleted in northeastern Missouri.

S. Louis Potosi in Mexico is changed to St. Luis Potosi for the province.

Library of Congress holdings:

Photostat positive (mounted) and negative (in 9 parts) of an original in the Provincial Library of British Columbia.       G3700 1820.M4e

## Seventh state (Martin's "eighteenth [actually twentieth] edition")

The following alterations are made in Maine: the international boundary is redrawn to the northwest of its former location; the sentence, "A very extensive Lake has been discovered here," is deleted; the headwaters of the St. Johns River are extended

to the southwest; six lakes are added in this area, one of which is named Bungah Quohene L. and another Aphmoojeene Gamook L.; the Penobscot River headwaters are extended north and northwest and eight lakes are added in that vicinity; one of the headwater tributaries is named Seboois R., and the only named lake is designated Chesuncook L.; in this same general area the words "Proposed Canal" are also introduced; a tributary, Dead Run, is added to the Kennebeck River, and Bath is introduced near the mouth of this river.

In Vermont a trail is added from the Canadian border to Johnsburg, with a branch extending to Greensboro.

Additions in eastern Canada include a town named "Hiatts," a trail from Quebec to Highgate, Vt., and a trail from the St. Lawrence River to the Vermont border.

In Pennsylvania the name Lehigh is replaced by Stoddartville, Stoys L. is introduced, and a new road joins Bedford and Greensburg.

Additions in New York are Canandaigua L., Crooked L., Seneca L., Cayuga L., and Skeneateless L.

Additions in present West Virginia include Burning Spring, Cedar Cr., Stear Cr., Woodsboro, Shenandoah R., and several new trails. In the same State "Branch Po." is replaced by "South Branch Potomac," and "Franklin" is relocated.

The southern boundary of North Carolina is relocated about 15 miles farther north.

In eastern South Carolina Chatham is replaced by Cheraw and Greenville gives way to Society Hill.

Modifications are made in the West Indies as follows: in Santa Domingo the names Seybo, Conception, and Monte Christi R. are added, "Mole SN" is replaced by "Mole S Nicholas," and a network of roads is introduced; in Puerto Rico the phrase "da Porto Rico" has been added to "St. Juan"; in Jamaica the towns Queens T., Crawford T., and Moora T. and a network of roads are added, and Savannah la Mar replaces Savannah; in Cuba the following changes appear: St. Pedro, St. Felice, Xagua B., Ochao, St. Jago R., Honduras, P. del Padre, Guibara, and Pto. de Nipa are added, a system of roads is introduced, Alta de Principe replaces Villa del Principe, and St. Juan has been extended to St. Juan Fernandez; new names on the inset map include B. of Campeche, B. of Honduras, Caribbee Islands, Windward Is., Leeward Is., and Virgin Isles.

Library of Congress holdings:

An original (mounted).       G3700 1820.M4f

## Eighth state (Martin's "nineteenth [actually twenty-first] edition")

The statistical table in the Gulf of Mexico is removed and "Gulf of Mexico" is relettered and relocated to fill the space vacated.

The general statistical table in the southwest part of the map is replaced by a "Statistical Table of the Several Countries Exhibited on the Map," which is laid out on a simulated scroll with curled edges.

New names along the coast of Yucatan include C. Catoche, Cosumuel I^d, Glovers Reef, Ruttan I., Bonaco I., and P^t Pedro.

Additions in Cuba are S. Filipe, Coco I., Pardon I., Cruz I., Guajaba, and Romano Is.

South of Cuba, Little Cayman is changed to Caymanchica, Caymanbrecha is introduced, Hogsties is deleted, and the name Grand Cayman is relocated.

C. Francois, C. Cabron, and C. Rafael are introduced in Santo Domingo, and Maliana Bay is changed to Juliana Bay.

Library of Congress holdings:

Photostat positive (mounted), a positive (in 12 parts), and 2 negatives (each in 12 parts) of an original once held by Edward Eberstadt of New York City and subsequently acquired by a Mr. Frost.                       G3700 1820.M4g

## 1822 EDITION

The two states of this edition have the note "Improved to 1822."

## First state (Martin's "twentieth [actually twenty-second] edition")

The designation "Sabine Lake" in southwestern Louisiana is removed from within the lake and relettered to the west of it.

The dash-dot U.S.-Mexican boundary has been removed from the west bank of the Sabine River, the south bank of the Red River, and the south bank of the Arkansas River.

The headwaters of the Arkansas River have been redrawn. The source is now at approximately 40°15' north latitude and 31°20' west of Washington, D.C.

A new section of the U.S.-Mexican boundary is introduced (as a dash-dot line) along the 31°20' meridian (west of Washington, D.C.) from the 42° parallel south to approximately 40°15'.

The upper portion of the Multnomah River, in the vicinity of latitude 42°, is cut off from the lower course of the stream. The betrunked portion, named Rio de San Clementi, is connected with the Pacific Ocean by an unnamed, broken line, west-flowing river that enters the sea at Port St. George.

Also deleted in this area is the note reading "Supposed Course of a River between the Buenaventura and the Bay of San Francisco which will probably be the communication from the Arkansaw to the Pacific Ocean."

Introduced in this region is a new dash-line stream named Timpanagos R. that rises in Lake Timpanagos then crosses the California Mountains and flows into the Bay of St. Francisco.

A short, dash-line stream is introduced between the California Mountains and the bay south of St. Michael.

"R. de las Truches," north of St. Michael, is renamed R. Buenaventura. The headwaters of the stream are extended to an incompletely drawn lake.

The designation "Western Territory" is introduced in the area of present-day Washington and Oregon.

The dash-dot international boundary on the parallel 49°40', from the Gulf of Georgia to the Lake of the Woods, is deleted as is the curved boundary from this parallel at Gt. Lake River to the 49th parallel at the front of the Rocky Mountains.

The Canadian portion of the Columbia River is relocated.

Two new partly dashed streams that drain into the Gulf of Georgia are introduced and named "Caledonia R." and "Tackoutche R.," respectively.

The north-south boundary in the eastern part of Northwest Territory is deleted.

The central part of the map, including Missouri, Missouri Territory, Arkansas Territory, and parts of New Mexico, Texas, Mississippi, Tennessee, Kentucky, Illinois, and Northwest Territory, has been reengraved with numerous changes in mountains, streams, and place names.

A line of dots designated "Steam Boat Route" is introduced in Lake Erie.

Additions in South Carolina include the town of Chesterville and a trail from Camden to Wadesboro, N.C., with a branch leading through Chesterville to Society Hill.

A swamp symbol is added in southern Florida, bordering L. Mayaco. The configuration of the lake has been changed and it is relettered "L. Mayaco" rather than "Mayaco L." as on earlier states.

The country names Colombia, Panama, and Costa Ricca [sic] and the province names Guatimala [sic], Veragua, and Vera Paz are added to the inset map.

The southern boundary of Yucatan is changed from a line of light dots to one of heavy dashes and dots. The eastern terminus of this boundary is moved to Port Cavallos.

A new dash-dot boundary is drawn between Costa Rica and Veragua, and new dotted boundaries are introduced between the other countries in Central America.

Library of Congress holdings:

a) An original (mounted).

b) Photostat positive (mounted) and negative (in 4 parts) of an original in the Boston Public Library.                       G3700 1822.M4

Second state (Martin's "twenty-first [actually twenty-third] edition")

"New California" is added in California between 38° and 32° north latitude.

"New Albion" is added in California between 41° and 39° north latitude.

The designation "Internal Provinces" is added in Texas and northern Mexico.

The name "Mexico" in large, broadly spaced letters is added across the southern part of that country.

Library of Congress holdings:

a) Original, mounted on cloth to fold in sixths, and photostat positive (mounted) and negative (in 8 parts) of same. Original acquired April 1969 at Streeter Collection auction.

b) Photostat positive (mounted) from an original in the John Crerar Library.      G3700 1822.M4a

This is Martin's "twenty-second [actually twenty-fourth] edition." It is the last identified state of Melish's large U.S. map. Martin believed, however, that there might have been an 1826 state for which A. T. Goodrich issued the 1826 edition of the *Geographical Description*. The 1823 edition differs from the previous state in the following respects:

"Published by John Melish Philadelphia" has been deleted at the bottom of the title cartouche.

The following new authority note has been added:

Published by James Finlayson, Agent Philadª Successor to John Melish."

The imprint note is changed to "Improved to 1823."

Library of Congress holdings:

a) An original (mounted).

b) Photostat positive (mounted) and negative (in 12 parts) from an original in the British Museum.
G3700 1823.M4

# The Hotchkiss Collection of Confederate Maps

## BY CLARA E. LEGEAR

Reprinted from the November 1948 issue of the *Library of Congress Quarterly Journal of Current Acquisitions.*

THE Library of Congress acquired in 1948 the maps, diaries, correspondence, and private papers of Maj. Jedediah Hotchkiss. A topographical engineer in the Confederate States Army attached to Gen. Stonewall Jackson's staff, Hotchkiss was also an educator and a promoter of Virginia's natural resources. The late C. Vernon Eddy, then Librarian of the Handley Library at Winchester, Va., learned of the existence of this collection some years ago, and, after a number of visits to Staunton and extended negotiations, was instrumental in having it listed and removed to fireproof quarters. Subsequently, it was placed at the disposal of the late Douglas S. Freeman, who made numerous references to the Hotchkiss papers in his *Lee's Lieutenants.* The collection was acquired by the Library of Congress from Mrs. R. E. Christian, of Deerfield, Va.,

Major Hotchkiss' last surviving descendant.

The collection contains some 600 maps, of which 340 are manuscript, relating principally to Virginia and West Virginia between 1861 and 1865. Many of them also reflect the postwar activities of Hotchkiss in the development of mines, railroads, and towns in both of these states. A number of the manuscript maps are annotated to show that they were actually used by Generals Lee and Jackson in planning their campaigns.

In addition to maps made by or under the direction of Hotchkiss, the collection includes a number of manuscript copies of Virginia county maps made under the direction of Maj. Albert H. Campbell, who was in charge of the Topographical Department, Confederate States Army. These maps are copies of some of the "Lost War Maps of the Confederates" about which Major Campbell wrote in the *Century Magazine* (vol. 35, 1888, p. 479–481) in protest against the many published criticisms that suitable maps had not been available to Confederate commanders. Major Campbell conceded that there was a lack of maps at the start of the war but explained that General Lee, upon taking command of the army, took steps to organize a topographical bureau for procuring accurate maps for his own use and that of his commanders. Major Campbell, being placed in charge, organized the work of surveying each county in detail and of preparing maps on comparatively large scales, giving due credit to the heads of field corps in the titles of the maps. When Richmond was evacuated on the night of April 2, 1865, Major Campbell packed up the master maps of the Engineer Office and placed them on an archive train bound for Raleigh, N. C., in the charge of an engineer officer and a draughtsman. He never thereafter learned of their whereabouts. It is particularly gratifying that the Hotchkiss collection contains copies of a number of these official Confederate maps not hitherto represented among "The Gilmer-Campbell Maps" described by Lawrence Martin in *Noteworthy Maps . . . Accessions [of the Library of Congress] for the Fiscal Year Ending June 30, 1926* (Washington, 1927, p. 7–17).

Many of the Hotchkiss manuscripts are so finely drawn as to give the appearance of printed maps. Much of the coloring was done with pencils, red being used for roads,

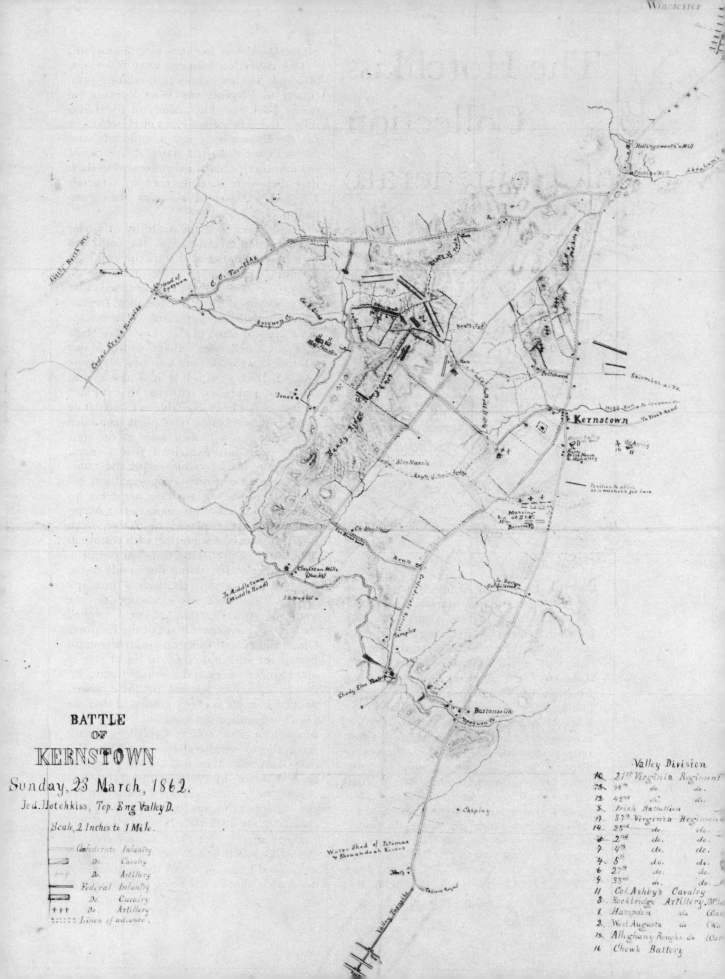

Winchester

Hollingsworth's Mill

Kernstown

Skirmish at Pk.

BATTLE
OF
KERNSTOWN

Sunday, 23 March, 1862.

Jed. Hotchkiss, Top. Eng. Valley D.

Scale, 2 Inches to 1 Mile.

Confederate Infantry
Do. Cavalry
Do. Artillery
Federal Infantry
Do. Cavalry
Do. Artillery
Lines of advance.

Valley Division

10  21st Virginia Regiment
7b  48th    do.    do.
12  42nd    do.    do.
8   Irish Battalion
17  37th Virginia Regiment
14  23rd    do.    do.
6   2nd     do.    do.
7   4th     do.    do.
4   5th     do.    do.
6   27th    do.    do.
9   33rd    do.    do.
11  Col. Ashby's Cavalry
3   Rockbridge Artillery (McL.)
1   Hampden    do.   (Cap.)
2   West Augusta   do.  (Wa.)
18  Alleghany Roughs do. (Car.)
16  Chew's Battery

Taranquel
Head of Opequon
C. C. Turnpike
Cedar Creek Turnpike
Opequon Cr.
Col. B. House
Maj. Funk
Jones
Sandy Ridge
Mrs. Massie
Route of Main body
Ch. Mosilla
Cloverdon Mills (Quak)
To Middletown (Middle Road)
J. B. Neyle

Pritchard
Hogg Run   To Opequon Cr.
To Flank Road
Position to which skirmishers fell back.
Massing at 2 P.K.
Reserve

To Bartonsville Col. Gilbert

Temples

Shady Elm Post

Bartonsville
Opequon Cr.

Chipley

Water Shed of Potomac & Shenandoah Rivers

To Front Royal
Valley Turnpike

*The three maps illustrating this article were drawn by Jedediah Hotchkiss. From the Geography and Map Division.*

blue for water, green for wooded areas, and brown for hachures indicating topography. On the larger-scale maps, dwellings and the names of their occupants are shown, as well as churches, mills, blacksmith shops, stores, railroad stations, courthouses, and post offices.

At the outbreak of the Civil War, Jedediah Hotchkiss offered his services to Gen. Richard S. Garnett as topographical engineer and on July 2, 1861, was assigned to duty under Col. M. M. Heck on Rich Mountain. Immediately, he began a survey of Camp Garnett and vicinity. A copy of the resulting map, in this collection, may be his first war map. The position was attacked by McClellan's troops and evacuated on a rainy night. Hotchkiss, serving as adjutant on the retreat, led the troops over mountains and through swamps to safety. When General Lee reorganized the army in the following month, Hotchkiss joined him at Valley Mountain and worked feverishly on a map of Tygart Valley for Lee's campaign. Although confined by an attack of typhoid fever for some weeks, he made maps while convalescing for the reports of the officers who conducted the Rich Mountain and Tygart Valley campaigns. In March 1862 he was assigned to the staff of Gen. T. J. (Stonewall) Jackson, as topographical engineer of the Valley District, Department of Virginia, with the rank of captain. His map of the Battle of Kernstown (March 23, 1862), made shortly after his arrival, has been preserved.

Complying with General Jackson's comprehensive instructions to "Prepare a map showing all points of offense and defense in the Shenandoah Valley from the Potomac to Lexington" he produced a masterpiece, performing this difficult task in record time. His familiarity with the region and his great facility in sketching were contributory factors in this notable accomplishment, for which he received high praise from General Jackson. The map is drawn on tracing linen, on the scale of 1:80,000, measuring 7½ x 3 feet, and is in an excellent state of preservation. Showing an infinite amount of detail useful for military tactics, it was frequently laid before Confederate commanders who were planning troop movements. When the Hotchkiss Collection was acquired in 1948, the original manuscript drawing of the Shenandoah Valley map was on loan to the Handley Library of Winchester, Va. Following the death in October 1963 of Mr. Eddy, Librarian, Mrs. Christian recalled the map from the Handley Library. In fulfillment of her wish that the Shenandoah map be reunited with the other Hotchkiss maps, she presented this historic and cartographic treasure to the Library of Congress in 1964.

Another remarkable item in the collection is Hotchkiss' field sketchbook. The cover bears this annotation over his signature: "This volume is my field sketch book that I used during the Civil War. Most of the sketches were made on horseback just as they now appear. The colored pencils used were kept in the places fixed for them on the outside of the cover. These topographical sketches were often used in conferences with Generals Jackson, Ewell and Early. . . ." The more than 100 pages of delicately executed sketches reveal an extraordinary ability and an artistic hand. How such fine work could be done in the saddle remains a marvel to everyone who examines it. The flyleaf and the first pages show positions on the Cedar Run Battlefield, dated March 23, 1862. The majority of the maps relate to various sections of the Valley of Virginia, centering on the Valley turnpike. Others show sections of the Blue Ridge, Massanutten, Powell's Fort Valley, and the road between Dawsonville and Darnestown in Montgomery County, Md., as well as regions in Virginia around Chancellorsville, Winchester, Orange County, Bristoe Station, and Warrenton.

Hotchkiss was directed on numerous occasions to choose lines of defense, to select troop positions for important engagements, and to perform other arduous and often extremely dangerous duties, all of which were faithfully executed. He was constantly on the move and more than once narrowly escaped capture. One night he rode 60 miles to block a mountain pass and at another time he rode 46 miles to report the progress of battle. He took an active part in the Battle of Winchester, May 25, 1862, riding with Jackson at the head of his troops and rallying the citizens to put out the fires started during the battle. His original map of troop movements on this day is preserved at the Handley Library. Several days later, he plotted troop positions around Richmond, as shown on a captured Federal map. On June 9, he led General Taylor's brigade in a flank movement at Port Republic and also in the attack that decided the battle. His map of the battlefield showing troop positions is in the collection.

When General Jackson went to Richmond, Hotchkiss went to Staunton to prepare a map of the Piedmont region for the Pope campaign. The collection includes several undated maps which may have been made at this time. Hotchkiss rejoined the army at Gordonsville, which he subsequently mapped; he was also at Cedar Mountain, in the Rappahannock operations, and at Chantilly, maps of which are represented in the collection. Later he was in the first Maryland campaign with General Jackson, blew up the Monocacy River bridge, and guided Gen. J. E. B. Stuart by concealed roads from Sharpsburg to Shepherdstown, for which General Jackson commended him to the Secretary of War for promotion.

Continual sketching, note-taking, and map-drawing filled the days of Captain Hotchkiss. While serving on Jackson's staff at the time of the Battle of Fredericksburg, December 12, 1862, he aided in planning troop positions. During the winter of 1862–63 at Moss Neck, he made numerous reports and maps to accompany them, including a large map of the lower Rappahannock showing the lines of the Second Corps.

In the spring of 1863, at the request of General Jackson, Hotchkiss secretly made a map extending "from the Rappahannock to Philadelphia." Attached to it are two labels: "Map made by Capt. Jed. Hotchkiss at Moss Neck—by order of Gen. T. J. Jackson," and "Used by Gen. R. E. Lee in the famous Gettysburg campaign." It is probably the most beautifully executed map in the entire collection, measuring 52 by 32 inches and containing a great amount of detail, so finely drawn as to be remarkably clear. It is represented in the Library of Congress collection by a photostat, the original being in the Handley Library.

Captain Hotchkiss reported to General Lee that General Jackson had been wounded at Chancellorsville on May 2,

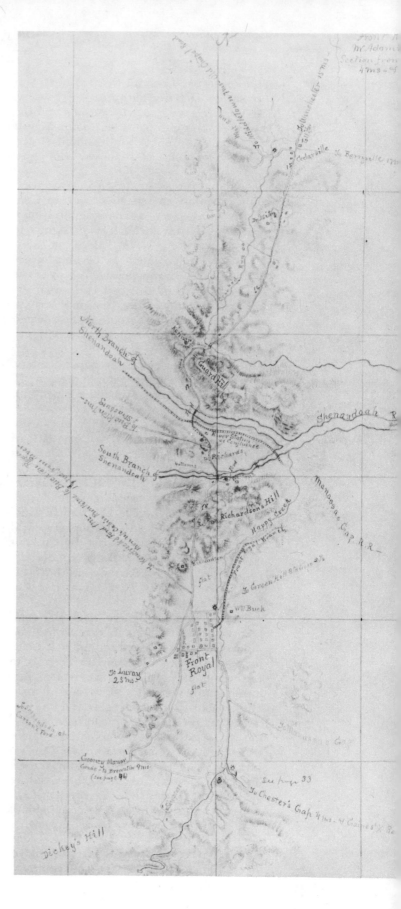

1863. Two days later he escorted the ambulance carrying General Jackson to Guiney's Station (Guinea), Va. At General Lee's request Captain Hotchkiss prepared complete maps of the Chancellorsville campaign, on which all subsequent maps have been based. The collection contains several maps made on this occasion.

While serving on General Ewell's staff, Hotchkiss prepared maps of the Second Battle of Winchester, June 13–15, 1863. He was in the first day's Battle of Gettysburg and then was ordered to watch and report from Seminary Ridge. A copy of the map of Gettysburg he made to accompany General Ewell's report is in the collection. A little later he prepared a "Sketch of Routes of the 2nd Corps A. N. Virginia, from Fredericksburg, Va., to Gettysburg, Pa., and return to Orange C. H., Va. June 4th, to August 1st, 1863," on the scale of 1 inch to 10 miles; this is likewise preserved in the collection. His map of the engagement at Bristoe Station was made after that action on October 14, 1863.

General Lee frequently required maps of Captain Hotchkiss and expressed great confidence in them. In the spring of 1864 he ordered Hotchkiss to select a line of defense and, in carrying this out, Hotchkiss rode hundreds of miles. The resulting report was specially complimented by General Lee and was adopted in large part. One of Hotchkiss' most strenuous feats was to sketch under heavy fire, in one day, the 10-mile-long line held by General Lee from the Chickahominy to the Totopotomoy and to deliver the map to the general that evening. A map answering this description is contained in the collection.

Captain Hotchkiss remained with the Second Corps when General Early took command and served on his staff in the Lynchburg-Monocacy-Washington and the Valley campaigns. A number of the maps in the collection reflect these activities.

*A Hotchkiss manuscript plan for the Battle of Chancellorsville.*

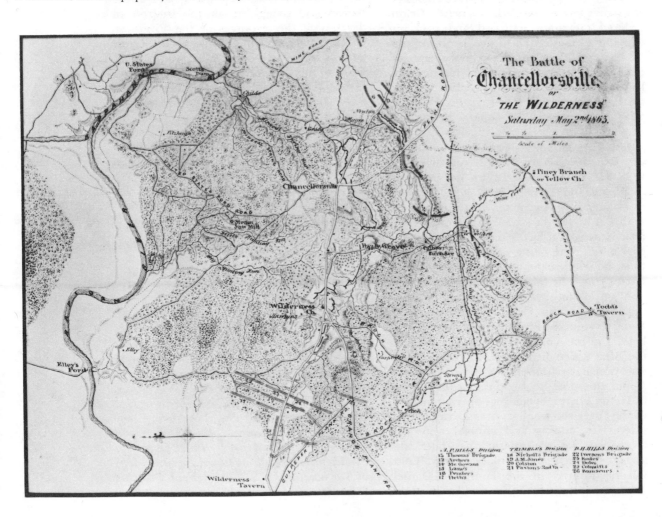

During the winter of 1864–65, Hotchkiss prepared beautifully illustrated reports of the operations of the Second Corps and made more than 100 maps for General Lee and other officers. The collection contains a manuscript report illustrated by an atlas of 63 plates of finely drawn maps of the Second Corps' camps, marches, and engagements during the campaign of 1864.

Major Hotchkiss was on the staff of General Early when General Sheridan attacked at Waynesboro and had to flee over the Blue Ridge, barely escaping capture. He was with General Rosser at Lynchburg when General Lee surrendered. Having sent his maps to a hiding place, he went home at once and was paroled on May 1, 1865 at Staunton, where he moved his family shortly thereafter. Later that year he was arrested and his maps were demanded by order of General Grant. He hurried to Washington and, in an interview with General Grant, protested against the confiscation of his maps, offering to make copies of any that were needed. General Grant ordered the maps returned and paid for copying all he desired to use in illustrating his reports. When the official documents of the Civil War were being prepared for publication, Major Hotchkiss supplied a number of the maps which were included in the atlas accompanying the *Official Records of the Rebellion*.

Jedediah Hotchkiss was born at Windsor, Broome County, N. Y., November 30, 1828. He was graduated from the Windsor Academy and early showed great interest in botany and in geology. In the winter of 1846–47, he taught school in Lykens Valley near Harrisburg, Pa., in a community where coal mines were being opened. In his spare time, he studied the geology of the anthracite region. The following summer, in company with another teacher, he made a walking tour of the Cumberland Valley of Pennsylvania, the Piedmont region of Maryland, and the Valley of Virginia, as well as the Blue Ridge, little realizing how well he was preparing himself for his life's work. About this time he made the acquaintance of Henry Forrer, owner and operator of one of the large iron smelters near Luray, whose interest in mining and mineral resources awakened the enthusiasm that later absorbed so much of Hotchkiss' energy. That fall he tutored in the family of Daniel Forrer at Mossy Creek, Va., and for the next ten years was principal of the Mossy Creek Academy. In 1858 he resigned to organize the Loch Willow School for Boys at Churchville, Augusta County, which flourished until the outbreak of the war. For two years after the war, Major Hotchkiss kept a school at Staunton and thereafter opened an office as topographical and mining engineer, which he continued until his death in 1899.

Major Hotchkiss' postwar activities and interests, too numerous to record here, are reflected in his voluminous correspondence, diaries, and papers. He wrote *The Battlefields of Virginia—Chancellorsville* with William Allen in 1867; *The Geography of Virginia* in 1876, published in many subsequent editions; and *Virginia*, volume 3 of the *Confederate Military History*, edited by C. A. Evans, in 1899. He edited *The Virginias, a Mining, Industrial and Scientific Journal* from 1880 to 1885. He compiled an *Historical Atlas of Augusta County, Virginia*, 1885, made many surveys, compiled and published maps, and wrote papers and pamphlets in the interest of developing the resources of the Virginias. In 1872 and again in 1874 he visited Great Britain and was influential in getting millions of northern and foreign capital invested in the development of his beloved State. He lectured on many occasions, organized the Stonewall Jackson Camp of Confederate Veterans, and was an ardent supporter of the Second Presbyterian Church and the Young Men's Christian Association in Staunton. His whole life merits the words of commendation General Jackson said to him on occasion, "Good, very good."

*A catalog of* The Hotchkiss Map Collection, *compiled by Mrs. LeGear, was published by the Library of Congress in 1951. It is out of print, but copies may be examined in many large reference libraries.*

*A comprehensive list of* Civil War Maps, *compiled by Richard W. Stephenson, is a 1961 publication of the Library's Geography and Map Division. Both Union and Confederate maps are described. Copies of the list are for sale by the Superintendent of Documents, U. S. Government Printing Office, at one dollar each.*

# South American Historical Maps

BY LAWRENCE MARTIN

REVISED AND EXPANDED

BY WALTER W. RISTOW

*Reprinted from volume 1, number 3 (1944), of the Library of Congress Quarterly Journal of Current Acquisitions.*

THE WEALTH and diversity of the Geography and Map Division's holdings may be illustrated by describing noteworthy items selected from the thousands of cartographic materials acquired in a particular year. Thus, in 1943 the collections were enriched by several distinctive accessions bearing on the history of South America. Included were a group of manuscript maps drawn in the late eighteenth century, a rare engraved map of the continent, dated 1775, and a portfolio of facsimiles of early historical maps.

The manuscript maps acquired by purchase were selected from among a number of cartographic items listed in Catalog No. 693 issued by Maggs Bros., Ltd., of London in 1940. Though separately described in the catalog, the individual maps, with some few exceptions, have an intimate relationship to one another. Most of them record detailed surveys made to delimit boundaries between Spanish and Portuguese possessions in South America. The maps, all produced by Spanish mapmakers, are skillfully and neatly drafted and many have watercolor washes.

For the first two centuries following the discovery of South America, European settlements were sparse and largely confined to the coastal regions. Spanish and Portuguese spheres of interest in the continent were initially prescribed in the Bull of Pope Alexander VI, dated May 4, 1493, which accorded to Spain territories lying to the west of an arbitrarily selected line, and to Portugal lands to the east. Pope Alexander's line, which approximated the 37° meridian west of Greenwich, limited Portuguese exploration to a small segment of the continent immediately to the west of Cape São Roque at the eastern extremity of present-day Brazil. The Treaty of Tordesillas, signed on June 7, 1494, made a more equitable division of the unexplored continent by establishing the boundary line along the meridian lying 370 leagues west of the Cape Verde Islands. The Tordesillas line, approximately 10 degrees west of the meridian designated by Pope Alexander, gave to Portugal dominion over much of the territory now embraced by the Republic of Brazil.

By the beginning of the eighteenth century the two Iberian monarchies had established administrative jurisdiction over their respective portions of the continent. The principal European settlements were still largely along the coasts, but Spanish Jesuit missions had been established in the upper reaches of the major streams. Portuguese explorers meanwhile had advanced inland from São Paulo and other Brazilian bases.

Disputes and conflicts between nationals of the two countries had become quite common by the early 1700's, particularly in the upper courses of the Paraguay and Uruguay Rivers, in the western part of the Amazon Basin, and around the headwaters of the Orinoco River. With the objectives of minimizing zones of conflict and establishing more realistic lines of demarcation between their respective dominions, representatives of Portugal and Spain signed the Treaty of Madrid, on January 13, 1750. Although the negotiators agreed on tentative boundaries and on cessions of various disputed territories, Jesuit leaders in Spain were strongly opposed to some parts of the Treaty of Madrid. Its provisions were accordingly never put into effect, and the treaty was officially annulled in a subsequent agreement, signed by the two nations on February 12, 1761.

Friction and conflicts in the several troubled areas, therefore, persisted and increased in number and intensity. Representatives of Spain and Portugal met again some 15 years later with the hope of arriving at a mutually satisfactory resolution of the basic problems. The points upon which tentative agreement was reached were summarized in the Treaty of San Ildefonso, signed on October 1, 1777. Its proposed boundaries were essentially the same as those prescribed in the Treaty of Madrid a quarter of a century earlier. The 1777 negotiators, however, considered the treaty boundaries to be preliminary and tentative and subject to revision following accurate surveys in the several disputed areas. The Treaty of San Ildefonso, therefore, stipulated that to delimit the boundaries more exactly and to ensure that there "might not be the least doubt about it in the future," a commission of experts would be named to survey and mark the line.

Commissioners were designated by the two countries and *Partidas* were organized to survey the several controversial territories. Spanish and Portuguese survey and arbitration teams operated in close conjunction in each region, but each group prepared its own maps and submitted separate reports to its respective officials. Agreements were reached in the field for some parts of the international boundary, but more often unresolved questions were referred to the Spanish and Portuguese Governments. The demarcation surveys continued over a period of 17 years. Notwithstanding the expressed desire of both parties to resolve the boundary question and the heavy expenditures of time, effort, and money on the work of the Joint Commission, Spain and Portugal never reached a final agreement regarding their conflicting claims. The official reports, letters, maps, and other documents submitted by the leaders of the several survey *Partidas* therefore were consigned to various archives and repositories in Spain, Portugal, and South America. No reports on the surveys or on the conclusions and findings of the Joint Commission or of the *Partidas* were ever published, and no impartial analysis was ever made of the Commission's work. Negotiations continued, however, until war was declared between Spain and Portugal in 1801. The 5,000-mile line described in the Treaty of San Ildefonso was, nonetheless, generally

Title from one of six manuscript maps in the Library surveying the Brazil-Uruguay frontier and prepared by Josef Varela y Ulloa, Chief Spanish Commissioner for the Partida Primera. Only this map carries the signatures of both Varela and his Portuguese counterpart, Cabral, on the title.

recognized for a century or more as an acceptable common boundary.

Parts of the San Ildefonso line also served to delimit the independent republics established in South America in the early decades of the nineteenth century. The many boundary disputes that have plagued every one of the countries may be traced, in large part, to limits vaguely defined during the colonial era. In arbitration proceedings for a number of the boundary differences the opposing governments have cited official reports of the Joint Commission and of the *Partidas* established under provisions of the Treaty of San Ildefonso. Unpublished manuscript maps prepared by Spanish or Portuguese survey teams have at times been offered as evidence to support the respective positions.

Included in the group of manuscript maps acquired by the Library of Congress in 1943 are original surveys prepared by the Spanish *Partidas* for the territory along the Paraguay and Uruguay Rivers, and for the upper Amazon River and a number of its major tributaries. Chief Spanish Commissioner for *Partida Primera* was Josef Varela y Ulloa, and his Portuguese counterpart was Sebastião Xavier da Veiga Cabral. Josef Varela y Ulloa was born on August 14, 1748, in Galice, Spain, of a noble family. He studied mathematics and science, and in 1776 he assisted Jean Charles Borda, the distinguished French astronomer and mathematician, in surveying the peak of Tenerife Island in the Canaries and establishing geodetic control betweeen it and the coast of Africa. Varela also engaged in geodetic surveys along the southeast coast of South America before his appointment to the Commission. His technical knowledge and experience were utilized to advantage in the boundary surveys, as is apparent in the official reports and maps that were prepared by him and under his direction. After completing the boundary assignment Varela returned to duty as a Brigadier de Marine in the Spanish Navy. He died on July 23, 1794, in Havana, Cuba, while on another surveying expedition.

Six of the manuscript maps now in the collections of the Geography and Map Division were prepared under Varela's direction and bear his signature. One map also carries the signature of the Portuguese Commissioner, Sebastião Xavier da Veiga Cabral da Camara, and a long note in his hand. Four of the maps are identified by the numbers 4, 5, 7, and 9 and two unnumbered maps seem to be part of the same series. Collectively the six maps show the Brazil-Uruguay frontier extending north and northwest from Laguna de Merin on the Atlantic coast.

The southernmost map of the series, which is unnumbered, is mounted on linen sectioned to fold to approximately six by nine inches. The edges are bound with blue linen, to which four brass rings are attached at the top. The map measures 35½ by 68 inches and is at the approximate scale of 1:210,000. River systems are drawn in considerable detail and physiographic features are shown in pictorial perspective. Coastal swamps are indicated with an appropriate symbol and a green watercolor wash. The ocean and major streams are likewise in green. The title, enclosed within a decorative cartouche, reads *Plano Topografico que comprende la parte septentrional de La Laguna de Merin con las vertientes que bajan à ella de la Cuchilla general El Sangradero de la misma Laguna: El Arroyo de Fahin: El Piratini: y la boca del Río Grande de Sⁿ Pedro. Levantado por la Primera Partida de Demarcacion de Limites del mando del Brigadier de la Armada Dⁿ Josef Varela y Ulloa.* Varela's signature is inscribed in the lower right corner of the cartouche. It is possible that the number originally assigned to this map was trimmed when the map was mounted. Because maps 4 and 5 are in sequence to the north, the number 3 is assigned to the southernmost map for purposes of identification.

"No. 4" is inscribed, in a bold hand, at the top of the adjoining map, which extends north to the Sierra de los Tapes, at approximately 29°30′ south latitude. The cartography and cartouche resemble these features on the previously described map. The title is *Plano Topografico que comprende las vertientes del Arroyo Ycabaquã: Las del Rio Negro: y la cresta que divide aguas al Yacuy y al Uruguay hasta la Sierra de los Tapes ó Montegrande. Levantado por la Primera Partida de Demarcacion de Limites del mando del Brigadier de la Armada Dⁿ Josef Varela y Ulloa.* Varela's signature is again below the title. The map, which measures 47 by 49 inches, has been mounted on muslin in the Library's preservation laboratory and sectioned to fold to approximately 24 by 17 inches. As on map No. 3, no scale is indicated but, reckoned from measurement of a degree of latitude, it approximates 1: 210,000.

In the same pattern and at the same scale is map No. 5, which shows the territory to the north of No. 4 extending to 27° north latitude, just beyond the Uruguay River. The 59 by 54 inch map has also been mounted on muslin, sectioned to fold in sixths, in the Library's laboratory. The title, within a decorative border, reads *Plano Topografico que comprende una parte del Montegrande: el Río Zacuy: los Establecimientos y Misiones del Uruguay: Los Yervales que actualmente poseen los Indios Guaranis: y el curso del mismo Uruguay desde la boca del verdadero Pepiri ó Peguiri hasta el Paso que llaman de Concepcion Levantado por la Primera Partida de Demarcacion de Limites del mando del Brigadier de la Armada Dⁿ Josef Varela y Ulloa.* The cartographer's signature is also within the cartouche.

Map No. 7, at the same scale as those described above, is on a sheet that measures

191

only 29 by 21 inches. Geographically this map lies to the west of parts of maps 4 and 5, but it does not abut either. It maps a segment of the Uruguay River downstream from the part shown on map No. 5. It is entitled *Plano del Rio Uruguay desde Yapeyu hasta La Estancia de Sⁿ Gregorio*

*Levantado por la Primera Partida de Demarcacion de Limites del mando del Brigadier de la Armada Dⁿ Josef Varela y Ulloa* and bears the signature Josef Varela y Ulloa.

Map No. 9, at the same scale, is on a sheet 40½ by 44½ inches. Following ac-

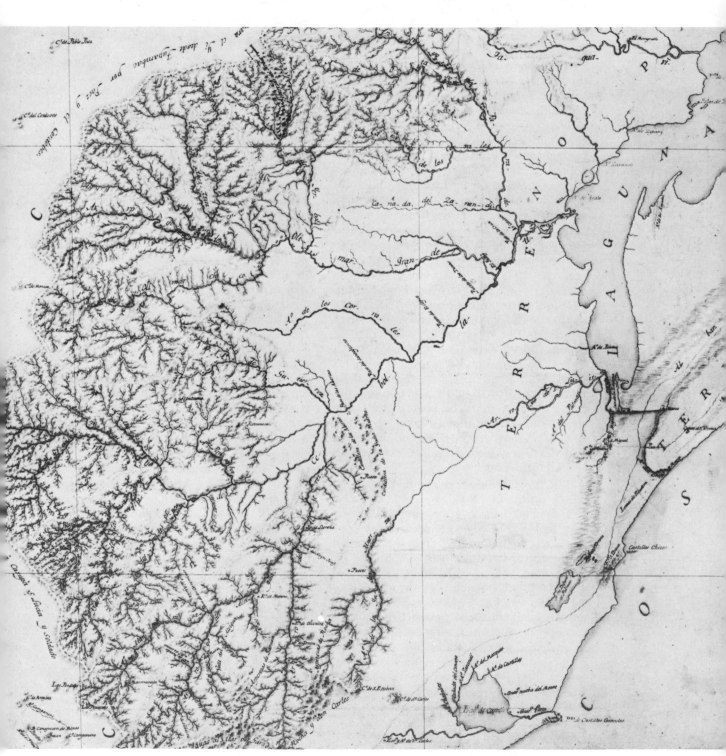

quisition by the Library it was mounted on muslin and quartered to fold. It adjoins No. 5 on the east and bears the title *Plano Topografico que conprende* [sic] *una parte de los Yervales pertenecientes à los Pueblos de las Misiones del Uruguay La Cresta que divide aguas à este Rio y al Yacuy: y la Picada que llaman de S<sup>ta</sup> Victoria por donde se sale à los Dominios de Portugal Levantado por la Primera Partida de Demarcacion de Limites del mando del Brigadier de la Armada D<sup>n</sup> Josef Varela y Ulloa.* It is signed by Josef Varela y Ulloa.

A large (approximately 80 by 45 inches) unnumbered Varela map extends from 27° to 34°25′ south latitude and embraces all the territory covered by maps 3, 4, 5, and 9, as well as the equivalent of an additional sheet to the south. Its title, enclosed within a plain rectangular cartouche, reads *Plano Topografico que comprende la costa del mar desde la ensenada de Castillos hasta el Rio Grande de S<sup>n</sup> Pedro: el Arroyo del Chuy̆: la Laguna de la Manguera, y la de Merin, contodos los Arroyos, que desaguan en esta: el Piràtini: las cabeceras del Rio Negro, y las del Ycabăcuà: las vertientes que bajan de la Cuchilla general al Yacuy̆, y al Uruguay: los establecimientos y Misiones Españolas del propio Uruguay: los Establecimientos Portugueses mas inmediatos a dichas Misiones: y el curso de una gran parte del Uruguay con la boca del Rio à que los Demarcadores pasados dieron el nombre de Pepiri; expresandose en el mismo Plano los terranos y demarcados, y los que estan endisputa entre los Comisarios Principales de los dos Soberanos, por cuya orden se hizo este trabajo, que empezò elaño de 1784, y se concluyò en el de 1788.*

This map is one of the most significant in the Varela group for, as the title says, it presents cartographically both Portuguese and Spanish positions regarding the boundary. A note below the title explains that a red line on the map shows Spanish claims and a yellow line the Portuguese. Territory between the two lines is designated as neutral. Unlike the other Varela items, this map has graphic scales graduated in meters and leagues, respectively. Calculated as a representative fraction, the scale is approximately 1:365,000. The official character of

*Lower left-hand corner of Varela-Cabral map, the only one of the Varela maps to designate both Spanish and Portuguese boundary claims.*

the map is indicated by the fact that it carries the signatures of both the Spanish Commissioner Varela and the Portuguese Commissioner Sebastião X. da Veiga Cabral da Camara. There is also a lengthy note, in Portuguese, signed by the latter, in the right-center. The map also establishes that the surveys for the detailed maps were made between 1784 and 1788.

Only one map among the group of manuscripts acquired in 1943 was apparently prepared by *La Segunda Partida* of the Joint Commission. It shows parts of the Uruguay and Paraguay Rivers lying between 21° and 31°20′ south latitude and undoubtedly incorporates within its limits data from several large-scale surveys. The unsigned map is 31 by 15 inches and is at the approximate scale of 1:1,700,000. It is identified by a small "No. 13" at the top right margin and by "N. 6" on the verso. The title reads *Plano Corografico de los Reconocimientos Pertenecientes á la Demarcacion del Art. 8° del Trat? Preliminar de Limites de 11 de Oct<sup>e</sup> de 1777 Practicados por las Segundas Subdivisiones Española y Portuguesa en orden á desatar las dudas suscitadas entre sus respectivos Comisarios.* The line drafting and lettering on the map were accomplished with skill and taste. Rivers are in green and the entire map surface is tinted with a light yellow wash. Groups of hills are drawn in low perspective. Red lines trace roads and crosses locate missions. There is no date on the map but, like the Varela maps, it was very likely made between 1784 and 1788.

Two unsigned manuscript maps, numbered on the verso XXXII-2 and XXXII-24, bear on the southwestern section of the Portuguese-Spanish boundary that was surveyed by *La Tercera Partida.* Both are neatly and attractively drawn and are beautifully tinted with watercolor washes. They are mounted on linen with the edges bound in green silk. Map XXXII-2 is entitled *Copia del Plano de la demarcacion que hizo la Tercera Partido reducido à punto pequeño. Comprehende la frontera con Portugal, desde el Salto grande en el Rio Paranà hasta la boca del Jauru, y la Provincia del Paraguay.* As on the Varela composite map, there is a note beneath the title stating that the boundary claimed by the Spanish is in red and that by the Portuguese is yellow. Enlarged maps of sections of the Paraná and Paraguay Rivers are inserted at the top of the sheet, and at the bottom there is an attractive view of the mouth of the Jauru River. The map is 34 by 15 inches and is at the scale of 1:1,700,000. It is focused on the Paraguay River and extends from the city of Corrientes on the south (latitude 27°30′ south) to the Cordillera de Joseph (latitude 16° south) on the north. The Rio Paraná parallels the east margin of the map. Spanish representatives on *La Tercera Partida* of the Joint Commission were Felix de Azara and Diego Albear, and map XXXII-2 was probably made under the direction of one or both of these men. Neither XXXII-2 nor XXXII-24 is dated, but both were probably made during the period 1784 to 1788. Untitled map XXXII-24 portrays the Paraguay River from Asuncion on the south to the Cordilheira de San Jozé on the north and is undoubtedly one of the larger scale surveys prepared by *La Tercera Partida*. The approximate scale is 1:700,000 and the dimensions are 62 by 15½ inches.

Two other manuscript maps acquired in 1943 are identified by the number XXXII-19, written on the verso of both of them. They have been mounted on muslin since they were purchased by the Library. Although they seem to be in the same numerical sequence as the two maps of *La Tercera Partida* described above and are within the territory it surveyed, the two XXXII-19 maps were apparently not prepared as part of the boundary survey. Drawn in 1794, they show the city and environs of Oran, in the northern extremity of present-day Argentina but near the late-eighteenth-century Spanish-Portuguese boundary. It is possible that Oran was settled by the Spanish as an outpost to protect and strengthen territorial and boundary claims in this region. Both maps are ascribed to Ramon Garcia de Leon y Pizarra, then Governor and Captain-General of the Spanish Province of Salta, who founded Oran in August 1794. The cartographer dedicated both maps to King Charles IV of Spain. The first map, which shows the environs of Oran, is entitled *Plan topografico del Valle de Centa, delineado p^r D^n Ramon Garcia de Leon y Pizarro* and contains a lengthy description, in Spanish, of the geographical and strategic advantages enjoyed by the region. It is at the approximate scale of 1:80,000.

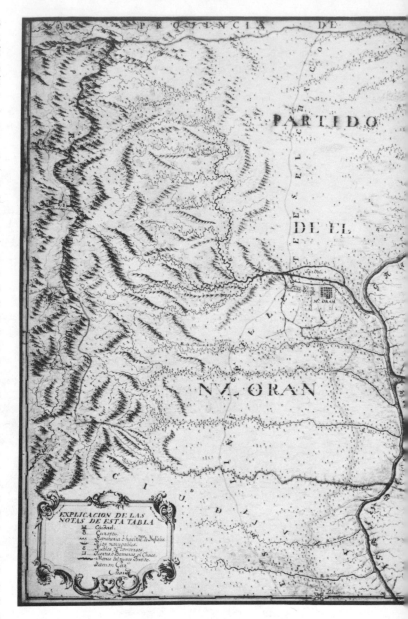

At the large scale of 1:4,000 is the *Plan de la Ciudad de la Nueva Oran, fundada en 31. de Agosto de 1794. p^r D^n Ramon Garcia de Leon y Pizarro,* which also contains a long note in Spanish. The title and inscription are within a border of native trees, and below the note there is a perspective view of Oran. Both maps are 20 by 28½ inches in size.

Because of the gaps in the numbering sequence it was inferred that the manuscripts acquired by the Library in 1943 did not include all the maps prepared by the Spanish members of the three *Partidas* concerned with the south and southwestern boundary between the Spanish and Portu-

*Environs of the city of Nueva Oran, drawn by its founder, Ramon Garcia de Leon y Pizarro. Maps illustrating this article are in the Geography and Map Division.*

guese jurisdictions. Some six or eight years later it was learned that the Mapoteca do Itamaraty, the map library of Brazil's Ministério das Relacões Exteriores, in Rio de Janeiro, had also purchased from Maggs Bros., Ltd., a number of the manuscript maps listed in their Catalog No. 693. In 1951 the Map Division acquired, on exchange, photostat reproductions of 11 maps in the Itamaraty purchase (see Library of Congress *Quarterly Journal of Current Acquisitions*, August 1951, p. 45). They sup-

plement and complement the Library of Congress maps described above.

Six of the reproductions were prepared by the Spanish *Partida Primera* and are signed by Josef Varela y Ulloa, and three of them also bear the signature of Sebastião Xavier da Veiga Cabral da Camara. The maps are identified by numbers, on either the recto or verso, that appear to fit into the numerical sequence of the Varela y Ulloa maps in the Library of Congress.

Map No. 1 (recto number) is entitled *Plano Topografico que comprende una parte del Río de la Plata, y la costa del mar desde la punta del Este de Maldonado hasta las cercanias de Castillos Grandes. Levantado por la Primera Partida de Demarcaciones de Limites del mando del Brigadier de la Armada Dⁿ Josef Varela y Ulloa.* It is 23½ by 43 inches and, like the other detailed Varela y Ulloa maps, is at the approximate scale of 1:210,000. It is the southernmost of all the maps prepared by *La Primera Partida* in the Library of Congress.

Map No. 2 (verso number) is 28 by 46 inches and is at the same scale as No. 1, of which it is a northward continuation. Its title is *Plano Topografico que comprende el Arroyo del Chuy la Laguna de la Manguera la parte medional [sic] de la Lagunas de Merín, las dos Lenguas de tierra adyacentes y las vertientes del Arroyo Cevollati Levantado por la Primera Partida de la Demarcacion de Limites del mando del Brigadier de la Armada Dⁿ Josef Varela y Ulloa.*

Map No. 8 (recto number) is long and narrow, 41 by 12 inches, and shows a section of the Uruguay River. Its title reads *Plano del Rio Uruguay desde la Estancia de Sⁿ Gregorio hasta el Arroyo de la China Levantado por la Primera Partida de Demarcacion de Limites del mando del Brigadier de la Armada Dⁿ Josef Varela y Ulloa.*

Three of the reproductions show parts of Laguna de Merin and the adjacent seacoast and are signed by both the Spanish and Portuguese Commissioners of *La Primera Partida*. The most southerly of the maps, numbered 28 near the upper right corner, is entitled *Plano Topografico de los Arroyos de Chuy S. Miguel y sus contornos hasta Castillos Chicos en que se manifesta la Linea perteneciente a los Dominios de España establecida en cum-*

*plimiento del Tratado Preliminar de Limites de 11 de Octubre de 1777 por los primeros Comissarios de las Coronas de España y Portugal en el Año de 1784.* The approximate scale of this map is 1: 75,000. Showing territory northeast of that on the above map but not directly adjoining is a map, identified on the verso as XXXII-3, entitled *Plano Topografico que comprende los Arroyos de Tahin Bayeta Parte de las Lagunas Merim* [sic] *Manguera y sus contornos.* Part of the territory on these two maps is shown, at the reduced scale of 1:210,000, on *Plano Topografico e individual que comprende los Arroyos de Chuy S. Miguel Tahin y Bayeta la Laguna de la Manguera la Lengua de Tierra que media entre ella y la costa del Mar y parte de la Laguna de Merim* [sic] *y sus contornos.* The top right corner of the sheet is numbered 3.

A small, unsigned map, identified on the verso as XXXII-31, is entitled *Mapa del Rio Grande y de las Tierras que estan por el Portugués.* It shows, at the approximate scale of 1:1,350,000, the coastline lying between 29°30′ and 35° south latitude. On the original map yellow and red lines indicate the respective claims of the Portuguese and Spanish Commissioners. It is oriented with the north at the right side of the sheet.

The remaining four photocopies acquired from the Itamaraty Library are designated Nos. 1, 2, 3, and 4. The sheets adjoin one another, with more or less overlap, and have varying scales, ranging from 1:1,200,000 to 1:950,000. Collectively they show coastal and inland regions of South America extending from Punta Negra (35° south latitude) on the south to the valley of the Río Guaporé on the north (about 14° south latitude). Nos. 1 and 3 bear the signature of Pedro Antonio Cerviño, No. 2 is signed "Inciarte," and No. 4 is unsigned. They were obviously prepared by Spanish representatives on the Joint Boundary Commission. No. 1, entitled *Carta Plana que comprehende la costa del Mar desde Maldonado hasta el Rio Grande de S<sup>n</sup> Pedro,* is 44 by 16 inches and is at the approximate scale of 1:1,000,000. Parts of the Uruguay and Paraná Rivers are shown in the northern section of the map. Part of the same territory is shown on No. 2, which overlaps the previous sheet and maps extensions of these two rivers to the north

and northwest. The map is 35 by 23 inches in size and the scale approximates 1:950,000. The title is *Carta Esferica de la Provincia del Paraguay Con los Rios que dividen Estos Dominios de los del Brasil, arreglado al tratado Preliminar de Limites del año de 1777. Levantado Por los Demarcadores Españoles.* In the lower left margin is inscribed "Del° por Inciarte A° de 1796."

No. 3 is a northern extension of No. 2 along the Paraguay River and also includes part of the Province of Chiquitos, to the west of the river. The scale is about 1:1,150,000 and the dimensions of the sheet are 30 by 20 inches. It is entitled *Mapa Geografico Que Comprehende parte de la Provincia de Chiquitos . . . con la confluencia de los Rios Guaporè y Sararè el curso del Jauru, y su desague en el del Paraguay por cuyos puntos debe pasar la Linea Divisoria segun el Articulo 10 del Tratado preliminar de 1777.* "Pedro Antonio Cervino lo delineo" is inscribed at the lower left margin.

The unsigned map, No. 4, extends to the west of No. 3 to show part of the Río Mamoré. It is designated as *Mapa Que Comprehende parte de las Provincias de Moxos y Chiquitos . . . Construida por algunas noticias que no tienen la mayor Exactitud para dar idea de los Rios Ytenes ó Guapore y Sarare . . . segun el tratado de 1777.* The map is 15 by 22 inches and at the scale of 1:1,200,000.

Descriptions of all the Itamaraty maps, including those of which the Library has photocopies, are given in a catalog published by the Brazilian Ministerio das Relaçoes Exteriores in 1960: *Mapas e Planos Manuscritos Relativos ao Brasil Colonial Conservados no Ministerio das Relaçoes Exteriores e descritos por Isa Adonias para as Comemoracoes do Quinta Centenário do Morte do Infante Dom Henrique.* I Texto.

One of the manuscript maps purchased from Maggs by the Library of Congress seems unrelated to any of the treaty series described above, in spite of its number XXXII-1, on the verso, in the same style as the others. It maps most of the Rio Uruguay from the mouth of the Rio Negro to beyond Salto Grande. The title of the map suggests that it, too, bears on the Spanish-Portuguese boundary surveys: *Plano de la Marcha hecha por el S<sup>or</sup> D<sup>n</sup> Jph. de Andonaegui Mariscal de Campo de*

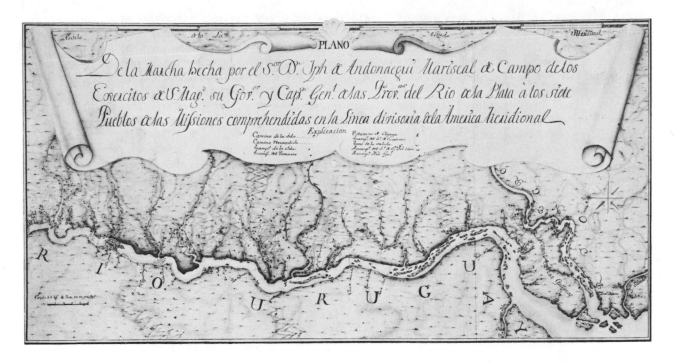

Andonaegui map of the Rio Uruguay.

los Exercitos de S. Mag$^d$ su Gov$^{or}$ y Cap$^n$ Gen$^l$ a las Prov$^{as}$ del Rio de la Plata a los siete Pueblos de las Missiones comprehendidas en la Linea divisonia de la America Meridional. The map, which is 15 by 28 inches, is mounted on linen, with the edges bound in green linen. It is oriented with north to the left. The scale is approximately 1:680,000. Drafting is skillfully and neatly done with green and brown washes emphasizing water and land features. The date "1767" is penciled in the lower right margin, although the map was probably prepared in the 1780's as were most of the other treaty maps.

Surveys of the northwestern Spanish-Portuguese boundary in South America, prepared for the Joint Commission, are recorded on a series of eight maps. They include detailed surveys of the upper Amazon River and several of its principal tributaries. Numbered consecutively 11 to 18, the maps were all prepared by or under the direction of Don Francisco Requeña, "primer comisario de la Quarta Partida Espanola de Limites." Except for the last one, prepared at Madrid in 1796, they were drawn at Ega (now Tefé), headquarters of the Spanish survey party between August 1788 and January 1789.

Francisco Requeña y Herrera, engineer, geographer, soldier, artist, cartographer, and administrator, was one of the most technically qualified of the Spanish and Portuguese Commissioners. Probably born about 1735, he was trained in mathematics and engineering and worked as an engineer in Spain and Africa before his service in America. By 1764 Requeña was in Panama where, as a military engineer, he drew plans of the streets and fortifications of the cities of Chagres, Darien, and Portobelo. In 1769 he was transferred to Guayaquil where he spent several years surveying and mapping that colonial city. Following this project Requeña was assigned the task of preparing a map of the Province of Guayaquil, on which he worked for some six years. He also served as quartermaster of a Spanish task force sent to the Popoyán region in Colombia to resist Portuguese territorial encroachments.

Meanwhile, the Treaty of San Ildefonso had been signed and the Portuguese and Spanish Governments were selecting their representatives for the Joint Boundary Commission. For administrative purposes, as has been noted, a *Partida* was organized for each division of the treaty line. In many instances the colonial administrator of a province or presidency within the region to be surveyed was given responsibility for organizing the survey parties. Thus, Don Ramon Garcia de Leon y Pizarro, Governor of the Province of Maynas, was named Spanish Commissioner for *La Quarta Partida,* which had jurisdiction over the boundary in the west and northwest parts of the Amazon Basin, described in article 11 of the treaty.

Shortly after he returned from the Popoyán foray, Requeña was named Deputy Commissioner by Don Ramon. He was at first reluctant to accept the assignment. Before the survey party was fully organized, however, Don Ramon was named Governor of the Presidencia de Quito, and Requeña became his successor as Governor of Maynas and Spanish Commissioner of *La Quarta Partida.* The Spanish survey party went into the field early in 1780 and established headquarters at Ega (present-day Tefé), at the junction of the Japurá and Amazon Rivers. For the next 11 or 12 years Requeña was occupied in surveying and mapping, in conjunction with the Portuguese repre-

sentatives, the upper Amazon River and its tributaries. There were many delays and frustrations due to the unfavorable physical and climatic conditions, the uncooperative position of the Portuguese Commissioner, the indifferent support of the Spanish authorities, and the slow and uncertain communications between the Ega headquarters and the seat of government in Madrid. Months, even years, elapsed before the Commissioner in the field was able to get a statement of the official Spanish position regarding some small disputed section of the boundary. Requeña was not idle during these periods but continued to prepare maps, reports, and views describing the geography of the upper Amazon Basin and to transmit them to his superiors in South

*Requeña map No. 17 charts several Colombian rivers which ultimately flow into the mouth of the Yapurá, which in turn joins the Amazon at Tefé in Brazil.*

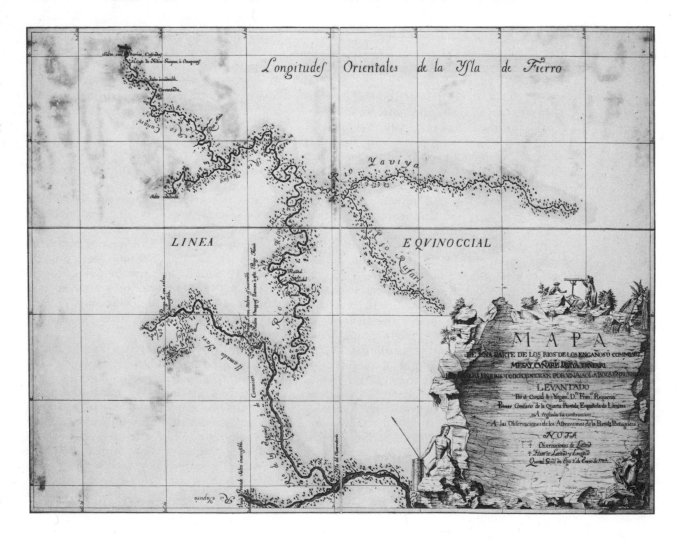

America or in Spain. Additional reports and maps were prepared by Requeña after his return to Spain in 1794. Although never published by the Spanish authorities, several of his reports were used as evidence in boundary disputes between South American republics and were published with other documents relating to arbitrations.

The eight Requeña maps acquired by the Library of Congress in 1943 are executed in a fine hand and are embellished with clear and brilliant watercolor washes. The titles are bordered by rococo ornamentation and sketches of Amazon fauna, flora, and landscapes. The first seven (Nos. 11–17) show sections of the Amazon River or of its several tributaries. No. 18 is a reduced scale map of northwestern South America, including the territory north of 18° south latitude, and west of 41°. longitude, reckoned from Tenerife. It includes all of the rivers shown on the seven larger scale maps, with geodetic control points indicated.

The Library's Requeña maps are here described:

**No. 11.** Mapa de una Parte del Ryo Marañon ó de las Amazonas Comprehendida entre la Boca del Rio Yavari, y la del Caño Avatiparanà, Levantado Por Dⁿ Francᵒ Requena Primer Comisario de la Quarta Partida Española de Limites y Areglada su Construcion A las observaciones de los Astronomos de la Partida Portuguesa. Ega 21 de Agosto de 1788. 73 by 21 inches. Approximate scale 1:210,000. Rococo title border. Green wash on rivers.

**No. 12.** Mapa de una Parte del Ryo Marañon ó de las Amazonas Comprehendida Entre la Boca del Caño de Avatiparana y la Villa de Ega ó Tefé, Levantado Por Dⁿ Francᵒ Requena Primer Comisario de la Quarta Partida Española de Limites y Areglada su Construcion A las Observaciones de los Astronomos de la Partida Portuguesa. Ega 8 de Septiembre de 1788. 59 by 21 inches. Approximate scale 1:210,000. Green wash on rivers, buff along river banks and on margins of islands. Ornamented title cartouche includes a palm tree and female figure, mounted on pedestal, blowing a trumpet.

**No. 13.** Mapa de una Parte del Rio Yapura Comprehendida desde su Entrada en el Rio Marañon por su Boca mas Occidental hasta el Pueblo de San Antonio de Maripi, Levantado por el Coronᵒˡ è Yngenᵒ Dⁿ Francᵒ Requena Primer Comisario de la Quarta Partida Española de Limites A Reglada su Construccion A los Observaciones de los Astronomos de la Partida Portugueza. Ega 12 de Octubre de 1788. 34 by 26 inches. Approximate scale 1:210,000. Watercolor wash along river and banks. Cartouche includes sketch of an Indian man, woman, and child, a man in European dress, and an alligator.

**No. 14.** Mapa de una Parte del Rio Yapurà Comprehendida desde la boca del Caño de Avatiparana immediata al Pueblo de Maripi Hasta la boca del Rio Apaporis proxima al Salto de Cupati, Levantado Por el Coronᵒˡ è Yngenᵒ Dⁿ Francᵒ Requena Primer Comisario de la Quarta Partida Española de Limites A Reglada su Construccion A los Observaciones de los Astronomos de la Partida Portugueza. Ega 12 de Octubre de 1788. 21 by 88 inches. Approximate scale 1:210,000. Wash on river and banks. The title border portrays a European, accompanied by two Indians, shooting at a flock of waterfowl.

**No. 15.** Mapa de una Parte del Rio Yapurà Comprehendida Desde la Boca del Rio Apaporis Hasta el Salto Grande, o cachoeira de Vuia, Levantado Por el Coronᵒˡ è Yngenᵒ Dⁿ Francᵒ Requena Poimer [sic] Comisario de la Quarta Partida Española de Limites A Reglada su Construccion A las Observaciones de los Astronomos de la Partida Portugueza. Ega 12 de Octubre de 1788. 26 by 75 inches. Approximate scale 1:208,000. Green wash on rivers, brown along shorelines. Two views form the lower corners of the ornamental cartouche: at the left two Europeans taking and recording geodetic observations and at the right a group of natives beside a crude shelter.

**No. 16.** Mapa de Una Parte del Rio Apaporis Comprehendida Desde su entrada en el Rio Yapura Hasta la Poblacion de los Yndios Corotus, Levantado Por el Coronᵒˡ è Yngenᵒ Dⁿ Francᵒ Requena Primer Comisario de la Quarta Partida Española de Limites A Reglada su Construccion A las Observaciones de los Astronomos de la Partida Portugueza. Ega 12 de Octubre de 1788. 17 by 26 inches. Approximate scale 1:210,000. Green and brown wash along rivers. A native about to spear a sleeping animal illustrates the right border of the title cartouche.

**No. 17.** Mapa de una Parte de los Rios de los Engaños ò Commiari, Mesay, Cuñarè Javiyà Yrufari los Quales, unidos todos, entran por una sola Boca en la Rio Yapura, Levantado Por el Coronᵒˡ è Yngenᵒ Dⁿ Francᵒ Requena Primer Comisario de la Quarta Partida Española de Limites A reglada su construccion A los Observacciones de los Astronomos de la Partida Portugueza Quartel Grãl de Ega 1° de Enero de 1789. 26 by 34 inches. Approximate scale 1:208,-000. Green and brown wash along streams. A native landscape serves as a background for the title, in which two surveyors take observations, an artist sketches, and an Indian peers around a rock to watch.

**No. 18.** Mapa de los Virreynatos de Buenos Aires, Lima, Sᵗᵃ Fe y Capitania Grãl de Caracas en la America Meridional con las Colonias Portuguesas Limitrofes Para acompanar Al Proyecto, y reflexiones Sobre la mejor Demarcacion de Limites Entre los Dominios de ambas Coronas Dispuesto, y Construido Por el Brigᵣ, e Yngenᵒ en Gefe Dⁿ Francisco Requena. Madrid 1° de Marzo de 1796. 33 by 26 inches. Approximate scale 1:4,260,000. Green wash colors rivers and oceans. Mountains shown with neatly drawn hachures. Numerous towns, cities, and missions are located and named. Geodetic control points used for maps 11 to 17 are marked with red crosses, single crosses for latitude and double crosses for both latitude and longitude. A landscape with several natives, a leanto, a small boat, and typical fauna and flora borders the title.

Longitude is measured from Tenerife in the Canary Islands, on No. 18, from the island of Fierro, in the same group, on maps 13, 14, 15, and 16, and from Paris on maps 11 and 12. Variations in style and orthography suggest that the eight maps were prepared by several draftsmen or copyists.

As noted in the title inscription of No. 18, this series of maps served to illustrate a report entitled "Proyecto y reflecciones sobre la mejor demarcacion de limites entre las coronas de España y Portugal presentadas en 10 de Marzo de 1796 por Don Francisco Requeña," which was one of the documents published at Caracas, in 1876, as *Titulos de Venezuela en sus limites con Colombia*. No maps accompany Requeña's report in this publication. In the presentation note preceding the report, the Spanish Commissioner wrote (as translated by W. W. Ristow):

> During the seventeen years that I have served in South America on the fourth boundary commission, I have forwarded to the attention of the Minister of State of Your Excellency various general and special maps with our respective representations, on which were portrayed the operations and surveys of the Demarcacíon, as well as all the obstacles and sad embarrassments with which the Portuguese Commissioners impeded agreements . . . .
>
> I now have the honor to present to Your Excellency a collection of maps of the rivers which were examined and surveyed by the combined Spanish and Portuguese parties. They are on a scale sufficiently large to be quite detailed, for they show the islands, channels, branches, and other details of these rivers, to permit Your Majesty to appreciate the injustice and ambitious pretensions of the Portuguese Commissioners.

In addition to the detailed maps, Requeña also prepared a number of watercolors picturing the geography, vegetation, animals, people, and culture of the upper Amazon Basin. Not long after the original version of this paper was published in the *Quarterly Journal*, a group of Requeña illustrations was described by Robert C. Smith in an article entitled "Requeña and

*Requeña map No. 18 is a composite that includes all the rivers shown on larger scale maps of the Amazon and its tributaries.*

the Japura: some Eighteenth Century Water Colors of the Amazon and Other Rivers." Published in the July 1946 issue of *The Americas* (Academy of American Franciscan History, Washington, D. C.), the paper includes descriptions and several reproductions of 10 Requeña watercolors from the collection of the Oliveira Lima Library, Catholic University of America. The watercolors were purchased by Señor Lima in 1914 from a Dutch dealer, who had previously acquired them from a Spanish source. The Requeña watercolors and maps admirably complement each other.

Following completion of the reports and maps covering his own surveys, Requeña, with the collaboration of Vicente Aguilar y Jurado, Second Secretary of the Spanish Foreign Office, prepared a report summarizing the surveys of the several Spanish groups: "Memoria Historica de las Demarcaciones de Limites en la America entre los Dominios de España y Portugal." To accompany the report Requeña compiled, in 1796, from his own original maps and from reports and maps by the other Spanish Commissioners in the custody of the Foreign Office, a map of the major part of South America showing the entire extent of the disputed Portuguese-Spanish boundary.

The Spanish Government published neither the report nor Requeña's map and they gathered dust for years in official archives. Not until the latter part of the nineteenth century were they published in various collected works. The "Memoria," without the map, appears in volume 4 of M. Charles Calvo's *Recueil Complet des Traites* (Paris, 1862). The report and the map were also included in *Titulos de Venezuela,* as cited above. The map, folded and tipped in following page 232 in this volume, is entitled "Mapa geográfico de la mayor parte de la América Meridional que contiene los paises por donde debe trazarse la linea que divida los Dominios de España y Portugal, Construido en virtud de Real Orden por el Teniente General Dⁿ Francisco Requeña en el año de 1796." Measuring 25½ by 19½ inches, the map was engraved by Jorge Laue, "Tatografia de H. Neun, Caracas." In the lower left portion of the sheet, under the heading "Adver-

# MAPA

...TE DE LOS VIRREYNATOS DE BUENOS AIRES, LIMA, S.ᵗᵉ FE
Y CAPITANIA GRAL DE CARACAS.
EN LA AMERICA MERIDIONAL
...ON LAS COLONIAS PORTUGUESAS LIMITROFES
*Para acompañar*
*Al Proyecto, y reflexiones*
*Sobre la mejor Demarcacion de Limites*
*Entre los Dominios de ambas Coronas*
*Dispuesto, y Construido*
*Por el Brig.ᵉ é Ingen.ᵒ en Gefe D.ⁿ Francisco Requena*

"MAR T. NORTE"

LINEA EQUINOCTIAL

L. Parime

Rio Caqueta ó Yapura

R. Negro

MAR. MARAÑON O DE LAS...

S.ᵗᵃ Fee de Bogota

R. Orinoco

R. Casiquiari

R. UCAYALE

R. MARAÑON

*El Pais Comprendido entre los Rios*
*Purus y Parari es enteramente*
*desconocido à todos los*
*Geografos*

O[CE]ANO DEL SUR

Caracter...
- Capital
- Capital
- Ciudad
- Villa, ó...
- Pueblo co...
- Poblacion...
- Poblacion...
- Arzobis...
- Obispad...
- Virreyna...
- Audienc...
- Govierno
- Guardia
- Observacio...
- Idem de...
hechiz...
Madrid S...

tencias Sobre Este Mapa General," are listed the source materials consulted by Requeña in compiling the map. Included are his own maps of the upper Amazon, the maps prepared under the direction of Jose Varela y Ulloa, described above, other Commission surveys, and earlier published maps of the continent. Below the list is an "Esplicacion de la Linea de Demarcacion y Puntas de Disputa," with some 20 unresolved boundary problems listed and keyed, by upper case letters, to specific locations on the map.

An enlarged (49 by 38 inches) facsimile of the same map was published, probably about 1860, by Frederick Bourquin, a Philadelphia map publisher. The inspiration for Bourquin's facsimile has not been determined. Two copies are in the collections of the Geography and Map Division.

One manuscript map included in the Maggs purchase has no relation to the other maps in the group or to the Portuguese-Spanish boundary surveys. Entitled *Mapa Coro-grafico de la Provincia de Cartagena de Yndias y parte de las de S^ta Marta, Jiron, Socorro, Velez, Antioquia, y Choco del Norte, sus Confines formado, y construido por D^n Vicente Talledo y Rivera, Tenyente Coronel Del R. Cuerpo de Ingeniero,* it is undated, but the map paper carries an 1804 watermark. The large (52 by 35½ inches) map is mounted on heavy linen, apparently done for the original owner, and is sectioned to fold to 9 by 13 inches. Its somewhat soiled condition suggests that it was frequently consulted. It includes part of the Caribbean coastline of present-day Colombia and extends eastward to Cape San Juan de Guia and south to 6° north latitude. The approximate scale is 1:430,000. Drafting is neatly and skillfully done and the ocean margins and rivers are colored with a green wash. Place names are liberally distributed, and six categories of towns, cities, and capital cities are differentiated. A gray watercolor wash is used to show generalized relief, and specific peaks and hills are outlined with neat hachures. In a 14-line note, inscribed below the title and legend, the author gives credit to the surveys of Spanish naval Captain Joaquin Fidalgo as the data source for the coastal regions. In an article published in 1952 Rozo notes that "En 1817 don Joaquín Francisco Fidalgo levantó la carta del Darién e islas Mulatas, tres años

después don Vicente Talledo y Rivera ejecutó el mapa corografico de la provincia de Cartagena de Indias y parte de Santa Marta, Girón, Socorro, Vélez, Antioquia y Chocó." [1] This establishes 1820 as the proper date for Talledo's *Mapa Corografico.*

Another rare South American acquisition, initially reported in the January-March 1944 issue of the *Quarterly Journal,* is *Mapa Geográfico de America Meridional Dispuesto y Gravado por D. Juan de la Cruz Cano y Olmedilla, Año de 1775.* Published in Madrid, this map is beautifully engraved on eight large sheets, each 35 by 22 inches. When joined they form a magnificent map of South America measuring approximately 88 by 70 inches. Its borders and corners are ornately decorated with coats of arms, fruit clusters, and mythical characters. Shortly after it was published the Spanish Government restricted its distribution because some of the boundaries did not accord with official claims and pretensions. The Cruz Cano *Mapa Geográfico* is accordingly quite rare, and before 1943 there was no original in the Library. Since that date several other copies have been acquired. The collections now also include several copies of a facsimile published in London in 1799 by Faden, and a nineteenth-century facsimile, apparently printed from the original plates. In 1967 the Geography and Map Division acquired a set of pulls of the Cruz Cano map from the original copper engraved plates, which are preserved in the Calcografia Nacional, Madrid. Several articles about the map have been published in recent years. [2]

Francisco Requeña listed the map among the source materials he used in compiling his 1796 *Mapa Geográfico.* It is interesting to note that the Spanish Government in 1802 appointed a committee, headed by Francisco Requeña, to reexamine Cruz Cano's discredited map. In his report Requeña declared that the map "did honor to the country, to the Minister who had ordered its execution, and to the geographer who prepared it with scientific precision, an abundance of detail, and meticulous care. At the time [the map] was published," he added, "it was impossible to produce a better one." [3]

The Geography and Map Division also reported in 1944 the acquisition of the first volume of a series of facsimile maps from originals in Spanish archives, published in

Madrid in 1942 under the general title *Monumenta Chartographica Indiana*. It was assembled, with pertinent notes, by Capt. Julio F. Tato, Director of the Naval Museum and Librarian of the Geographical Society of Spain. In a prologue to volume one, Don Pedro Novo y Fernandez Chicarro indicated that the projected series would comprise 50 or more volumes and include reproductions of a thousand significant historical maps. The first volume, for which Julio F. Guillen prepared an introduction, features maps of the Rio de la Plata region and southern South America. There are catalog descriptions for a number of maps, and attractive facsimile reproductions (a few in full color) of selected items. Among the facsimiles is Juan de la Cruz Cano's 1775 map of South America, which is reproduced, with some reduction in scale, on eight plates of the *Monumenta Chartographica*. It is with regret that we report that the ambitious hopes of the sponsors expressed in the prologue were not realized, and no additional volumes in this series have been published.

## NOTES

[1] Dario Rozo, "Historia de la cartografía de Colombia," in Sociedad Geográfica de Colombia, *Boletin*, 10:179 (1952).

[2] See, for example, José Miguel Pérez de Villaoz, "El mapa de la América Meridional de Don Juan de la Cruz Cano y Olmedilla," *Revista Chilena de Historia y Geografía*, no. 131, p. 121–175 (1963); and Walter W. Ristow, "The Juan de la Cruz Map of South America, 1775," *Festschrift: Clarence F. Jones*, edited by Merle C. Prunty, Jr. (Evanston, Ill., 1962), p. 1–11. This article was also published in Spanish under the title "El mapa de Sud América de Juan de la Cruz Cano y Olmedilla" in *Revista Chilena de Historia y Geografía*, no. 132, p. 95–109 (1964). See also Thomas R. Smith, "Cruz Cano's Map of South America, Madrid, 1775: Its Creation, Adversities and Rehabilitation," *Imago mundi*, vol. 20, 1966, p. 49–78.

[3] Quoted in Gabriel Marcel, *Le Géographe Thomas López et son oeuvre* (Madrid, 1908), p. 51.

Reprinted, with extensive revisions, from volume 5 of *Treaties and Other International Acts of the United States of America*, edited by David Hunter Miller and published by the Department of State in 1937.

JOHN DISTURNELL'S map of Mexico is of historic importance because it was the official cartographic reference consulted in negotiating the peace treaty of February 2, 1848, which terminated the Mexican War and is commonly referred to as the Treaty of Guadalupe Hidalgo.[1] The map actually became a part of the treaty and has figured prominently in settling border disputes. It is described in the English version of the treaty as "Map of the United Mexican States, as organized and defined by various acts of the Congress of said Republic, and constructed according to

# John Disturnell's Map of the United Mexican States

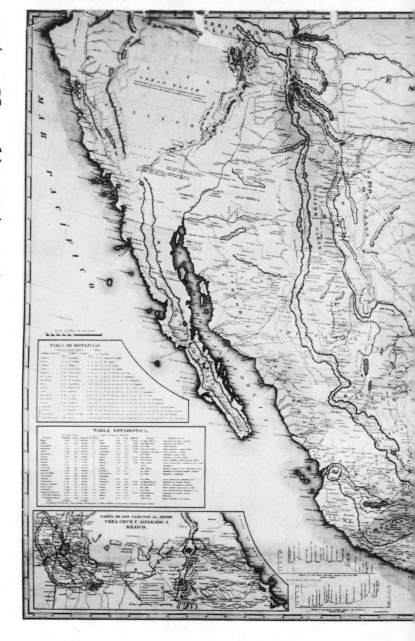

BY
LAWRENCE MARTIN
EDITED AND ABRIDGED
BY WALTER W. RISTOW

the best Authorities. Revised Edition. Published at New York in 1847 by J. Disturnell." In the Spanish version it is referred to in the same general terms, and its title is given in Spanish, including a translation of the words "Revised Edition."

At least seven variants of Disturnell's map were published at New York in 1847, all of which are designated "Revised Edition" and bear the same title. It is essential, therefore, to identify the exact editions of Disturnell's map which were consulted in the negotiations and ratification of the Treaty of Guadalupe Hidalgo.

It is unfortunate that the map title was translated in the English version of the treaty, for no Disturnell map bears the English title specified in the treaty. A map by Tanner, however, also published at New York, closely resembles in title that described in the treaty:

A Map of the United States of Mexico, As organized and defined by the several Acts of the Congress of that Republic, Constructed from a great variety of Printed and Manuscript Documents, by H. S. Tanner. Fifth edition, 1847.

The similarity in title of the two maps is not solely coincidental, for Disturnell's map is a reprint of the first of two independent plagiarisms of Tanner's map.

Variations occur between the title of the Disturnell map used in the negotiation of the treaty—

Mapa de los Estados Unidos de Méjico, Segun lo organizado y definido por las varias actas del Congreso de dicha República: y construido por las mejores autoridades. Lo publican J. Disturnell, 102 Broadway. Nueva York. 1847. Revised Edition.

and the title given in the Spanish version of the treaty—

Mapa de los Estados-Unidos de México, segun lo organizado y definido por las varias Actas del Congreso de dicha República y construido por las mejores autoridades: Edicion revisada que publicó en Nueva-York en 1847 J. Disturnell.

In the Spanish version of the treaty, the only two English words in the title, "Revised Edition," have been translated, the spelling "México" is used, and there are minor changes in punctuation, capitalization, and order of bibliographic data. No edition of Disturnell's map has been identified that includes in its title the Spanish words "Edicion revisada" or the spelling "México."

Since Disturnell printed at least 23 editions of the map of Mexico, seven of them in 1847, and there has been some confusion concerning which one is the treaty map, since Disturnell's map is a reprint of an earlier map by White, Gallaher & White, since their map is a plagiarism of a map of Mexico by H. S. Tanner, and since the latter in turn was taken literally from the

*Seventh edition of John Disturnell's map of Mexico, 1847. Maps illustrating this article are in the Geography and Map Division.*

southwestern part of Tanner's map of North America, the history of the successive editions of all four maps is recorded to place the Disturnell maps of 1847 in their proper setting and to identify with certainty the two versions of the treaty map.

H. S. Tanner published in 1822 *A Map of North America, Constructed According to the Latest Information.* The state names "Cohahuila" and "New Santander" are lettered astride the Rio Grande, since these subdivisions of the former Intendencia of San Luis Potosí appear to have terminated at the Rio Nueces rather than at the Rio Grande. The boundary between Upper California and Lower California is a hand-colored northeast-southwest line from the mouth of the Rio Gila to El Rosario on the Pacific coast, some 150 miles south of San Diego. Tanner issued new editions of this map in 1829 and 1839 and perhaps in other years. The 1822 edition was included in Tanner's *New American Atlas,* published in 1823. The geographical memoir at the front of the atlas says that the Mexican portion of the map of North America was based on Pedro Walker's *Map of New California,* Alexander von Humboldt's *General Map of the Kingdom of New Spain,* Z. M. Pike's *Map of the Internal Provinces of New Spain* and his *Chart of the Internal Part of Louisiana,* William Darby's *Map of the*

*Disturnell's map is a reprint of this map of Mexico issued by White, Gallaher & White in 1828.*

The White, Gallaher & White map is a plagiarism of H. S. Tanner's 1826 map of Mexico shown here.

*Southern Part of the Province of Texas,* Bernardo de Orta's *Plan of the Port of Vera Cruz,* and Juan de Langara's *Chart of the Gulf of Mexico.* In view of the subsequent dispute concerning the latitude of the southern boundary of New Mexico, it is interesting to observe that the latitude of "Paso" on the Disturnell map is nearly the same as on the Humboldt and Tanner maps. Humboldt, however, placed the southern boundary of New Mexico even farther south than did Disturnell.

A map of Mexico which Tanner published in 1825 was based on the southwestern part of his map of North America. The scale, approximately one inch to 120 miles on the North America map, was enlarged on the map of Mexico to one inch to 84 miles. The latter was also reoriented on a new central meridian. The map of Mexico contained all the descriptive notes printed on the face of the trans-Rocky Mountain and Mexican portions of the other map.

Between 1825 and 1847 Tanner issued at least 10 variants of one or another of five editions of his *Map of the United States of Mexico,* with the following dates and designations: (a) 1825; (b) 1826; (c) an impression of the second edition but not labeled as such, copyrighted April 2, 1832; (d) 1834, second edition; (e) 1838, second edition; (f) 1839, second edition; (g) 1846, second edition; (h) 1846, third edition; (i) 1847, fourth edition, and (j) 1847, fifth edition. The Library of Congress copy of the map designated "1846, second edition" belonged to Millard Fillmore and bears his autograph and the date May 21, 1846. If we assume that Fillmore purchased his map on this date, the map designated "1846, third edition" must have been published later than May of that year. Beginning with that edition, the Tanner maps show an engraved boundary between Upper California and Lower California which extends in a northeast and southwest direction from a point on the west bank of the Colorado River opposite the mouth of the Gila River

207

to a point on the Pacific Ocean near "Pt Mondrains," some 120 miles south of San Diego. All variants published before May 1846 have a hand-colored line in the same position, except Fillmore's copy, which places the boundary on the parallel of 32° north latitude. Fillmore's copy of the map of Mexico is probably without historical significance because when he acquired it he was no longer a Member of Congress and did not hold any other public office. He was obviously interested in the Mexican War, however, for he had at least four other maps of Mexico showing battles. In 1848 Fillmore was elected Vice President on the ticket with Gen. Zachary Taylor, and in 1852, as President, Fillmore took an important action pertaining to Disturnell's map.

The southern boundary of New Mexico on Tanner's 1822 map of North America and on the 1825 edition of his map of Mexico evidently was based on Baron von Humboldt's map of New Spain published in 1809. On his 1826 map of Mexico, however, Tanner deleted the southern boundary of New Mexico west of the Rio Grande and introduced a new boundary about 8 miles farther north in the western part and 80 miles farther north in the eastern part. It is this latter boundary which was accepted by White, Gallaher & White in 1828 and by Disturnell in 1846 and 1847. All the Tanner maps of Mexico dated 1825 to 1847 are copyrighted. They are important to this study because they represent the original data source for Disturnell's map.

An independent plagiarism of Tanner's 1834 map of Mexico, known as Rosa's *Mapa de los Estados Unidos Mejicanos Arreglado a la distribucion que en diversos decretos ha hecho del territorio el Congreso General Mejicano,* was published in Paris in 1837. This map was brought into the argument concerning the boundary marking in 1853. It differs from Tanner's map of Mexico in the following respects: (a) the statistical table in the Gulf of Mexico is omitted; (b) in the table of distances, Cordova is replaced by Ayotla, but the distance from Mexico City is not modified; (c) the hand-colored northeast-southwest boundary between Upper and Lower California is replaced by an engraved boundary in the same position. Another edition of Rosa's map was printed in 1851.

In 1828 a plagiarism of Tanner's map of Mexico was published under a Spanish title by White, Gallaher & White, of New York. Eventually some 24 different editions of this map were published at New York, all but the first by Disturnell, and the map has become widely known as Disturnell's map. That the White, Gallaher & White map was plagiarized from Tanner's is suggested not merely by the similarity in titles. The two maps share common errors, for example in the outlines of the coast and the courses of the rivers, and they have the same insets: a large-scale map of the area between Vera Cruz and Mexico City, a highly individual table of statistics, and a long table of distances. The later map used all of Tanner's explanatory remarks, which were translated word for word. The following notes, for example, were printed in the area between the Colorado River and Santa Barbara, Calif., on Tanner's map and on White, Gallaher & White's map, respectively:

These mountains are supposed to extend much farther to the North than here shewn but there are no data by which to trace them with accuracy.

Se supone que estas montañas se estienden mas al Norte de lo que se ezhibe aqui; mas no eziste dato alguno con que poderlas trazar con precision.

It is curious that, although White, Gallaher & White's map was an obvious plagiarism of Tanner's copyrighted map and both were published in the United States the later map was also copyrighted. Outside its lower neat line, near the right border, appear the words "Entered according to Act of Congress, May 31st, 1828, by White, Gallaher & White." This suggests that Tanner's map may have been used by friendly agreement to compile the slightly enlarged Spanish language map, but it seems odd that White, Gallaher & White made no public acknowledgment to Tanner.

The earliest identified edition of Disturnell's reprint was published in 1846, doubtless because of the outbreak of the Mexican War. Its title information is identical with the White, Gallaher & White map except for date and publisher. The two maps were printed from the same plates, as is indicated by the faint copyright notice, which was incompletely eradicated and shows on the borders of all but two of Disturnell's editions printed between 1846 and 1858.

During negotiation of the Treaty of Guadalupe Hidalgo, at least three different editions of Disturnell's map were used, of which the seventh edition, dated 1847, was made a part of the American original of the treaty and now is in the National Archives at Washington. The twelfth edition, also dated 1847, and now with the original treaty in the archives of Mexico, was also consulted. There is no evidence that either Nicholas P. Trist, who represented the United States, or the Mexican Plenipotentiaries knew that they authenticated and placed with the treaty originals two different editions of Disturnell's map or, indeed, that they suspected there were at least seven editions, all dated 1847, and all designated "Revised Edition." As a matter of fact, although the variations between the seventh and twelfth editions are numerous, none of the differences apparently caused complications in the boundary marking by John B. Weller, John Russell Barlett, and their Mexican colleagues.

A third significant edition of Disturnell's map is one of those published in 1846. Robert E. Lee used and commented upon it in January 1848 when he was assisting Trist in determining whether San Diego was in Upper California or in Lower California. We do not know which of the several 1846 editions Lee had in hand.

Since 1848, 20 or more facsimiles of Disturnell's map have been produced, most of them in connection with international boundary studies relating to the acquisition by the United States of the territory now comprising California, Nevada, Utah, Arizona, New Mexico, and parts of Wyoming, Colorado, and Texas. Facsimiles issued before 1936 are described in the original version of this study published in volume 5 of *Treaties and Other International Acts.*

In the act of Congress approved August 31, 1852, making appropriations for the civil and diplomatic service of the United States for the year ending June 30, 1853, there was an important proviso relating to Disturnell's map, as follows (10 Stat. 94–95):

For running and marking the boundary line between the United States and Mexico, under the treaty of Guadalupe Hidalgo, one hundred and twenty thousand dollars: *Provided,* That no part of this appropriation shall be used or expended until it shall be made satisfactorily to appear to the President of the United States that the southern boundary of New Mexico is not established by the

commissioner and surveyor of the United States farther north of the town called "Paso" than the same is laid down in Disturnell's map, which is added to the treaty.

The proviso was introduced as an amendment in the Senate on August 27, 1852, by Senator James M. Mason, of Virginia, chairman of the Committee on Foreign Relations. The record of the debate does not show that a copy of Disturnell's map was laid before the Senate by either Senator Mason or his colleagues (*Congressional Globe,* 21: 2402–2407, August 27, 1852; *Daily National Intelligencer,* August 30, 1852). The other Senators who discussed the amendment were Clarke, of Rhode Island; Pearce, of Maryland; Weller, of California; and Underwood, of Kentucky. Senator Weller had himself been a U.S. Boundary Commissioner in 1849.

On October 11, 1852, the Secretary of the Interior, Alexander H. H. Stuart, in response to an inquiry from President Fillmore dated September 10, 1852, wrote to the President concerning this proviso and the President's duty in the matter. The Secretary included in his letter the following statement (Senate Executive Document No. 6, 33d Congress, special session of the Senate, serial 688, p. 21):

To enable you to fulfil this duty, I respectfully submit the following report of the facts of the case, accompanied by a copy of Disturnell's map, and other documents bearing on the question.

The particular copy of Disturnell's map then transmitted to the President of the United States has not been identified.

The Secretary of the Interior pointed out to President Fillmore (ibid., p. 24, 25) that—

the line, as established by the joint commission, is but about seven geographical miles north of the position of Paso, as marked on the map. But when Paso is transferred from $32°15\frac{1}{2}'$, its place on the map, to its true position, which is $31°45'$ north latitude, or more than 30' south of its supposed position, then the distance between the line and El Paso is increased to more than thirty-seven geographical miles.

· | · · · ·

I do not see how, by a fair construction of the law, any part of the money can be drawn from the treasury, and I am therefore compelled, respectfully, to submit to you the propriety of at once suspending the operations of the commission, as there are no means at your disposal to maintain it in the field.

President Fillmore replied on October 14, 1852, saying (ibid., p. 164):

I herewith return your report on the subject of the Mexican boundary commission, with my concurrence, together with the papers accompanying the report. It seems to me that, in justification of the course which the Administration has been compelled to pursue, it might be well to give publicity to the report through the papers.

You will, of course, notify the Secretary of State.

In accord with the President's suggestion, the Secretary of the Interior published in the *National Intelligencer* of October 16, 1852, his letter of October 11 to the President. With it he did not print Fillmore's letter quoted above, but an entirely different document, a formal note in the nature of an Executive order, dated October 13, 1852, and reading as follows:

After a careful perusal of the foregoing Report and an anxious consideration of the question involved in it, I am reluctantly constrained to concur in its result; and consequently no part of the appropriation therein referred to can be drawn from the Treasury. The Secretary of the Interior will immediately notify the Secretary of State of this decision that he may inform the Mexican Government of the causes which compel this government to suspend the further prosecution of this work until Congress shall provide the requisite means.

With these documents should be read the report of the Senate Committee on Foreign Relations which led to the amendment concerning Disturnell's map, together with editorials respecting the Mexican boundary situation, and all the documents in the report of the Secretary of the Interior dated March 21, 1853 (*Daily Union*, August 28, 1852, p. 3; August 31, 1852, p. 3; and September 1, 1852, p. 3; *Daily National Intelligencer*, August 31, 1852, p. 3; and October 18, 1852, p. 2; and Senate Executive Document 6, 33d Congress, special session of the Senate, serial 688).

Finally, President Fillmore, in his third annual message to Congress, dated December 6, 1852, quoted the proviso concerning Disturnell's map in the act of August 31, 1852, and went on to say:

My attention was drawn to this subject by a report from the Department of the Interior, which reviewed all the facts of the case and submitted for my decision the question whether under existing circumstances any part of the appropriation could be lawfully used or expended for the further prosecution of the work. After a careful consideration of the subject I came to the conclusion that it could not, and so informed the head of that Department. Orders were immediately issued by him to the commissioner and surveyor to make no further requisitions on the Department, as they could not be paid, and to discontinue all operations on the southern line of New Mexico.

Disturnell's *Mapa de los Estados Unidos de Méjico*, then, in its use in 1852 by the Secretary of the Interior, the President of the United States, and the Congress, made unavailable an appropriation of $120,000 and led to the discontinuation of boundary demarcation by the Commissions of the United States and of Mexico.

The man whose name is associated with this influential map, John Disturnell, was born in Lansingburg, N. Y., and began his professional career in Albany as a printer, probably around 1825. Five years later he moved to New York City where he established a bookselling and publishing business. He continued operations in New York until 1870 when he apparently relocated his firm in Philadelphia. In 1877, however, he was back in New York, where he died on October 2 of that year.

Disturnell was a prolific publisher of popular handbooks, directories, gazetteers, statistical compilations, guidebooks, and maps. He capitalized on the growth and development of railway and steamship transportation, on the growing tide of immigration, and on the California Gold Rush. His *Traveller's Railroad Guide,* published in 1840, is the earliest American railroad guide. Disturnell also found time in a busy career to write several quasi-scientific works, including *Influences of Climate in North and South America* (1859) and *The Great Lakes or Inland Seas of America* (1863).

John Disturnell had no personal competence in mapmaking. In common with

*This title decoration on the White, Gallaher & White map was reproduced exactly by Disturnell.*

other commercial publishers of the day he drew upon all available published and unpublished cartographic sources to compile his maps. Plagiarism and pirating of information were accepted practices. Before the 1840's most maps were printed from copper engraved plates. A limited number of impressions were periodically made from the plates, and as new data were received the plates were revised to bring the map up to date. The haste to get a revised map in the hands of prospective purchasers did not permit verification of information, and errors and inaccuracies were numerous. Disturnell's maps were no exception. In 1849 Randall B. Marcy, U. S. military leader and explorer, described Disturnell's map of Mexico as "one of the most inaccurate of all those I have seen, so far as relates to the country over which I have passed. He makes a greater error than most others in laying down the Pecos, and has the Colorado, Brazos, and Red river all inaccurately placed. Upon the Red river he has a very large branch coming from the far west, near El Paso, which he calls 'Ensenado Choctow.' This is altogether an imaginary stream, as no one who has been in the country ever heard of it; neither does any branch of the Red river extend to within three hundred miles of the Rio del Norte" (Senate Executive Document 64, 31st Congress, 1st session, p. 62).

Notwithstanding its apparent shortcomings Disturnell's *Mapa de los Estados Unidos de Méjico* was undoubtedly a popular and widely consulted map in 1847. It is not surprising, therefore, that it was selected as the official treaty map by the United States and Mexican negotiators.

### NOTES

[1] This study of an important American treaty map was made in the Library of Congress at the request of the Department of State. It was originally published in *Treaties and Other International Acts of the United States of America*, vol. 5, 1937, edited by Hunter Miller, Historical Adviser, Department of State. The paper has been revised, abridged, and edited for inclusion in this volume.

# TABLE FOR IDENTIFYING VARIANT EDITIONS OF
## JOHN DISTURNELL'S MAPA DE LOS ESTADOS UNIDOS DE MEJICO

Because the initial version of the Mexican map published by Disturnell in 1846 was derived from a map published originally in 1828 by White, Gallaher & White, the latter is designated as the first of 24 identified editions of the *Mapa de los Estados Unidos de Méjico*. The White, Gallaher & White map, as has been noted, was itself derived from Tanner's 1826 map of Mexico. The variants noted for the first edition represent modifications from Tanner's map.

Martin designated each variant as a separate *edition*, and this term has been retained here. Other investigators limit the term *edition* to different engraved plates or to specific years. Variants within an edition are more appropriately identified as *states*. (See article on Melish's United States map in this volume and Coolie Verner's article on "The Identification and Designation of Variants in the Study of Early Printed Maps" in *Imago Mundi*, no. 19, 1965, p. 100–105).

## First edition

Mapa de los Estados Unidos de Méjico, Segun lo organizado y definido por las varias actas del Congreso de dicha República: y construido por las mejores autoridades. Lo publican White Gallaher y White. Nueva York, 1828. Grabado por Balch y Stiles, Nueva York.

The title, place names, and legend are in Spanish (all in English on Tanner's map).

The scale has been enlarged to approximately one inch to 70 miles (one inch to 85 miles on Tanner's map).

In the east and northeast, Cuba, Florida, Georgia, and parts of South Carolina have been added, increasing the overall size of the map to 41 by 29 inches (as compared with 28 by 23 inches for Tanner's map).

Library of Congress holdings:

Original, mounted on cloth, sectioned to fold to 29 by 20½ inches. Division stamp: Apr 27 1911.

## Second edition

Mapa de los Estados Unidos de Méjico, Segun lo organizado y definido por las varias actas del Congreso de dicha República: y construido por los mejores autoridades. Lo publican J. Disturnell, 102 Broadway. Nueva York. 1846.

The date has been changed to 1846.

"J. Disturnell, 102 Broadway" has been substituted for "White, Gallaher & White." The type for "Lo publican" has been changed from script to block lettering.

"Grabado por Balch y Stiles, Nueva York" has been deleted.

The copyright notice outside the neat line has been removed.

The names "Oregon," "Missouri," and "Arkansas" have been relocated.

A number of names and features have been added to the map, among them "Iowa," "Indian Territory," "Balize," as well as a number of cities. Boundaries have been added for Iowa, Indian Territory, Missouri, Arkansas, and Louisiana. Several new lakes and streams are shown, hachures have been introduced for certain mountains, and the coast of California has been substantially corrected.

Because later editions of Disturnell's map were used in treaty negotiations, the following features in the critical boundary area, unchanged or modified from the White, Gallaher & White map, are noted.

Along the Rio Grande have been added in English the words "Boundary as claimed by the United States."

Along the Rio Nueces and the headwaters of an unnamed stream between it and the Rio Puerco have been added an engraved boundary and the English words "Original Boundary of Texas in 1835."

Between these streams and the Rio Grande have been added the words "Prior to the revolution Texas & Cohahuila were united to form one of the Federal States of the Mexican Republic."

The part of the engraved boundary of the State of Tamaulipas north of the Rio Nueces in Texas has been imperfectly eradicated.

In the "Tabla Estadistica" the Spanish words "y Tejas" have been eradicated from the rubric "Cohahuila y Tejas" but the areas and populations remain unchanged.

An engraved highway marked "Gen. Taylors Route 1846" and the words "Ft. Brown" have been added near the mouth of the Rio Grande.

An engraved boundary between Alta California and Baja California extends east and west, near the parallel of 32°15' north latitude, from a point on the Colorado River about 50 miles south of the Gila to a point on the Pacific coast about 50 miles south of San Diego. This boundary is not present on the White, Gallaher & White map, which has in color, but without an engraved line, the same northeast-southwest boundary between Upper and

Lower California that appears as an engraved line on the 1846 and 1847 editions of the Tanner map. It is a debatable question whether, if Disturnell had engraved this northeast-southwest boundary upon his map in 1846, as Rosa did upon his plagiarism of Tanner's map in 1837, the southern boundary of the United States at the Pacific might have been fixed some 120 miles south of San Diego rather than only a little over a dozen miles south.

Library of Congress holdings:

> An imperfect, colored original, mounted on cloth, sectioned to fold to 31 by 22 inches. Lacks the upper right corner, including part of the title. Division stamp: May 8 1913. Below the title is the rubber stamp impression "U.S. Geological Survey Library 9922 1887."

## Third edition

[Same title as second edition.]

A trail some 135 miles in length has been added in central Texas, between the city of "Sⁿ Antonio de Bejar" and the city of Austin.

At the head of the first branch on the east side of the "Rio Sⁿ Marco" north of the city of Gonzales a small lake has been introduced.

Library of Congress holdings:

> Photostat positive, mounted, and negative in four parts of original in possession (in 1936) of Dr. Herbert M. Evans of Berkeley, Calif. Division stamp: Dec 15 1936.

## Fourth edition

[Same title as second edition.]

The city of Monterrey, Mexico, has been moved southward from 26° north to 25°40' north, and westward from 23° to 23°35'.

A group of roads, villages, etc., have been added in the vicinity of Monterrey.

Rinconado Pass is shown.

The city of Saltillo has been moved southward.

The boundary between the states of Durango and Coahuila has been moved southward from a position north of La Concepcion to a new position close to the letters "G" and "O" in "Durango."

Library of Congress holdings:

> Original, colored, mounted on cloth, sectioned in 32 parts to fold to 8 by 5½ inches. Transferred from U.S. War Department, July 10, 1935. Manuscript title affixed to verso: Map of the United States of Mexico New York 1846.

## Fifth edition

Mapa de los Estados Unidos de Méjico, Segun lo organizado y definido por las varias actas del Con-

greso de dicha República: y construido por las mejores autoridades. Lo publican J. Disturnell, 102 Broadway. Nueva York. 1846. Revised Edition.

The words "Revised Edition" have been added in small letters below and to the right of the date.

There is a scale of English miles below the date that reads "Scale of Miles."

The phrases "Carolina del S" and "Florida del O" and the words "del E" in "Florida del E" have been deleted.

Engraved Florida-Georgia and Alabama-Florida boundaries have been added.

Many roads, railways, and cities have been added in Cuba, Florida, Georgia, and elsewhere.

Various additions to and corrections in lakes and rivers have been made in Florida and elsewhere.

The coast line of Texas has been redrawn.

The word "Tejas" has been shifted southward.

Names of many Indian tribes have been added.

Hachures and names have been added for peaks and mountain ranges.

Notes have been added on the face of the map, in English. A note lettered between the Arkansas River and the Ramo de Smoky Hill near longitudes 24° to 26° west of Washington and reading "The 'Army of the West' left Fᵗ Leavenworth June 30ᵗʰ reached Santa Fe Aug. 18ᵗʰ 1846" fixes the date of publication of this edition of the map after August 1846.

Of interest with reference to the use of later editions of the map in treaty negotiations are the following changes and continuations in the boundary area.

The state name "Tamaulipas" has been moved so that no part of it is lettered in Texas between the Rio Nueces and the Rio Grande.

In the "Tabla Estadistica" the area of Cohahuila has been reduced by 100,000 millas cuadradas to allow for the subtraction of Texas and the footing of the column has been corrected accordingly, but the population remains unchanged.

The name "Rio Grande or Bravo del Norte" has been added to the lower course of the river.

The words "Rio del Norte" have been erased from the mouth of the same stream.

The designations "Battles of Palo Alto & Resaca de la Palma 1846" and "Salt Lake" have been added and the phrase "Gen. Taylors Route 1846" has been deleted in the boundary vicinity.

Library of Congress holdings:

> Two positive photostat copies (one mounted in one piece and one in four parts), and two negative photostat copies (each in four parts), of original in New York Public Library.

## Sixth edition

[Same title as fifth edition.]

The type in "Revised Edition" has been enlarged.

"Scale of Miles" has been replaced by "Scale of English Miles."

The names "Miami," "L. Macoco," "L. Monroe," and "L. George" have been added in Florida.

The words "Route of Gen. Taylor 1846" have been added in southern Texas.

A road near Corpus Christi has been changed.

"Sandy Desert," "Chaparel," and "Colorado C" have been added.

"S. Theresa" has been added in northern Tamaulipas.

"Tabasco" has been substituted for "Villa Hermosa" in the state of Tabasco.

"Sumasinti R" has been added nearby.

Library of Congress holdings:

Colored original, mounted on cloth, sectioned to fold to 31 by 32 inches. Division stamp: Mar 4 1914.

## Seventh edition

Mapa de los Estados Unidos de Méjico, Segun lo organizado y definido por las varias actas del Congreso de dicha República: y construido por las mejores autoridades. Lo publican J. Disturnell, 102 Broadway. Nueva York. 1847. Revised Edition.

The earliest of seven or more maps published in 1847, this is the one that was sealed, authenticated, and added in February 1848 to the originals of the Treaty of Guadalupe Hidalgo, now in the National Archives. This is *a* treaty map but not exclusively *the* treaty map. The words "Revised Edition" are quoted, as will be recalled, in the Treaty of Guadalupe Hidalgo, but this does not mean that an edition of Disturnell's Map was published in 1847 without these words. Some 18 editions, beginning with two of those in 1846, including all seven of the editions published in 1847, and continuing through the four editions published in 1848 and five published in 1849, 1850, and 1858 are likewise designated "Revised Edition."

Two inset maps in the western part of the Gulf of Mexico show the Bay of Vera Cruz and "the battle grounds of the 8th and 9th May 1846" near Palo Alto and Resaca de la Palma.

The word "Golfo" has been replaced by the letter "G" in the phrase "G. de Méjico."

"Ft Jupiter" in Florida, a railway east and north of New Orleans in Louisiana, and several roads, railways, and cities in Cuba have been added.

In southern Texas the word "Chaparel" has been deleted, "Salt Lake" has been changed to "Salt Lakes," and "Colorado C." has been extended toward its head.

In Mexico figures for population have been added for many cities.

At the bottom of the map two profiles have been added for the routes between Mexico City and Vera Cruz and between Mexico City and Acapulco.

Extensive changes have been made in drainage, roads, and city names in the northern parts of the states of Nuevo León and Coahuila near the Sabinos and Salado Rivers, whose courses are changed from northeasterly to southeasterly.

The symbol for "Cross Timbers" has been extended across the Red River from northern Texas into Indian Territory.

Hachures and the name "Washita Mts" have been added in southwestern Indian Territory.

Hachures have been added along the south bank of the "Ensenada Choctau," the east bank of the "Rio Puerco," and the east bank of the unnamed stream east of it which is designated as part of the original boundary of Texas in 1835.

"Range of the" has been introduced before "Comanches" in western Texas.

"El Toro" has been added near Monterey, Calif.

"Pletel" and "Coco" have been added in southern Tamaulipas.

Rivers, roads, cities, hachures, and other modifications have been added in Central America and southern Mexico, including "R. de Segovia," "R. Ulloa," "Yzabal," "Comayagua or Nueva Valladolid," "Guatemala," "Guastatoya," "Telonicapan," and "Escuintla"; "Mosquito Coast" has been substituted for "Costa Mosquito"; the western boundary of Guatemala has been moved eastward and the country name shifted; and the names "Honduras," "Tlasila," "Zepilitan," the fort north of Tabasco, "Tonala," "R. Alvarado," "R.S. Juan," "Lalana," "Tutla," "Sierra de la Madre," "Ixtlan," and the highways from La Puebla to Oajaca and from Yzabal to N. Chiapa have been added.

Roads have been added and trails have been converted to double-line roads in central and northern Mexico.

The following modifications in the boundary region on the seventh edition are of particular interest with relation to its use as a treaty map.

Part of the Rio Nueces has been moved southward to a new course nearer the Rio Grande.

A portion of the old course of this stream has been designated as the "Rio Frio."

A road southwest of San Antonio de Bexar has been deleted.

A new road has been added between San Antonio de Bexar and the Presidio de Rio Grande to which are transferred the words "Gen1 Wool's Route 1846," which were formerly printed along a road farther south.

On the north side of the Rio Gila, near 33° west longitude, a river crossing is identified as "Ford."

"Agua Sola," "Carizal," and "S. Jose" have been added along the trail from San Diego to the junction of the Colorado and Gila Rivers.

A trail leading from "S. Diego" to "S. Miguel" and southward throughout Baja California has been changed to a double-line road.

"S. Maria," "Buena Vista," "Sario," and "Cocospera" have been added south of the Gila River in northwestern Sonora.

In northeastern Sonora the Gila River has been given a new headwater tributary, "R. Suanca," which rises close to the south boundary of New Mexico and upon which a village named Suanca has been added.

The seventh edition was published by John Disturnell in the early months of 1847. We know this because Nicholas P. Trist received his instructions as American Commissioner on April 15, 1847, and left Washington the next day, and because on October 25, 1847, James Buchanan, Secretary of State, wrote to Trist, referring to "the division line between Upper and Lower California as delineated on the map which you carried with you" (D.S., 16 Instructions, Mexico, 79–83; serial 509, p. 95). Moreover, Trist quotes in his memorandum of January 4, 1848, those words of the Secretary of State concerning the map he carried with him from Washington to Mexico, and then goes on to say: "The map referred to by the Secretary of State as the one I brought with me, is the 'Revised Edition' of the one published at New York, in 1847 (forty seven) by J. Disturnell, 102 Broadway, and bearing, in spanish, the following title: 'Map of the United States of Mexico, as organized & defined by various acts of the Congress of said Republic, and constructed according to the best authorities.' " In the same memorandum he noted that the Secretary of State "had the map before him" when he wrote certain words concerning the boundary between Upper California and Lower California. Trist also said that this boundary "is *erroneously* laid down in your map" and called it the line "laid down in our map."

This earliest of the 1847 editions was probably used in discussing the boundary of Texas as well as that between the two Californias, for Trist said in his report of the conference between the Mexican Commissioners and himself on September 2, 1847, that General Mora y Villamil illustrated certain of his remarks by running his finger "over the territory comprehended between the Nueces & the Bravo, on the map before us."

The seventh edition of the map of Mexico was published not long before April 15, 1847, for Trist observed in his memorandum of January 4, 1848, that the inclusion of San Diego in the territory claimed by the United States had its origin "in *accident*, in pure accident: the accident of the Secretary of State's having before him one map instead of another. That map was the one just published at New York, as an engraver's speculation, to meet the demand which put it into the hands of every body." On January 7, 1848, Trist enlarged upon his mistaken idea that this seventh edition was a new map, a mere speculation, and not based upon the best among earlier maps like that of Baron von Humboldt. Disturnell's map, he then thought, was "a map, suddenly got up, as the mere speculation of an engraver or bookseller, to meet the demand in our country for Maps of Mexico. And this is the character of the one I brought with me."

Library of Congress holdings:

Colored original, mounted on cloth, sectioned to fold to 32 by 22½ inches. Division stamp: Aug 7 1935. Received by transfer from U.S. Corps of Engineers.

## Eighth edition

[Same title as seventh edition.]

There are four inset maps in the Gulf of Mexico, as compared with two on the previous edition.

The name "Buena Vista" is missing from the southeast corner of the state of Coahuila, near Saltilla, but is found in the five subsequent editions dated 1847.

In northern Tamaulipas a trail has been added between La Como and Nuevo Santander.

"San Fernando" has been relocated slightly to the south.

Library of Congress holdings:

Colored original, mounted on cloth, sectioned in 32 parts to fold to 7½ by 5½ inches.

## Ninth edition

[Same title as seventh edition.]

"Buena Vista" has been added in southeast corner of Coahuila near Saltillo.

The following villages in Durango, Coahuila, and Chihuahua appear for the first time on this edition: Aqua Nueva, Hedionda, Bueno Ventura, Patos, La Punta, Joya, Santiago, Lienegas.

In the same area the following trails have been added: a) from Aqua Nueva to Bueno Ventura by way of Hedionda, b) from San Filipe to Encarnacion by way of Castañuela, Patos, and La Punta, c) from La Punta through Santiago and southwestward to the main road from Chihuahua to San Luis Potosí, d) from Lienegas to Hornos, and e) from Monclova to Lienegas and northwestward to S. Pablo in Chihuahua.

Library of Congress holdings:

Colored original, mounted on cloth, sectioned to fold to 31½ by 22 inches. Presented as gift by Thomas W. Streeter. Division stamp: Jan 31 1938.

## Tenth edition

[Same title as seventh edition.]

"S. Pablo" added in northwest corner of Sonora, approximately on the site of present Yuma, Ariz.

In northwestern Baja California the name of the first coastal indentation south of S. Miguel has been changed from "Bahia S. Francisco or All Saints Bay" to "Bahia Todos Santos or All Saints Bay."

Library of Congress holdings:

Colored original, mounted on cloth, sectioned to fold to 31½ by 21 inches, and an imperfect original, colored, mounted on cloth, in two parts, each 31½ by 24½ inches, which lacks the bottom margin and a segment of the map. Division stamp: 3-Mar 1961. Note in upper right margin, in pencil, reads "Office Sec. of Senate U.S."

## Eleventh edition

[Same title as seventh edition.]

Adjacent to the international boundary in Coahuila, Nueva León, and Tamaulipas the following modifications have been made:

At Loredo, Tamaulipas, a circle has been added for the village site.

The circle on the bank of the Rio Grande at Revilla has been deleted and a new circle for this village has been introduced eight miles farther west.

The circle for Presidio de Rio Grande has been deleted and a new circle for this place has been introduced three miles farther west.

The northern part of the road from Seratvo, Nuevo León, to Revilla, Tamaulipas, has been altered in position.

The road from Revilla to Loredo has been moved westward.

A new road 110 miles in length has been introduced between Loredo and Presidio de Rio Grande.

Library of Congress holdings:

Colored original, mounted on cloth, sectioned to fold to 31½ by 21 inches, and another colored original, mounted on cloth, sectioned to fold to 30 by 21 inches. On latter is division stamp: Transfer 90 Nov 15 1944. Also includes rubber stamp impressions "Adjutant General's Library" and "General Staff Map Collection File Copy." Several pencil and ink annotations in an unknown hand.

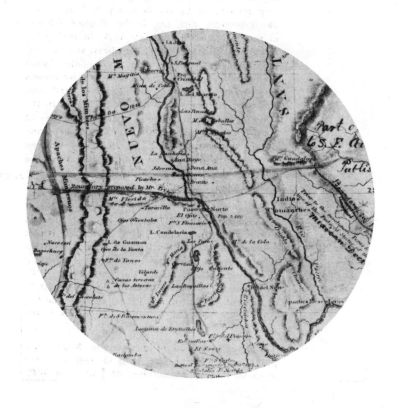

*Detail of United States-Mexican border before and after correction on Disturnell's map. Above, from the seventh edition, 1847; below, from the fifteenth edition, 1848.*

## Twelfth edition

[Same title as seventh edition.]

The following towns have been added in Texas: Milan Falls, Boston, Marshall, Liverpool, Egypt.

New roads or trails, also in Texas, have been added a) from Baston to Henderson by way of Marshall, b) from Washington northwestward to Franklin, c) from Franklin northward to Chihuahua Trail, d) from Nashville to Milan Falls, e) from Virginia via Liverpool to Columbia, f) from Port Calhoun southwestward for the full length of St. Joseph Island, g) from Port Cavallo to Quintana, h) from Quintana to Matagorda, i) from Columbus to La Grange, and j) from Houston to Richmond and southwestward to the Egypt road.

This twelfth edition of Disturnell's Map shares with the seventh edition the distinction of being a treaty map. The twelfth edition is preserved in the archives of the Government of Mexico as number "C-1-2-22-2" and is certified in Spanish and in English. The English certificate, signed by Trist, stands on the right and reads as follows:

> This is the Map, referred to in the Fifth Article of the Treaty of Peace, Friendship, Limits and Settlement, between the United States of America and the Mexican Republic, signed this day.
>
> Witness our hands and seals, at Guadalupe Hidalgo, this second day of February, one thousand eight hundred and forty-eight.

Library of Congress holdings:

> Three colored originals mounted on cloth. One, sectioned to fold to 31 by 21½ inches, was purchased from Edward Eberstadt, New York City. Division stamp: Dec 15 1936. Of the two sectioned to fold to 30 by 21½ inches, one bears the division stamp "Jul 1958" and the rubber stamp impression "U.S. Geological Survey Library 9922 1887."

## Thirteenth edition

[Same title as seventh edition.]

The following changes have been made in southern Coahuila: "Buena Vista" has been erased and relettered farther north and the circle for this locality has been replaced by a larger circle with a dot; at the left of this new symbol crossed sabers have been introduced, below which appear the word "Battle" and the dates "Feb. 22 & 23, 1847"; the place name "Patos" has been moved northward; new trails leading westward and northwestward from Patos have been added; and "S. Antonio" has been introduced on the trail from Castañuela to Alantos.

The following modifications have been made on the inset chart of the Bay of Vera Cruz: southwest of the city of Vera Cruz a curved line of dashes has been introduced, along which appear the words "Vera Cruz invested by the American Army under Gen. Scott, March 1847"; south of the city appear the words "City & Castle Surren[d] March 27. 1847"; near the bottom of the map, east of the anchor symbol, appear the words "American Fleet"; and west of this point on the shore there is a short line of black dashes, labeled "American Forces Landed here March 9th 1847."

Along the international boundary the following changes have been made in Texas: "Goliad" moved northwestward, "Refugio" moved northward, "Preston" added, a road southwest of Victorio deleted, the road from Victorio to Refugio relocated, a new stream introduced near Refugio, "Laredo," Texas, added opposite "Loredo," Tamaulipas, and "Head of Nav" introduced south of Laredo, Texas; and these changes have been made in Mexico: "Guerreo or" introduced before "Revilla" in Tamaulipas and "Guerreo" deleted in Coahuila.

Library of Congress holdings:

> Colored original, mounted, sectioned to fold to 30 by 21½ inches.

## Fourteenth edition

Mapa de los Estados Unidos de Méjico, Segun lo organizado y definido por las varias actas del Congreso de dicha República: y construido por las mejores autoridades. Lo publican J. Disturnell, 102 Broadway, Nueva York. 1848. Revised Edition.

Inset, "Diagram of the Battle Ground Feb. 22[d] and 23[d] 1847," has been added in Atlantic Ocean.

Adjacent to the international boundary the following additions are noted: in southern Nuevo Méjico and Alta California a road or route from the Rio Grande to the Rio Colorado starting at "Mina de Cobre" and following the "R. Suanca" and the "R. Gila," the eastern portion of which is designated "Gen. Kearney's Route Oct. 1846"; near the junction of the Gila and the Colorado the words "Note The Gila on its Northern side is bounded by a range of lofty Mountains"; along the road from the junction of the Gila and the Colorado the words "Gen. Kearney's Route Dec. 1846"; northeast of San Diego the place name "S. Maria" and nearby the words "Battle of San Pascal Dec[r] 6th 1846"; a trail northwestward from "S. Jose" to "Ciudad de los Angelos" and the name "Temascal"; in northern Sonora, south of the Gila, the words "Gen. Kearney's camp Nov 11th 1846"; in northern Chihuahua, along the road south of Paso, the words "Col Doniphan's Route 1847"; between Chihuahua and Saltillo, the words "Doniphan's Route 1847."

Library of Congress holdings:

> Photostat positive, mounted in one piece, and negative, in four parts, of an original in the American Geographical Society.

## Fifteenth edition

[Same title as fourteenth edition.]

"Boundary pro<sup>d</sup> by Mr. Trist" has been printed in the Gulf of Mexico, opposite the mouth of the Rio Grande.

In Alta California a dotted line, identified as "Boundary Proposed by Mexico," follows the 37th parallel of north latitude eastward from the Pacific Ocean to the 23d meridian west of Washington, D. C.

Also labeled "Boundary Proposed by Mexico" is a dotted line in Texas that extends due south from the Red River to the Nueces River.

"Pikes Peak" has been added where the Arkansas River flows from the Rocky Mountains.

"Battle Jan 9<sup>th</sup> 1847" has been added near "Ciudad de los Angelos."

"Sandy Desert" has been added west of the junction of the Colorado and Gila Rivers.

A new dotted boundary line extends the full length of the Gulf of California.

The southern boundary of Nueva Méjico west of the Rio Grande has been deleted.

North of the parallel of 32° north latitude and about 90 miles west of the Rio Grande, the place name "Corepelado" has been deleted.

A new southern boundary of Nuevo Méjico, designated "Boundary proposed by Mr. Trist," has been drawn on the parallel of 32° north latitude except at the east end, where it bends a little farther south.

The Rio Grande is shifted westward some 25 to 35 miles in the 200 miles of its course from "Fra Cristobal," north of "Paso," to "F<sup>te</sup> S. Eleazario," south of that place.

A hachured mountain range nearly 70 miles long has been added between the old and the new course of the Rio Grande.

The road along this portion of the Rio Grande and for some miles farther south has been relocated.

"Brazito" has been moved southward to a point on the east bank of the Rio Grande near the site of "Paso."

"S<sup>n</sup> Diego" has been moved southeast and relettered "San Diego."

"Robledillo" has been deleted.

"Dona Ana" has been added north of "La Salinera."

"La Canada" has been deleted.

"F<sup>te</sup> de Carizal" has been relettered "Carrizal."

A lake and stream have been added nearby.

Hachures have been added for the northward extension of "M<sup>te</sup> Barrigon."

"L. S. Martin" has been deleted and a larger body of water, called "Laguna de Encinillas," has been added a little farther south.

The dotted boundary extending westward from "M<sup>te</sup> Guadalupe" to the Rio Grande has been replaced by a new dotted boundary extending southwestward from "M<sup>te</sup> Guadalupe" to the Rio Grande, with the words "Boundary Proposed by Mr. Trist" engraved and then imperfectly erased.

The name "Paso" has been deleted.

The name "F<sup>te</sup> Paso del Norte" and the population "P. 5,000" have been deleted from their position near 32°10′ north latitude and the name and the symbol for this place have been added on the west bank of the relocated Rio Grande near 31°50′ north latitude, with the population "Pop. 5,000" nearby.

Library of Congress holdings:

Imperfect original, lightly colored, mounted on cloth sectioned to fold to 29 by 21 inches, which is badly worn and lacks small pieces. Transferred from General Land Office June 13, 1935. Has numerous annotations including, above the title, "This map forms part of the Mexican Boundary Commission." It may be inferred that the map was used in the field by John R. Bartlett, the Boundary Commissioner who worked under the direction of the Secretary of the Interior in 1850 and soon after, or by his predecessor, John B. Weller, in 1849.

## Sixteenth edition

[Same title as fourteenth edition.]

The designation "Boundary Proposed by Mexican Commissioners" replaces "Boundary Proposed by Mexico" below the word "California," in "Alta California."

The east-west boundary between the Pacific Ocean and the Gulf of California, represented by heavy dashed lines on several previous editions, has been replaced by a line of fine dots in exactly the same position, i.e., north of the parallel of 32° north latitude and south of the place name "S. Miguel."

On the southern boundary of New Mexico the words "U.S. Commissioner" have been added between the phrase "Boundary proposed by Mr. Trist" and "M<sup>te</sup> Florida."

In western Texas "Original Boundary of Texas in 1835" has been altered to read "Boundary of Texas in 1835 (See S. F. Austin's Map)."

The northwestern headwaters of the San Antonio River are designated "Medina R." and a dashed boundary has been added between the head of this stream and the head of the Nueces River, continuing thence northwestward, eastward, and northward to the Red River northeast of "Waco Village." Along this boundary have been added the words "Spanish Boundary 1786 between Coahuila & Texas."

From the head of the Nueces River a dashed boundary extends southwestward to the Chihuahua-Coahuila boundary on the south bank of the Rio Grande.

To the phrase "Prior to the revolution Texas & Cohahuila were united to form one of the Federal States of the Mexican Republic" have been added the words "(Mexican Decree May 7. 1824)."

Along the meridian of 23°45′ west longitude, between the Red River and the Nueces, the phrase "Boundary Proposed by Mexico" has been amended to read "Boundary Proposed by Mexican Commissioners."

"R. Colorado," near the head of the Red River, has been amended to read "R. Colorado or Red R."

The headwaters of the "Rio Colorado de Bajar" have been truncated on the northwest and supplemented on the southwest by the inclusion of a stream formerly shown as a tributary of one of the branches of the Rio Grande.

"Loredo," Tamaulipas, has been deleted.

At the mouth of the Rio Grande "Boundary pro^d by Mr. Trist" has been amended by the addition of the words "U.S. Commissioner."

Library of Congress holdings:

Colored original, mounted on cloth, sectioned to fold to 29½ by 21 inches. Division stamp: 3-Nov 1961. There are also rubber stamp impressions reading "Adjutant General's Library" and "General Staff Map Collection File Copy." Received on transfer from National Archives.

## Seventeenth edition

[Same title as fourteenth edition.]

The east-west boundary along the 37th parallel from the Pacific Ocean to the meridian of 23° west longitude has been deleted, along with the sentence "Boundary Proposed by Mexican Commissioners."

The east-west boundary from the Pacific Ocean to the Gulf of California, between the place name "S. Miguel" and the 32d parallel, has been deleted.

A new boundary running eastward from San Diego Bay to the junction of the Colorado River with the Gila has been identified as "New U.S. Boundary."

The country name "Méjico" and the words "Gold Region" have been added for the first time.

Library of Congress holdings:

Colored original, mounted on cloth, sectioned to fold to 31 by 21½ inches.

## Eighteenth edition

Map of California, New Mexico and Adjacent Countries Showing the Gold Regions &c. New York. Published by J. Disturnell. 1849. Printed at Ackerman's rooms, 120, Fulton S^t N.Y.

This map was issued to accompany the second of three editions of Disturnell's *Emigrant's Guide to New Mexico, California, and Oregon*, which was published in 1849 as an 80-page pamphlet. The first edition, a 46-page pamphlet likewise published in 1849, had been accompanied by a folded map by J. Calvin Smith entitled "Map of North America," on which appeared a large-scale inset map entitled "Map of the Gold Region California." The map in the first edition and also in the third edition (1850) was published by Disturnell but is not a version of the "Mapa de los Estados Unidos de Méjico."

Covers only the western half of the "Mapa de los Estados Unidos de Méjico." It was made from a new plate and seems to have been printed from stone rather than from copper. It was mechanically reproduced from the copperplate of the seventeenth edition or from a paper negative derived from that plate, since all the corrections and incomplete erasures on the seventeenth edition also appear on the eighteenth.

A number of the major geographical names have been translated from Spanish into English, e.g., "New Leon" for "Nuevo León," "New Mexico or Santa Fe" for "Nuevo Méjico ó Santa Fe," "Gulf of California" for "Golfo de California," "Lower California" for "Baja California," "Pacific Ocean" for "Mar Pacífico," and "Mexico" for "Méjico."

"United States" has been lettered boldly across the upper part of the map.

The name "Texas" has been added, together with additional streams, lakes, mountains, trails, place names, and notes in Upper California.

The north-south dotted boundary in Texas which extended from the Nueces to the "R. Colorado or Red R" on the seventeenth edition, has been deleted along with the words "Boundary Proposed by Mexican Commissioners."

The trail from San Diego to the mouth of the Gila River and thence southeastward through Sonora has been changed to a double-line road.

From "Mina de Cobre" on the Rio Grande to the junction of the Gila with the "R. de las Asencion" a long trail, designated "Lieut. Col. Cooke's Wagon Route," has been added by way of "Terrenate" and "F^te Santa Cruz" in the part of northern Sonora acquired by the United States in the Gadsden purchase.

In New Mexico the word "Apacheria" has been deleted.

Library of Congress holdings:

Two colored original maps, mounted on cloth, 31 by 23½ inches. One of them bears the call no. G4300 1849.D5.

## Nineteenth edition

[Same title as eighteenth edition.]

A dotted trail extending from western Texas to "F^te Santa Cruz," added in northern Sonora, is identified in two places as "Col. Hays' Route."

"Fredricksburg" has been added in central Texas.

"San Pedro" has been added in northern Sonora.

A new dotted trail, identified as "Gregg's Route," extends from the eastern edge of the map near latitude 36° to the "Route of the Santa Fe Expedition 1841" on the "Ensenada de Trace."

Trail and creek symbols and the words "Goose Creek" have been added at the north edge of the map between longitudes 36° and 37° west of Washington.

The words "Lawson Pass" and a dotted east-west line have been added near the north edge of the map in the valley west of "Fremont's Route."

The words "to Oregon" identify a trail near the north edge of the map at approximately longitude 42° west of Washington.

Library of Congress holdings:

> Photostat positive, mounted on cloth, 31 by 22 inches. From negative supplied by Carl I. Wheat. Division stamp: Dec 15 1936.

## Twentieth edition

Mapa de los Estados Unidos de Méjico, California &c. Segun lo organizado y definido por las varias actas del Congreso de dicha República: y construido por las mejores autoridades. Lo publican J. Disturnell, 102 Broadway. Nueva York. 1849. Revised Edition.

In contrast with the eighteenth and nineteenth editions, names on this edition are in Spanish.

Like the first through the seventeenth editions, the twentieth was reproduced from copper engraved plates.

This is the first Spanish edition dated 1849.

The additions made on the eighteenth edition, notably in Upper California, are carried over to this edition, but none of the changes recorded for the nineteenth edition appear here.

Library of Congress holdings:

> Photostat positive, slightly reduced (23 by 32½ inches), of original in collection of Edwin Grabhorn, San Francisco, Calif. Division stamp: Dec 15 1936.

## Twenty-first edition

[Same title as twentieth edition.]

In California these additions have been made: the names "Webster," "Benicia," "Martinez," "Suisan," "Stockton," "N. York," "Fremont," "Vernon," "St Louis," "Gold Region," "Mt Linn," "Laguna," and "Coast Range," and a trail symbol running northeast from "S. Jose," California.

In Texas these additions have been made: "San Marcos," a road from San Marcos to Seguin, "New Braunfels," a road from San Marcos to Austin, "Fredericksburg," a road from Fredericksburg to Austin, a road from Corpus Christi to Laredo, Texas, and a road from Corpus Christi to Mier, Tamaulipas, with a branch leading to Comargo.

Also in Texas "Seguin" has been moved northwestward to a new position, the road from San Antonio de Bexar to Bastrop is moved so as to pass through San Marcos, and the trail from San Antonio de Bexar to Austin and the road from San Patricio to Mier have been deleted.

In Oregon these additions have been made: a new course of the "Rio Luis or Snake R" from "F^t Hall" westward to 37°30', a road on the south bank of this stream, and two new tributaries of the Snake River, one of which is called "Goose Cr."

Near 38° north latitude and 28° longitude west of Washington a short trail and the words "Fremonts Route Dec 1848" have been added.

Library of Congress holdings:

> Colored original, mounted on cloth, sectioned to fold to 31½ by 21½ inches. Purchased in 1936 from Attic Book Shop, Washington, D. C. Division stamp: Dec 15 1936.

## Twenty-second edition

Mapa de los Estados Unidos de Méjico, California &c. Segun lo organizado y definido por las varias actas del Congreso de dicha República: y construido por las mejores autoridades. Lo publican J. Disturnell, 102 Broadway. Nueva York. 1850. Revised Edition.

Along the Missouri-Arkansas boundary the words "Missouri Compromise Line 36°30'" have been engraved.

Between the top of the map at longitude 43° west of Washington and the junction of the Rio Virgin with the Rio Colorado two dotted lines similar in form to the Nevada-California boundary but in different positions have been added.

Library of Congress holdings:

> Positive photostat, mounted, and a negative photostat, in four parts, of an original in the Bancroft Library, Berkeley, Calif. Division stamp: Dec 15 1936.

## Twenty-third edition

Mapa de los Estados Unidos de Méjico, California &c. Segun lo organizado y definido por las varias actas del Congreso de dicha República: y construido por las mejores autoridades. Lo publican J. Disturnell, 157 Broadway. Nueva York. 1850. Revised Edition.

"Eagle Pass" has been added in northern Coahuila.

"Trinity or" has been added before "Smiths R" in northern California.

"Sacramento City" has been substituted for the words "Nueva Helvetia."

"S. Jose" has been relettered in capitals.

To the right of the title this has been added: "*Note*. In the 1847 edition of this map which was appended to the Treaty of Guadalube Hidolgo, dated Feb. 2, 1848, a geographical error was discovered and corrected in regard to the true position of Paso del Norte situated near the 32$^d$ degree of North Latitude."

Below the boundary which extends eastward from San Diego to the junction of the Colorado River with the Gila this note has been added: "North West Boundary of Mexico As defined by the Commissioners in October 1849. North Latitude 32°31' 59" Longitude 7 H. 48 M. 21 S. W. from Greenwich being about 17 miles to the Southward of the town of San Diego in Upper California."

"S. Miguel" is moved westward.

Library of Congress holdings:

Colored original, mounted on cloth, sectioned to fold to 31 by 22 inches. Purchased in 1936 from Edward Eberstadt, New York City. Division stamp: Dec 15 1936.

## Twenty-fourth edition

Mapa de los Estados Unidos de Méjico, California &c. Segun lo organizado y definido por las varias actas del Congreso de dicha República: y construido por las mejores autoridades. Lo publican J. Disturnell. Nueva York. 1858. Revised Edition.

Between the Rio Grande and the Gulf of California the present southern boundary of the United States has been indicated by a dash-dot line, designated "Gadsden's Treaty Line."

The territory between this dash-dot line and the Gila River has been designated "Ter. of Arizona."

The initial letter of the country name "Méjico" has been left in Arizona.

A number of railroad lines have been added throughout the map.

Library of Congress holdings:

Colored original, mounted on cloth, sectioned to fold to 30½ by 21 inches. Division stamp: Sep 19 1904.

# How to Order Photoreproductions

Photocopies may be obtained of all illustrations appearing in this publication. Orders should be addressed to the Library of Congress, Photoduplication Service, Washington, D.C. 20540. Requests should specify the title of this publication, *A la Carte;* the page number and position of the item; a brief identification; and the photographic negative number or location of the negative as cited below. Prices are available from the Photoduplication Service; all orders must be prepaid.

Negatives for all illustrations in this publication are located in the Geography and Map Division of the Library of Congress, with the following exceptions.

| Page No. | Negative No. or Location |
|---|---|
| 91 | LC USZ62–10751 |
| 115 | LC USZ62–1943 |
| 126 | LC USZ62–4702 |
| 141 | LC USZ62–1804 |
| 145 | LC USZ62–42493 |
| 150–51 | Manuscript Division, George Washington Papers, Series 2 (microfilm) |

# Index

Aa, Peter van der, *D'Engelze Volkplanting in Virginia*, 127
Acoliuhyan, 20
Acre, Israel, 58
Adams, President John, 104, 138, 141, 142
Adams, Randolph G., *British Headquarters Maps and Sketches*, 88
Adams County, Pa., 157, 158
Adams-Onis Treaty, 162, 169
Addison, Col. John, 129
Africa, 197; maps, 34, 35, 62, 65, 70–75
Agnese, Battista, 34–38, 79
Agricola, Rudolphus, 2
Aguilar y Jurado, Vicente, 200
Ahuaxpizin, Carlos, 9
Alameda, Fray Juan de, 19
Albear, Diego, 194
Alden, James R., 140
Alexander's Island, 127
Alexandria, Va., 121, 124, 128, 129, 130, 137, 140, 144, 145, 147
Algiers, 58
"Aligany" region, map, 116
Allardt, Hugo, 65
Allegheny River, 121
Allen, William, and Jedediah Hotchkiss, *The Battlefields of Virginia—Chancellorsville*, 188
Altantse, Luc, 3
Alvarado, Pedro, 11
Amazon River, 190, 197–199, 202; Basin, 189, 200; maps, 201
America, 2, 3; maps, 38, 39, 42, 43, 46, 47, 65–68, 74, 78–90
American Geographical Society, New York, 61, 79
American Revolution, maps, 86–90
Amherst, Jeffery, 109
Anacostia River, 127
Anacostien Island, 127
*Analectic Magazine*, 167
Andonaegue Mariscal, Joseph de, 197
Annapolis, Md., 122, 129
Anthiaume, A., 41, 43
Antioquia, Colombia, 202
Antonio, Don, 15, 19, 23
Antwerp, Belgium, 42
Apian, Peter (Petrus Apianus), 2–4, 48
Apucupa, 24
Aragon, map, 60
Archivo General de Indias (Seville), 79
Argentina, 194

Arizona, 209
Arkansas River, 169
Arnoldi, Arnoldo de, 43
Asia, maps, 46, 65, 74
Asuncion, Paraguay, 194
*Atlantic Neptune*, 88, 89
Atlantic Ocean, 34, 35, 37, 41
Atlases, 34–38, 45–61, 63, 64, 79, 84
Atlxocopan, 24
Averdunk, Heinrich, 50, 56
Azara, Felix de, 194
Aztecs: land measures, 16; maps, 5–33

Bagrow, Leo, 4, 40, 41, 43, 50, 52, 56
Ballendine, John, 121–124; "Map of Potomack and James Rivers . . .," 122–125, 128
Baltimore, Lord, 83, 98, 99, 129
Baltimore, Md., 144, 145; map, 88
Barlow, R. H., 19
Barnes, Joseph, *A Map of Virginia; With a Description of the Countrey, the Commodities, People, Government, and Religion; Written by Captaine Smith, sometimes Governour of the Countrey, etc.*, 93
Bartlett, John Russell, 209
Batchelder Collection, 149
Bavaria, maps, 52
Beale, Col. Ninian, 129
Beall, Alexander, 130
Beall, George, 129
Beatty, Charles, 129
Beck, George, 126, 130, 142
Belhaven, Va., 127, 130; *see also* Alexandria, Va.
Bellin, J. N., 84
Beneventanus, Marcus, 78
Berey, Jeanne, 70
Berey, Nicolas, 70, 71
Berkley, Dr. Henry J., 129
Berks County, Pa., 158
Bertelli, Ferdinando, 39
Besançon, France, 58
Bibliothèque Nationale (Paris), 60, 65, 74, 84, 97, 101
Birch, William Russell, 139, 141
Bladensburg, Md., 129, 144
Bladensburg Road, 129
Blaeu, Cornelis, 65
Blaeu, G. I.; *see* Blaeu, Willem Janszoon
Blaeu, Joan, 63, 65

Blaeu, Willem Janszoon, 63–68, 74, 94
Blair, John, 116
Blanchard and Langdon, map of New Hampshire, 85
Blathwayt Collection, 127
Blodget, Samuel, 135, 140
Blodget, Samuel, Jr., 148
Blodget's Hotel, 141
Blue Ridge Mountains, 185, 188
Böyë, Herman, 160, 161; *Map of the State of Virginia Constructed in Conformity to Law From the Late Surveys Authorized by the Legislature and Other Original and Authentic Documents*, 159
Bohemia, map, 60
Bohemia Manor, 99
Bologna, University of, Italy, 58
Bologne, Virgil de, 42
Borda, Jean Charles, 191
Botetourt, Governor, 119
Bourquin, Frederick, 202
Braddock, Gen. Edward, 86
Bradley, Abraham, 90
Braun, Georg, 43, 54; and Franz Hogenberg, *Civitates orbis terrarum*, 42, 43, 51, 53, 58, 60
Brazil, 189, 190–192, 197–199; maps, 192, 201; Ministério das Relacões Exteriores, 195, 196
Brazos River, 211
Bristoe Station, Va., 185, 187
British Board of Trade, 105
British Colonial Office, 127
British Isles, maps, 48, 49; *see also* Great Britain
British Museum (London), 39, 44, 61, 64, 84, 101, 107
British Public Record Office, 84
Brooks, Philip Coolidge, 162
Brussels, Belgium, map, 54
Bull of Pope Alexander VI, 189
Burgoyne, Gen. John, 86
Burnes, David, 129, 140
Bussemecher, Johannes, 58–60

Cabot, John, 79
Cabot, Sebastian, 41
Cacamatzin, 9, 11
Cairo, Egypt, 53, 58
Calcogra a Nacional (Madrid), 203
California, 209; Gold Rush, 210; map, 80
Calvo, M. Charles, 200
Camara, Sebastião Xavier da Veiga Cabral da, 195
Camers, Solinus, 4
Campbell, Maj. Albert H., 183
Canada-Newfoundland (Labrador) boundary case, 105
Canary Islands, 191, 200
Candisch, Thomas, 68
Caño de Avatiparana, 199
Cape São Roque, Brazil, 189
Cape Verde Islands, 189
Caracas, Capitania Grãl de, 199
Caraci, Giuseppe, 44
Carey, Mathew, 136
Caribbean, 37
Carleton, Osgood, 90, 161
Carlos, Don, 9, 11, 13, 18–20
Carroll, Charles, 132
Carroll, Charles, Jr., 129
Carroll, Daniel, 129
Carrollsburg (D.C.), 130, 132

Cartagena de Yndias, Provincia de, 202
Cartwright, T., 142
Casa de la Contratación, 41
Castile, Spain, map, 60
Catholic University of America, Oliveiro Lima Library, 200
Cedar Mountain, Battle of, 186
Cedar River, 118
Cedar Run Battlefield, 185
Cerne Abby Manor, 129
Cervini, Cardinal Marcello, 57
Cerviño, Pedro Antonio, 196
Ceynos, Francisco, 17, 18
Chagres, Panama, 197
Chaix, Paul, 40
Champlain, Samuel de, 80, 82
Chancellorsville, Va., 185, 186; map of campaign, 187
Chantilly, Va., 186
Charles II, King of England, 64
Charles III, Duke of Lorraine, 50
Charles V, King of Spain, 42, 48, 49, 194
Charts, 84; eastern coast of North America, 89; St. Augustin, 89
Chaudiere, Guillaume, 42, 43
Chaves, Alonso de, 41
Chesapeake and Ohio Canal, 129
Chesapeake Bay, 90, 93, 99, 121
Chester, Pa., 144, 147
Chester County, Pa., 158
Chicago Historical Society, 43
Chichimecatecotl, Don Carlos, 7, 12, 22–24
Chickahominy River, 187
Chinquitos Province, 196
Choco del Norte, Colombia, 202
Christian, Mrs. R. E., 183, 185
Christoph, 57
Chubb, Thomas, 54
Churchman, John, 90
Churchville, Va., 188
Ciuaiunti, Benito, 11, 13
Civil War, maps, 183–188
Clark, Edward, 139
Clark, William, 168
Clarke, T., 130
Clinton, Sir Henry, 86, 88
Clinton Collection, William L. Clements Library, 88
Coatlecouztin, Don Carlos, 20
Cock, Hieronymus, 41, 42
Cock, Mathias, 41
Cohuanacochtzin, Pedro Alvarado, 9, 11, 12
Colbert, Jean Baptiste, 74
Colles, Christopher, *Survey of the Roads of the United States of America*, 90, 129
Collet, Capt. John, 85
Colom, Jacob, 65
Colombia, Republic of, 170, 202; map of rivers, 198
Colorado, 209
Colorado River, 207, 208, 211
Columbia River, 170
Columbus, Christopher, 37, 68, 69
Colvin, Sidney, 44
*Congressional Globe*, 209
Connecticut, map, 85
Contreras, Alonso de, 18, 20
Cornell University Library, 90
Cornwallis, Gen. Charles, 86
Cortés, Fernando, 8, 11, 12, 24
Cosa, Juan de la, 78

Cóven, I., 110
Cozcacoah, 24
Cratander, Andreas, 2
Crawford County, Pa., 157
Cristóbal, Don, 9
Cruz Cano y Olmedilla, Juan de la, 202, 203
Cuauyacac, 26, 27
Culpeper County, Va., 161
Cumberland, Fort, 146
Cumberland County, Pa., 157
Cumberland River, 114
Cuñare Javiyà Yrufari los Quales, 199
Cupati, Salto de, 199
Cutler, Manasseh, 90
Cuzco, Peru, 53, 58

Daily Union, 210
Dalton, Tristam, 145
Danckerts, Cornelis, 65
Darby, Pa., 144
Darby, William, 206, 207
Darien, Panama, 197, 202
Darley, Felix Octavius Carr, 115
Darnestown, Md., 185
Dartmouth College Library, 88
Dauphin County, Pa., 157, 158
Davidson, Samuel, 138, 140
Davis, John, 141
Dawsonville, Md., 185
Deakins, Francis, 132
Delaware, maps, 90
Delaware Bay, 98; maps, 80
Delaware County, Pa., 158
Delaware River, 147
De L'Isle, Guillaume, 85
Denmark, maps, 58, 60
Denucé, Jean, 4, 52, 71
Dépot des Cartes et de la Marine (Paris), 41, 84
Dermott, James R., 130, 138
Des Barres, Joseph Frederick Wallet, 88
"Description dv pais des Hvrons, 1631," 81
Deutsche Staatsbibliothek, Berlin, 65
Deventer, Jacob van, 42
DeWitt, Simeon, 89, 129
Dinwiddie, Gov. Robert, 114
District of Columbia: early history and maps, 90, 126–152, 175; Ellicott plan, 146, 147; Jefferson plan, 131, 132; L'Enfant plan, 90, 130, 135, 136, 138, 147; see also Alexandria; Georgetown; and Potomac River
Disturnell, John, 204–221; Map of the United Mexican States (1847), 103, 204, 205
d'Ogerolles, Jean, 58
Donck, Adriaen van der, 100
"Doted Line" map, 134, 135
Drake, Sir Francis, 68
Duddington Manor, 129, 140
Dumbarton House, 140
Duncanson, William Mayne, 140
Dunk, George, Earl of Halifax, 105
Dunlap's American Daily Advertiser, 148
Dutch West India Company, 98

Early, Gen. Jubal A., 187, 188
Eastham, Melville, 45, 51, 56, 61
Ebeling, Christoph Daniel, 142

Eddy, C. Vernon, 183, 185
Ega, Brazil, 197–199
Elizabeth I, Queen of England, 55
Elizabethtown, N.J., 144
Ellicott, Andrew, 90, 136–138, 146–148; plan of Washington, D.C., 148
El Paso, Tex., 211
Engaños ò Commiari, 199
England; see Great Britain
English Pilot, Fourth Book, 84
Erie County, Pa., 157
Erskine, Robert, 89, 129
Erskine-DeWitt Collection (New-York Historical Society), 89, 90
Europe, 58; maps, 34, 35, 46, 49, 65, 74
Evans, C. A., 188
Evans, Lewis, 85, 90, 114, 119
Ewell, Gen. Richard S., 187

Faden, William, 84–86, 203
Faden Collection (Library of Congress), 86
Faehtz, Ernest F. M., 130
Fairfax Corner Stone, 161
Fairfax, Lord, 90, 122, 127, 130
Faithorne, William, 99
Fauquier, Gov. Francis, 116
Federal City; see District of Columbia
Fendall, Gov. Josiah, 98
Fidalgo, Capt. Joaquin, 202
Fierro (Canary Islands), 200
Fillmore, President Millard, 207, 209, 210
Filson, John, 90
Finaeus, Orontius, 58, 79
Finlayson, James, 171
Fischer, Father Joseph, 78
Flanders, map, 48
Florence, Italy, Biblioteca Nazionale, 44
Florida, maps, 80, 85
Florida State Historical Society, 85
Ford, Worthington C., 91
Forlani, Paulo, 43
Forrer, Daniel, 188
Forrer, Henry, 188
Fort Cumberland, Md., 121
Fort Pitt (Pittsburgh), Pa., 118, 121
Fort Pleasant, Va., 121
Foster, John, 82
Four Mile Creek, 127
France, maps, 58, 60; colonial possessions in America, 84
Franklin, Benjamin, 85, 104, 105, 118, 122
Franklin County, Pa., 157
Franquelin, Jean Baptiste Louis, 84
Frans, Peter, 42
Frederick, Md., 124, 131
Frederick County, Va., 161
Fredericksburg, Va., 93, 187; battle of, 186
Freeman, Douglas S., 183
Freeman, T. B., 142
French and Indian Wars, 86
Friendship (estate), 129
Frogland (estate), 129
Front Royal, Va., maps, 186
Fry, Joshua, 83, 90, 122, 127
Fürstliche Stollberg-Wernigerodische Bibliothek, Wernigerode, Saxony, 35
Funk, Jacob, 131, 132
"Funkstown," 131
Furtènbach, Hans, 2

Gabry, Peter, and Sons, 98
Galarza, Joaquín, 17, 18
Gallatin, Albert, 107
Garcia de Leon y Pizarro, Ramon, 194, 195, 197
Garnett, Camp, 185
Garnett, Richard S., 185
Gaspare a Myrica, 48
Gastaldo-Bertelli: 1565 map, 39, 40, 43; "Vniversale descrittione di tvtta la terra conoscivta fin qvi," 43
*Gazette of the United States* (Philadelphia), 136, 148
Gemma Frisius, Regnier, 48, 58
Gendt, A. L. van, 4
Geographical Society of Spain, 203
*George Washington Atlas*, 90
George Washington Bicentennial Commission, 90
Georgetown (D.C.), 121, 124, 126, 128, 129, 130, 132, 140, 142, 144–147
Georgia, 165; map, 86
Gerbel, Nicolaus, 57, 58
Germany, map, 58
Gettysburg, battle of, 187
Ghymmius, Gualterus, 46
Gila River, 207
Gilpins, Col. George, 130
Glasgow, Scotland, 165
Globes, 48, 49
Gloucester Harbor, Mass., map, 80
Goodrich, A. T., 167, 170, 171
Goodspeed's Book Store, 121
Goos, Pieter, 84
Goose Creek, 127
Gordonsville, Va., 186
Gotha, Duke of, 40
Grand Ohio Company, 123
Grant, Gen. Ulysses S., 188
Grave (The Hague), 58
Great Britain: colonial possessions in America, maps, 84, 90, 114; England, maps, 58, 60; Saxton's county maps, 55
Great Falls of the Potomac, 127, 129, 145
Great Kanawha River; *see* Kanawha River
Great Lakes level case, 105
Great Meadows campaign, 114
Greatorex, Eliza, 140
Greece, maps, 57, 58
Greenleaf, James, 144, 147, 149
Griffith, Dennis, 90, 136
Grynaeus, S., 79
Guadalupe Hidalgo, Treaty of, 204, 205, 209
Guatemala, 170
Guayaquil, Ecuador, 197
Guillen, Julio F., 203
Guiney's Station (Guinea), Va., 187
Gulf of Mexico, 37, 86, 167, 169
Gutiérrez, Diego, 39, 41, 42

Hadfield, George, 139
Hale, Edward Everett, 86
Hale, Nathan, 86
Hallet, Etienne Sulpice (Stephen), 139
Halley, Edmund, 85
Hamburgh (D.C.), 130, 131
Handley Library (Winchester, Va.), 183, 185
Harbaugh, Leonard, 140
Hardy County, Va., 161
Harper, Lathrop, 35
Harpers Ferry, Va., 161

Harrisburg, Pa., 158, 188
Harrison, J., 142
Harrison County, Va., 161
Harrisse, Henry, 40, 41, 80; *Bibliotheca Americana Vetustissima*, 2; *Découverte et évolution cartographique de Terre-Neuve*, 40; *The Discovery of North America*, 4, 80
Harrisse Collection, 79
Harvard University, 80; Press, 90, 129
Havana, Cuba, 191
Havre de Grace, Md., 144
Hawkins, George F., 131
Heber, Richard, 4
Heck, Col. M. M., 185
Henrico County, Va., 160
Henry, John, map of Virginia, 85
Hernando, Don, 11
Herrman, Augustine, 83, 87, 100, 127; map of Virginia and Maryland, 96, 127
Hildebrand, F. I., 60
Hill, Clement, 129
Hill, Samuel, 90, 135, 136, 148; *Plan of the City of Washington in the Territory of Columbia*, 135
Hills, John, 88
Hind, Arthur M., 55
Hinks, Arthur R., 69
Hispanic Society of America (New York), 36
Historic American Buildings Survey, 140
Hoban, James, 139, 140, 142
Hogenberg, Franz, 39, 43, 50, 51, 54; "Americae et proximarvm regionvm orae descriptio," 43; *see also* Braun, Georg
Hogenberg, Hans, 43
Hogenberg, Remigius, 55
Holbein, Hans, 2
Hole, William, 93
Holland, Samuel, 90
Hollar, Wenceslaus, 99
Holman, Richard B., 82
Holme, Thomas, 83
Holmead, Anthony, 129
Holston River, 116
Homann, Johann Baptist, 127
Hondius, Henricus, 47, 68; *Nova Virginiae tabula*, 127
Hondius, Jodocus, 47, 63, 65
Hooch, Pieter de, 64
Hosier, J. Walter, 161
Hotchkiss, Maj. Jedediah, 183–188; *The Geography of Virginia*, 188; *Historical Atlas of Augusta County, Virginia* (1885), 188; *see also* Allen, William
Houghton, Arthur A., Jr., 96, 144
Howe, Adm. Richard, Lord, 88
Howe, Sir William, 86
Howe Collection (Library of Congress), 88
Howell, Reading, map of Pennsylvania, 90
Howlett, Dr. Freeman S., 28
Hubbard, William, *Narrative of the Troubles with the Indians in New England*, 82
Hudson River, map, 80
Huehuexoxol, 22–24
Hueyatl, 22, 24
Humboldt, Baron Alexander von, 14, 18, 208; *General Map of the Kingdom of New Spain*, 206
Humboldt Fragment VI, 13–15, 17, 18, 20, 26, 27; Fragment VIII, 20
Hungary, map, 60
Hunting Creek, Va., 130, 137
Huntingdon County, Pa., 158

Huntington Library (Pasadena, Cal.), 36
Hus, Jan, 98
Hutchins, Thomas, map of the western parts of
Virginia, 85, 90
Huttich, I., 79
Hydrographic charts, 84

Ihuan, Hernando Pimentel, 9
*Imago Mundi*, 57
Ingham, S. D., 157
Institut de France, 44
Irving, Washington, 115
Istanbul, Turkey, 53, 58
*Italiae, Sclavonia, et Grecia* (Gerard Mercator), 51
Italy, map, 58
Itamaraty, Mapoteca do (Rio de Janeiro), 195, 196
Ixtlilxochitl, 7, 12, 23, 26
Ixtlilxochitl, Fernando Alva, 8
Ixtlilxochitl, Fernando Cortés, 9, 11
Ixtlilxochitl Ometochtli, 9
Izcutecatl, Pedro, 23

Jackson, Gen. T. J. (Stonewall), 183, 185–187
Jaillot, Alexis Hubert, 70, 71, 74
Jaillot, Simon, 70
Jamaica, 129
James River, 93, 100, 121, 123, 124
Jamestown Colony, 92
Jansson (Janssonius), Jan, 47, 54, 63, 65, 94
Japura River, 198
Jared Sparks Collection (Cornell University), 90
Jauru River, 194
Jay, John, 107
Jay, William, 107
Jefferson, Peter, 83, 127, 128; "Map of the North-
ern Neck of Virginia," 128
Jefferson, Thomas, 90, 104, 114, 128, 132–135, 138,
139, 141, 148, 160; *A Map of the Country be-
tween Albemarle Sound and Lake Erie*, 90; *Notes
on the State of Virginia*, 90; plan of the city of
Washington, 132, 133
Jefferys, Thomas, 84, 86, 109, 121, 122, 127; *Cata-
logue of Drawings & Engraved Maps, Charts &
Plans; the Property of Mr. Thomas Jefferys;
Geographer to the King* (1775), 121
Jenkins (Capitol) Hill, 130
Jerusalem, 53, 58
Jiron, Colombia, 202
Jode, Gerard de, 60, 61
John Carter Brown Library (Providence, R.I.), 2,
4, 36, 96, 99, 101, 127
Johnson, Sir William, 116, 118
Johnson, Thomas, 122, 124

Kanawha River, 90, 116, 118, 123
Karpinski, Louis C., 82
Keith, Sir William, *History of the British Planta-
tions in America*, 127
Kent, James, 144–147, 149
Kent, William, 144
Kentucky, 90, 114
Kernstown, Battle of, 184
Keuning, J., 50, 56, 57
King, Nicholas, 130, 138
King, Robert, 138
King, Robert, Jr., 140
Kitchin, Thomas, 109
Klencke, Johan, 64

Koeman, Cornelis, 63
*Königen Buch oder Register darinfein ordentlich
erzehlt werden die Koenige aller fuernemsten
Koenigreichen des Christenthumos*, 60
Kohl, Johann Georg, 40, 79, 80, 81
Kohl Collection (Library of Congress), 40, 79
Kratz, Provost Philipp, 59
Kremer, Gerhard, 47; *see also* Mercator, Gerardus
Kremer, Gisbert, 48
*Kurfürsten Atlas*, 65

Lagarenne, Charles, 144
Lancaster, James, 127
Lancaster County, Pa., 158
Langara, Juan de, *Chart of the Gulf of Mexico*, 207
Lange, Otto, 36
Lanzas, Pedro Torres, *Archivo General de Indias*,
84
La Roncière, Charles de, 84
Latin America, maps, 81
Latrobe, Benjamin H., 137, 139
Lauc, Jorge, 200
Law, Thomas, 140
Lear, Tobias, 145–147, 150, 151; *Observations on
the River Potomack*, 144
Leavitt, George A., & Co., 4
Lebanon County, Pa., 157, 158
Lee, Gen. Robert E., 185–188, 209
LeGear, Clara E., 84
Lehigh County, Pa., 157
Lemaire, Strait of, 69
L'Enfant, Maj. Pierre Charles, 90, 134, 135, 142,
147, 148; "Plan of the City Intended for the
Permanent Seat of the Government of the United
States," 90, 130, 135, 136, 138, 147
Le Rouge, George Louis, 84
Lewis, Andrew, 116
Lewis, Meriwether, 168
Lewis, Samuel, 136
Lewis and Clark expedition, 168
L'Huillier, Pierre, 43
Liancourt, Duc de La Rochefoucauld, 140, 141
Lima, Peru, 199
Line of Demarcation; *see* Bull of Pope Alexander VI
Lingan, James M., 129
*Literary Magazine* (London), 136
Little Falls, Va., 124, 127
Loaysa, Didor Francisco de, 17, 18
Loch Willow School for Boys, 188
Lochaber Line, 119
Löw, Conrad, 61
London, England, plans, 53
London Company, 92
Loon, Jan van, 84
Lords Commissioners of Trade and Plantations, 85,
105
Lorraine, 1564 map, 50
"Lost War Maps of the Confederates," 183
Loudon, Samuel, 149
Louis XIV, King of France, 70, 74
Lowery Collection (Library of Congress), 44
Loyal Land Company of Virginia, 114, 116, 118
Luray, Va., 188
Luzerne County, Pa., 158
Lykens Valley, Pa., 188
Lynchburg, Va., 188
Lynchburg-Monocacy-Washington campaign, 187
Lyon, France, 58

McAfee, Byron, 19
M'Carty, Daniel, 118
McClellan, Gen. George B., 185
McGee's Ferry, 217
Madrid: Naval Museum, 203; Treaty of, 189, 190
Maerschalck, Francis, 85
Maes, Nicolaes, 64
Magellan, Ferdinand, 68
Maggs Bros., Ltd., of London, 189, 195
Magnaghi, Alberto, 37
Maine, map, 90
Manatus map of 1639, 80
"A Map of Potomack and James Rivers in North America Shewing their several Communications with the Navigable Waters of the New Province on the River Ohio," 121
*A Map of the Genesee Tract . . .* (1791), 136
*Map of the Middle States of North America* (1791), 136
*Map of the Middle States . . . Showing the Position of the Geneseo Country,* 136
*Mapa Geográfico de America Meridional,* 202
"Mapa geográfico de la mayor parte de la América Meridional que contiene los paises por donde debe trazarse la linea que divida los Dominios de España y Portugal," 200
Mapa Tlotzin, 26
Mappe Quinatzin, 15
Mappe Tlotzin, 8
Marcel, Gabriel, 74
Marchi, Capt. Francesco di, 42
Marcou, Jules, 74
Marcy, Randall B., 211
Margaret of Parma, 42
María, Dna., 23
Mariscal, Jph. de Andonaegui, 196
Martin, Col. Lawrence, 90, 103, 162, 164, 168, 183
Martyr, Peter: *Decades,* 4; *De Orbe Novo,* 4
Mary, Queen of England, 42
Maryland, 98; maps, 83, 90, 96–99, 136
*Maryland Journal,* 136, 149
Mason, Senator James M. (Virginia), 209
Mason and Dixon line, 101
Mason's Island, 127, 142, 145, 147
Massachusetts: maps, 80, 90; town plats, 161
Massachusetts Historical Society, 147
*Massachusetts Magazine,* 136, 148
Massanutten, Va., 185
*Maurits Atlas,* 65
Maynas Province, 198
Mayo, William, 127
Medina, José Toribio, 41
Mela, Pomponius, *De orbis situ libri tres,* 2, 3
Melish, John, 154–158, 165, 166, 168, 170; *A Description of the Roads in the United States,* 167; *A Geographical Description of the United States,* 154, 165, 168; *A Geographical Description of the World, Intended as an Accompaniment to the Map of the World on Mercator's Projection,* 168; "Map of Pennsylvania," 154, 155, 157, 158, 170; *Map of the United States* (1816–23), 103, 154, 162, 164, 165, 168–170; *Map of the World on the Mercator Projection,* 168; *A Military and Topographical Atlas of the United States,* 167; "Prospectus of the State Map & County Maps of Pennsylvania," 158; *The Traveller's Directory Through the United States,* 167; *Travels in the United States of America in the Years 1806 & 1807, and 1809, 1810, & 1811,* 165

*Memoria Historic de las Demarcaciones de Limites en la America entre los Dominios de España y Portugal,* 200
Mendoza, Don Hurtado de, 57
Mendoza, Viceroy Antonio de, 17, 26
Mercator, Gerardus, 45–50, 56, 58, 61, 63, 79, 84; *Amplissima Terrae Sanctae descriptio,* 48; *Atlantis pars altera. Geographia nova totius mundi . . .,* 46; *Atlas sive cosmographica meditationes de fabrica mvndi et fabricati figura. Gerardo Mercatore Rupelmundano,* 45, 52, 56, 127; *Belgii Inferioris geographicae tabule,* 56; *Chronologia,* 50; *Galliae tabule geographicae,* 57; *Germaniae tabule geographicae,* 56; *Italiae, Sclavoniæ, et Græciæ tabule geographice, Per Gerardum Mercatorem . . .,* 47, 57
Mercator, Gerardus, Jr., 46
Mercator, Johannes, 50
Mercator, Michael, 46
Mercator, Rumoldus, 46, 47
Merin, Laguna de, 191, 195
Mesay, 199
Mexico, 8, 9, 11, 14, 170; maps, 5–33, 204–221
"Mexico" (estate), 130
Mexico City, 8, 9, 11, 15, 53, 58, 59, 208
Mexican War, 208
Millar, Andrew, 109
Miller, David Hunter, 104, 162; *Treaties and Other International Acts of the United States of America,* 104
Mississippi River and valley, 86, 170
Mitchell, John, 85; *A Map of the British and French Dominions in North America With the Roads, Distances, Limits, and Extent of the Settlements . . .,* 85, 103–107; "A New Map of Hudson's Bay and Labrador," 107
Mochiuhquecholtzomatzin, Don Francisco, 12
Moll, Herman, 127
Monocacy River bridge, 186
Monongahela River, 121, 123
Montanus, Arnoldus, *Die unbekante neue Welt,* 127
Montezuma, 11
Montgomery County, Md., 185
Montgomery County, Pa., 158
*Monumenta Chartographica Indiana,* 203
Moore, "Tom," 127
Morgan Library (New York City), 36
Morse, Jedidiah, *American Geography,* 136, 142
Mortier, C., 110
Mortier, Pieter, 71, 127
Moss Neck, Va., 186
Mossy Creek, Va., 188
Mossy Creek Academy, 188
Mount, William, 84
"Mount Pleasant" (estate), 130
Mount Vernon, Va., 90, 132, 146, 147
Mouzon, Henry, map of North and South Carolina and Georgia, 86
Müller-Reinhard, J., 50
Münster, Sebastian, 60; *Cosmographia,* 42, 57, 58
Mulatas, Islas, Panama, 202
Munich Cathedral, 58
Murphy, Henry C., 4
Museo Naval (Madrid), 78

Nacotchtanck, 127
Nagel, Heinrich, 60

Nansemond County, Va., 161
Naples, Kingdom of, map, 58, 60
Nassau, Johan Maurits van, 64
*National Intelligencer,* 149, 209, 210
Natural Bridge, Va., 161
Navarrete, M. F. De, 41
Necoametl, 24
Netherlands, maps, 64
Neun, H., 200
Nevada, 209
New Amsterdam, 98
New Brunswick, N.J., 144
New England, 94; maps, 80–82, 94
New Hampshire, maps, 85, 90
New Jersey, maps, 85–87
New Jersey-Delaware boundary case, 105
New Mexico, 209; southern boundary of, 207, 208
New Netherland, map, 100
New Spain, 19; map, 208
New Troy, 129
New World, maps, 39, 78
New York (State), 165
New York, N.Y., maps, 80, 83, 85
New-York Historical Society, 89, 107, 129
*The New-York Magazine,* 136, 148, 149
New York Public Library, 36, 79
Newark, N.J., 144
Newberry Library (Chicago), 36
Newport, Capt. Christopher, 93
Nezahualcoyotl, 8, 9, 15, 23, 26; Palace, 15
Nezahualpilli, 8, 9, 11, 12, 15, 23, 26; heirs of (chart), 10
Nicholas, Gov. Wilson C., 160
Nightingale, Atkinson, 142
*Niles' Weekly Register,* 157, 167
Nopaltzin, 9
North America, 37; maps, 34, 35, 46, 47, 85, 89, 102, 103, 108, 206
North Atlantic Coast Fisheries Arbitration, 105
North Carolina, map, 85, 86
Northampton County, Pa., 157
Northern Neck (Va.); *see* Virginia
Nova Scotia, maps, 80–82
Nova Terrae-Maria tabula, 83
*Nova totius Americae sive novi orbis auct: G. Janssonio,* 68, 69
Novo y Fernandez Chicarro, Don Pedro, 203
Nueva Oran, Argentina, maps, 194, 195
Nunn, George E., 78

Ochtervelt, Jacob, 64
Octagon House, 140
Octicpac, 20
Ogilby, John, *America* (1671), 127
Ohio, 129, 165; map, 90
Ohio Company, 114
Ohio River, 121
Ometochtli, 22
Omyzlato, Lucas, 24
"Onoyda Lake" (Lake Oneida), 118
Oporinus, Johannus, 57
Oran, Argentina, 194
Orange County, Va., 185
Orange Court House, Va., 187
Orinoco River, 189
Orme, Archibald, 129
Orta, Bernardo de, *Plan of the Port of Vera Cruz,* 207

Ortelius, Abraham, 52, 54, 57, 60, 61, 63, 74; "Bavariae olim Vindelicae delineationis compendivm," 52; "Maris Pacifici," 43; *Theatrum orbis terrarum,* 42, 43, 51, 60, 63; "Typus Vindelicae sive Vtrivs qve Bavariae," 52
Ortroy, Fernand G. van, 4, 50
Otumba, 11, 12
Oztoticpac Lands Map, 5–33

Pacific Ocean, 39, 43, 167, 208; Tatton map (1600), 42
Page, Thomas, 84
Palestine, 1537 map, 48
Palmer, G., 167
Panama, 170, 197, 202
Paraguay River, 189, 190, 193, 194
Paraná River, 194
Paris, France, map, 58
Park, Moses, map of Connecticut, 85
Parkman, Francis, 84
Parkyns, George Isham, 142
Pecos River, 211
Pedro, Don, 12, 13
Penn, William, 142
Pennsylvania: Bureau of Land Records, Department of Internal Affairs, 156; county manuscript maps, 156–158; Legislature, 168; maps, 85, 90, 118, 121, 152–161, 170
Perrenot, Nicolás, 48
Perry County, Pa., 157
Perth Amboy, N.J., 144
Peter, Robert, 129, 130, 142
Petersburg Academy, 160
Pforzheim, Germany, 58
Philadelphia, Pa., 129, 144, 165
Philadelphia County, Pa., 157, 158; maps, 155, 156
Philip II, King of Spain, 42
Philippine Islands, 84
Phillips, Philip Lee, 44, 78, 81, 84, 85, 91, 101; *List of Geographical Atlases in the Library of Congress,* 84; *List of Maps of America in the Library of Congress,* 78; *Notes on the Life and Works of Bernard Romans,* 85; *The Rare Map of Virginia and Maryland by Augustine Herrman; Bibliographical Account With Facsimile Reproduction From the Copy in the British Museum,* 101
Phillips, R., 140
Piankitank, Va., 160
Pickering, Timothy, 136
Pictet, Charles, 142
Pierce, Edward, 129
Pierce, William, 129
Pike, Zebulon, 168; *Chart of the Internal Part of Louisiana,* 206; *Map of the Internal Provinces of New Spain,* 206
Pike County, Pa., 157, 158
Pilot guides, 84
Pimentel, Don Antonio, land grants of, 19
Pinet, Antoine du, 58, 59
Pittsburgh, Pa., maps, 166
"Plan, Exhibiting the Squares on Which Robert Peter's Building Stood . . .," 130
"Plan of Alexandria in the Territory of Columbia . . .," 130
Plantin, Christopher, 52
Pocahontas, 92
Pocahontas County, Va., 161

Poland, map, 61
Polar regions, maps, 47, 68
Pomar, Juan Bautista, 15, 26–28
Popayán, Colombia, 197
Popple, Henry, *Map of the British Empire in America* (1733), 85
Portobelo, Panama, 197
Portolan chart, 44
Port Republic, 186
Port Tobacco (Potopaco), Md., 93
Portugal, map, 61
Potomac River, 93, 121–124, 127, 129, 130, 136, 142, 145, 146, 161; Eastern Branch, 127
Powell, Nathaniel, 94
Powell's Fort Valley, 85
Powhatan, Chief, 92
Pownall, Thomas, 105, 122
Pratt, Frederick W., 130
Price Brothers & Company, Limited, 105
Priggs, John F. A., 129, 131
Prince Georges County, Md., 129
Princeton, N.J., 144
Ptolemy, Claudius, 46, 50, 57, 61, 78, 79
Public Record Office (London), 114
Punta Negra, 196
Putnam, G. P. & Co., 115
Putnam, Ruth, *California: the Name,* 40

Quad, Matthias, 60; *Europae totius orbis terrarvm partis praestantissimae, vniversalis et particvlaris descriptio,* 58; *Fasciculus geographicus,* 60; *Teutscher Nation Herrlichkeit,* 60, 61
Quad-Bussemecher atlas, 59
Quauhximalco, Mexico, 26
Queen's Hazard (estate), 129
Quesada, Antonio Rodríguez, 17–19
Quinatzin, 15
Quinatzin Tlaltecatzin, 9
Quito, Presidencia de, 198

Raemdonck, Jean van, *Gérard Mercator, sa vie et ses œuvres,* 50
Raleigh, N.C., 183
Rappahannock River, 93, 186
Rebellion, Official Records of the, 188
Red River, 169, 211
Requeña, Don Francisco, 197–201, 203
Rich Mountain, 185
Richmond, Va., 121, 124, 161, 183, 186
Riddell, Henry, 123
Ridolfi, Cardinal Nikolas, 57
Rijks-Archief (Amsterdam), *Inventaris der verzameling Kaarten berustende in het,* 84
Rio Apaporis, 199
Rio de Janeiro, Brazil, 195
Rio de la Plata, maps, 203
Rio del Norte, 211
Rio Grande, 20, 196, 208
Río Guaporé, 196
Río Mamoré, 196
Rio Marañon, 199
Rio Negro, 196
Rio Roxo of Natchitoches, 169
Rio Uruguay; *see* Uruguay River
Rio Yapurà, 199
Rio Yavari, 199
Ristow, Walter W., 90, 129

Riverol, Vicencio de, 18
"Road from the Yadkin," 121
Roanoke River, 100, 118
Rochambeau, Comte de, 86; manuscript atlas, 128
Rochambeau, Marquis de, 86
Rochambeau Collection (Library of Congress), 86
Rock Creek, 127, 129, 134, 135, 140
Rockefeller, John D., Jr., 84
Rockville, Md., 131
Rocque, Jean, *Set of Plans and Forts in America* (1763), 85
Rodriguez, Antonio, 17
Roland, François, 71
Romans, Bernard, *Concise Natural History of East and West Florida,* 85
Rome, Italy, 129
Rosenwald, Lessing J., 39
Rosenwald Collection (Library of Congress), 3, 56
Ross, Lieutenant, 86
Rosser, Gen. Thomas L., 188
Royal Geographical Society (London), 69, 70, 121
Royal Library and Museum (Berlin), 14
Rozier, Notley, 129
Ruffault, Heronimous, 35
Ruge, Walter, "Älteres kartographisches Material in deutschen Bibliotheken," 35
Ruscelli, 58
Ruysch, Johann, 78

Sabine River, 169
Sahagún, Bernardino de, 8
St. Augustin, Province of Georgia, chart, 89
St. James' Creek, 127, 132
Salta Province, Argentina, 194
Salto Grande, 196, 199
San Antonio de Maripi, Pueblo de, 199
San Diego, Calif., 208, 209
San Ildefonso Treaty, 190, 197
Sandoval, Francisco Tello de, 19
Sans, Carlos, 78
Sanson, Adrien, *Atlas nouveau,* 71
Sanson, Guillaume, 71
Sanson, Nicolas, 71
Santa Barbara, Calif., 208
Santa Maria Nativitas Tetzcocinco, 26
Santa Marta, Colombia, 202
Santillan, Gómez de, 18
São Paulo, Brazil, 189
Sardinia, Kingdom of, map, 58
Sauthier, Claude J., map of New York, 85
Saxton, Christopher, *Atlas* of English and Welsh counties, 55, 56
Scavenius Collection (Dartmouth College), 88
Schuster, Ernest A., 138
Schuylkill County, Pa., 158
Scotland, 165; maps, 58, 61
Scott, Joseph T., 138
Scull, Nicolas, map of Pennsylvania, 85
Seckford, Thomas, 55, 56
Seibert, S. R., 131
Seler, Eduard, 14, 15, 17
Seller, John, 84, 99
Seminary Ridge, 187
Senex, John, 127
Service Hydrographique of France (Paris), 84
Sharpsburg, Pa., 186
Shenandoah Valley, map, 185
Shepherdstown, W.Va., 186
Sheridan, Gen. Philip H., 188

Sicily, Kingdom of, map, 58, 60
Smith, Capt. John, 91–94, 99, 127; *A Description of New England*, 94; *The Generall Historie of Virginia, New-England, and the Summer Isles*, 94, 127; *A Map of Virginia. With a Description of the Covntrey*, 82, 91, 96, 127; *Virginia Discouered and Discribed by Captayn John Smith 1606*, 127
Smith, Robert C., 200
Smith, William, 131
Sociedad de Geografía of Mexico, 36
Société Royale de Géographie d'Anvers, 4
Socorro, Colombia, 202
Solinus, Caius Julius, *Polyhistor*, 3
Somerset County, Pa., 158
Sophianos, Nicolaos, 57
Soto, Hernando de, 79
South America, 37, 170; maps, 34, 35, 46, 47, 84, 189–203
South Carolina, map, 86
Southack, Cyprian, *New England Coasting Pilot*, 84
Spain, 197
Spangler, Jacob, 157
Stadtbibliothek at Breslau, 43
Staunton, Va., 186, 188
Stevenson, Edward Luther, *Terrestrial and Celestial Globes*, 49
Stewart, J. W., *Map of the City of Washington*, 130
Stockdale, J., 136, 141
Stone House (Georgetown), 140
Stuart, Alexander H. H., 209
Stuart, Gen. J. E. B., 186
Stuart, John, 116
Stuyvesant, Gov. Peter, 98
Sullivan, James, 104
Susquehanna River, 158
Sussex County, Va., 161
Sweden, map, 60
Swift, Jonathan, 75
Swords, James, 149
Swords, Thomas, 149

Tacuba, 9
Talledo y Rivera, Don Vicente, 202
Tanner, Benjamin, 157
Tanner, Henry S., 154, 158, 161, 167, 168, 171, 205–207; *A Map of North America, Constructed According to the Latest Information*, 206; *A Map of the United States of Mexico, As organized and defined by the several Acts of the Congress of that Republic*, 205; *New American Atlas*, 206
Tassin, Nicolas, 71
Tatham, William, 129
Tato, Capt. Julio F., 203
Tatton, Gabriel, 39, 43, 44; map of Pacific Ocean, 42
Taylor, Gen. Richard, 186
Taylor, Gen. Zachary, 208
Taylor, George, Jr., 148
Techotlaltzin, 9
Tecocoltzin, Fernando, 9
Tefé, Brazil, 197–199
Tejada, Alonso de, 18
Tempatzin, 26
"Ten Mile Square," 127, 137
Tenerife Island, 191, 200
Tenizcin, 23
Tenochitlan, 8, 9
TerBorch, Gerard, 64

Tetlahuchuctzin, Pedro, 19
Tetlahuehuetzquitzin, Don Pedro, 9, 11, 20, 23
Tetzcocinco, 19, 20
Teutzquitzin, Diego, 9
Texas, 209
Texcocan palaces, 15
Texcocinco, 27
Texcoco, 7–9, 12–14, 18–20, 26, 28; rulers (chart), 8
Tezcatlipuca, 26
Tezcocinco, 26
Thackara, James, and John Vallance, engravers, 90, 135–138, 146–149, 165
Thevet, André, 39, 42, 43
Thomas, John V., 130
Thomas and Andrews, publishers, 148
Thornton, Dr. William, 138–140
Thornton, John, 84
Thornton, Mrs. William, 140, 142
Tiber Creek, 127, 134, 140
Tiebout, Cornelius, 129, 136, 149
"Tin Case Map," 138
Tindall, William, *Standard History of the City of Washington*, 148
*Titulos de Venezuela en sus limites con Colombia*, 200
Tixicomotecatl, 22
Tlacocoua, Zacarías, 12, 13, 20
Tlacopan, 9
Tlahuilotzin, Antonio Pimentel, 9, 11–14, 17, 18, 20, 26
Tlailotlaque tribe, 26
Tlaxomulco, 26, 27
Tlotzin, 26
Tlotzin Pochotl, 9
Tochatlauhtli, 20
Todeschi, Pietro, 66, 67, 69, 70
Tollancinco, 11; estate, 7
Toltec Indians, 26
Tonal, Inés, 23
Toner, Dr. Joseph M., 130, 131
Tooley, R. V., 43, 55
Toppahanock (Rappahannock) River, 93
Tordesillas, Treaty of, 189
Totocinco, 22, 24
Totopolomoy River, 187
Traver's Tavern, 147
*Treaties and Other International Acts of the United States of America*, 162
Trenton, N.J., 144
Trist, Nicholas, 209
Tudor Place, 140
Tunnicliff's Hotel, 140
Turkey, map, 60
Turkey Buzzard Point, 127

Ulloa, Francisco de, 79
Union County, Pa., 157
United States: early cartography, 153–182; maps, 90, 162, 163, 169
U.S. Coast and Geodetic Survey, *The King Plats of the City of Washington . . .*, 138
U.S. National Archives, 160, 209
U.S. Office of Strategic Services, 164
United States-Mexican boundary, 162, 169, 170, 216
*The Universal Asylum, and Columbia Magazine*, 148, 149
*Universal Magazine* (London), 136
University of California Press, 162

Uruguay, colonial, 190–192
Uruguay River, 189, 190, 192, 193, 195–197
Utah, 209


Vadianus, Joachim, 2
Vallance, John, 168; *see also* Thackara, James
Valley of Virginia, 185, 188
Vandalia, 122, 123
Varela y Ulloa, Josef, 190, 191, 193, 195, 202
Veiga Cabral da Camara, Sebastiao X. da, 191, 193
Velez, Colombia, 202
Venango County, Pa., 157
Veracruz, Mexico, 208
Vergara, Pedro de, 18, 20, 26, 27
Verlett, Janneken, 99
Vermeer, Jan, 63, 64
Vermont, map, 90
Verner, Coolie, 91
Vespucci, Amerigo (Americus Vespucius), 68, 69, 78
Vienna, Austria, 58
Vignaud, Henri, 112
Villegagnon, Nicolas de, 43
Vingboons, Joan, 80, 83; Manatus, 83
Virginia, Colonial, 92, 121; Executive Council, 114,
    129; House of Burgesses, 114, 119; maps, 80, 82,
    83, 85, 86, 90–93, 96–99, 101, 106, 118, 121–123,
    127–130, 153–161, 170, 183–188; Northern Neck,
    90, 127; State Library, 114, 160; University of, 147,
    160, 161
Virginia-North Carolina boundary, 118
*The Virginias, a Mining, Industrial and Scientific
    Journal*, 188
Virreynatos de Buenos Aires, 199
Visscher, Nikolaus, 63–65, 74; map of New Nether-
    land, 100
Voogt, Claes Jansz, 84
Vopel, Caspar, 60
Vrients, J. B., 52


Waghenaer, Lucas Jansz., 60, 84
Wagner, Henry R., 35, 43, 79
Waldburg-Wolfegg, Prince, 78
Waldron, Resolved, 98
Waldseemüller, Martin, 3, 78
Wale, Peter de, 4
Wales, Saxton's *Atlas* of counties, 55
Walker, Dr. Thomas, 114, 116–119
Walker, Pedro, *Map of New California*, 206
Walker-Washington map, 114–120
Walpole, Thomas, 122, 123
Walton, Elisabeth, 64
Wansey, Henry, 140
Warner, John, 127
Warren County, Pa., 157
Warrenton, Va., 185
Washington, D.C.; *see* District of Columbia
Washington, George, 86, 87, 89, 90, 114–119, 122–
    124, 132, 134, 135, 138, 139, 147, 150, 151
Washington, John Augustine, 114
Wayne County, Pa., 157, 158
Waynesboro, Pa., 188
Weaver, Isaac, 155
Webster-Ashburton Treaty, 105

Weeks, Mangum, 130
Weld, Isaac, 141
Wellens, Jan, 41
Werner of Gymnich, 50
Werowocomoco, 92
West, John, 130
West Indies, 165, 170; map, 80
West Virginia, maps, 183; statehood centennial, 121
Wharton, Samuel, 118, 122
Wheat Row (estate), 140
White, Gallaher & White, 205, 206, 208, 211
White, Zachariah, 131
Whitelaw, James, map of Vermont, 90
Whiteside, Jno. C., 156
Widow's Mite (estate), 129
Wieder, Frederik C., 65, 68
Wilbur, James B., 84
William, Duke of Juliers, Cleves, and Berg, 46
William L. Clements Library (Ann Arbor, Mich.),
    88
Wills, E. Penissa, 114
Wilmington, Del., 144
Winchester, Elhanan, *An Oration on the Discovery
    of America Delivered in London, October the
    12th 1792*, 136, 149
Winchester, Va., 185, 187
Windsor, N.Y., 188
Winsor, Justin, 80
Winterbotham, William, *Historical . . . View of
    the American United States*, 136
Wisconsin-Michigan boundary case, 105
Wit, Frederik de, 63, 65
Wolfegg Castle (Württemberg), 3, 78
Woltersdorf, Ernst G., *Reportorium der Land- und
    Seekarten*, 59
Wood, John, 160, 161
Wood-Böyë map of Virginia, 170
Woodward, Fred E., "Chart Showing the Original
    Boundary Milestones of the District of Colum-
    bia," 138
World, maps, 2–4, 36, 37, 40, 41, 46, 48, 50, 52, 53,
    58, 78, 79, 169
Wright, Benjamin, 42, 44
Wright, Edward, *Certain Errors in Navigation,
    1599*, 50
Wroth, Lawrence C., 96, 101
Wyoming, 209
Wytfliet, Corneille, *Descriptionis Ptolemaicae
    avgmentvm*, 79


Xocotlan, 20
Xolotl, 9
Xoxul, 23


Yndios Corotus, 199
York County, Pa., 158
Young, Notley, 149
Young, William, 148
Yoyotzin, Jorge Alvarado, 9, 11


Zacco, Bartholomio, 43
Zumárraga, Bishop Juan, 9, 20

☆ U. S. GOVERNMENT PRINTING OFFICE : 1975 O - 587-872